THE PRODUCTION OF
POLITICAL TELEVISION

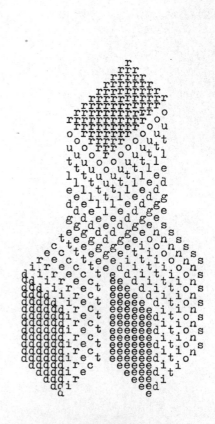

THE PRODUCTION OF POLITICAL TELEVISION

MICHAEL TRACEY

ROUTLEDGE DIRECT EDITIONS

ROUTLEDGE & KEGAN PAUL
London, Henley and Boston

First published in 1977
by Routledge & Kegan Paul Ltd
39 Store Street,
London WC1E 7DD,
Broadway House,
Newtown Road,
Henley-on-Thames,
Oxon RG9 1EN and
9 Park Street,
Boston, Mass. 02108, USA
Printed by Thomson Litho Ltd
East Kilbride, Scotland
© Michael Tracey, 1977

British Library Cataloguing in Publication Data
Tracey, Michael
  The production of political television.
  1. Television in politics - Great Britain
  I. Title
  791.45'5   HE8700.7.P6   77-30176

ISBN 0-7100-8689-X

*Owing to production delays
this book was published in 1978*

CONTENTS

ACKNOWLEDGMENTS

I must first of all thank all those communicators who were kind
enough to talk to me about their work. I entered this work with a
good deal of pessimism as to the likely success in obtaining the
necessary access to the world of the professional broadcaster.
Having completed it I can only say that I was met everywhere with
great kindness and patience.

I should like to thank the Centre for Mass Communication Research, University of Leicester for providing the comfortable
facilities within which this book could be prepared and written.
In particular I must thank the Centre's secretarial staff - Jean
Goddard, Anna Howse, Heather Brown, Enid Nightingale - for typing
much of the various drafts of the work. I wish also to express my
gratitude to Dr Richard Dembo for help in the early stages of the
work, and my friends and colleagues Dave Morrison, Phil Harris and
Dennis Howitt for many periods of stimulating conversation. The
BBC's Written Archives Centre provided not only a good deal of help
but also a most appealing location in which to work.

Tony Smith, broadcaster, academic, controversial theoretician of
broadcasting, has that great gift of both encouraging one's work yet
providing always pertinent observations as to its weaknesses and
limitations.

The supervisor of my doctoral thesis on which the book is based,
Peter Golding, needs to be singled out for special praise. His
many comments and always perceptive insights into barely legible
drafts made smoother a difficult path, and his confidence that it
was actually possible to complete the work at all was a great
stimulant.

Finally, I can only say thank you to the person without whom I
quite literally would never have been able to complete this work,
my wife Jane.

PREFACE

The purpose of this book is to consider the ways in which political
television programmes are shaped and formed within the multitude of
contexts and conditions which prevail at any one moment. The definition of 'political television' entails those programmes whose content and central purpose is involved, however obliquely, with the
policy-making process within Britain – whether that be at the
national, regional or local level. I developed this particularly
broad-ranging brief for my work largely because it seemed clear to
me as I sat at home watching the television that many programmes
which were not traditionally defined within the context of political
television – a definition which has tended to begin and end with the
news and 'flagship' programmes such as 'Panorama' and the late,
lamented (by some) '24 Hours' – were in fact highly political. Thus
my search for the 'truth' about this most crucial form of
television led me not only into the legendary portals of the BBC's
Lime Grove building but also into the small regional companies which
span the country from Aberdeen in the north to Plymouth in the
south. My intention was wherever possible to make use of evidence
drawn from the actual production setting or from lengthy interviews
with those directly responsible for controlling that setting. The
central question throughout this work has been 'what factors deter-
mine or influence what will and will not be made available as programme material?', why study political television in the first
place?

The first and most straightforward reason for focusing on political TV is rather idiosyncratic – a personal interest in the political process. Political television in general is of interest to
the political scientist in so far as it does provide the single
most important source of political information for the audience
(Butler and Stokes, 1969, p.220). Being aware of these high levels
of exposure, the parties within the political system now more than
ever define the coverage they receive as significant and increasingly gear their activity to the needs of the media. It is often
argued now that the presence of television has changed the whole
nature of elections, though it may be more accurate to say that
television has affected the form of elections but not necessarily
the content.

Political television is also one of the more controversial areas of broadcasting, again something resting on the assumed importance of television in influencing the decisions people make about politics. For this reason then it is worth studying the internal mechanisms of media organizations in order to test the truth or falsity of the various assertions about the nature of production.

At a higher level of abstraction, it is hoped that an analysis of the generation and utilization of ideas by individuals working within organizations geared to the purveyance of what are essentially intellectual processes - i.e. news and current affairs departments - will facilitate some understanding of the central problems of sociology, namely the origin of knowledge in society, and in particular the relationship between the individual-within-society and those ideas-within-society that provide his understanding of the social process. In what way for example are the criteria employed for decision-making within the production setting articulated to wider organizational and social meaning systems? How does this fit with other criteria for decision-making which may be rooted in technocratic, financial, editorial and institutional structures. Does the interaction change over time as well as within time - and in relation to what does it change? What is the nature of the relationship between the production, the organization, the wider social power structures and the ideologies characteristic of the society?

There is considerable interest within society or more accurately within certain sections of the cultural, intellectual and political establishments in the future organization and direction of the whole structure of broadcasting. It may well be an interesting exercise to discuss at length such questions as the overall goals of broadcasting and the types of broadcasting structures that might be 'best for society'. The point has to be made, though, that such a debate within society - institutionalized as it is within the Annan Committee - rests on a number of assumptions which are far from articulated in any meaningful sense and which in many ways may be downright fallacious. As our knowledge stands at present - both about the nature of audience taste and expectations and about the real nature of programme-making - proposals for change are predicated on an understanding of media processes which just does not exist. It is rather like trying to institute changes within schools without having any understanding of the nature of learning. It is to holders of those wider suppositions and assumptions about television that this work is ultimately addressed.

No single research method was adopted during the course of this research - not, one might add, for any notably theoretical reason, but rather because of the exigencies of the situation. The initial aim had indeed been to undertake a participant-observation study, in a programme production that fitted my definition of political television, but unfortunately this was not, in the end, possible, simply because no one at that time was willing to grant the necessary access. The alternative to watching producers actually working was talking to them about their work and hoping that that would in the end produce a degree of access which, combined with the interview material, would provide insight into the situation of programme production. This is in fact what happened. In the end three main

methods, or sources of information, were employed during the course
of the study; these were:
1 interviews with producers of 'political television';
2 observation of several programme productions;
3 archival work – analysis of various pieces of documentary
   material, and in particular material in the BBC archives relating
   to the General Strike, 1926.

THE INTERVIEWS

A sample of two weeks' programmes that fitted the initial definition
of political television was taken from the 'Radio Times' and 'TV
Times'. (1) The 'producers' (2) of the particular programmes were
contacted and interviews requested. The titles of those people
varied, but all are here referred to as 'producer'. Having established a listing of all the programmes and those responsible a
standard letter was sent requesting an interview. The total number
of programmes included on the list was forty-seven. As on some
programmes the responsibility was shared by more than one producer
the total number of possible interviews was fifty-two. Of these,
thirty-nine interviews were carried out. In addition, a number of
other interviews were carried out with presenters, executives and
radio producers. The interviews were, when possible, taped and
then transcribed, the mean length being 1 hour 10 minutes. One of
the interviewees objected to taping, and so notes were taken, and
on the one occasion when even note-taking was not possible, notes
were taken immediately after the interview. After several of the
interviews an opportunity was available to talk informally with the
interviewee, and often, when this took place in the bar, to talk to
various other broadcasters. While there are often difficulties with
the information gathered in such an informal setting, not the least
of which is the difficulty of retention, I did feel that often some
of the information gathered in this more informal setting was as
useful as the taped material, and definitely provided a useful opportunity to test the consistency of responses, generally to establish a 'feel' for the situation of the producer, to develop new
ideas and confirm established notions. It was particularly interesting to listen to fairly animated conversations between the producer and his colleague, always goaded by the presence of the
researcher-as-outsider.
   The interviews were structured, in the sense that the same basic
interview schedule was used for each interview, though the questions
were open-ended, the interviewee being allowed to develop his own
line of thought if he or she so wished.
   There are clearly many difficulties involved in using material
gathered in formal interviews, but the interesting feature as one
proceeds is the way in which general themes and ideas begin to
emerge; hints of possible lines of analysis, leads to follow up,
confirmation of one's own suppositions and explanations, denial of
other ideas that one holds, all begin to develop out of the material
that is accumulated. In summing up the methodology behind this part
of the work, I can do no better than quote Ivor Crewe (1974, p.43),
who in discussing 'new approaches' to the study of elites, declared:

'elites need to be interviewed. The best way of finding out about
people is talking to them. It cannot guarantee to secure the truth,
especially from people well practised in the arts of discretion,
but it is surely superior to any alternative way of discovering what
they believe and do.'

OBSERVATION

During the course of the interviews several producers asked if I
would like to spend some time with their programme 'to see what it's
really like'. Periods of observation were thus spent in the newsrooms of the regional BBC and ITV, and in the current affairs
department of the BBC. The period of observation in ITV fortunately
coincided with the General Election, a prime time to study the functioning of political television and the sorts of ideas that structure the coverage of political affairs.
     The method of participant observation is really a combination of
several methods 'in embryo'. Much of the time was spent just observing and listening, noting activities, conversations, decisions and
the like. There were innumerable short 'interviews', questions that
became lengthy talks, questions that were answered with a good deal
of brevity, information that was offered unsolicited but that was
most welcome – a series of sources that gradually begin to add up
to a reasonably accurate picture of what is 'really happening'. The
observation was invaluable in adding the flesh to the skeleton constructed from the interview material, introducing new elements in
need of scrutiny and close consideration. For example, I never
really understood or appreciated the role of the film editor in
programme-making until I actually spent time in the cutting room.
I had never understood the relationship between a programme's day-
to-day activity, the immediate perspective of the editor-of-the-
day or the programme organizer, and the wider perspective applied
by the news editor until I actually saw it happening. Two separate,
but inextricably linked, levels of decision-making were clearly
evident, whereas initially I had formulated a notion of the news
editors being responsible for general policy and all everyday decisions.

AN HISTORICAL PERSPECTIVE

As a background to the research, I initially thought it would be
useful to describe the historical background to the present situation of political broadcasting. It rapidly became clear that not
only was a historical narrative a useful backdrop to the central
arguments, but the analysis and understanding of those historical
materials was a critical step toward the intended analysis of the
connections between the process of production and the wider social
and political context.
     I have, therefore, looked at the general development but have
also focused on particular periods and events in order to try to
tap, and adequately explain, the connections between an institution – particularly the ideas generated within that institution –

and the society within which it exists: the four central events are
the BBC and the General Strike, 1926; the Retirement of Sir Hugh
Greene; the 'Yesterday's Men' incident; and the coverage by ATV of
the 1974 (February) General Election.

INTRODUCTORY

INTRODUCTION

The following pages of this book are, I suppose, an exercise in exploration into the relatively unknown world of political tele-vision. This is essentially a study of production within political television, an attempt to understand and explicate the fashioning of political images within the confines of the television organi-zation. The ubiquity of 'the box' within our everyday lives is clear and yet the most surprising fact which faces the new student of the medium is the relatively sparse body of real information which one has as to the forces which shape the actions and motiva-tions of these key institutions within our culture. Their nature, their purpose, their operations remain mysteries. At the same time, though, the formulation of theories about television and the forces that shape it abound, and everyone, from that curious aggregate the 'man in the street' to the most distinguished social theorist, is willing to offer his version of what it is that generates and influ-ences programme-making practices. And with each and every critique the single most telling fact is that they operate from what is in effect a position of almost total ignorance. Principally this work was always intended to be an attempt to confront the problem of the nature of political television through what Edward Thompson has described as the 'collisions of evidence and the awkward confron-tations of experience'.

In many ways this work could be seen as a coherent whole in the sense that all its various parts are concentrated on the one point - the nature of the production of political television. In another sense, though, it would be seen as a series of many parts drawing on different types of evidence and looking at different aspects of the same problem. Either way it is hoped that some understanding of television production will emerge.

POLITICAL COMMUNICATION AND POLITICAL TELEVISION

The use of broadcasting as a means of transmitting political mes-sages has long both troubled and excited politicians. Concern over the amount of time to be allocated to the discussion of politics, to news about affairs in Westminster, to the type of material to be

transmitted and the amount and type of coverage of elections, goes
back to the very infancy of broadcasting, even though the coverage
of the political affairs was until relatively recently somewhat
circumscribed. This is clearly a long way from conditions today
where politicians crave for the attention of the media (particularly
television), where a good deal of broadcast time is given over to
political affairs and where it is not unreasonable to argue that the
whole style of politics is very much influenced by the presence of
the camera and the microphone.

If one considers the range of news and current affairs programmes
made available by the broadcasting organizations and the size and
types of audience which watch them, one is left with the impression
that the broadcasting diet of large sections of the population consists of substantial chunks of political matter. (1) The problems
that are involved in deciding the actual significance of all this
in the formation of attitudes and behaviour are, of course, difficult and contentious areas of discussion that lie beyond the scope
of this work. It is sufficient here to point out that a substantial
amount of political information is made available to the viewing and
listening audience. It is clear that broadcasting in general, and
television in particular, have emerged as key elements of what is
described as the 'process of political communication'. What, however, does one mean when talking of 'political communication', and
how much do we know about the broadcasting aspects of it?
Lord Windlesham described political communication as (1966, p.17):

'the deliberate passing of a political message by a sender to a
receiver with the intention of making the receiver behave in a way
that he might not otherwise have done. This definition contains
three components: a political message; the method of passing or dis-
tributing the political message; and an intention to make the
receiver respond in a particular way.'

Utilizing this definition and attaching it to Oakeshott's definition
of politics as the activity of attending to the general arrangements
of a set of people, a political message in the context of national
politics becomes one concerning the arrangements of the State
(Windlesham, 1966, pp.17-18). The purposive criteria which Windlesham includes within his definition do not fit the ideology, and
some of the reality, of the broadcast media, but nevertheless the
core of his definition that political communication is the transmission of a message, from X to Y, concerning the arrangements of
the State, seems reasonably adequate.

Two recent students of the political process in Britain discussed
the role of information in the process of change and the way that
channels for the transmission of that information relate to political activity among the electorate (Butler and Stokes, 1969,
p.215):

'Political activity must depend in large part upon the flow of political information. New information sets in motion the processes by
which individual attitudes are formed and modified. Exchanges of
information alter the political outlook of the family and other
small social groups. The information about politics reaching the

public through the mass media changes the support accorded to the
parties and their leaders.'

If it is possible to assert that the flow of information is an
integral feature of political change - 'in the short term, marked
changes are scarcely imaginable except in response to some information flow' (Butler and Stokes, 1969, p.215) - then the channels
through which that flow takes place take on a good deal of importance.

   Before delineating those channels, however, it is important to
point out that the dominant notions underpinning the process of
political communication are integral parts of the concepts of a
liberal democracy - the social and political arrangements that are
deemed to characterize British politics in the twentieth century.
The idea of individuals communicating with each other, settling the
affairs of society through rational discussion and decision is a
view which still characterizes much of the discussion about political communication; witness the words of Lord Windlesham: 'The
distinguishing feature of democratic politics is the dialogue
between the governing and the governed, each attempting to influence
and persuade the other' (1966, p.9), and where that discussion has
recognized that the model of liberal democracy no longer fits the
reality of twentieth century political life the 're-establishment'
of some level of meaningful interpersonal communication through the
creation of an 'adequate' communications system is postulated as
the solution for the restoration of the democratic process - for
example, Anthony Smith, a prominent writer on the mass media, wrote
recently that for 'alienated' man, industrial, urban man, the mass
media can be a means by which the articulate can reconnect themselves to the stream of active consciousness and a means by which
the inarticulate, if truly served by the community of broadcasters,
can see their experience actually being made to carry weight (Smith,
1973, p.285).

   It was clearly recognized that in an industrial society the
classic model of public discourse could not apply. Yet the structure of power in the society was still to be one where the governors
were ultimately responsible to the governed. Clearly in such a
situation the information that the latter had about the former, and
the sources from which that information was obtained, became significant. The channels for the provision of this essential information became necessary components of the democratic process, and
'This channel of communication was the press, which could report
and interpret the business of the Government to the public, behaving
in a neutral way' (Seymour-Ure, 1968, p.18).

   Gradually the press became not just the transmitter of the information but also the translator of that information, the definer of
'truth' for the audience-electorate (Seymour-Ure, 1969, p.19):

'The Press did more than enable the electorate to hold the Government responsible; it held the Government responsible itself, safe-
guarding the people against corruption, incompetence and despotism.
It too then was the Public's representative, elected in the sense
that people chose to read it; and it too therefore became 'responsible' to its readers for fulfilling the function it set itself up
to perform.'

While such a theory of the press may not bear too much similarity
to 'reality', it does I think, illuminate some of the latent signi-
ficances of the political communications process: the implicit
assumption that it is the essential key linking those who govern and
those who are governed, a unifying web for the democratic process.

Of what exactly, is one talking when referring to the process of
'political communication'? Of what is the process constituted? It
consists, broadly speaking of channels for the transmission of messages from political actors to their political audience. One can
perhaps best distinguish between channels whose sole function is the
act of communication – for example, the broadcast media, the press,
publishers, advertising agencies – and those institutions who have a
variety of functions one of which is political communications, for
example, political parties, interest groups, governmental agencies.
There are, then, within the channel of political communication not
one but many streams each seeking to transmit information to broadly
the same audience, each having varying degrees of success.

Is it possible to begin to delineate one 'channel' of communication as being more important than another in absolute terms of the
number of people reached and in terms of the influence exerted? In
terms of actual importance probably not, in terms of assumed importance most certainly yes. Focusing on what they believe to be the
two main sources of political information – personal conversation
and the mass media – Butler and Stokes (1969, p.218) state that the
'electorate itself sees the mass media as a more important means of
following politics', and in their survey only 12 per cent in 1964
and 14 per cent in 1966 said that they did not follow the campaign
from either television, newspapers or radio. Television has the
largest audience of the three and in the 1964 and 1966 elections
25 per cent of the population over the age of five watched each of
the nightly party braodcasts and even more saw the specially extended daily news bulletin (Butler and Stokes, 1969, p.219). While
nearly as many people say that they follow politics in the press as
follow it on television – 66 per cent in 1964 and 59 per cent in
1966 – when asked to evaluate their relative uses of press and television, television was much preferred; in 1964, 64 per cent of those
who followed the campaign at all said they relied more on television, and 28 per cent said they relied more on the press (Butler and
Stokes, 1969, p.219).

TABLE 1.1   Percentage of homes with TV in GB

1950	10
1955	40
1959	75
1964	88
1966	90
1970	95

(Source: Seymour-Ure, 1974)

Radio was much less important, with only 23 per cent in 1964 and
20 per cent in 1966 saying that they followed the campaign on radio,
and of those who followed the campaign by any medium only 7 per cent

reported that they relied on radio most. The increasing percentage
of homes with television is shown in Table 1.1 and the various
findings about the relative importance of the different sources of
political information are brought together in Table 1.2. (2)

TABLE 1.2   Sources of political information

	Percentage following politics/campaign by given medium or channel			Percentage saying given medium or channel most important 1964	
	Summer 1963	Autumn 1964	Spring 1966	Of all media	Of all channels
Television	55	75	72	65	48
Newspapers	48	66	59	28	20
Radio	19	23	20	7	5
Conversation	27	60	63	-	19
Didn't follow campaign/politics	30	8	8	-	8
				100	100

(Source: Butler and Stokes, 1969)

    Clearly there are many problems with findings of this nature -
not least of which is the difficulty of establishing the discrete
effects of particular processes in a general situation: 'A great
deal of common information flows out to the mass British electorate
through media which are heavily overlapping and which are describing
political issues and events that they have sledom done anything to
shape' (Butler and Stokes, 1969, p.244). Many would argue that the
media do indeed define issues, and that because more people spend
more time watching television, and place more faith in the veracity
of 'the pictures of the world' that television provides, that medium
is the most significant definer of issues, not defining issues in
the tradition of the fourth estate, however, but rather providing
limited and partial views of reality that result from the technological and ideological structures that underpin the process of
image formation. (3) Other writers have pointed to the way that
the very presence of the medium in the political process alters that
process (Seymour-Ure, 1974). Another problem is that the data gathered usually originates from work done during the course of elections when from the broadcast media's point of view they are really
at their most circumscribed, bound as they are by the limitations
of the parties' requirements and the electoral laws. It may well be
that political communication is more significant during the period
between elections when the messages communicated by the various
channels are less tangible, more discreet, rather than in the partisan atmosphere of the election.
    These are all important questions, all firmly rooted in what is
known as the study of 'media effects'. What has become clear, however, is that television now occupies centre stage in the world of

political communications simply in the sense that it is defined as
occupying centre stage by politicians and public alike. But what
does the process of political communication 'look like'? Figure
1.1 (4) is an adapted version of a schema developed by Jay Blumler
from a basic model presented by Westley and MacLean (1957).

Now we can say several things about this schema:

1 we are aware of the essential components of the process;

2 we are aware of the fact that there are a whole series of limi-
ations on the efficacy of the 'messages';

3 we know that it is not just a question of uni-directional flow,
that 'feedback' is an important part of the process;

4 we know that in many ways the model is something of a fiction
in the sense that the structures of power- and decision-making
within society are such as to not require the assent of the electorate except on routinized occasions e.g. elections. Communication
within the political elite, on a private basis, may be far more significant than communication between the elite and the electorate. (5)

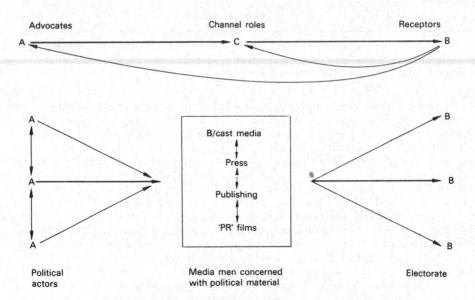

FIGURE 1.1 Political communication as process: a model

The messages are received within a particular context that alters,
reduces or eradicates the intended meaning. C is receiving messages
from A and passes them on to B. In implementing the role, C 'acts
as an agent of B selecting the abstractions of (messages) suited to
B's needs, transforming them into symbols shared with B, and then
transmitting them by some medium to B'. There is also feedback as
to the level of satisfaction B has with the messages.

This is obviously limited in that C often acts more as an agent
of A than an agent of B - and in fact is very often, in the case of
the broadcast media, required to be so legally.

Source: Blumler 1970.

5 Of the three main components - A, C, B - we know a good deal
about A - the internal structuring of the institutions concerned,
the background and beliefs of their members, the decision-making
procedures, the declared intentions of their personnel. (6) We
know a good deal about B - the composition, structure, beliefs of
those receiving the political messages, the types of political
behaviour they engage in and the relationship between that and the
messages. We know next to nothing about the primary components of
C, the broadcast media. It is a remarkable fact that there has only
been one systematic study of the internal functioning of the medium
of political television published in Britain (Blumler, 1969), and
if, for example, one goes to look at one of the leading books or
collections of papers on mass communicators, Halmos's 'Sociology of
Mass Media Communicators'(1969), out of fourteen papers presented
there are only three based on systematic study of mass communicators
in their organizational context, only two out of the three are based
on work in British media, and one of these two (Burns, 1964) is only
part of a work the full text of which has never been published.
The one remaining work is Blumler (1969). There are, of course,
books and articles by people who have worked as political broadcasters that draw heavily on their actual experience, and there are
the various biographies and autobiographies of media personnel - but
these are really the stuff upon which more systematic research
should build.

The organizational channels through which the messages from A to
B flow tend to be treated as 'neutral' and 'value'-free (Windlesham,
1966, p.223):

'tv is no more than one of the mechanical devices regularly used to
distribute political information to a mass audience ... if tv cannot
easily be distinguished from other media by an investigation of the
nature of the process, this is because the central process is that
of political communication: a continuous flow of political information not essentially altered by the peculiarities of the channel
selected for the transmission of messages.'

They are also treated as channels that may indeed be value-laden
but whose process can be adequately defined through analysis of its
product; for example, the increasingly prominent notion that news
organizations select, interpret, and present items in accordance
with a pattern ordained by their organizational social and cultural
setting. Quite how they do this, who does it and why they do it -
if indeed they do do it - is often left more to the imagination than
to any systematic study of organizational procedures.

One of the key features of the broadcasting media in this, and
indeed any other, society is their visibility. The percentages of
homes in the advanced industrial societies actually possessing at
least one television set has reached what is to all intents and purposes saturation point (Emmett, 1972, p.197). The television screen
is an obvious part of our environment. We are told by various polls
that television is by far the most popular pastime in the country,
that nearly half the population devotes most of its leisure time to
viewing television (Emmett, 1972, p.200; SMC, 1973, p.13). The fact
of wide-scale and intensive exposure to broadcast material has led

many people to infer that because it is visible and all too present
in our lives it therefore has a dominant role to play in the formation of our attitudes and behaviour. Even given the acknowledged
reservations by media sociologists about the perspectives employed
in their research, (7) it is still true to say that research into
the mass media has been largely dominated by the assumption of the
media's persuasive and influential power. In discussing this point,
Halloran (1969, p.8) stated that: 'The early development of both
mass media and research into mass media coincided with the emergence
of an image of mass society which was to influence research and
thinking about the media for many years.' This, together with the
view that behaviour could be explained in terms of instinct and
'human nature', combined with the apparent success of propaganda
campaigns in the war of 1914-18, tended to reduce communications
theory to a mechanistic stimulus-response theory. It is true to
say, then, that while man's knowledge of his psychological processes
becomes more and more sophisticated, mass-communications theory was,
and is still, dominated by the implicit conception of 'persuasion' -
Halloran (1969, p.9) again: 'They (i.e. comm. researchers) are
basically concerned with effects and it might be more appropriate to
refer to developments in "models of the persuasion process" rather
than to developments in mass communications research.'

The bulk of this effects research has involved a short-term,
stimulus-response, direct-effects approach, and even though innumerable studies and the expenditure of large amounts of research funds
have produced little in the way of conclusive evidence of the
alleged impact of the broadcast media on the lives of the population, the work on 'effects' still predominates in mass-communication
research.

The reasons for this are not difficult to pin down and stem from
the types of questions which have traditionally been asked about the
media and society by academics working in this area, which broadly
speaking have tended to remain the same. (8) In effect, four
factors have underpinned this state of affairs and have shaped the
types of research that has been conducted, to the detriment of our
understanding of the media institutions, their processes and practices. There is in the first instance the nature of public attitudes and concerns; there is also the particular attitudes of
academic researchers who for both intellectual and mercenary reasons
tended to be influenced by the final factor which has been the
reluctance of media controllers to allow the researcher into the
institutions in order to do the necessary research. For all these
reasons the making of television programmes and the social contexts
within which that happens remain obscure.

This then, very briefly, is the historical context for the development or rather non-development of research into the individuals
and institutions responsible for producing the mass-mediated messages and images which are alleged to have such impact on the popular consciousness. The generally lopsided nature of mass communications research is by now widely recognized within the discipline
(Halloran, 1969; McQuail, 1972), though it would probably be true to
say that the discipline still finds it relatively difficult to rectify the situation.

There have of course been a number of studies of the history and

development of the mass-media industries (Schramm, 1960; Petersen
1965; Murdock and Golding 1974), and there have also been a number
of studies of the communicator in his organizational environment
(White, 1950; Breed, 1955; Gieber, 1956, 1964).   There have also
more recently been some interesting observational studies (notably
Blumler, 1969; Elliott, 1972; Cantor, 1972; Epstein, 1973), and in
fact, one might argue that a leading characteristic of these works,
apart from their academic merits, is that they ever appeared.   They
are somewhat special in the overall tradition of mass-communications
research.   The limitations of the situation have, however, taken
their toll in that findings have tended to be either fragmented,
atheoretical, ahistorical or all three, a fact which tends to
reflect the limitations imposed on research of this kind rather than
any failing on the part of the person conducting the research.
Halloran (1969, p.6) states: 'The problem is not so much that there
is a lack of studies but ... that the studies have been confined,
on the whole, to the lower level of mass media operation.'
    A position that was echoed in Denis McQuail's observation that
the discussion of communication organizations (1969, p.67):

'has focussed on a fairly narrow area of enquiry where some evidence
is available.   Clearly there is a need both for a systematic exploration of the effects of variations in structural context on the work
of communicators and also for studies of the external, political,
economic and social pressures in the mass communication organization ... and the tradition of enquiry has remained an empirical one
and theory available is of a fragmentary and ad hoc kind.'

    What is clearly needed, then, when confronting the processes by
which media material is made available is to build the research into
a coherent body of theory so that one's findings do not hang alone
but rather offer the distinct possibility of generalizable conclusions.
    It would be wrong to create the impression that mass-communica-
tion research has avoided altogether the institutional aspects of
the process, and indeed while the actual activity of media research
may have devoted much of its time to investigations of the effects
of the output of the mass media, the need to place the communications organizations and the communicator in their wider social setting has been central to the various models of the communications
process that sociologists have devised.   Wilbur Schramm (1961),
George Gerbner (1956), Westley and Maclean (1957), Riley and Riley
(1959) and De Fleur (1966) have all developed elaborate models of
the processes of mass communications, one of whose features has been
an attempt to integrate the communicator and his organization into
the model.   At the level of model building there has been a recognition as indicated by Jeremy Tunstall's point that (1970, p.15):

'a more organization-oriented view of the media in general seems
essential if we are not to perpetuate the predominant view in which
the media messages sometimes appears to be reaching the audience
members' eyes and ears as if from heaven above or (in some perspectives) hell below.'

Rooted in social-systems analysis and functional analysis, a central feature of these theoretical formulations has been the placing of the communicator and his organization within their particular contexts wherein the processes of mass media production actually take place. That there has been little empirical validation of the actual meaning of these contexts - how the various influences of the wider society, the organization, the production setting, professional and personal ideologies actually relate to decision-making and how they interact to structure and direct programme production - is an unfortunate outcome of the practical and theoretical difficulties of research in this area.

The lack of readily available information on media institutions combined with the pervasive belief in the significance of the media in our daily lives has underpinned the development of the three dominant models of the mass communications process: 1. mass-society theory; 2. the process as a form of interpersonal communication; 3. a flow model. The dominance of particularly the mass-society model has tended to obscure any meaningful understanding of the media organizations and their operations. The concepts of the elite-mass relationship and the purposive manipulatory role of the media in this has led to various explanations of the processes of production within the media organizations rooted more in a priori assumptions than in any meaningful analysis of information gathered from within the organizations themselves. The mystification at the heart of much of the discussion of the processes of mass communication, and in particular at the level of organizational 'analysis', was and is really the starting point of the work of this work. (9)

While I have not here offered a particularly detailed review of the literature relevant to this study, I want briefly to indicate the way in which my reading of that literature and my sense of how it is built around implicit conceptions of the general processes involved (10) framed my own work.

Two central themes have characterized the literature on media institutions and their processes, though often more implicitly than explicitly. These are (a) views of the institutional restraints on media productions - drawing in particular upon aspects of organization theory, and decision-making theory, such work seeks to answer the question 'why is this media product as it is?' by detailing the requirements of the institutions within which the production actually takes place; (b) on examination of the media product as a 'cultural form', approaching the study of media institutions as a problem in the sociology of knowledge. These are only analytically distinct areas of study, and are both often included or at least implied in the research literature. It does suggest, though, two dominant lines of analysis: 1. the structure of decisions within the media institutions; 2. the culture of media institutions and media personnel, and how they relate to what Parkin (1972) has usefully described as socially available 'meaning systems'.

Subsumed within this rather broad bracket are a series of 'descriptions' of media institutions: the concept of 'gatekeeper', tinged as it is witn functionalism in one school of thought, elite conspiracy in another; the notion of the creative individual operating in the organizational setting (a popular description among media professionals); a phenomenological description of the media

process, a school of thought which is becoming prominent in the
United States; a great deal of the work on media institutions has
been concerned to delve into the relationship between the communicator and his audience, employing the concept of reference groups
and developing the concept of transactional analysis. Other descriptions are rooted in no particular theoretical formulation, but
rather consist of detailed – often journalistic – accounts of particular programmes or careers. There is finally a line of analysis
which argues that media organizations are part of the institutions
of a ruling class or elite and that therefore media processes must
be interpreted as the mechanisms by which the ideology of that class
or elite is encoded, transmitted and made dominant.

Thus one of the two central themes has concerned itself with the
inhibitions placed on production by the institutional and social
order. The sorts of questions asked are of the order 'who is the
controller, who is being controlled, how are they controlled, why,
with what effect?'. It is a world of determinations, a heavily
structured process whereby the end product results from something
other than the simple transmission of a 'pure' message – the 'noise'
in the system is, as it were, deafening. The only sop to a concept
of autonomous action (i.e. the communicator acting as communicator
with something he wishes to say rather than the communicator as
'organization man', 'commercial man', 'political tool' doing and
saying what others wish) is in terms of controls being relaxed, or
of the broadcaster routinizing the operational and ideological precepts of his situation, thus neutralizing the controls. As we shall
see, a total understanding of the television process may require
more than just a description of the control mechanisms which impinge
upon the production, important though they are.

The question that is always posed when people talk about the
effects of mass media is, in one version or another, 'what is the
relationship between media output and social consciousness?' One
or two writers, have been enticed by the possibility of reversing
the statement and of posing the question: 'what is the relationship
between social consciousness and media output?' – that is, to what
extent is the intellectual/cognitive domain of the mass communicators' world inhabited by particular 'meaning systems' (Parkin,
1972) or what Stuart Hall has provocatively called the 'mode of
reality of the state' (Hall, 1972).

It has been observed previously (Langs, 1968; Halloran et al.,
1970; Hall, 1972) that news practices incorporate a whole series of
beliefs, a frame of mind, within which the news content is rooted.
This work is only partly involved with news programmes since the
scope of 'political television' is broad and spans the whole departmental structure of television. (In any research of the nature
undertaken here one is of course dealing with both politics and
television – the content of news, current affairs etc. – and the
politics of television, i.e. the attitudes and effect of the political system on television.) Various writers have described the
particular values possessed by communicators, going on to explain
the final product as consisting of the fruits of that value structure. We will need to examine the whole question of the structure
of beliefs within broadcasting: is there a coherent value structure
within broadcasting (as various interviews in the Bakewell-Graham

(1970) book suggest)? If so, what are its main components, if not, what are the counterposing value structures? What role, if any, do belief structures play? Do they change over time, and in relation to what do they change? In short, the literature on media institutions has cohered into two principal perspectives; what we can term, the institutional and cultural determinants of television content.

Research into the institutions of the mass media did not really commence until the 1950s at which time a concept emerged that has figured prominently ever since: that is the concept of the 'gatekeeper', first fully articulated in White's classic study of 'Mr Gates'. (11) While there have been many critiques of this approach, the concept did offer the hope of conceptual clarity with its central observation that media products – whether that be a television programme or a story in a newspaper – are, in part at least, about the intervention of individual subjectivities into the communication process. It is probably true to say that most institutional research in broadcasting has involved variations on this basic theme.

White's Mr Gates was a wire editor on an American newspaper and what he illustrated was the enormously subjective nature of the selection of copy for inclusion in the paper. It will become clear in later stages of this paper that selection embodies much more than making subjective decisions, but what remains significant about this early work is that, by emphasizing that media production was about process, it created the possibility for other and later studies to emphasize that these processes extended beyond the individual consciousness, and were in fact embedded in a number of specific contexts. In short, the essential relativity of media production became the framework for analysis and the function of all research since has been to fill in the details of that framework – emphasizing the importance of technology, the role of organizational superiors, the difficulties of 'time', the role of particular sources of information and so on. (12)

And what did all this add up to? To the general conclusion that although the 'pictures of the world' presented by broadcaster or journalist were necessarily distorted they were a distortion born of the 'mechanics' rather than the politics of production. Having said that, a caveat is called for, since a number of gatekeeper studies did show the way in which production is a social construction in the sense that it takes place within institutions that possess their own goals and needs. For example, at a rather obvious and simple level it was shown in studies in the United States that there was a significant interaction between the social purpose of the news process and the private purpose of owners and controllers. A useful elaboration of how this operates is Breed's study of newspapermen in the north-east USA in which he delineates numerous control mechanisms open to the employer: the initial socialization of the young journalist into the dimensions and meaning of the organization's policies; the use of sanction; the importance of career ambitions; a general feeling of esteem and obligation for his superiors; the perpetual state of urgency about the news process and so on (Breed 1955). (13) It was on the basis of studies such as this one that a number of writers, ante-Marcuse, began to conclude that because of the operation of these processes the media tended to support existing social mores and values, to favour elite groups within the community and generally to underpin the status quo. (14)

If gatekeeper studies drew our attention to the communication system operating within the media institutions as well as between them and the audience they also pointed to the particularities of organizational control. Various studies have now taken up this theme and considered the communications process from the perspective of the internal operations of the bureaucracies within which it happens. The question of how the organizational context influenced the product necessarily entailed the further questions of which way decisions flow within the organization and the extent to which the individual broadcaster is an autonomous actor.

As a general proposition, research has argued that decisions flow down from senior executives to programme-makers whose situation is therefore heavily constrained by organizational criteria, and that this denies the very purpose for which the organization exists, that is, communication. There is, then, at the heart of all broadcasting, and indeed of all institutionalized communication, a profound paradox embodied in the conflict between institutional needs and production needs - in short, between the theory and practice of communication. It has to be said, though, that there is a tendency on the part of academics to seek a black and white solution to the question of control: either programme-makers are essentially autonomous, as for example, Jay Blumler's study of '24 Hours'' election coverage in 1966, (15) or they are seen as total 'victims' of the structural contexts within which they must work - as suggested for example in Halloran and his colleagues' study of the October 1968 Vietnam Demonstration (16) and in Epstein's recent study of the American news networks. (17) I would merely suggest that the dichotomy is too bold and that the operation of influences from above in the form of policy statements, the creation of standards and norms, instructions as to what to cover and not to cover and so on, and the operation of the individual motivations of programme-makers should be seen as interlocked processes, differentially important historically and institutionally, whose interaction forms a central feature of production. Blumler's work, excellent as it is, I find particularly intriguing since his argument - that in an organizational world in which human action is a complex interplay of individual autonomy and structural constraint there is an increasing tendency for programme-makers to operate free of restraint - challenges the theoretical orthodoxy which I have been expounding and in many ways echoes the orthodoxy of the 'fourth estate'.

In arguing that production in broadcasting is structured, restrained and inhibited and therefore partial, the proposition is not that this is a function of conspiracy or conscious distortion, rather that partiality is a consequence of the routines by which organizations and their employees operate on a daily basis. For example, Halloran and his colleagues argue that the fact that the media presented the Vietnam demonstration as a violent one (when, they claim, it was not so violent) related to the way in which the news angles of the story were selected and developed prior to the demonstration. This in turn was rooted in the wider organizational need to utilize scarce resources, the dependence on newspapers for

ideas and information through which to define items, conceptions of
the nature of the technology, expectations of the audience and the
kinds of material which would sustain interest and attention (Halloran et al., 1970). Epstein tries to define precisely the structures within which programme-making is encased and sees three:
organizational, political, the nature of the medium. The world 'out
there' is refracted through these structures and its presentation
becomes a unique but distorted construction of the 'true' picture
(1973). A simple example of this within news programmes would be
the emphasis on visual stories, the use of familiar images, a focus
on conflict, an emphasis on action rather than talking heads, the
presentation of stories in a fictional form, with a beginning,
middle and end. A number of other studies have shown the way in
which a whole range of programme output is dominated by organizational perceptions of what will be commercially viable and politically suitable. (18) Perhaps the most accomplished study along
these lines in a British context has been Elliott's description of
how subjective, institutional and televisual factors limited Stuart
Hood's attempts to produce a series of programmes dealing with 'the
nature of prejudice'. (19) Interspersed with such telling observations as 'the film sequence was intended to attract the viewers'
attention so (the producer) instructed the film editor to pick out
scenes of action and violence that would make an arresting sequence
...' (1972, p.72), his final conclusion is harsh: 'the dominant
means of communication in society is tending more and more to be
controlled and operated by people who have nothing to say, or if
they have cannot use the media to say it' (1972, p.166).

Research on the role which institutions external to broadcasting
play in the making of content is, in an academic sense, much less
thorough than that which has specifically looked at the internal
operations of broadcasting. In considering the role of what we
might call 'externality' a number of studies stand out. The significance and centrality of the State within the affairs of broadcasting is best evinced by Anthony Smith's lengthy study. (20) In
particular I would point to an article by Smith in which he discussed the coverage of the Ulster crisis by British broadcasting,
which in its depiction of the complex interweaving of operational
practice and political requirements is by far the best account to
date of that troubled area. (21) The central theme here is that
pressures from the political structure - and broadcasting is potentially the vassal of a political master - have become internalized
and understood as given routines of programme-making which, though
they do not overtly threaten the sense of autonomy prevalent within
broadcasting institutions, nevertheless remain as a permanent underlying state of crisis.

Two other pieces one would wish to mention are by Kumar (1975)
and Hood (1972). The problem of broadcasters as these two writers
see it is that they are constantly faced with the question of the
relation in which they stand to a situation where the moral and
political consensus - the stability of which is an essential prerequisite for the maintenance of the illusion of impartiality,
autonomy, etc. - is challenged by increasingly powerful and dissi-
dent groups. Broadcasting, they argue, will always tend to occupy
the same intellectual locale as the representatives of dominant

political groups – Hood's 'ruling classes' – and stand against those
oppositional forces which are a necessary component of the process
of change.

The importance of the commercial environment has been elaborated
in relation to the commercial television companies, and, for
example, Murdock and Golding (1974) have recently demonstrated not
only the framework but also the consequences of what they describe
as the 'political economy of the mass media'. They have, one might
say, a passionate interest in the life and times of Lew Grade.

Popular opinion holds that the operations of broadcasting are
heavily influenced by the intellectual dispositions of those
involved in making programmes. At the same time among important
sections of political and cultural elites, occupying very different
positions along the political spectrum, there is a powerful belief
that the nature of broadcasting, and particularly the nature of
television, is a function of its domination by a particular set of
political ideologies. The research literature, however, has argued
that the question of the intellectual location of broadcasting, the
means by which it is arrived at and the processes by which it is
sustained and reproduced are far more complex than this simplistic
view. Two distinct types of belief need to be considered: 1. professional ideologies drawn from the very heart of the occupation of
the broadcaster, and 2. the political ideologies drawn from the
individual broadcasters' membership of the wider political culture.
In looking at the role of belief structures in broadcasting one is
tapping the intellectual framework of the broadcaster's occupational
being and his social being.

A pastiche of the ideological self-image of the professional
broadcaster is that of a creative individual, serving, informing,
educating and entertaining his public but doing so in an impartial
and above all responsible manner. The adherence to such views by
professional braodcasters has been documented on numerous occasions,
but what is particularly interesting is that the attachment to such
norms is very high indeed whereas the attachment to expressed political beliefs is very low. It would of course be logically difficult for the broadcaster to articulate both sets of belief. Placed
in the context of the previous findings of research, what is being
argued is that the precise interpretation and meaning of the professional codes of practice are actually defined by institutional
criteria and that in effect individuality and creativity count for
little unless they function in accord with the concerns and ideas
of senior personnel. In short, professional descriptions of what
they do, how they do it why, are little more than an operational
fiction.

An interesting twist to this view is provided in a study by
Sigelman (1973) of American newspapers. He posed the question of
how journalists could sustain their attachment to professional norms
when they functioned within newspapers which pursued distinct editorial lines and ensured that the news content of the paper reflected that line. How does one alleviate such an apparently tension-
inducing situation? What Sigelman argued is that the whole process
of recruitment, socialization, working arrangements, and ideological predispositions is such as to ensure a compatibility between
employer and employee. Thus viewed, the canons of the profession

remain mere mythology since the employer and employee both function within a common framework of understanding. This is an important paper, since previous studies have discussed the means by which inconsistent beliefs are neutralized by the hierarchy. Here the two groups are in fundamental agreement and the interests of both are served: the one to sustain a particular line, the other to sustain the illusion of the professional norms.

In a number of pieces Hall (1971, 1972, 1973) has written of the cultural location of the mass media, arguing that the broadcasting organizations are embedded within society's dominant institutions and are therefore enclosed by its dominant ideas. That this does not strain to breaking point the professional rhetoric of broadcasters is because of the potent mystique of such mediating concepts as objectivity, impartiality and balance which retain viability because broadcasters operate within the confines of a 'sanctioned terrain' defined by the precepts of the liberal democratic order. The point is, of course, that the central precepts of the professional ideology of broadcasting arose within the context of an emerging theory of the press which was not only compatible with the political ideology of liberal democracy but part of that structure.

It is not too difficult to see why such authors as Hall and Hood can outline with a sense of exasperation the apparent ease with which communicators can declare their 'objectivity' when to Hall's and Hood's minds their whole life and code is geared to the interest and wellbeing of one political order. Communicators, on the whole, favour liberal democracy and work comfortably within the intellectual frameworks which it provides. Hall and Hood clearly do not favour its political and social arrangements and employ very different frameworks for explicating its nature. These two authors and others of a similar disposition are perfectly aware of all this and quite rightly point out that explanatory frameworks or, in sociological terms, paradigms, only survive and operate so long as they do explain the world, when new explanations are called for so are new paradigms and when that happens the broadcaster is totally compromised.

Chapter 2

THE PRODUCTION OF POLITICAL TELEVISION
A conceptual framework

Within the broad framework of discussion about political communication two main themes can be identified. One connects historically
with a conception of newspapers in a liberal democratic society as
organizations which through their ability to scrutinize the governing elites, and their provision of information for the electorate,
are able to act as a 'fourth estate'. Counterposed to this view is
what one might term the sanctioned media model, which views the
broadcasting media as an appendage of the State or of commercial
interests and thus largely geared to the needs and interests of
those dominant groups. One can perhaps separate these positions
into camps which employ either a liberal democratic world view, or
a class-based or elite-based analysis. It is possible to see the
distinctions between the opposed explanatory structures in the very
language which they employ, the one speaking of 'civic culture',
'accountability', 'watchdog', etc., the other speaking of 'ideology', 'control', 'elites', etc. The one sees the media as a means
by which the political institutions are held responsible, the other
sees the media as a means by which these institutions sustain an
'irresponsible' position by legitimating the position of dominant
groups within public consciousness.

THE VIEW FROM LIBERAL DEMOCRACY: POLITICAL BROADCASTING AS
FOURTH ESTATE

Models of political communications are usually composed of three
basic elements: A. political actors, B. the electorate, and C. the
institutions through which messages are transmitted (of which the
mass media are the most prominent example) resting somewhere in
between the two. The flow of information is seen as moving from
A, the political actors, to B the electorate, via C the media
institutions, though the media also create information themselves
by casting a critical eye over the operations of government. This
is the 'watchdog' role so ably described by Seymour-Ure (1968) in
the context of the print media. Likening the press to a pressure
group which has the ability to enforce certain sanctions, he states,
'The sanction of a newspaper is the power to publish what a party

or Government wants to keep private, which is ultimately connected, probably, to an estimate of electoral advantage' (1968, p.304). Thus the criteria for judging a healthy press in this view is not the sheer number of press outlets, points of view, etc., but whether the existing press is able to carry out fully and efficiently this watchdog role. Discussion of the precise role of broadcast journalism has involved variations on a similar theme. Should the broadcast journalist function as a mouthpiece for the State, the neutral purveyor of someone else's information, a source of non-partisan comment and criticism or as an overtly partisan editorializer (Blumler, 1970). The proposition offered by Blumler is that British television moved 'from the more subdued second function, which predominated in the 1950s, towards an enthusiastic application of the third in the 1960s' (1970, p.72). Referring to his own work in the 1966 Election, he develops a position which encapsulates and reproduces one view of the broadcast media, that of the liberal democratic theory of the press. In other words, that the broadcasting media in Britain, having emerged from the dark age of Reithian paternalism, have actually begun to incorporate certain functions that attach to the role of the press in a liberal democracy - not only the transmission of the information with which the electorate can begin to make its decisions, but also the establishment of a critical presence within the political process. A century after the print media, and four decades after its own birth, the broadcast media gained membership of the fourth estate.

What, however, is the fourth estate, what precisely is this 'theory of the press', how does it apply to the broadcast media and what implications does it have for a discussion of the nature of programme-making?

A THEORY OF 'THE PRESS'

On considering the substance to the 'theory' which underpins certain conceptions of the role of the press in Western political culture, one has to consider the proposition that there was an evolution from a libertarian view of the press to a view which holds that the press has a number of 'social responsibilities'. (1) This argument embodies a rather genteel view of history and differs somewhat in its view of the development of the press from such works as Williams (1965). It involves a rather Whiggish view of the gradual accretion of constitutional changes and the gradual emergence of a liberal democracy. It avoids the harsh realities of the means by which the press actually gained its politicized role, constantly hampered by the State, and ignores the connections with changing economic structures and attendant changes in the structure of power between rising and declining classes. Beneath the emerging world of liberal democracy lay the historic clash, Williams would argue, between the class in the ascendancy, the urban middle class, and the class in decline, the landed aristocracy. Williams notes, 'The newspaper was the creation of the commercial middle class, mainly in the 18th century. It served this class with news relevant to the conduct of business, and as such established itself as a financially independent institution' (1965, p.197). However, though there may be a

degree of difference in the explanatory frameworks, the differences
are more of emphasis than substance and relate to the details of the
precise sequential ordering of events and change. The views
embodied by this 'theory' provide one dominant explanation of the
situation of the press and it is at that level that they need to be
considered, as the summation of a historical position which only
approximates to historical reality.

With the radical transformation in the seventeenth and eighteenth
centuries of man's view of man — the emergence of rationalism, the
development of the middle classes, and the preponderance of market
forces, the attribution of significance to the individual per se
and his possession of natural rights, with the refocusing from the
deity onto the laity, the ground was well prepared for the emergence
of a press liberated from the authoritarian attachment to the State.
'By the end of the (eighteenth) century libertarian principles were
enshrined in the fundamental law of the land, in constitutional
phrases protecting freedom of speech and of the press' (Siebert,
1956, p.44). The vision embodied in the work of John Milton, John
Erskine, Thomas Jefferson, John Stuart Mill, a developmental image,
spanning three centuries, was of a society of rational men engaged
in the pursuit of truth (Siebert, 1956). Since a rational decision
was deemed to require information upon which to dwell before arrival
at that decision, particular unpolluted sources of information
became crucial. The first purpose of the press thus became the provision of information; 'Basically the underlying purpose of the
media was to help to discover truth, to assist in the process of
solving political and social problems by presenting all manner of
evidence and opinion as the basis for decision. The essential
characteristic of this process was its freedom from government control or domination' (Siebert, 1956, p.51). Thus, while one view
would see the emergence of the press as dependent on the fact that
it served the specific interests of the urban middle class, the
tendency here is to view the emergence as the fruition of a view
as to the actual intellectual desirability of a free press. Siebert
says that the purpose of the press was and is to 'discover truth',
others might argue that the purpose was to discover the state of
business and the latest share prices.

The immediate problem, however, was how one could guarantee the
'truth' of the information provided? The solution was seen to lie
in the inescapable logic, the self-righting mechanisms, of the free
marketplace of ideas, 'let the public at large be subjected to a
barrage of information and opinion, some of it possibly false, and
some of it containing elements of both. Ultimately the public could
be trusted to digest the whole, to discard that not in the public
interest and to accept that which served the needs of the individual
and of the society of which he is a part' (Siebert, 1956, p.51).
Jefferson articulated the point: 'The discernment they have manifested between truth and falsehood, shows that they may safely be
trusted to hear everything true and false, and to form a correct
judgement between them' (quoted in Smith, 1973, p.36). Thus, in the
free marketplace of ideas — always assuming that any individual who
so wished had the facilities with which to market his ideas — truth
would drive out falsehood. The key factor was that the press was
divorced from the government, it stood as an apparently autonomous

entity in the midstream of social and political affairs. In this
situation the press could r.ot only be the purveyor of information
about the government but could also act as a watchdog on the government. With the development during the nineteenth century of a
British governmental system which emphasized the accountability of
the government and its attendant institutions to the people, with
advances in education and increased awareness of and activity in
political affairs, the press was lauded as a central institution in
the political process. Through its ability to transform the complexities of government the press was seen as an ideal means of
communication between electors and their representatives, enabling
the former to arrive at rational decisions in choosing between rival
claimants to being the latter. It was only a short step from the
press enabling the electorate to hold the government to account,
to its holding the government to account itself by seeking out corruption and attacking abuses of power. Thus in this full-bloodied
conception of the fourth estate, the press was not only a broker of
information, but also potentially a breaker of governments.

Such briefly was one view of the historical development of a
political press. It was very clear, however, to even the most fervent advocate of the fourth estate that the nineteenth century did
not only bring changes in the political structure and that a number
of developments in the organization and economics of the press
rendered meaningless the very notion of a libertarian press even as
it was apparently achieving its rightful position in the political
process.

Carey (1969) argues that one witnessed in the late nineteenth
and early twentieth centuries in, for example, the American news
media what one might describe as the rebrokerization of the press.
Arising from a 'fetishism of objectivity', which itself derived from
the need for the news agencies to serve an ideologically heterogeneous readership (Carey 1969, p.32-3) it led to the assumption
'that the highest standard of professional performance occurred
when the reporter presented the reader with all sides of an issue
(though there were usually only two), presented all the 'facts',
and allowed the reader to decide what these facts meant'. The press
in this view became a passive link in a communications chain, and
not, as the theory of the press so far outlined would have had it,
as an active watchdog, a constituent of the fourth estate. The difficulty and inherent danger in this development would clearly be
that in abandoning its interpretive and critical role, in transmitting 'untouched' information from society, then the press would
reproduce that information in all its confusion and contradiction.
This would in itself rest on a 'development' in the dominant view
of the audience since, as we have seen, libertarian theory rested
on the premise of the individual's capacity to detect truth from
falsehood.

The idea of a libertarian theory of the press suffered a further
blow with the incorporation of broadcasting within its ambit in the
early decades of the twentieth century. The theory had assumed the
existence and availability of numerous outlets, and yet here was a
new medium, the central characteristic of which was that it was
physically impossible, given available technologies, to have numerous outlets. Every broadcasting organization therefore had built

into the principles upon which it was established a clear element of
State control - the very antithesis of the then dominant libertarian
theory of the press. As Smith states (1973, p.45), the emergence
of broadcasting was a midwife to what became known as the 'social
responsibility' theory of the press.

It was also the case that the axiomatic basis of the libertarian
theory did not stand too close an inspection, in the context of the
advanced industrial society of the twentieth century concepts of
rationalism, natural and individual rights, free enterprise, all
seemed to wither before the realities of industrial society. Above
all else the economic logic of libertarian theory - that outlets
were available to all who wished to possess them - became patently
nonsensical in the face of the immense costs entailed in publishing.
Thus the concentration of the press into fewer and fewer units, the
increasing criticism of the press's role in society as that concentration increased, the undermining of the rationalist assumptions
of man, the challenge to the efficacy of the 'free marketplace' of
ideas, that is the general intellectual challenge to the basic
assumptions of the Enlightenment which had provided the intellectual
justification for libertarian theory, all served to chip away at the
foundations on which the old theory had rested. As much as anything
else it was noted that nowhere in libertarian theory was the public
accorded a right to receive information. In response to such
changes the press began to express a commitment to the general welfare and to express a responsibility to their audience (Peterson,
1956, p.83).

Theodore Peterson (1956, p.75) described the social responsibility theory as 'largely a grafting of new ideas onto traditional
theory'. He was making the point that social responsibility accepted libertarian view that the press services the political system
with information, discussion and debate; that it should enlighten
the public and therefore encourage self-government; act as a watchdog of government; facilitate commerce through the use of advertising; entertain; and be financially self-sufficient. What the
emerging view did not accept was that the press actually did perform
those roles.

The theory of a socially responsible press received its clearest
articulation in the Commission on the Freedom of the Press in the
United States, which published a number of reports in 1947, and in
Britain by the Royal Commission on the Press which sat from 1947-9.
The implication of the movement from libertarian to social responsibility concepts was that 'Press freedom was a freedom to provide a
certain kind of service to society, it retained no freedom to please
itself' (Smith, 1973, p.45). The Canons of Journalism adopted by
the American Society of Newspaper Editors in 1923 called on newspapers 'to practise responsibility to the general welfare, sincer-
ity, truthfulness, impartiality, fair play, decency and respect for
the individual's privacy' (Peterson, 1956, p.85). The emergence of
this theory and the codes of practice which it entailed and which
were attached in particular to the broadcasting institutions, its
exponents would argue, reflected a developing view that man was far
from rational, was, in fact, immature and irrational. It is in this
historical context that one can situate one view of the position of
the broadcasting institution in general and their political broad-

casting sections in particular, as being autonomous units guided by
a number of key principles.

It is useful to illuminate the point by listing the five requirements which the Commission on the Freedom of the Press saw embodied
in social responsibility theory:

1 That the press provide a 'truthful, comprehensive and intelligent account of the day's events in a context which gives them
meaning'. In this we can perhaps see the division between 'fact'
and 'comment' which was underpinned by the notion of objectivity.

2 The press should serve as 'a forum for the exchange of comment
and criticism'.

3 It should project a 'representative picture of the constituent
groups in society'.

4 It should be responsible 'for the presentation and clarification of the goals and values of the society'.

5 It should provide 'full access to the day's intelligence'.

This, then, was the articulation of a guiding framework within
which the press should function. While it was still felt that the
press retained its independence from the State, the concept of freedom implied in this autonomy subtly changed. Peterson describes the
position: 'Libertarian theory was born of a concept of negative
liberty which we can define loosely as "freedom from" and more precisely as "freedom from external restraint". The social responsibility theory, on the contrary, rests on a concept of positive
liberty, "freedom for", which calls for the presence of the necessary implements for the attainment of a desired goal' (1956, p.93).
Crucially, whereas in libertarian theory under no circumstances
should the State intervene in the affairs of the press, social
responsibility theory holds a view that the State must not only
allow freedom but must actually promote it. 'Government', Hocking
of the Commission tells us, 'remains the residuary legatee of responsibility for an adequate press performance' (Hocking, 1947).
By extension it is clearly within this context that one can see
the enabling acts and charters of British broadcasting as an exemplification of the fulfilment of this duty. However subtle, and
to many critics of broadcasting, exasperating, relationships between
the Minister responsible for broadcasting in Britain and the broadcasting institutions themselves are well known and the following
statement might well have been culled from the record in Hansard of
a Minister's response to a question of, for example, the BBC: 'If
the freedom of the Press is to achieve reality, government must set
limits on its capacity to interfere with, regulate, or suppress the
voices of the press or to manipulate the data on which the public
judgement is formed' (Commission, 1947).

Broadcasting became a prime exemplification of the social responsibility theory: too powerful, too scarce a resource to be allowed
to operate completely unfettered and 'irresponsible', a whole
battery of guidelines was laid down – educate, inform, entertain, be
impartial, balanced, objective, act in public service, be fair,
operate codes on taste and violence. Yet great pains were made to
create broadcasting systems which visibly functioned beyond the
control of governments. The argument of the Commission was that
absolute freedom of the press to do as it pleased 'wears the aspect
of social irresponsibility. The Press must know that its faults

and errors have ceased to be private vagaries and have become public
dangers. Its inadequacies menace the balance of public opinion. It
has lost the common and ancient liberty to be deficient in its functions or to offer half-truths for the whole.' This view was more
sardonically echoed in the opinion of Anthony Wedgwood Benn that
broadcasting is far too important to be left to the broadcasters.
Thus what one view would - as we shall see - interpret as a system
of control, is here felt to be the very mechanics by which broadcasting autonomy is actually sustained and operated.

The notion of socially responsible autonomy, which is what the
social responsibility theory actually involves, is readily apparent
in the numberous public statements by senior broadcasting executives. Charles Curran quotes with approval Sir William Haley's view
that the BBC 'remains an independent body. It has charge of its own
affairs. Its programmes are safeguarded from outside interference.
Its position within the community and the corollary of its trust of
impartiality remain' (BBC Handbook, 1973, p.9). Curran challenges,
however, the rather patrician, neo-Reithian view of Haley that the
intent of broadcasting is to raise public taste, and sums up the
position in a manner which is a classic exposition of the doctrine
of social responsibility (BBC, 1973, pp.9-10):

'The BBC does not exist to shape society to some predetermined pattern. Supplying that society with an accurate and comprehensive
service of impartial broadcast journalism is not shaping it to a
pattern. Setting out to "raise taste" would be. We have a continuing duty to educate as well as to inform and entertain ... it is
providing a service; it is not setting itself up as an arbiter of
taste or a manipulator of society. But, if it is doing its job
responsibly and well, it will give its audiences a clear picture of
the prevailing scale of values within society, and will reflect the
order in which society as a whole (often described as 'the consensus') classified those values. By being truthful and responsible,
it achieves more than it could ever achieve by setting itself up as
the nation's guide in matters of taste or morals.'

Freedom and detached observation, comment and the provision of
information, these provide the framework for this liberal democratic
view of the situation of broadcasting in British society.

The position taken here is one reply to the question of how near
the institutions of the mass media are to society in general and to
the dominant institutions within that society in particular, notably
the government and State structure. By implication it denies that
these structures are able to influence programme content. The central proposition within Curran's statement is that broadcasters are
of the nation, but not of the government. Broadcasting becomes in
this view the 'representative' of the nation, one means by which the
notion of the accountability of rulers to ruled is implemented. A
former senior TV news executive, Donald Edwards (1962, p.12) stated:

'If broadcasting is to reflect the nation, we must include matters
in dispute. We must communicate the views of others, however dis-
tasteful or embarrassing they may be to some. This is our duty as
honest reporters. The public is entitled to the truth as inter-

preted by all sides — and so on behalf of the public we put probing, searching questions to Cabinet Ministers, railway chiefs, industrial bosses — all "them who push us around". The public have not the opportunity of putting the questions themselves. We do it for them.'

This is, of course, the 'accountability' function referred to by Blumler (1970) and is a clear exposition of the 'requirements' of the press as outlined by the Commission (1947). Kenneth Lamb (1974) in a lengthy account of numerous crises and the difficulties involved in covering political affairs, brackets his discussion with the statements that 'The BBC is in every proper sense of the word a national broadcasting service, but it is not and never has been government-controlled or government run.... The BBC is independent, and its independence is vital to its credibility. But it is also a corporate citizen. It is not above or outside the nation, but a part of it,' sentiments echoed by Sir Michael Swann (1974) in his reflections on his first twelve months as chairman of the BBC.

One could reproduce many similar statements by broadcasting personnel about the position of broadcasting. Broadly, they add up to a position in which the broadcasting organization, particularly through its news and current affairs department, is able from its independent position to provide information and 'explain' events and processes for the citizenry which comprises its audience.

There is also another interesting strand to this argument about the situation of broadcasting, and this is reflected in the academic formulation of the situation of political television in, for example, elections. The position is exemplified in the work of Seymour-Ure (1968, 1974) and Blumler (1969, 1970, 1974), and their work provides a detailed and sophisticated formula of the view of broadcasting as consisting of autonomous but responsible institutions.

In Seymour-Ure's illuminating book on the press (1968) he argues that of the various functions which the press can fulfil the most important is the question 'whether the newspapers we do have are properly equipped to assemble, interpret and criticise information about politics and Government' (1968, p.307). In this way the press is able to sustain the democratic basis to British political life. The only real problem which the press faces in this view is whether it is suitably equipped for its role, which is presented as analogous to that of the opposition in Parliament. The structure of Seymour-Ure's argument is of the press fulfilling the role assigned to it by the social responsibility theory of the press, the watchdog of the democratic process. It may have one or two teeth missing, it may be rather insipid occasionally and guard the wrong doors, but watchdog it nevertheless is. Now, the interesting feature is that when one comes to read Seymour-Ure's and Blumler's accounts of political television, similar themes emerge.

In a rather perceptive and certainly most useful account of the development of the media's coverage of the general elections between 1945 and 1970, Seymour-Ure (1974) identifies several dominant trends in that coverage: the general growth of election broadcasting, instigated by the rise of television as the principal political medium, the break up of the parties' monopoly over political broadcasting and the rapid expansion of the broadcasting institution's

own programme. At the centre of his analysis is the notion that
broadcasting quickly came to occupy the centre of the electoral
stage to the general chagrin of the parties who saw television as
being a, perhaps superior, rival in the definition of the issues of
the election and in shaping the campaign. The campaign-of-the-
parties, or so the scenario goes, became the campaign-of-the-media,
and particularly the campaign-of-television as a new independence of
the broadcaster emerged during the last years of the 1950s and the
decade of the 1960s (Seymour-Ure, 1974, pp.212-13).
 Blumler (1974, pp.135-6) makes a similar point when discussing a
number of the features which distinguished the coverage by the
British media of elections in the 1970s. He points to the

'evolution of both television and the press - the former mainly
since 1959 and the latter unevenly throughout the post-war period -
towards a more autonomous relationship to the party system ... Thus,
less emphasis has been placed in recent years on the more passive
media functions of transmitting party-originated messages, and more
on the active provision of frames of reference that serve to filter
and interpret such messages. Consequently, British elections have
appeared to become increasingly media affairs rather than party
affairs. Of course, no such contrast should be pressed too far.
The main outlines of electoral choice in Britain are still set by
records, policies and rhetoric emanating from party activities and
decisions. Nevertheless, the presentation of that choice to the
public has recently been shaped more by the values, attitudes and
forms of audience service of media men than by the politicians more
partisan concerns.'

Seymour-Ure refers to Blumler's work on the election of 1966,
(Blumler, 1969) which Blumler spent in the BBC current affairs
group, to make the point that the new independence of the broadcasting organizations often created a situation where the priorities
of the two groups, broadcasters and politicians, would clash, what
he terms 'a lack of identity between the strategies' (Seymour-Ure,
p.214). Blumler, in fact, also made this point in a piece on the
general process of television in political communication (Blumler,
1970, p.94) in which he argued that there is a lack of clear 'role
definitions which enhances the potential for conflict'.
 By 1970, Seymour-Ure states (1974, pp.234-5), the

'media as a whole were detached as never before from the party
system. In 1954 they stood towards one end of a spectrum: there
were still a few 'official' party papers, and on the air the parties
had absolute control over the very limited number of election programmes broadcast. By 1970 they had shifted far towards the other
end. In an era of universal suffrage the parties had paradoxically
lost control over the means of appealing to the electorate.'

He concludes that we can expect to see even more expansion in the
significance of broadcast journalism since it would be too much
trouble for the politicians to force a reversal in the developments
of election broadcasting. We look forward to a future where 'broadcast programmes (are) increasingly free of rules imposed from out-

side about party balance at election time; and (where there is) an
orientation in current affairs broadcasting ... that was similar to
what has just been called "positive criticism" in the press' (1974,
p.237) – positive criticism being the adoption of an 'anti-govern-
ment stance regardless of party', 'suspicious of government and well
equipped to expose it' (1974, p.236). The general drift of Seymour-
Ure's thesis is clear: through a gradual process of change in the
setting of the media institutions, with the corollary of much expanded and improved election broadcasting, a detachment has arisen
between the political and media spheres, to the extent that the
media have now become potent forces in themselves and challenge the
sovereignty of the Parliamentary process. Blumler's conclusion
about the overall state of the media in general, and broadcasting
in particular, is in similar vein. Discussing a number of indications in the February 1974 election of the increasing flexibility
of the coverage of elections – increased coverage, more time for
minorities, experts, ordinary voters, new news programmes – he says
that this is heartening when so much of the analyses of the mass
media emphasize the constraints which inhibit their actual operation. Speaking of the·relatively free hand which producers in
broadcasting had in covering the February election, he states by
way of conclusion (1974, pp.161-2):

'Some part of the explanation for this must lie in the public service model of organization that Britain has sustained in the broadcasting field for many years. This has ensured that financial constraints do not stifle innovatory impulses at source, and has helped
to keep alive the principle that communication should serve citizen-
ship.'

THE VIEW FROM THE OTHER SIDE: THE 'COLONIZATION' OF THE FOURTH
ESTATE

    By controlling every major opinion moulding institution in the
    country, members of the upper class play a predominant role in
    determining the framework within which decisions on important
    issues are reached (Domhoff, 1967, p.83).
    Two central themes emerged from the literature on media institu-
tions which reflect the more overtly radical perspectives of many
writers on the situation of broadcasting as opposed to those numerous authors referred to in the 'view from the fourth estate'. That
view of broadcasting in general, and political broadcasting in particular, emphasized the approximation to a 'theory of the press' in
liberal democratic societies paying particular attention to the
sense of autonomy which pervades the position. The view from what
I have called 'the other side' – implying its generally 'radical'
base – emphasizes a very different view of the historical development of 'the press', the constraints, the actual lack of autonomy,
the sheer inability of broadcasting to achieve what the rhetoricians
of the fourth estate claim it does achieve, the attachment to dominant institutions within society – be they political or commercial –
and to society's dominant ideology. Within this explanation twin
themes also emerge. One, that the restraints on, or 'structuring'

of, the production process derive from other social institutions or
social groups - for example, the State, institutional elites, social
classes, etc. - as exemplified in the work of, for example, Smith
(1973), Hood (1972) and Miliband (1973). The other theme, while in
broad agreement with the overall conclusions of these writers,
derives from the more 'sophisticated' pastures of media research and
points to the structuring of the programme-making process by particular routines and ideologies that derive from the occupational setting of the organization and from the general structure of ideas
within society, as, for example, in the numerous works of Stuart
Hall (1971, 1972, 1973) and in a recent paper by Murdock and Golding
(1974).

Overall, these views imply that political broadcasting is bound
to the dominant institutions and ideologies by an actual subordination in power terms, by an intellectual disposition to acknowledge the role and centrality of those institutions and ideas and
by occupational practices which serve the status quo rather than
'alternative' views of, say, the political process and history.
This latter notion of 'occupational practice equals status quo' is
clearly defined in Elliott's perception that the programme-making
process is locked into a rehash of conventional wisdom and has much
quoted observation that programme-making has more to do ith the
contradictions than the conspiracies of capitalist society (Elliott,
1972).

What I wish to isolate here are the central points of this
explanation and to indicate how one might begin to consider their
implications in the light of evidence gathered.

The premise of the elite position is that any analysis of the
context within which broadcasting occurs - and by implication within
which programmes are made - necessarily involves a consideration of
the political, economic, and cultural factors which inhibit and
ultimately control what happens. Because of the integration of the
broadcasting institutions within the framework of a ruling class or
elite, (2) to accomplish its tasks as envisioned by the fourth-
estate view, it would necessarily have to place its very existence
in jeopardy. Such a line of analysis reflects a more wide-ranging
observation that interaction within society is about conflicts
between social units of unequal power. This view approaches the
'problem' of media production from the perspective of political
sociology - though this is often not explicit - and sees the treatment of the media as one part of the discussion of the nature of
social order. As Dowse and Hughes (1972, p.13) state, the 'area of
substantive concern for the political sociologist is the problem of
social order and political obedience'.

If one view of the world sees social order as sustained by a commitment to a set of common norms and by agreement between the plura-
lity of groups within society as to the basic legitimacy of the
values which characterize society, the implications of this alternative view of the situation of the media involves a different perspective altogether. The social structures of Western society, the
position states, are heavily stratified, with an unequal distribution of power and wealth between the different strata. In such a
society social order may be maintained through the use of force but,
as Rex (1974, p.213) notes, 'the use of bullets and prisons, has on

the whole not been seen as necessary elements in British capitalism'. The implicit observation is that those societies in which
the mass media are both most visible and discussed, are characterized by a high level of agreement as to 'legitimate' values, even
though the structure of rewards according to available evidence is
manifestly unequal. Thus the dominant orders need not exercise
their institutional power to sustain their dominance since they
rule, however ironically, with the acquiescence of the lower orders.
By extension it is argued that 'the ideas of the ruling class are
always in any age the ruling ideas' - and our age is no exception-
not because of any rational convergence at a point of mutual agreement by two different classes (or elite/non-elite, etc), nor because
of the persistent use of force, but rather because one class/elite,
through its command of power and privilege will be in a position to
legitimate its world view. Hence 'those groups in society which
occupy positions of the greatest power and privilege will also tend
to have the greatest access to the means of legitimation. That is
to say, the social and political definitions of those in dominant
positions tend to become objectified and enshrined in the major
institutional orders, so providing the moral framework of the entire
system' (Parkin, 1972, p.83). Thus, there is, in this view, beneath
every moral order a political order from which the moral framework
is derived and by which it is sustained. Through that moral framework one witnesses the intellectual subordination of one group to
the values and ideas of another. Should command of the processes
of legitimation - the assumption that the existing order of things
is rational, objective and therefore legitimate - fail, the institutionally privileged groups are able to fall back on their command
of 'power' to maintain the order that the mechanics of legitimation
failed to achieve. In this view the press would either be ideologically in tune or suffer the fate of being politically/commercially
out of order.
    Parkin (1972), whose book is rapidly emerging as something of a
minor classic in the discussion of the dynamics of stratification,
does not in fact refer to the role of the mass media as an agency of
legitimation. It is, however, within this explanatory framework
that one can situate what I have here referred to as the 'colonization thesis' of media institutions.
    In a review of the state of elite studies in Britain, Rex (1974,
p.216) asks what are the

'institutional and ideological means whereby the elites relate
themselves and the classes which they represent to those over whom
they exercise hegemony. Three phenomena of importance here would
appear to be the political labour movement, the non-elite institutions of higher education and the media. The central process here
is the incorporation into or co-option of the leading figures in the
these spheres into the elite world.'

The point was made somewhat more stridently and with none of Rex's
professional skill in a recent book by a Canadian sociologist who
claimed to be providing 'a political sociology of the Press' (Hoch,
1974), and who subtitles his work 'An enquiry into behind-the-scenes
organization, financing and brainwashing techniques of the news
media'!

In a recent paper Murdock and Golding sought to integrate the broad implications of this form of analysis within an empirical analysis of the functioning of media institutions. Clearly and correctly they recognize that there could be no 'theory' of mass communications sui generis and sought to place their analysis within the framework of a political economy of the mass media: a description of the economic dynamics of media institutions and the consequences of that dynamic for public consciousness. They declare: 'The mass media ... play a key role in determining the forms of consciousness and the modes of expression and action which are made available to people', a serious accusation and, if true, a mightily important one. They continue (Golding and Murdock, 1974, p.226):

'There is a limited range of information made available by the media. The range of interpretive frameworks, the ideas, concepts, facts and arguments which people use to make sense of their lives, are to a great extent dependent on media output, both fictional and non-fictional. Yet the frameworks offered are necessarily articulated with the nexus of interests producing them, and in this sense all information is ideology.'

In substance - that levels of taste, information, etc., are related to media output - this is not a particularly unique description. What is original in the context of media sociology is the fusion of the concepts of political (with its implication of 'power', 'interest', etc.) and economy (with the implication of the material ordering of society). Bonded together they provide an analytic framework within which at a broad level the institutions of the mass media can be situated and explained. Within this, though, lies the need for another explanatory structure. 'It is not sufficient simply to assert that the mass media are part of the ideological apparatus of the State, it is also necessary to demonstrate how ideology is produced in concrete practice' (Murdock and Golding, 1974, p.207). What would be required then from this perspective is a political sociology of media institutions that will focus attention on the way in which these institutions, in reproducing the precepts, values and ideas of ruling elites, actually operate. It is precisely the lack of such an approach upon which to build that has defined much of the work on media institutions. One can detect in these numerous writers a coherent position on the functioning and situation of the broadcasting institution within society, one that is in sharp contrast to the fourth-estate view. Both views, if only by implication, entail a view of the formation of content, but never adequately articulate that view. There are a number of difficulties with the positions and it is the general conclusions to be drawn that form the basis for the next part of the discussion.

CONCLUSION

Two principal and opposed themes about broadcasting are detectable amid the numerous statements and analyses available and it is these which provide the basis for this book. The liberal democratic

viewpoint argues that the political process is a system that falls
into a number of discrete parts, of which the media form one part of
one relatively autonomous system, the political communication system
system. The counter view, taking its basic perspective from the
observation of Wright Mills that any such liberal democratic view of
the political systems of advanced industrial societies is little
more than a 'fairy tale', argues that the systemic view of the political communications process is meaningless because it fails to
account for the structure of power within these societies. The
system is weighted in favour of dominant groups and dominant institutions and this is necessarily reflected in the communications
system. The starting point for this discussion then about the
nature and circumstances of communication are the opposed views that
power within society is diffused, and that power is concentrated.

   Two recent pieces of work illuminate the tendencies pointed to
here. In a recent paper Gurevitch and Blumler (1975) state in a
discussion of the roots of media power that one root is 'normative':

'This springs from the respect that is accorded in competitive democracies to such tenets of liberal philosophy as freedom of expression and the need for specialized organs to safeguard citizens
against possible abuses of political authority. This tends to legitimate the independent role of media organizations in the political
field and to shelter them from overt attempts blatantly to bring
them under political control.'

Murdock, in developing work along opposed lines, states (1974):

'The nature and extent of recent changes in the social structures of
advanced capitalist societies have been the focus of considerable
argument and remain a matter of debate. The position taken here,
however, is that on balance the available evidence tends to support
the view that despite modifications, the class system remains 'the
fundamental axis of the social structure' and the source of 'ramifications which are generally more widespread and intricate' than
those produced by other structural dimensions.... Hence because of
its centrality and pervasiveness, a consideration of the relations
between the class system and the mass media system provides the most
fruitful starting point from which to begin exploring the relationship between mass communication and social structure.'

   The implications of this discussion can be presented graphically.
In chapter 1 a fairly simple diagrammatic representation of the
political communication process was established. In the light of
what I have here described as the dominant trends in the explanatory
framework as it applies to the broadcast media in particular, one
can reformulate the process: is it

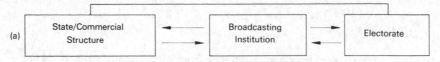

or

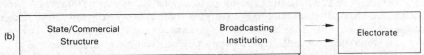

(b)

State/Commercial Structure   Broadcasting Institution   Electorate

in which (a) represents the broadcasting institution as an autonomous unit interacting with but being divorced from the political
sphere, and in which (b) represents a view of the media as being
colonized and controlled by the dominant political and economic
institutions within the society?

There is an interesting observation to be made which illuminates
the differences between the two points and this is that as a general
proposition when political scientists have studied 'power' they have
detected its pluralistic distribution; when sociologists have
studied 'power' they have concluded that it is concentrated (Crewe,
1974, p.34-5). In this context it is noticeable that the two writer
writers in the British academic discussion of the media organizations who have described the 'autonomous' situation of the media -
and autonomy can be seen as an institutional corollary of a 'pluralist' society - are Blumler and Seymour-Ure, both of whom are political scientists. Those who have emphasized the non-autonomous
nature of the media - and lack of autonomy of one form or another
would be an obvious corollary of an elite view of society - are on
the whole sociologists. Ralph Miliband would seem to be something
of an exception.

The distinction lies partly in the 'fourth-estate' view's attachment to formal processes and formal relationships, to the proposition that the text-book description of a 'free press' has a basis in
fact. Thus, the tendency would be to look at the formal distribution of roles in the political system, the assumed connections
between the political communications system, the governmental structure and the electorate - indeed the very use of such concepts as
government distinguishes the position. The sociological perspective
emphasizes the informal distribution of power, the 'real' as opposed
to assumed practices of social and political activity. Sociologists
would therefore argue that power in broadcasting does not lie in
its formal place, i.e. the public service corporation, the board,
the editor, etc., but actually lies in other institutions and persons, the State, the 'advertiser', the 'class', etc. However, it
would be wrong to suggest that such writers as Blumler are unaware
of informal processes, and what one needs to add is that the two
views begin from different perspectives; the one looks to the actual
day-to-day operation, the other looks to the connections between the
media and other social institutions with the assumption that having
detected the link the former is somehow logically subordinate to the
latter.

Is it possible to argue, and ultimately this could prove to be a
most persuasive argument, that there is actually no real difference
or disagreement between the two viewpoints and that they are actually talking about twin levels of the same overall process. The
point is, in fact, similar to that made by Wright Mills of the pluralist arguments that their analysis of power within American society
leads to the broad conclusion that power is diffused rather than

concentrated. Mills, identifying pluralism as an intellectual ana-
logue to the broad theories of liberal democracy, argues that though
there is an apparent functioning of these principles at one level
this fact does not negate the overall distribution and meaning of
power, nor does it deny the conclusion that the notions of liberal
democracy within the context of Western power structures are fundamentally incorrect (see, for example, Mills's 'Structure of Power in
America' in his 'Collected Essays', Horowitz (ed.), 1967). Thus one
might extend this and argue that the media do indeed function as a
fourth estate within the context of the rather narrow confines provided by the Parliamentary system, but not within the broader framework of the political, economic and moral order that underpins that
Parliamentary system.

In turn, this Millsian proposition begs the question of how that
broader framework – the political, economic and moral order – is
actually integrated within the programming process. For this one
has to move from the macro-perspectives of general explanation to
the micro-perspectives of the actual operation of programmes. What
is the nature of programme-making, who is involved, who makes decisions and in relation to what are those decisions made – who is consulted, what factors are weighed against other factors, what resources are or are not available for implementing decisions? In what
ways do organizational requirements influence programme-making, and
just what are those requirements and in relation to what are they
formed? Are the interests of the maker of political television and
his organizational superiors diverse or unified? In what ways are
other facets of the external setting of political television significant in influencing decisions about programme content? These are
the kinds of questions which formed the basis for this work.

Problems created by the absence of a micro-perspective are only
too apparent in the work of Miliband (1973). This work has received
immense praise as the exemplification of the elite perspective on
the social process. It clearly embodies the position that the mass
media in general, through a series of mechanisms, are one means by
which the dominant social orders reproduce their social power.
Along with the educational system, they are an instrument used by
the State (in its capacity as the institutional rendering of the
power of a ruling class), and are therefore for the State, but not
of the State (Miliband, 1973, pp.50-1).

Commenting on Miliband, Poulantzas (1972) adopts a position developed by Althusser (1971) that the media, along with other institutions, constitute the 'ideological apparatus of the state', a view
which is similar to that developed by Miliband in the sense that the
function of the media is to legitimate the power of the dominant
social orders. It differs, however, by placing the media within the
state structure – contrasted with Miliband's description of the
media serving the State from without. Poulantzas criticizes Miliband for simply counterposing bourgeois concepts with his own 'concrete facts' and thus functioning within a bourgeois frame of reference, 'placing himself on their own terrain' (Poulantzas, 1972,
pp.240-1).

There is a good deal of irony in Poulantzas's critique, notably
when Miliband takes up the defense, albeit in an oblique manner, of
'abstracted empiricism'. Countering Poulantzas' accusation that he

fails to develop an appropriate 'problematic' Miliband retorts
(1972, p.256):

'I think it is possible to be so profoundly concerned with the elaboration of an appropriate "problematic" and with the avoidance of
any contamination with opposed "problematics" as to lose sight of
the absolute necessity of empirical enquiry, and of the empirical
demonstration of the falsity of the opposed and apologetic 'problematics'.'

Just what constitutes 'empirical enquiry' is itself 'problematic'
but there is a strong propensity when dealing with his thesis for
Miliband to resort to 'intellectual sleights of hand' (Crewe, 1974,
p.39) and 'imaginative speculation' (ibid., p.43). By no means
could his description of the operation of the mass media - whether
defined as ideological apparatus or instruments of legitimation -
be described as 'empirical enquiry'. Rather it constitutes a series
of useful theoretical assertions employing unsystematic data, which
potentially form the framework for an enquiry.
    The view from the left tends not to employ data systematically
gathered from within the media institutions and thus had no attendant practice for its theory. Ironically - because they are interested in power and control within society - there is little or no
theory of process, of the practice of power within the institutions
themselves, and only when that is achieved will there be any adequate understanding of the relationships between the mass media and
the wider political, economic and cultural structures. Analysis
has not gone much further than the application of sometimes insight-
ful, sometimes erroneous, inferences. For example, analysis of the
social background of media personnel often entails an assumption
about 'control'. Wakeford et al. (1974) include among a list of '18
selected elite groups', 'Controllers of the Media', 'The Governors
of the BBC. Members of the ITA and the proprietors of the seven
national daily newspapers'. Whether these do or do not constitute
a distinctive social grouping is not the point here. What is interesting is that the concept of elite is so readily attached to a concept of control which would necessarily embody an understanding of
decision-making procedures, which is totally absent from their analysis. Thus it might be interesting to know that all these people
came from certain sorts of background - indeed it would be amazing
if they did not have a number of distinguishing characteristics,
since members of these bodies are selected from the usual Civil-
Service criteria of the 'great and good' - but it logically tells
us nothing about their actual function. This reflects a general feature of studies which employ a ruling class/elite analysis of
society and its institutions where a detailed picture of the social
composition of assumed controlling elites necessarily entails assumptions as to their actual functioning, their actual possession of
power and their use of it to further their own specific class/elite
interests. The importance of this point can be seen in Wakeford et
al.'s inclusion of the governors of the BBC. As can be seen from
the later discussion of Greene's retirement, one of the principal
themes in the history of the BBC has been the lack of control which
the governors actually have. The flaw - and it is a central diffi-

culty with many elite studies - is to consider only formal status
and to fail to account for informal processes. There is no logical
connection between social composition and decision-making procedures, nor between social origins and social behaviour and if we
wish to situate the media within the social process, and to explain
the way the one relates to and is influenced by the other, it is to
an analysis of decisions and behaviour which we must look.

At the same time it is at least arguable that the fourth-estate
view is unreal in its assessment of the extent to which the 'logics'
of other social structures actually impinge upon the political
broadcaster. For example, immense formal power over broadcasting
actually accrues to the State, and most sections of the 'press' now
form part of large industrial combinations. Protestation that that
power is never used or that the interests of the parent company are
unimportant may be either true or remarkably naive, but they are
certainly unsubstantiated.

It is plausible to argue that view of the socially responsible
fourth estate is then divorced from the more fundamental processes
which have underpinned the development of the media. Its implication within the present context ignores division within the media -
for example, the historical division between 'quality' media (put
crudely, 'The Times' and BBC 2) and 'light' media (again put
crudely, the popular press and most television). It also avoids the
observation that the media, having been a vehicle for the political
assertion of a middle class - and therefore in their time reformist -
now form the voice piece of an established class. Thus one could
understand that they may be divorced from the established political
structures, but this does ignore the fact that they still exist
within the social milieu of the urban middle classes. There is, of
course, that area of publishing and broadcasting whose purpose is
not the articulation of a class world-view, but rather whose purpose
is derived from the entrepreneurial activity of that class, that is
the media as commercial enterprises. They will reproduce that
class's world-view as a consequence of their activity and not as a
purpose of their activity.

One, therefore, needs to consider the diferential between intended and unintended consequences. Are the media attached to State/
commercial interests and therefore fulfilling a clearly purposive
function, or are they inhibited by a number of occupational routines
and practices which effectively mean that they serve dominant interests, or are they detached from, and intended by the logic of a
liberal democratic society to hold to account those interests? The
evidence contained within this book is geared to the notion that
while the second proposition holds a good deal of attraction, that
is, that what is evidenced is a kind of historical or evolutionary
coincidence between the paths taken by political broadcasting and
the needs and interests of dominant institutions within society, one
has also to allow for both a good deal of actual autonomy and also
of real pressure and subordination. What I think will also become
clear is that the pressure from the external environment is internalized within the taken for granted practices of programme-making.

Discussion of the broadcasting polarities of autonomous institutions and State/commercial appendages obscures the complexities of
the relationship between the internal and external features of pro-

gramme-making and has tended to detract from a discussion of the way
in which programmes are made - and in the context of the overall
discussion of broadcasting in society, unless one is talking about
programming, the whole discussion of media institutions is futile.
One could not discuss the school in the context of a political
sociology of British society without considering what happens in
the classroom, because whatever it is that schools 'do' to children
they 'do it' largely in the classroom. Neither could one have a
'theory' of 'the classroom'; the framework would be provided by a
discussion of, for example, socialization. Thus one could seek an
integration of the treatment of data gathered within the classroom
and a discussion of socialization so that the former informs the
latter. Thus, to draw the parallel with the media, one is placing
the discussion of the programme-production process within the
broader discussion of a political sociology of broadcasting. Just
as one cannot have a 'theory' of the media institutions per se -
something recognized by Murdock and Golding (1974) who sought to
establish their discussion within the framework of a political
economy of Western capitalism - so one could not have a 'theory' of
production. Rather one has at some point to link it to the broader
framework of the political sociology of British society. It is for
this reason that the two positions which I have drawn, though
opposed, are both vitally important because they both seek to place
the media institution - though not the production process - within
the general structure of British political, economic and social
life. By thinking in terms of the relationship between the programme-making process and the much larger question of, for example,
structures of power and processes of legitimation, one would be more
able to treat the media as integrated within the wider dynamics of
a social process.

While both views implicitly recognize that no view of the situation of the media is possible without a 'theory' of society,
neither view has adequately recognized the necessary connections
between a theory and its practice, or 'empirical validation' for
those who deny the Marxist implications of 'practice'. Until the
linkage is made, such views of broadcasting are at best interesting
propositions and at worse ill-founded beliefs.

What we need to understand are the internal and external dynamics
of programme-making rather than the mere appearances. The position
adopted here, though it stems from a different academic tradition
and is employed in a different context, is not dissimilar to that
adopted by Silverman (1968) in calling for a more actor-based perspective and methodology and a more ready recognition of the presence and role of an 'environment'. Thus knowledge of production
should in the first place stem from the perspectives and experiences
of those directly involved. To use a simple but relevant example,
it is no good pointing to pressures from advertisers and politicians
if one cannot at the same time show some kind of response or
display how this is integrated within the activity of the programme-maker. Neither, however, can one sustain a view that programming operates only at the level of the individual disposition
of producers because the prime minister, to use a crude but obvious
example, is, much to their regret, a keenly felt part of the total
production environment. Wilson's occasional and much advertised

rage at a broadcaster may not have immediately or directly impinged
upon that broadcaster but may have entailed a series of events which
were of consequence for that broadcaster in the long run. The particular formulation of those 'events' are then the visible, though
subtle, representation of a system of power.

It is necessary therefore to consider the individual perspectives
and life experiences of producers - in the sense in which Becker
has stated in discussing the 'naturalistic perspective' in sociology
(1971, p.64) that 'to understand why someone behaves as he does you
must understand how it looked to him, what he thought he had to contend with, what alternatives he saw open to him' - and the way that
shapes, and is shaped by, their functioning within an internal context with its own (or its controllers') perspectives, goals, resources, etc. At the same time one has to consider the outer or external context with which the inner is in constant and involved contact. The premiss of this work is that one can in fact begin to
make a number of clarifying statements about the situation of political broadcasting and therefore about the nature of the political
material with which the bulk of the population is presented. By
inference it will tell us much also about the institutional arrangements which characterize the British social structure and therefore
go some way towards receiving the implied conflicts between the
'liberal democratic' view and the 'elite' views of the situation of
broadcasting in general and political broadcasting in particular.
By confronting empirically the numerous statements made from entrenched and opposed traditions, one can establish a degree of understanding of the actual as opposed to the assumed determinations in
the making of political television. Focusing on the relationship
between the internal features of programme production, from the
perspectives of those involved, and their relationship with external
factors, will I think draw attention to a number of difficulties in
the view of the 'autonomous' institution by indicating that programme material is produced by a number of processes and frameworks
which to an extent at least inhibit the making of messages for communication. At the same time, the perspective will also indicate
that the view that the broadcasting organizations are effectively
within the grip of the dominant institutions within society is, in
the present context, unnecessarily simple and crude, notably in
terms of the imputation of purposive action, rooted in elite interests, as being the basis for programme content.

The subject of this book is defined by a problem within a problem. The first involves the nature of the political television
process, and this implies the second problem, one which is at the
heart of the political process, the problem of order - the means by
which a political system functions and, most crucially, sustains its
own existence. Does analysis of the nature of production lead to a
conclusion that broadcasting fits within a view of the political
system within which political television provides the necessary
linkage between individuals and groups at all levels of society?
Crucially, does political television ential an exchange of information and response between leaders and led? Or does the analysis
lead to the conclusion that broadcasting as political communication
serves dominant interests within society rather than the abstracted
requirements of an abstract entity, the political system? The

discussion contained within these pages, as with most discussion of
political television, is then one further rehearsal of a persistent
'battle' between the tenets of pluralist views of liberal democracy
and Millsian/Marxist view of an 'elite-ridden' society.

Part two

THE INTERNAL CONTEXT OF POLITICAL BROADCASTING

Chapter 3

THE PRODUCERS
Autonomy or servitude

The perspective of this part is clearly implied in the title. In
response to a written request for an interview, one current affairs
producer wrote that:

'I don't have any clear idea of how I produce television programmes,
and although I can see that it might be useful to you to analyse
the way in which I operate, I don't actually think that it will be
useful to me. In fact I think it would make it more difficult for
me, because I find this type of self-analysis 'stuntifying' (sic).
So I am sorry to appear churlish but I am afraid I have to refuse
your invitation to be interviewed.'

Another very senior news executive wrote in reply that he wasn't
sure what I meant by production, nor what he himself meant by it.
That the factors which influence programme making in television are
somehow mysterious and obscure was a common initial reaction, frequently summed up by a shrug of the shoulder and the observation
that it somehow 'just happens'. Conversely it was frequently
pointed out that I was wasting my time, as are most academics, in
looking for the 'hidden meanings' since it was really all rather
simple and straightforward.
    Neither version comes near to explaining how political messages
are made. Through talking to people actually responsible for making
programmes, through watching them actually at work, one can detect
a number of forces which operate within the immediate setting of
programme production, 'forces' which stem from the nature of the
medium, from the technology that has to be employed, from the previous history of broadcasting, from the organization and from the
profession of the broadcast journalist. This discussion will be
of those forces which together constitute one level of an answer to
the question 'why is political television as it is?'

Of central importance is 'the producer' of political television,
since he provides the creative heart around which the formal organizational and programme structure is built and from which the artefact we recognize as political television emerges. The central premiss here is that an analysis of the role of the producer, an

elaboration of programme-making from his perspective, can provide
important clues to the various forces which shape and mould political television. It is then necessary to provide more detail on that
role and to answer the question 'just what does the producer actually do?'. Does he serve the whims of his political masters or is
his role that of the free-floating intellectual plugged in to an
advanced technology?

The information gathered during the course of this research concentrated on decision-making about programmes (including both the
origination of the programme itself and the subject matter for the
programme); on the role of particular power holders; on the requirements of the law and the organization, and on the attitudes towards
these requirements; on the particular conception of the audience and
the role that the viewing audience played; and on the technical and
financial resources available to the programme.

'Producer' is used here in a generic sense and embodies the
actual job description of 'producer', 'news editor', 'editor', 'executive producer'. Persons occupying these positions are the central
characters of British political television. Through them and their
work experience flow all the forces operating on and forming the
programmes made available as political content. While the titles
may vary the job is similar in all cases and was described in the
following way by the producer of a major current affairs programme
on BBC television:

*'What duties go with your position, What is entailed in being 'pro-
ducer' of the programme?'*

'I think I make it possible for other people to work, though I don't
delegate everything. I like to put my handwriting on the finished
product. I like on the day to have a hand in writing some of the
script.... Apart from that I spend my time in conferences with
everybody in the programme. I'm a great one for reviewing progress,
so that if an idea comes up I say "That interests me, go away, give
me a treatment". They come back a few days or a few hours later
with a written treatment. That's good for them, it's good for me.
It disciplines their mind and also it's easier for me to understand.
We then have an argument about that. I then say "Well go away and
do some more about this". And this process is repeated several
times, by which time we've got to the point of no return and we are
actually committed to doing something because we are spending money.
Anyway, we are spending their time so if I pulled them off there'd
be too short a time scale for them to do anything else....
'We also have formal meetings; I have a couple a week. Monday
mornings - there is an hour, maybe two hours, we have a general
thrash around in the hope that I may get some good ideas, and it's
also boss-bashing time. About Thursday - Friday's too late because
we are tied up if we have a programme on Friday. Thursday morning
we ought to, and we usually do have a meeting in the morning to
recapitulate on everything that we are going to do in that week, and
review progress. But in between there are lots and lots of informal
meetings. It's exit one or two people, enter one or two more people
all day long. In between that I sort out the hire and fire policy
of the staffing. I'm responsible for my budget which is about

£300,000 p.a., which I'm always overspent on. I'm trying to find
out new ideas, and constantly looking for new people - people will
ring me up and say "there's this, this and this story you ought to
know about".

'I spend some time going out on recces myself to keep my hand in.
Also, if there's something very, very awkward, I wouldn't like to
have somebody going solo, and if there's nobody else I will go with
him as a witness. We wouldn't bug the conversation, we'd simply
have somebody like myself who would be able to stand up in court
afterwards and say what really went on. I try to read myself into
the problem, but most of this is done at home. If people are away
from the office they talk to me by telephone. I have to be always
available, always contactable. A certain amount of it is mildly
enjoyable, like I get lunch with various people - I find that's a
great strain on the liver and on the head.

'Part of my job must be, of course, keeping people happy: my
front men, my reporters, making them think that this is the most
worthwhile job that they could be doing, the best programme they
could be on. Taking decisions about who to favour on the staff
knowing that you will upset the other man - you've got to be a bit
like Solomon. If there's only one reporter for two jobs - who has
him? Can a man have a crew for Timbuctoo, no he can't, it's too
expensive, we'll have to do it some other way. Bad news for him.
I have to cope with my staff, who have to do the best job possible
because it's their professional career at stake, which means the
most expensive job possible. They want perfection. I want it good
and I want it on the day and it's my job to keep the cost down as
far as possible.

'Also I find myself saying to people "Now, I think you are not
imaginative enough, go out and think of something else". Or I'll
deliberately float an idea - I hope everyday to float a few ideas,
to suggest more exciting, more original ways of doing it. Scripts
come back to me, I sub them,I sub them very carefully. I sub everything I can put a pencil to. I'm a great re-write man; I have a
typewriter on my desk and I'll rewrite anything that's put in front
of me. I will go through a film reporter's script very carefully.
I have my own very strong convictions about English language and
house style and the way we say things in television journalism....

'I will keep relations outside (i.e. the department) with the
rest of the BBC - like, I'll consult the lawyer on something dodgy
about the law of libel or something. Other departmental relations.
I'm always looking for more real estate, more television time, other
programmes we could do as spin-offs, this kind of thing. I spend
some time closeted with the administration, mainly on financial and
staff matters; and also with my leadership, my boss, on everything
including editorial matters. But I get a very, very free hand. I'm
the one that decides in the end, and has a responsibility in the end
for what happens. There's very little pressure on me, partly due to
the skill of my group head who keeps it away from me.'

This is a rather elaborate, and unusually reflective description
of the job, but it does reflect the basis of producing at this
level. There are of course minor distinctions to be made, few producers for example would be involved in quite the 'heavy subbing'

that is implied here. The basic similarity of the job of producing
even across different organizations was detailed by a producer
working on one of independent television's more prestigious current
affairs programmes.

'What duties go with your position as executive producer?'

'Well, it's the same role that's called different things on different programmes: "World In Action", it's called executive producer.
"This Week", it's called producer. "Panorama", it's called editor
... It's all the same job and there is no real difference between
any of these functions ... What it means in terms of responsibility
is that I am just like the producer of a small programme except that
on a large programme you need a number of producers, (1) you need
someone who is in charge of the producers and the programme; you
have the final responsibility in the programme and are ambassador
to the outside world - to the IBA, to the company, and take full
management and editorial responsibility for it....
   'On a week-to-week basis I run the programme in quite some
detail. Obviously with a (long) programme there are a number of
items you have to delegate, but I keep quite a close eye on most
things. It varies a little and I have a sort of deputy on a weekly
basis, a sort of producer of the week, and we work in partnership
together. But I keep either a detailed eye on most items or a
general eye where nothing of importance would escape me. I decide
which ones should go ahead. I'm like the editor of a newspaper, but
whereas in the newspaper you have departments ... here we are much
smaller; though we are a very large programme, we still only have
around twenty people, so it's not too big....'

   These references are taken from producers of large programmes
with substantial resources. The descriptions differ in the smaller
programmes, though only marginally, even on one programme in the
sample where there were only three people, including the producer,
actually producing it. The young producer of that programme, in
which contributors were allowed to discourse on any topic of contemporary relevance, noted that while technically his grading within
the BBC was as acting assistant producer he was on this programme
'not working direct to a producer, I'm doing a producer's function.
I work to an executive producer'. He had working for him only one
assistant and a researcher, which given his own personal inclinations, meant that the whole process of producing that programme was
'very conversationally based'.
   The situation in regional broadcasting, the position and role of
the maker of political television in the non-London ITV companies,
and in the regional stations of the BBC, was complicated by the fact
that news and current affairs tended to be produced within the same
department. Interviews with regional producers produced the following broad description of their position and the general conclusion that, as with their London-based colleagues, they make most of
the important decisions about programmes.

'I'm responsible for two things basically: one is the regional news
output - which in television consists of a nightly news magazine

programme ... The brief basically is to report the news of the area
and to reflect the life and interests of the people in it. We also
have a late-night television news which is about three minutes long
and goes out at closedown. We have a Saturday sports programme....
So I'm responsible for all those. I'm also responsible for radio
news. The second part of my job is to be responsible for supplying
the network with regional news.'

A number of other producers in the regions alluded to the relationship with network news, though opinions were divided. All the
BBC producers felt that they had to serve the network, but the ITV
producers, who of course are in no way required to serve the interests of ITN, argued that they would keep the 'best' stories to themselves, or would serve ITN so long as it didn't conflict with their
own interests, or felt that they had a moral responsibility to provide ITN with anything they wanted even if in so doing they affected
their own interest. Of overriding importance in all this, however,
was the fact that any relationship with London on news matters was
essentially a financial relationship, that if London wanted a story
or an item then they covered the costs, a fact which the hard-
pressed producer, constantly fighting to make ends meet, was eager
to exploit:

'Our relationship with London revolves around a financial relationship. If I cover a story for London, even if, as I almost
inevitably would, I take some of it for myself, they pay for the
whole operation. They hire my cameraman and reporter for the day
and I ride on their coat tails because there's a system in the BBC
which put simply says richest user pays.'

The editor has responsibility for what goes into the programme.
He also takes responsibility for the programme budget, 'if budgets
go over I get an initial rocket from upstairs, which is not difficult to deal with, because basically we are allowed to average our
budget so if I go over badly one week I can save the next'.
If the 'producer' is of central importance to a programme production in the sense of having financial and editorial responsibility, how important is he in the origination of 'ideas', and how
autonomous is he within the wider context of the organization? What
is clear is that there is much of substance to their declarations
of autonomy and to the argument that the formation of programme
content cannot be explained in terms of the persistent imposition by
the hierarchy within the organization of its view of programme content. A conspiracy theory of media production does not get us very
far in explaining the process, nor does the proposition that producers are a body of docile hacks, haplessly responding to pressures
from all sides. David Dimbleby (1972), who has himself been in a
number of controversial situations, once described the current
affairs programme as the 'battlefield where the struggle for the
independence of the broadcaster and the freedom of the BBC goes on
day after day'. He was talking about the difficulties of producing
from Lime Grove, the BBC's main current affairs department. Go
beyond the portals of that building and the perspective on production changes somewhat, the immediacy of political intrigue sinks

into the background before the more pressing harassment of an
awkward technology, a limitation on resource and survival itslef in
a hostile, competitive environment.

It is interesting to discuss the question of autonomy with producers in different situations, with those working within Lime Grove
and those working within an ITV company or in the BBC regions.

Six of the interviewees had produced or were producing major programmes from Lime Grove. They all claimed a similar degree of autonomy, though the details varied slightly. The producer of a rather
distinguished programme was asked:

*'Do you ever find that you do something because someone above you
wishes that you do something, or you don't do something because that
same person doesn't want it done? One hears a lot about interference or undue pressure being applied.'*

'Not true. Absolutely. Nobody says you ought to be doing this or
you ought to do that. We did a film on the British Communist Party,
a very delicate film. My idea to do it. Nobody suggested it and
nobody interfered at all. No sort of hierarchical anxieties at all
on Northern Ireland etc. No one vetting me at all. It's very much
your own responsibility and if you get it wrong you get it wrong.'

His assertion that there were no anxieties about Ulster was a trifle
bizarre, as there most clearly are. (2) Other producers venturing
an opinion on the Ulster coverage stated that their own feeling was
of a need for responsible attitudes towards covering affairs in the
province - summed up by the statement, 'Northern Ireland, I'm very
much aware myself, is a very problematical field'. A BBC producer,
when discussing the question of balance, had said that 'the programme can do anything because you can balance over a period, except
over certain issues like Ireland where you can't say you will
balance over a period because it's going to produce a riot before
you've got time to. So over that you do feel an obligation to
balance in a very conspicuous way, everything, all the time.'

A producer working in Scotland described the particular difficulties presented by the Northern Ireland situation:

'One night these two funny men went into the Apprentice Boys Hall in
Bridgetown on a Saturday night and hid some gelignite in the stove.
The caretaker came in, lit the stove to heat the pies for the dance
and blew the place apart. Nobody was seriously hurt, but it was a
bomb explosion in a hall of an affiliated organization to the Orange
Lodge in the East End of Glasgow. It could have given rise to lots
of bother.

'On the second mention of this on the television on the Saturday
night we said that the police were saying that it was nothing to do
with the IRA, and it wasn't really, it was two crooks. That night,
the Assistant Chief Constable and others intercepted a group of
people coming up from Ervin to Glasgow to do a church. Now if you
are facing that kind of situation there are obviously cautionary
feelings that come up in the back of your mind about delving too
deeply into this. There's no direct pressure. I've never had any
direct pressure on me at all with this sort of thing but I console

myself with the thought that I know what is to be covered and what
is not to be covered on these sorts of things.

'We know that the volunteers have been sent to fight in Northern
Ireland; we know that the bulk of the detonators used by the Provos
are stolen from the national coal board in Scotland; other things of
this kind we know. We know of people arrested in Glasgow for other
offences who have been traceable to the UDA or the Provos. We've
reported cases where there was a hold-up by a fund-raising team for
an Ulster extremist group. You can report things like that, but not
necessarily dig into it. We don't ask "How many others are there of
them about?" We don't do that sort of thing.'

This is a rather unusual situation, but what it does make clear
is that a keenly felt caution over this area inhibited the news
magazine from becoming involved in this area.

The dominant view among those involved is that the producer
operates within a field of autonomy, freedom if you like within prescribed frameworks, restrained flexibility:

*'As a producer, what would you say the role of the producer in tele-
vision is? For example, how autonomous is he in determining the
content of a programme?'*

'If you are talking about "the" producer of a programme ... he has
quite a lot of freedom I would say. Well, take this programme I
have been producing recently. I can't think of a single occasion
when I was stopped from doing what I wanted to do. There are
various checks which happen in this bit of the BBC, which are routine - e.g. cabinet ministers, you have to get it cleared at a
higher level. That is usually routine and is sensible, actually,
because you don't know what other producers are doing, and Robert
Carr might appear on five different programmes in the course of two
night and that would be silly.

'I don't remember ever being stopped from doing what I wanted to
do. Occasionally I've been discouraged; occasionally if there have
been two roughly equal propositions my bosses have suggested that
one might be better than the other. The other form of control over
one is money.... I think on the whole I've not been interfered with.
Mind you, this is partly because I've been in the BBC long enough
to be pretty sensitive to what is or isn't on, and compared with a
bloke who's come in straight from newspapers or ITV, I probably
have an almost unconscious awareness that something is not on
because of a row there's been about something or other, so I probably don't even start to do it. So you can't take my answer
totally at face value. There's a watch; I'd say a watch is kept on
one.'

The producer of a large current affairs programme pointed to a
particular incident which may seem trivial, but in being trivial
introduces an element of perspective to any discussion of autonomy
of the producer. In responding to a previous question he had indicated his feeling that there was a good deal of autonomy enjoyed by
the working producer in the BBC, and commented 'At the end of the
week you've got a programme that may or may not be good, but you've

done your best and that's a marvellous way of getting it out of your
system. It's like writing a book every week or every day, that's
not bad.'

'You give the impression of being fairly autonomous within?'

'I think so - yes. I made a case for what I was doing by example -
by saying, "This is what I'm doing - just watch this space". When
I came to the (programme) just over a year ago, when (the previous
producer) left, I changed it first and then argued - I didn't really
need to argue because my boss said "I think that's right, what you
are doing". I then found there was aggro about the change of title
which was, in the end, not as important as all that, (but) at the
time I was very upset about it and lost a lot of sleep over it and
got very cross with the senior management in this place.
   'When it was all over, I found I was far too busy anyway getting
the show on the air, and we were able to keep up morale by saying
"look, the last thing you should worry about is the title, we are
not changing our policy, because no one wants us to". Actually, it
was a bit of a cock-up at a very high level, whereby certain people
were imagining that they were asking for one thing when they were
asking for something else. There was no malice in it. There was no
wish as far as I could see, to interfere with me or my predecessor.
There was a communication fault, but then it's a busy world, and one
can forgive this. There was a bit of maladroit bungling here and
there, but then no more than you'd find in comparable organizations
- it's all water under the gate. From that argument onwards we've
had nothing really but general support for the line we are taking.'

*'Would you say that the situation of the producer is similar in
other programmes in current affairs?'*

'No, I think I get more autonomy ... because there's still this
feeling that the "fellow has got a lot of very specialist contacts
and specialist knowledge, he must know what they are doing" ... Now
if you are producer of "Panorama", I don't know, but I suspect that
you are much more in the public eye - by public I mean the management, they are looking at you very hard indeed, because it's on
BBC1, it's a twenty-year-old show, it's very, very important that it
shouldn't put a foot wrong. This must be a terrible strain on the
producer....'

   The question of whether or not the change of title of a programme
is significant is more important, at least in some eyes, and was a
point raised by Anthony Smith when discussing the change from
'Tonight' to '24 Hours' to 'Midweek" - the view implied is contentious but is interesting enough to deserve an airing, since it is a
view of the producer's lack of creative autonomy. Smith's point is
that changes in the BBC are never abrupt, always subtle. Discussing the end of '24 Hours', he describes the attitude of those responsible for taking it off the air in terms of their expressed
feeling that the programme had had its day:

'The powers that be were beginning to look at "24 Hours" and say:

"Well, it's time to make a change." There's a change of some inde-
finable kind in the public attitude towards it and its material;
it's gone on for seven or eight years, as long as its predecessor
and there were similar motives in the change from "Tonight" to "24
Hours" eight years previously. Then they wanted to have a brighter
later programme, avoiding the repetitive trendy leftism of "Tonight"
in its last period, which had lost much of its audience to the
rival, early-evening programmes of the commercial companies. But
then "24 Hours" went the same way, constantly accused of liberal-
radicalism and there was a change of editor, bringing me in; for a
while I think it, in fact, contained less of the "leftism" of which
it was constantly accused. Then came Northern Ireland, the Six-Day-
War, May 68, and the whole student rebellion around the world, all
the issues of police and authority in general - that whole range of
issues which supposedly left in its aftermath a public feeling that
indulgence of the left had gone too far; the way "24 Hours" chose
its issues was deemed to be no longer fashionable, although it
seemed from inside that history rather than producers had chosen the
issues. But you could only produce a change by altering the title,
the producers, the format, the principal personalities. The feeling
that a change was due was dictated by a recognition of a change in
society plus a demand for a creative shift, seen through the prism
of institutional imperative.'

'But what is the "institutional imperative"?'

'The institutional imperative is that this particular man, this programme, this formulation of issues has become dangerous to us, us
the BBC.... There are too many rows, there's too much pressure directed against us because of this man, because of this position,
because of something.' (3)

   This description by Smith was particularly interesting, since I
was informed by a former head of current affairs group, BBC TV,
quite independently and without prompting that towards the end of
the 1960s, Attenborough, director of programmes, television, and
Wheldon, managing director, television, argued that people were
becoming bored with politics and that therefore their output should
reflect this. It is, of course, difficult to judge with any degree
of certainty the relevance or accuracy of these observations. The
sense of hostility they conjure up was both supported and denied by
other producers. Another statement, for example, declared that
there had been a veritable campaign in the late 1960s by the then
director general to emphasize the need for 'exposition' and less
'argy-bargy' in current affairs programmes. The generally rather
optimistic view of the producer's position was denied by one senior
producer. In reply to the observation that a frequent impression
held by outsiders of the BBC is that the producer is not that autonomous, he observed that within the programme staff no one was autonomous, in the sense that they were working for a producer. But he
concluded that the producer himself is not in effect autonomous
since, with any programme, there are a number of institutional demands, the central ones of which are the fact that the organizational hierarchy has a view of what it thinks the programme should

be doing, and that 'there is the knowledge that somebody above one didn't want that kind of treatment of subject a particular reporter or producer would apply. And these can be quite complex. These can change from month to month. One might feel terrible inhibitions from sending a particular person to cover a particular story one month, but the next month feel that their particular cloud had cleared.' This response is similar to that of a previous respondent who argued that he had been around the BBC for a number of years and knew if there had been a row some things were 'not on'. The difference lay in the general acquiescence of this respondent and the general hostility of the one just cited to this illusive but binding 'knowledge'.

There are in the life of any producer incidents he can point to where his own editorial responsibility was impinged upon by a decision made by a superior. These do not, however, form a particularly clear pattern. What did form a pattern was the seriousness with which the regulations relating to political coverage were taken. A close watch is kept on the number of MPs appearing in programmes, and particularly close attention is paid to the appearances of Enoch Powell for whom, in the case of the BBC, permission had to be sought from the editor, news and current affairs. The producer of a specialist programme, however, covering political affairs made the point that:

'We get quite strong reactions from MPs, though on the whole the programme doesn't attract outright antagonism. In fact, I can't remember a time when any particular item was attacked. Their suggestions are usually in the realm of what angles we should have taken, or what aspects emphasized.... I've had eighteen years in this thing and I don't think the pressures are as great or frequent as people would think.'

Are we to conclude that this interviewee is wallowing in a false sort of consciousness? What is probably significant is that his programme was small scale, viewed by a small audience and therefore not likely to attract the kinds of public and organizational attention given to other, more 'significant' programmes. The same theme of relative non-interference and freedom from pressure was forcibly made, with two notable exceptions, by other interviewees working within the news department of Television Centre and in the BBC's features and presentations departments.

A senior producer in BBC television news described decision-making as an osmotic process among a number of people rather than an oligarchical tyrannical operation. A producer who had worked in the news division since 1942, declared in terms which are by now familiar that:

'I have, in effect, total say in what has gone into this week's edition.... By that I don't mean that I am completely free to do what I like, I've - I was going to say that I've learnt the rules, but that's not quite right - I was aware of the general policy of the news division. I am aware of my own involvement in news. I am aware of my own interests. And taking all of these things into consideration I produce what will go on the air tonight with a certain

belief that I've been as honest in my selection and approach as one
can expect a human being to be.'

' You say that you are aware of these various elements; in what way
would you be aware?'

'Simply that I've spent thirty years in the news division, one way
and another. For the last fifteen of those years I've been at a
high enough level to know what the general thinking is at any particular time about anything that happens to be going on.... I would
be aware of what is going on simply from talking to my colleagues on
the sixth floor, which is, as it were, the editorial section. I
don't necessarily agree with everybody's point of view, but I
wouldn't do something that went against the accepted policy of the
day unless I had a very good reason for doing so.'

The situation of the producer is not that of a person under
siege, rather it is one of an experienced inidvdual who is aware of
limitations, accepts them, but formulates their nature and meaning
in vague terms: 'What is going on', 'accepted policy' etc. He tends
not to view these limitations in terms of the 'Principles and Practices' (4) and memoranda with which any broadcasting organization is
festooned. When pressed he talks of 'news and news values'. A much
younger producer working in the BBC presentation department who,
though he told of an incident in which a controller had threatened
to take off one of his programmes because he thought it too controversial, felt that though the use made of the medium was disastrous,
his own personal autonomy as a programme-maker was assured. The
limitation of which he was most aware was that due to limited
resources:

'in return for the limitations we live with I would say that we probably have more freedom and more autonomy as a department and that
filters down. I, as a producer, probably have more freedom and more
autonomy than a producer would in another department.'

The only imposition or restriction deriving from the organization
which he could think of when prompted were those relating to moral
standards. He pointed out for example, that three or four years
ago, he would have been able to use four-letter words, but that now
the climate had changed, even though there had been no formal ruling
on it, and the use of four-letter words is now unwise:

'I want whatever I film to go on the telly. If it said "fuck" and
I had to bleep it, it would be a silly convention because everybody
would know what was being said.... At the moment the broadcasters
seem to have conceded, and they seem to accept that the collective
standards demand a certain sort of standard on television, and the
collective standards seem to be that you don't say "fuck" on TV.
I don't actually, as it happens, think that that is particularly
important.'

The only restrictions that he could think of related to an area
which he didn't think was particularly important. Producers' aware-

ness of these limitations is through the much-vaunted system of
'referral' espoused in doom-laden terms by the managing director,
television (Wheldon, 1973, p.11): 'the wrath of the Corporation in
its varied human manifestations is particularly reserved for those
who fail to refer'. One ITV producer noted, when asked about contact with people higher up in the organization:

'Well, it depends. They are very good. They operate this sort of
retrospective censorship. I'm supposed to know what is not permissible to transmit and if in doubt I'm supposed to refer it up. If
I have something which I'm worried about, for example, some particularly gory killing in a fox hunt is the sort of thing that everybody moans about, then I'm supposed to refer it up. But nobody sees
the programme except me before transmission, though my boss does
quite often out of interest. But I'm in charge of it until it's
gone out, then, if the shit hits the fans I have to carry the can.
If any of the rules have been broken and if I do it often enough,
then of course, they'll take me off the job, they'll stop me doing
it. But I mean, there's no one between me and transmission, unless
it's something very, very inflammatory like Northern Ireland or
South Africa, where I'm supposed to know that I should refer it up.'

The impression created is of an essential mutuality between the
producer and his employers only occasionally disturbed by a contentious issue. It was interesting to note that the interviewees
working in ITV contrasted their own autonomy with the restrictions
imposed upon their BBC counterparts. Yet, as I have tried to show,
there is no great sense within those ranks of any particularly repressive situation, merely an acknowledgment of the various political and moral boundaries within which they had to function, and a
sense of the bureaucracy within which they had to work. ITV producers were eager to mention the informal relationships they had
with management:

'What about contact with executives?'

'Yeah ... Unlike some organizations one could name beginning with
B, there is no question of notes, memos, hierarchial structures,
anything like this. There is one man I will talk to and go in and
see; I will go in now if I want to see him and he will come in here
if he wants to see me. He lets one run it the way one wants, but if
he's interested in something he rings me up and says "What do you
think?", and I'll say "Terrible". Sometimes he says something which
is quite a good idea and I'll follow it up, but that's the only outside thing. He knows what's going on all the time, obviously, but
he's not the person who says "This week we do so and so, this week
we do something else".'

Earlier in the interview the same producer declared:

'I've never been stopped from doing anything, but there are two ways
of seeing that: one is that it's because I've never been nasty or
you could say that it's because it's a very easy-going company with
a good deal of autonomy. And I think the autonomy in this company

is quite high really. I'm self-sufficient, there is no one over
me.'

There were no responses from other ITV producers challenging this
view.

A VIEW FROM THE REGIONS

There is a strong metropolitan flavour to political television, as
there is to all broadcasting. The regions are nevertheless vitally
important in the process of political communication. A number of
regional producers were interviewed, principally those responsible
for the 6 p.m. news magazine programmes put out by both ITV and BBC.
These producers and the departments for which they were responsible
occasionally produced other forms of political television, and a
number of them produce programmes involving local MPs or discussing
local current affairs. What is the position of the producer in the
regional setting, how does it compare to that of his counterparts in
the capital? In the course of nineteen interviews with producers
responsible for regional political output a familiar theme replayed
itself: they regarded themselves as essentially autonomous but
recognized that this was structured within boundaries defined by
their superiors.   All argued that editorial responsibility was in
their hands, but also indicated that lapses in taste or a decline in
the viewing figures would inevitably lead to their superiors questioning their fitness to have that responsibility.
     'If you consistently do things in a way which they don't think it
right and proper, obviously they will look at you again and say "Do
I want this guy to work for me?"' Another typical reaction was:

'Obviously if the controller of programmes has an opinion about
something he lets it be known. Equally if the company's chief executive has an opinion on something he lets it be known, but I must
say in all honesty we don't get the kind of editorial interference
that you are talking about. I'm not denying that occasionally they
say "Didn't like that," but we don't get the kind of thing that
folks somehow imagine happens, where somebody says you must do such
and such ... On the other hand you can't ignore the fact of where
executive responsibility finally lies'

and

'By and large my boss leaves me on my own to do the programme and
either kicks me or pats me after it every now and then ... I have a
very good relationship indeed editorially with my boss here. I feel
that when we are talking we are talking more or less as equals. I
accept that he is the boss and that if he says "do this" then ultimately I do that. I don't believe that he has ever done more than
suggest that a particular story should be pursued in a particular
way. I don't think he's ever imposed anything on me. I've certainly never felt it. He may have done it with such diplomacy I
wasn't aware of it happening. In my previous job I used to have
more clashes with the person who was in a similar situation. This

is when I was a producer elsewhere, and I worked to a manager who had the same responsibilities as the manager (5) here ... and we used to clash quite strongly about films and cutting films and the way subjects were treated sometimes. But even there, though I would go home absolutely grinding my teeth, looking back at it I don't now think it was an unhealthy relationship, it was simply a different one.'

A somewhat rosy picture is painted here of the position of the producer of political television in both a metropolitan and regional setting and it does seem that on the whole the person seeking political intrigue in the making of these programmes will be disappointed; the truth of the process is much more prosaic. One cannot explain production in terms of the imposition of clear-cut hierarchical will, save in the broad sense of the establishment of a programme's working budget, general rulings on standards of taste and the control of the numbers of appearances by MPs. The structures and impositions of the political institutions of British society are by no means as frequent, forceful or important as is often argued. Hall's point that the 'broadcasting institutions exercise a wide measure of editorial autonomy in their programmes' (Hall, 1972b) is substantially correct. Hall sees this autonomy as occuring within and ultimately defined by 'the underlying structure of ideological and institutional constraints', which means that media institutions (presumably he is referring principally to news and current affairs departments) are both autonomous and constrained - a 'complex formation' indeed. The meaning of Hall's description is obliquely stated - broadcasters and politicians are ideologically in tune; when they are not, conflict is inevitable. When either the purpose of the broadcaster or his overt ideological inclinations lead him onto ground which the politician regards as sacrosanct, the 'real' structure of power, the ultimate subordination to the State, is made apparent. In 'normal' times, though, Hall tells us the reality of this relationship is masked by the operation of a number of key concepts - objectivity, balance, impartiality, professionalism and consensus.

Hall's theorizing has a certain elegance and yet retains a certain explanatory inadequacy. His point is that broadcasting avoids certain fundamental issues and that this blindness to real issues is mediated through the routines which constitute the pretence of objectivity and its attendant codes. That the range of available discussion is limited is clear, but what one would wish to argue is that Hall's formulation of what can be called the determinations of content ignores a number of key elements. Specifically it tends to ignore certain features of programme-making which militate against consideration of what the academic and radical mind might see as fundamental issues. The 'eunuch form' of political television, if eunuch it be, derives to a large extent from a number of features internal to the process of making programmes. The dominance of a particular form of broadcasting, the news magazine, the pursuit of audiences, the nature of the medium, etc., have all militated against the act of political communication by providing a determining framework within which the political communicator must operate. The sense of autonomy, which I so lengthily described, is on

the whole real when viewed from the perspective provided by questions that relate to political and editorial interference, but
unreal when viewed from the perspective of actually making programmes. Any producer (and therefore any programme) in political
television operates with a particular identity for his programme, a
limited amount of resources, a series of ground rules with which he
must concur, and a series of loosely held ideas about the purpose of
political television within the wider purpose of the organization as
a whole and the method by which that purpose will be achieved. His
life and work is a continuing debate with stylistic, technical,
legal-political and ideological structures. The setting for the
operation of these inhibiting frameworks is provided by the absence
of another framework encompassing the producer and the audience –
that is, the almost total alienation of the audience from the process of production. The congruence between the requirements of
cultural and political conformities and the mode of political television derives in large part from the unintended consequence of the
routines by which programmes are made.

Chapter 4

THE FUNCTIONING OF IDENTITY

The most frequent observation of sociologists who have written or talked about the mass media in contemporary society, and notably that part called 'news', has been that they detect within the over-all flow of messages a coherence and a patterning. Numbers of criteria are repeatedly - the repetition is the key - employed by communicators to select those messages that they will transmit from the mass of messages that theoretically are available to them. (1) The sociological analysis of news thus becomes a problem of elaborating the nature of those criteria. Hence news, from this sociological perspective, becomes not a 'mirror' to reality, an objective description or whatever, but a manufactured 'product' (i.e. an artefact resulting from a process) to be 'consumed' by an audience. It is a description of the world whose reality has more to do with the process by which it is created than any accurate or objective depiction of that world.

There is, however, far more to the formulation of programmes, even news programmes, than the operation of a series of news values. Clearly from a sociological perspective the analysis should be about the origination of those values. At the same time there is more to political television than news, so any treatment of the formation of political messages must go beyond consideration of only the news process. The treatment of news values often begs many questions about the social processes that underpin them. There is, for example, the simple but immensely important observation that the criteria applied to news, that is the dominant news values, changed drastically in the late 1950s and early 1960s (Smith, 1973). (2) It was, however, not only the content which changed during those key years, but also the whole style and pace of television news and current affairs.

It is remarkable but true that the first use of television newsmen in a form which we would now recognize - familiar anchorman in the studio, filed reports from television reporters, the use of specialist correspondents - did not emerge until 1961 with the 'Big News' at the Los Angeles station KNXT. (3) The point was well described by Greene (1969, p.11):

'the face of broadcasting in this country was fundamentally changed

in the Sixties. Movement in the Fifties was much slower. ITV
started in the autumn of 1955, but a good BBC man who was at home in
the late Forties would still have been at home in the late Fifties.
He might not be at home in the late Sixties.'

This is not so difficult to comprehend when one considers that in
Britain the BBC's news service always led, if one were available,
with a royal news story, and until 1959 would not mention any aspect
of election news. Change at Alexandra Palace was slow in coming,
and only began to emerge with the appointment of a former journalist, Hugh Greene, as director of news and current affairs in 1958.
When developments did come the impact was felt first not in news but
in the current affairs division. A number of developments, for
example, created new possibilities - satellites, compact cameras,
videotape, new editing techniques - and produced the possibility of
more lively (because immediate and visual) television. Technology
did not, however, provide the central drive. This came from the
pursuit of an audience in a competitive market - it was the initial
formulation of new formats followed by their success in terms of
audience size which provided the shift in form that characterized
the movement of television from one historical context, an essentially pre-war one, to the present historical context, a commercial
environment which emphasizes the maximization of audience size.
There was no way, for example, that Robert Wood, when he began the
'Big News' in 1961, or the BBC current affairs group when they
started 'Tonight' in 1957 in response to the end of the 'Toddler's
Truce', or ITN when in 1967 they were more or less forced by the ITA
to start 'News at Ten' could have known that these particular formulations would be successful. (4)
    Much has been made in the British context of the reactionary role
of Tahu Hole (Smith, 1973, p.81) who was head of the BBC's news
division, and the liberalizing impact of Hugh Greene. It is true
that it took only three years of not noticeably strong competition
to sweep Hole from that office (he became director of administration
in 1958) and it is true that in the context of a coming review of
broadcasting (Pilkington) a different approach was required. The
point, of course, is that the careers of these two men were merely
the figurative representations of the 'epistemological rupture'
engendered by the transition from monopoly broadcasting with all the
manifestations of Reithian paternalism to a competitive situation
with all the manifestations of the commercial ethic. Change lay in
the whole attitude to the subject matter and its presentation, and
was clearly spelled out by a senior broadcasting executive:

'You've got to think in the 1950s of the coming of television. I
think that the BBC badly needed that shake-up, and particularly in
the field of news. The whole development of television news in the
BBC was very slow indeed, and the whole attitude was extraordinarily
stuffy. Television news was to be a version of a radio news bulletin with a few pictures. The journalistic attitude was very
strange indeed. I remember the head of OB in television talking to
me one day in Alexandra Palace, and boasting of the fact that at the
Cenotaph ceremony in November (1952) when a man ran out towards the
King in an apparently hostile manner as the King was about to lay

the wreath, that immediately, as if by nature, without a word of command, the cameras were turned away from the incident so that it wasn't shown. Well, to me as an old journalist that seemed a very strange thing to boast about and I can assure you that the attitude changed in that sort of matter, and today there'd be no turning of cameras away from an incident like that.'

In a situation where only 30 per cent of the viewing audience was watching BBC, this conservatism could not prevail, not only because it might affect the possibility of raising the licence fee - the recurrent theme in the post-ITV years, nor just because the BBC wanted a second channel, but also because low audiences might call into question the very right of the BBC to exist. It is as if there had been an anomaly at the heart of broadcasting which rapidly shrivelled under the new conditions. What we can detect in the making of contemporary political television is the petrified form of the programmes which came to prominence in the years of flux following the emergence of ITV. The programme forms which arose from this situation provide the blueprint for contemporary political television embodied within what one might term a series of programme values that together constitute a number of specific identities - the news, the news magazine, current affairs, the feature, the documentary. Producers, it is argued, operate with a clear notion of what their programme 'is like', a concept which they both develop and inherit, and employ in making a programme along with the available resources, the technology etc. Into this is built a keenly felt, but poorly developed sense of the audience.

CONTENT AND STYLE AS IDENTITY

Producers have clearly worked-out views on the stylistic appearance and subject matter of their programmes. Derived from a number of sources, these provide an important framework within which political content must fit. A means is thus provided by which the affairs and happenings of the political process beyond the walls of the broadcasting organization are transformed into the representations of that process which emerge from within those walls.

I approached the question of identity by asking producers to talk about the way in which they made decisions about subject matter for the programme. With great facility producers were willing to detail numbers of factors which they took into account. A typical if notably articulate presentation was provided by a news editor at ITN. As with most respondents, he argued that there was an element of randomness to news, though he, like various other interviewees, was willing to acknowledge the point that patterns and routines are detectable. The news editor raised a number of criteria which he felt to be important: 'the most important events', though this, he felt, was not really suitable since it begged a whole number of questions. The problem as he saw it was that what was important in Edinburgh might not be regarded as news in Bolton or London. Therefore, he declared, 'we have to use stories that appeal to everybody, that are of interest to everybody. You have to remember that we are serving a mass audience and that, therefore, we must maintain their

"interest".' This led to his second criterion, a keen and persistent theme in all the interviews, of entertaining and interesting
stories. 'Interesting' he interpreted in a largely political sense,
questions of national political importance, happenings in Westminster etc. Industrial news he thought was tremendously important,
in two senses: stories in this bracket (strikes being the most notable example) are politically important and thus interacted with the
preceding category: at the same time the audience actually likes
them. 'There are at present a whole series of strikes and disputes,
in which perhaps we take an unrepresentative interest, but this is
because we have a largely working class audience, and they are
obviously interested in this.' Action stories provided his next category, and he included within this Ulster, plane crashes, car
crashes, other disasters. His next criterion was provided by background stories, where he felt that the news organization should
provide information on government papers and reports, etc. His
final criteria were picture stories, by which he meant those stories
which, though they fitted none of these previous criteria, must be
included because of their visual quality.

All these, he argued, were instantly recognizable by any journalist, since 'there is a kind of running consensus in the whole media
as to what is and isn't news'. The producer is strongly imbued with
this consensus, since he sees copy from the agency wire and is
therefore aware of what everybody is thinking. He would 'need a
very good reason for breaking out of the general feeling. This consensus also tends to reflect to a considerable extent the wider
social and political status quo. Therefore, we tend not to cover
the activities of minority groups.'

He consciously pursued a certain stylistic presentation based on
the use of two newsreaders, 'packages' of filmed reports of two to
two-and-a-half minutes length in which the reporter does everything,
'wraps' which are bunches of short stories, where possible utilizing
film, 'we use these to change the gear of the programme,' and an
'easy and informal style of spoken word though we still have a very
serious programme, especially when you consider that our viewers are
basically a 'Daily Mirror' readership type, we do, in fact, manage
to achieve a higher level than that paper.' The 'understanding' of
this style was, as with that other illusive element 'news value',
seen in terms of an instinctive feeling viewed in terms of 'this is
boring' or 'this isn't an ITN story'.

The operation of a number of news values is, even by their own
account, not in question. The focusing on elite figures, the searching for the dramatic and visual are clearly perceived influences.
What is not perceived, but what I think is vital, is that the operation of these values along with the particular form of presentation
constitute a stylistic paradigm that persists because it produces
what is the central concern of the broadcaster, an acceptable audience size. The relationship which is often implied in political
television is that 'news' forms a frontispiece to the other dominant
forms of political television, the news magazine and the current
affairs programme. The interesting feature, however, is that while
these are meant to complement the news-form (in-depth discussion,
background analysis, etc.) the central problem they have to face
also is the relevance of their form in audience terms, i.e. can they
obtain and sustain one?

A preoccupation with style of presentation has figured prominently in the recent history of BBC television news, whose audience
figures were decimated by ITV and by ITN after 1967. The assertion
that their change in style, exemplified by the introduction of two
presenters for the main 9 p.m. news and its extension to twenty-five
minutes, was a response to changing external circumstance, was
denied by the editor of Television News:

*'Was the change in television news a conscious process of competing
with ITN?'*

'Not really. The style, where there is one, and there isn't much
of one, is normally about getting the ritual gestures right, that
we introduce people in this form rather than that form; that we call
them "Mr Thing" instead of "old Fred Thing". It's a fairly marginal
sort of activity. Changing the style, the overall style, was not
all that radical, you would think we hadn't been doing it since
1964, which we had been on BBC2. It was two newsreaders because it
is very difficult for one newsreader to command the right tone, and
the longer a programme gets the more difficult it is. He's constantly finding himself caught out in more changes of intonation
within a given length than he can cope with, and so it's easier to
have two newsreaders. The newsroom in the background was simply to
make the point that this operation doesn't take place in a splendid
vacuum. (5) It is the result of a great deal of effort.'

The interesting point is why it was felt necessary to say that it
is the result of a lot of effort by many different people, and who
had suggested that it took place in a vacuum anyway. The answer, of
course, is that no one had suggested this, but the BBC's news division was sorely affected by the emergence and effectiveness of ITN.
The news programme - the public figure of the presenter(s), the
limited length of items, the use of short, filmed featurettes, the
knowing familiarity of the newsreader, the placing of 'serious' news
at the beginning of the bulletin, the conclusion with a light or
sporting piece (unless that happens to constitute a serious item) -
is a carefully prepared package within which the events of the world
are made to fit. If the function of news values is to limit the
views of the world made available, that of programme values successfully ensures the length and style in which that view will be presented.
Programmes other than news programmes also operate with clearly
specified identities, existing editorial briefs, which indicate what
they can and cannot do. This theme began to emerge during the
course of an early interview with the producer of one programme he
related an incident which I think clearly illuminates the point.
The programme he had previously worked on was what might be described as a rather sophisticated pop programme on BBC2. It identified clearly with the world of the so-called 'pop culture' and thus
was much intrigued by the Warhol affair - it put out a documentary
on ATV about the artist and film-maker Andy Warhol and made by
photographer David Bailey, which produced a good deal of threatened
and real litigation in relation to the possible banning of the programme. It was temporarily delayed by court order but was ulti-

mately allowed to be braodcast. The interviewee had thought that
as Warhol was such a significant cultural character it would be
useful to devote one programme to a discussion of Warhol's life and
times rather than to the usual line-up of rock groups. The night of
the programme discussion - with an audience that could be measured
in thousands rather than millions - there were nine phone calls of
complaint (in the BBC a log is kept of all phone calls, and this is
available to production staff and their superiors). The following
day the controller of the channel sent a memo to the producer saying
that though he hadn't seen the programme himself, he 'had heard'
that they had had a discussion on Andy Warhol, that theirs was a
music programme and not a discussion programme and that, therefore,
there were to be no more discussions on the programme.

There are obviously important questions about the nature of
editorial control and the quality of the judgment involved in the
controller's ruling. What is interesting is the way in which the
possible content of the programme was sharply defined by a specific
ruling about its nature.

It may be, of course, that the controller was also re-establish-
ing the programme format in order to suppress content. If, for
example, the discussion had been about a pop group, the 'aesthetics
of pop' say, one is left with a doubt as to whether the memo would
ever have been sent. The producer himself was in no doubt that the
memo was prompted by the change in format rather than the specific
content - the issue of the Warhol programme had after all, been
widely discussed throughout the whole of the media.

A similar insight was provided during an observation of a programme produced by the religious department of BBC2. The Warhol
episode had led to consideration of the way in which a programme's
subject matter was made to fit within a tightly prescribed area,
even though the inclination of those producing it was to develop the
content in particular ways. Discussion of the news had also led to
the proposition that the treatment of any subject matter had to meet
and satisfy certain stylistic features. What I wanted to do in the
context of this particular programme was to explore these propositions further. The results are, I feel, most illuminating.

The period was December 1973 when a major preoccupation of the
media was the alleged 'energy crisis'. The producer of a regular
programme with the religious department had been offered an extended
time period of an hour and ten minutes in which to discuss the question of 'has the God of growth failed?' The idea behind the programme was that they hold a debate between those in the country who
said that of course we had to have growth in the economy and those
who argued that it would be suicidal to continue with growth and
that what was required was a radical restructuring of values and a
new social contract. (6) They had been given by Alasdaire Milne,
the director of programmes, only one working day (they had been
informed at 9.30 a.m. and had to 'convince' him by 5.30 p.m.) to
assemble two 'suitable' panels - one pro-growth, one anti-growth.

That eight-hour period was marked by a continuous stream of suggestions, principally from the producer and the researcher. Possible 'names' were repeatedly swapped, 'Well, what about...? He/she
would be very good on this.' The name was then contacted: 'This is
the ... programme. We are mounting a special programme on the topic

of "has the God of growth failed?" Do you happen to think it has?
... Oh, you are not available on that date. Could you suggest anybody then, who might have something to say on this?' And so the
process was repeated - Philip Sherard, Dick Taverne, Barbara Ward,
Powell, etc., the names emerged, were checked and noted as yea or
nays. There was constant talk about the sort of people wanted.
When asked about the criteria they would employ in deciding which
people to contact and include, the researcher said, 'it's people
you know and those that are suggested to you. Of course at the
moment there are the added problems of the three-day week and transport difficulties.' (They had, for example, approached the editor of
'The Times'. He was holidaying in the family cottage in Somerset
and pointed out that a return to London might entail certain difficulties. They offered to send a BBC car to pick him up and return
him. He declined the offer.)
     Their first task was to assemble the anti-growth panel. 'We need
Bloom, Ward and Montefiore.' 'No, not Montefiore. What about
Galbraith?' 'No, he's in the States.' 'Try Trevor Huddleston, or
what about Barbara Wootton?' 'No. She's sensible, but that is
about all.' 'What we need are two practical men along with a
visionary.' More names poured forth, a litany of the more visible
personalities of the British social and political culture - frequent
reference is made to a well-thumbed copy of 'Who's Who'. The producer remarked that they must 'remember that we only want one
socially involved person!. One reason employed for excluding names
was that they 'are not big enough'. A response to one suggestion,
for example, was 'Who's he? He's just a second-rate journalist. He
hasn't got the stature to be on the programme.' Desmond Morris's
name was broached but was rejected by the producer on the grounds
that 'He's more anti-city than anti-growth. Also, he's not really
accepted intellectually, though I admit he would be very interesting.' The choice for the anti-growth panel gradually hardened
around Trevor Huddleston ('frightfully good') and Bernard Levin
(they had noticed from his column in 'The Times' that he was now a
'no-growther', and he was also a seasoned television performer),
balanced by a 'philosophical ecologist'.
     Having arrived at this point of decision they began the process
of assembling a pro-growth panel. The names again were familiar,
trade union leaders and government ministers predominating. They
faced a problem in that they were trying to get names who were
'good' and had 'stature' but who weren't overexposed in the media.
This becomes something of a contradiction in terms, since in effect
stature is increasingly determined by media exposure. It was a
particular problem in the closing months of the 1970-4 Heath administration, when industrial problems were massively important in the
realm of public affairs discussion. William Whitelaw was suggested
as a possible panellist by the researcher, 'he would be nice - he's
so much more than a politician'. It was while they were contacting
Whitelaw's office that the producer began to define the implicit
identity of the programme. I have shown how panellists were asses-
sed according to their particular compatibility with certain categories - 'philosopher', 'politician', 'pragmatist', 'visionary',
'stature', etc. The programme's identity was an underlying premiss
as to what it would contain, not in terms of the specific subject

matter and how it would be treated. For example, describing to the
press officer in the Department of Employment that the programme
would be about the whole question of growth, the producer added: 'As
you will understand from my department, religion, we won't talk
about this question of growth in wholly economic terms, but also in
more philosophical terms. Mr Whitelaw will be on the panel with two
others who share his views about growth.' He didn't, however, mention that the two others would in all likelihood be trade unionists.
The producer had declared prior to this that Robin Day (who was to
chair the discussion) was apoplectic about the thought of getting
the unions and the government on the same bench. There was then the
enticing possibility that the programme's attractiveness would stem
from not just the discussion between the pro- and anti-growthers, but
but also from the irony of having trade unions and government supporting the same argument at a time when in their normal affairs
they were involved in a conflict of huge proportions.

It might be argued that the attraction lay in the possibility
that their being on the same bench would typify the 'consensus politics' which, it is often argued, is the position sought by the
media. I am convinced, however, that a more immediate factor was
the assumed attraction of the ironic.

There was a built-in paradox in using well-known personalities
on a panel that might be summed up in the aphorism that personality
reproduces personality. This became clear when the researcher suggested a trade unionist who was not particularly well known. The
producer replied ... 'if we have a small trade unionist among the
big fish, we are going to be accused of setting them up. The higher
up the economic and political scale we go - the more Robin Day-type
people we use - the more high powered a trade unionist we will have
to have.'

They agreed that the pro-growthers should include a trade unionist, a member of the government and an 'A.N. Other figure'. Enoch
powell and Jimmy Reid were suggested. The researcher thought 'a
professor' would be useful to have on the panel, someone like
Vaizey - whose credentials were checked in 'Who's Who' - or a philosopher like Runciman or Hampshire. These were all possibilities for
the A.N. Other name and had the distinctive characteristic that they
were, among other things, 'non-institutional', that is, they had no
apparent connections with any of the two main power blocks, industry
(trade unions/business) or political (government/opposition).

In the course of these efforts word was received from the editor
of news and current affairs, via the head of department, that 'the
programme won't go ahead if it's too current-affairish, so we'll
have to sail pretty close to the wind on this, particularly on the
growth side. We can't have a boring pragmatist and we can't have
anybody who is too political.' It was suggested to the head of
department, that they have someone who was in space research and was
a bit of a visionary, which would keep them away from current
affairs. By asserting the implicit identity of the programme - that
it wasn't current-affairish but was 'sort of philosophical' they had
effectively ruled out the possibility of using many of the people
they had originally intended to use - notably the senior trade
unionists and politicians. It was interesting that the reaffirma-
tion of the identity of the programme emerged after their intention

to use these panellists had been made clear to the departmental head
and through him to ENCA. The particularly sensitive point - though
is, of course, difficult to be absolutely certain about - was the
possible inclusion of Powell. Far from happy with the situation,
the head of department declared:

'I'm being forced closer and closer to the icicle of Des Taylor
(ENCA). All political matter has to be cleared with the chief
assistant to the DG and by ENCA, who weigh it up in the light of
outside political affairs.'

    Despite the overall political conclusions to be drawn from this
incident, the programme had a declared purpose, which meant that
participants were excluded not on the grounds of political unsuit-
ability, but rather on the grounds that they had no relevance to
that programme. Whether one sees this as a control process skilfully operated or a rather unfortunate consequence of rigid adherence to programme identity is problematic. Its consequences in
influencing the content of the programme were nevertheless profound.
    The problem was then to find an 'economist with a philosophy of
life' which led to consideration of 'Christians involved in industry
- what about Sir Roy Geddes or Alan Davies of RTZ?' And so, after
several hours they were left with 'Christian industrialists': they
were Christians, and therefore fitted one feature of the programme,
the religious factor: they were industrialists, therefore pro-growth
and therefore fitted the immediate need of the panel: they weren't
overtly political and therefore not 'current-affairish'. They
therefore satisfied the proscriptions of the organizational hierarchy, and they had the necessary qualification of being proven performers, therefore satisfying the requirements of good broadcasting.
Their possible presence did not in the long run counter the objections of senior personnel and the programme was not broadcast.
    In discussions like this, there is a constant interplay between
the style of presentation of a programme - its visual identity -
and its content - what I wish to call the intellectual identity,
sometimes characterized as a 'house style'.

'You mentioned the phrase "house style". Is this a particular set
of ideas you have about the programme,'

'Oh yes. The way it looks - is it going to look like BBC2, is it
going to look like current affairs; is it going to look like its
own self, as a recognizable product? For example, the set, the
graphics, the way we position the lettering in the graphics on the
screen, the kind of shots we have of our studio set, the way we
introduce things and people, the way we shoot the film; certain
house rules. We always have an opening shot that is very,very wide
indeed, on film as well as in the studio, because then it gives me a
chance to do this and that and the other. To set out my stall.
This last season, I've always tried to start the show by saying -
"Tonight, we are going to tell you all about so and so. And we've
got the Chancellor of the Exchequer here..." and somebody else will
say "and I have got the Minister for Trade and Industry", or whatever it might be, "over here". "And over here, we've got another

group of people who don't like what the Chancellor has done about
this, that and the other. And we've got some jolly films as well."
That kind of thing. A recognizable way of introducing people, a set
of cliches, I suppose. We have to make the show hang together, as
if it were a service in a big cathedral, with lots of lady chapels,
so that there's a service going on in each part of the building.'

*'Would there be a house style in relation to the ideas side rather
than the stylistic aspects of the programme?'*

'Yes, it's ideas as well. Communication, the language, is very
important to me. The way we say certain things, the way we present
certain bits of information. Though, of course, in terms of ideas,
anything about the economy as far as my programme is concerned is
relevant. How do I want to tackle it? For the last twelve months,
I've been running a thematic presentation. That's to say every
week I say "This week, it's all about so and so." After years of
current affairs programmes I was bored with the presenter or reporter saying "I'm sorry folks, that's all we've got time for, and now
to something completely different", There's always a break. If
it's worth talking about, you may as well continue talking about it,
and you might get out some more information, so that poses stylistic
changes and ideas, and the way we put ideas up because it excludes
certain things.'

'If you broadcast to experts, you aren't broadcasting, you are
narrow casting in my view. You are infuriating the expert by not
telling him enough because he knows it already. And you are going
over the head of the individual, the ordinary man who doesn't know
as much as the expert. Anyway, I think you can forget about the
experts.'

His approach to his programme - albeit at an abstracted level - fed
on a notion of the kind of person he had to 'sell' it to; a person
who was not particularly informed, who liked seeing the Chancellor
saying something, rather than having someone saying what the Chancellor had said, liked pictures, but liked a theme to be developed
through rather than cut short. He added:

'We could do a very objective, cold, tepid piece about the balance
of payments, but what we really want is the Chancellor of the
Exchequer in the studio; so in a sense, then, I'm not doing what a
newspaper does, a journal or record or something like that. For
obvious reasons, I'm in the theatrical business really. If I want
the Chancellor of the Exchequer, it's a set occasion, he's being
interviewed, it's an important thing. If they can interview him in
a newspaper, then they can sub it down. If they want, they can make
it quite different, whereas you can see the dandruff on the Chancellor's collar, which is dreadfully important. You can also get him
in a different mode from the blanc presentation in a newspaper,
because if you read a newspaper, you can cut from one paragraph and
one story to another entirely, but you can't do that in television,
you've got to stay with it to the bitter end. Therefore, the style
of presentation is very much tied up with my intellectual approach
to the story.'

    The comment here, which throws most light on the making of pro-
grammes is 'I'm in the theatrical business really'. By using such
a description, the producer is being both literal and figurative.
He is implying that his foremost task is to keep his viewer enter-
tained and therefore to retain him as a viewer. This does not mean
that he suffuses the programme with a sawdust and greasepaint air,
rather that his programme is essentially a composition, within which
the content rests. Underlying his firm opinions about how the programme looks, what kind of items will be presented, how they will be
presented, who is involved, etc., is the key to his thinking, a
feeling about who it is that is actually watching. The focus of the
programme was economic affairs but the producer wished to interpret
his brief in a very loose manner so that it didn't just appeal to
city financiers, but also to 'ordinary people'.
    A suggestion was made to this particular producer by one of his
production team that they do an American trip. The producer had
already indicated to me that he tried to arrange trips abroad for
his people from time to time since this kept them happy and also
produced 'pretty pictures' for the programme. This suggestion was
for a three- or four-week stay during which time they would shoot
several film stories. The cost would be high and the producer made
it clear that they would have to talk very hard on this. The
ensuing discussion, however, provided a fascinating glimpse of the
centrality of the operating brief of the programme.
    A number of stories were suggested: the US postal service; the
Securities and Exchange Commission, which it was felt might feed
into a piece they were preparing on the role of the City in the
British economy; the railroad system, how the American experience
provides an insight into our own: 'Pictorially, it will be very good
good. The thing that will come out is that they don't have a transport policy,' black capitalism, or as one put it, 'coon capitalism'.
This latter was certainly the most favoured suggestion and, as with
the railway story, an interesting feature was that the broad conclusions of the story were predetermined, 'Let's face it. The conclusion we are going to come up with is that it is the system versus
the blacks.'
    No idea was forthcoming, however, for the producer's request for
a theme to cover the whole trip. Given the impasse, the discussion
moved onto another possible area for a programme, the energy crisis.
They saw two possible stories here: one, the overall situation from
a political perspective; two, the details of the energy crisis - how
much coal Britain held in stock, etc. The producer observed: 'I
like the political story, but it's not economic. The one that is
economic, we don't like.' The discussion then returned to its original area by the observation that: 'What we should be doing is the
money background to the Watergate story,' though none of the others
present agreed with this view. He rejected the idea of the 'economics of being black' story, on the grounds that it was 'just another
race story', and felt that the situation of the blacks didn't really
impinge upon him, and therefore, didn't impinge upon the audience.
The originator of the idea disagreed and felt that it: 'doesn't
matter whether it's relevant to the GB experience, it's still good
news and current affairs material'.
    The task, then, was to fit a particular type of content into a

particular programme brief, and at the same time to satisfy a number
of other criteria, such as visuality, interest level, etc. The
argument that the 'black' story was 'good news and current affairs
material' failed to take into account the fact that this particular
programme did not have a broad current affairs brief within which to
function - as with the previous programme, it couldn't be too 'cur-
rent-affairsish'. It seems to be the case that what we know of as
political television programmes operate a number of programme values
which are in part extractions from and elaborations of events as
determined by the news division, the translation of which into content is influenced by the programme's relationship to a particular
programme department. Where the producer functions with a programme
form and brief established by the particular department, within
which he works, we can see this as a derived identity. Within that
broad bracket, the producer is able to formulate a specific identity
by developing the details of his programme. A producer of a programme within a features department declared:

'We have vague terms of reference. The controller said recently
that we could do almost anything, so long as it's good, which is a
rather nice redefining of our brief. Basically, I suppose we are
human-affairs oriented. We spend a lot of our time looking at the
problems of the underdog and people who get pushed under by the
system, but really we work by a process of exclusion. We don't do
something that obviously belongs to light entertainment or obviously
belongs to plays or current affairs, or politics or religion or anything the other departments should be doing. Occasionally, if we
feel they've slipped up, we'll nip in there and pinch it, for
example, the big two-and-a-half-hour programme we did on a review of
the Welfare State thirty years on, that could equally have come out
of current affairs department. We think we did it in a much more
human way than they would have done. We think they would have had
far more politicians and done it as a sort of political shouting
match. In all the film we shoot, you'll find out more ordinary
people than in anything that comes out of current affairs.'

By human-affairs oriented he implied the focusing on non-elite
figures and an avoidance of abstractions which the viewer would
avoid because they were 'boring'. He saw himself and his programme
as contrasted with the sin of boredom as perpetrated by current-
affairs programmes. His conception thus led him to focus not only
on particular sorts of subject matter, but also on particular treat-
ments of that subject matter. The following account gives some of
the details which lie behind this point:

'I hope my programme is a way of presenting an overpowering abstract
idea in a way which is understandable and really brings it home to
ordinary people. Our biggest success in that way was the Welfare
State programme. We were wallowing around in the problem of how to
do it. The obvious thing to do was to pick out all of the bits that
had gone wrong and which didn't seem satisfactory. But we were
worried in that, whatever we selected, we would be editorializing
it in a way which we didn't want to be seen to be doing. Then the
researcher came up with the very bright idea that solved the problem

for us. He suggested that we choose two families, one fairly poor, and one fairly rich, and just compare them in every area where they came into contact with the Welfare State, and that really brought it home to people. People could sit down in the corner and look at the programme on the telly and they could identify with it.

'That seems to me the real thing and I think a lot of current affairs coverage fails to do this. It's actually very boring listening to politicians talking about abstract ideas, it's much more interesting listening to people talking about what really matters to them. I believe that all we are really doing is a sort of popular education job, if you like. If we are failing in that, because people are either bored, or because they don't understand it, or the subject isn't of any interest to them, then there's not much point in doing the programme, it seems to me.'

The producer in this kind of situation, where he is involved with political material, is faced with a dilemma: how to make entertaining programmes in an area in which he believes people are not particularly interested. The responses in many ways reflect their ituation, and this producer was able to develop a programme style and format which he feels avoided the pitfalls of 'boring' television. In other words he employs tried and tested formulae, particular formats which he has derived from the whole tradition of his area of broadcasting, from his department, and which he has developed during the course of his programme-making. In so doing, however, he may dilute and even prevent the transfer of political information, which is still his main task - the 'popular education job'. From this producer's point of view the main difficulty was not conflict with political elites but rather the development of an entertaining format. His problem was rooted ultimately in a strong identification with that mysterious person, the 'ordinary man' and an implicit concept of his likes and dislikes. Out of this abstraction emerges a solution to what he feels to be the problems posed by the abstractions of the political process. Beginning with the assumption that the audience is bored by much of the political material with which it is presented, and contrasting his own programme with a number of other types within which he does not fit, he depicts the programme as a feature, using film focusing on 'human interest' problems and 'ordinary people' rather than abstractions and boring politicians, and thus able to make the complex world of public and human affairs intelligible. Only through sustaining this particular identity can he sustain interest among his audience, the key word in his vocabulary.

The development of identity through the development of a particular stance vis-a-vis public issues, through an identification with certain types of participants and with certain types of subject matter is one means by which the producer establishes a programme identity. At the same time, however, a humber of other strategies are open to him, such as the use of particular broadcasters and reference to supervisors.

PROGRAMME IDENTITY FROM OTHER BROADCASTERS

It became clear from the research carried out that the professional broadcaster around whom any actual broadcast takes place effectively embodies within his own person both a type of subject and the way in which the subject will be treated. (7) The point was made by a producer in the BBC current affairs group:

'"Talk-In" varied considerably when Robin Day was presenter and when David Dimbleby was presenter. With Robin Day, we tended to be much more topical, much more political. This meant we couldn't plan the programme until pretty late - frequently not before the week concerned, and sometimes as late as the day before. We had a much smaller format for most of those programmes, using only three or four people. So we could work right up to the day before. But with Dimbleby, the programmes are much bigger, with a big invited audience. Programmes are prepared at least a week before or at least it is off the ground by then in the sense that you can get a number of people whom you can confirm. We did start with Day in the first place with an audience show, and they were all right. But we came to the conclusion that, given the fact that the viewer identifies Day with politics, we weren't actually getting a bigger audience and on the whole his particular skills were not really being exploited and so, in a sense, we retreated and did what he is good at which is the more formal debate and "Minister, tell me, what the hell you are up to?"'

The basic decision is the employment of particular personalities. That having happened, the programme is constructed around him in accordance with a number of characteristics he is felt to possess: he is, then, the embodiment of the programme's identity. The programme is still, at one level of definition, current affairs, but whether the audience will be seeing a discussion with the Chancellor of the Exchequer, or whether they will be seeing a discussion with a large number of people on the subject of wealth depends wholly on the person around whom the programme is being formed. The irony is that, though it is felt by the producer, by the rest of the programme staff and by the department, that the two versions are what the audience wants, they in fact remain the assumptions by the programme-makers about what the audience wants.
    Producers also tend to pursue their interpretation of their superiors' own feelings about the direction and subject matter for the programme. I asked producers about the role of comments from their colleagues and superiors, of how this influenced their own assessment of the programme and how the programme should develop in the future. I have repeatedly emphasized the connection with the audience, of how the formulation of the programme related to the pursuit of the chimera of the entertained ordinary man. On occasion, though, the necessary pursuit was of the entertained organizational superior. One producer summed up the situation in the following way:

'The fact of the matter is that, although one would like it otherwise, the comments and attitudes of one's senior colleagues are

bloody important because ultimately they are the ones who decide
whether a series continues and whether you are the right guy to produce it.   You get a programme that people you meet at home will say
"Oh, God, that was boring".   You will then find later on that your
BBC high-ups have said "Great programme, fascinating programme".
For example, we did a programme with Franz Joseph Strauss, which
really did send most people fast asleep straight away.   It read very
well in "The Listener" for people who knew about European Institutions but as a television programme, I don't think I met anybody who
stayed with it.   But I said at the time, and I knew I was right, "I
bet you the BBC hierarchy will like this," and sure enough they did.
Every week we get minutes of a meeting in which they go through different programmes and sure enough it was commended.   That happens
very, very often.'

*'Do you find then, that this would begin to influence you in terms
of later programmes? You have the organizational success of the
Strauss programme, do you say "we'll repeat that type of programme"?'*

'There is no completely straightforward and simple answer to that.
What I try to do is, I try to get a brief out of the people above
me, and that isn't all that easy.'

*'How do you do that?   Is it in the form of a formal request, or is it
over a drink?'*

'Oh no, informal.   The head of current affairs is very accessible.
I see him frequently, but on an entirely informal basis.   I say
"Well, what do you want the programmes to be? Who do you want them
to appeal to?"   In the BBC, as opposed to ITV, we don't have the
same necessity to obtain majority audiences across the board.   We
want them in some of our programmes, but we do have the constitutional responsibility to cater for minorities and so it is a valid
question to ask one's boos "Well, is this meant to be for the intellectual two million or do you want me to appeal to a much bigger
audience?"'

A BRIEF IDENTITY

The appearance and purpose of a programme may be a function of a
brief laid down at the programme's beginnings, combined with a
general sensitivity to the prevalent or dominant styles of programming, fused to the producer's own personal interjection of style.
A programme studied within the BBC's news division was particularly
interesting in this sense.   Its initial brief was that it would be
a 'review of the best of the week's news film', that it would cater
for the deaf as well as the hearing - which meant that it would
have captions as well as the spoken word - and would be broadcast
on a Sunday.   These various factors had a number of consequences for
the production in terms of what they could do and how they could
do it:

'So, compared to the people producing the nightly news, I have a different approach to things. The things that have been important day after day are not necessarily the stories which are going to take a lot of space in this programme. There are other reasons why my standards have to be different. Indeed, in the programme today, I've felt the need to go into a bit of explanation. At the end of last week's programme I got a call from somebody in the "Guardian" who wanted to know why we had said, "Now, the Watergate affair. In the last couple of weeks, we've tried not to overplay this," and a little later on in that programme, we used the phrase "is it going to be the most boring or the most exciting story of the century?" He wanted to know why we had used the words "boring" and "overplay" in this connection. Well, the fact is that it's perfectly legiti- mate for people night after night in a news bulletin to run minutes of talk about Watergate, but at the end of the week such as this, what you need if you are a normal viewer wanting to know more about Watergate are the pages and pages of print in the quality news- papers. I can't possibly do this even if I could find some way of summing up the Watergate affair in ten minutes of somebody's head and three or four lines of print, quite apart from the problems of printing would not be on for this programme. Anybody who wanted to read that amount of print would do far better to go to the news- papers for all the details.

'So that was what I meant when I said "try not to overplay it"; we would have been going over the same ground for the sake of it. It would have been broing, not because the events themselves are boring, but because a constant repetition of the same facts is boring. That applies to this week's programme as well. Obviously, the big story is the Lambton-Jellico affair. Well, what the devil can I do that isn't available in much more sensible detail in news- papers? I can't compete. So my standards are different, they are not ordinary news standards.'

There are a number of factors tied up in this description to which I will have need to return. Perhaps the most interesting is the observation that he couldn't compete with the press for detail because of the limitations of space and time. Within this was a slight implication that his colleagues elsewhere in the news divi- sion were, in fact, more able to compete. In reality, the time available to this programme was greater than the time available to main news bulletins, which leads one to conclude that his difficulty lay elsewhere or that he was totally wrong about his colleagues. I think the answer involves both these. When asked if his standards weren't normal news standards, just what standards did apply, his comments were revealing:

'This used to be more of a problem than it is now. When I changed the programme a few years back, I got approval for changing the billing. We used to be a "review of the week's world news"; this meant that we had to review the week's news, however boring this might be. I eventually got this changed to "the best of the week's news film and other matters of interest". This gave me scope and it meant that I could throw out important stories that in my terms were not important stories. Although I don't necessarily throw out a dull, but important, story it does mean that I don't necessarily feel that I've got to devote a great deal of length to it. How do I choose things? Well, this week, I came in knowing that there would be something about Watergate to be considered but I didn't know what on Wednesday.

'Obviously, the Lambton-Jellicoe story, but again, I didn't know what to say about this. What I'd seen on the news bulletins, I didn't much care for. I have my own feelings at times about what we should do and what we are wasting our time and money doing. You know, I see absolutely no reason or point in wasting money and resources and air time in showing exterior shots of the houses where people involved in scandals may or may not be. This doesn't seem to me to add one atom of information, excitement or enjoyment. Anyway, I knew I was going to have to do something about that. There was the Skylab story coming. I knew there was going to be the Paris Air Show, and there would be Iceland possibly, and as it turned out, yes.

"On the features side, I had a lot of very good film from our team who had flown out to India for the drought there, and this would be available. Also, it was the week of the Chelsea Flower Show, and there would be film of that. There were also various other items which, on Wednesday, I was gathering and thinking about and looking at.'

He indicated a number of other possible film stories which were visually appealing, such as a bank robbery in Germany, 'a bit of drama', which he would probably use (and did in fact, use in the end), and concluded:

'At the end of the week I don't think that detailed facts of the week's news stories are what a review of the week's news is all about. The basic facts are not necessarily as important as the overall feeling of the thing.'

And 'the thing' is the sum total of the week's news, represented not by the most salient or important points, but rather the most visually appealing pieces. This is not because, as the cliche goes, all of television is dependent on visualization, but because he has a brief from which he works. The particular formation of this brief created a number of difficulties. The positioning at the end of the week left him with the feeling that everything which could be said had been said on almost every issue. He was, therefore, in the ironic position of being made redundant as a news programme. At the same time, the brief entailed his using film. At the time of the interview, for example, there were a number of stories which exemplified his difficulties in this area - he refers particularly to Watergate and the Lambton-Jellicoe affair. Neither of these were compatible with the programme brief, in the sense that neither of them were particularly visual stories. Their explication would have been difficult in that the captions which had to accompany the spoken word for the use of the deaf viewers made it technically impossible to use lengthy explanations. This particular producer's solution to the problems was to have the brief changed slightly, so that it became the 'best' of the week's news film rather than the

more prescriptive 'review of the week's film'. In transforming the
brief he alleviated a series of potentially contentious areas. This
particular case does indicate the way in which the content of political television is shaped to accommodate workable programme formulae.

This particular programme had emerged during the formation of
BBC2 in 1964. Each of the existing departments of BBC1 were asked
to put forward ideas for programmes which would fit within the 'minority taste' brief of the new channel. It was suggested that a
special news programme which would appeal to the hearing, but would
also provide a service to the deaf and which would be able to use
film might be useful. The perspective of the programme was thus
heavily structured by its original formulation. It is not always
the case, however, that the idea behind the programme is so clearly
formed before the real work of producing it begins. The initial
formulation of some quite notable programmes has been vague, leaving
the producer, in effect, with little or no brief: 'Tonight', 'TW3',
and 'Pebble Mill At One' were all formed in this way. (8) A brief
look at the origins of 'TW3' throws further light on the process
described here. Given its success - at its peak, something like
twelve to fourteen million viewers watched the programme - the
beginnings of the programme were remarkably simple and ill-defined.
In a recent interview Sir Hugh Greene described how he saw the programme's origins.

'I had just got this as a vague idea in my mind that in the atmosphere of the early 60s, it would be very good to have a programme
which did something to prick pomposity, and show politicians and
others in their true character. I had got this vague idea from
Berlin in the back of my mind, I talked to Kenneth Adam about this,
he sympathized with it, and I talked to the people in the television
light entertainment department, informally at parties and so on,
just throwing in a few words of encouragement to start thinking
about this.

'Then came in some ways the other decisive incident. There was
an American comedian called Mort Sahl, who was associated with satirical programmes in the United States, he visited England and was
asked to do one programme for the BBC, done by light entertainment.
I remember this; it wasn't very good at all - Mort Sahl hadn't been
in England long enough to get the flavour of England. I remember
listening to this at the television centre, and what infuriated me,
really made me lose my temper which I don't do often, was the framework provided by Muir and Norden in which this was put on, with
either Muir or Norden, I forget which, standing on one leg, and
saying "Fancy Aunty BBC daring to put on something like this." For
someone in the BBC to talk about Aunty BBC on the air, with that
sort of coy approach, enraged me so much that I told light entertainment to stop thinking about this and put it, with Kenneth Adam's
association and agreement, into the hands of the current affairs
department. There you had all the bright young people of "Tonight",
and so on, and they then set to work thinking about the new format,
and from that point on, I didn't interfere at all, I didn't ask to
see anything in advance and whatnot. On the night of the first
number I watched it with some nervousness, unclear as to what it was

going to be like and was delighted. Seldom had a programme begun so
splendidly. But that was the real genesis of it all.'

*'Did you go to current affairs because that seemed the only logical
alternative to light entertainment given your disillusion with light
entertainment?'*

'Yes.'

*'When you went over to current affairs, you must have presented
Baverstock and Co. with a basis of the model of a programme.'*

'No. I didn't. They produced their model of a programme. I can't
remember my exact words after all these years, but all that I did
was to suggest to them that they should think in terms of a programme which took an irreverent look at what was going on in the
country, or in the world. It was up to them to work out how to do
it. And then as I say, I didn't take part in the discussions, I
didn't see anything in advance, I left it entirely to them.' (9)

In another interview, Baverstock sought to play down the role of
Greene and Adam, and yet his responses were remarkably in keeping
with Greene's. (Greene anyhow plays down his own role in the formulation of the sort of programme it should be.) He ridiculed the
notion that Greene had been influenced by the pre-war German caba-et
ret, but said that the central thrust of the programme was an attack
on cant, the unctuous hypocrisy which characterized post-war British
society. It was also, he declared, particularly important that the
programme be on Saturday evening, 'because then people are twenty-
four hours from having finished work, and twenty-four hours from
going to work', and are therefore, at their least public and most
private, in a position to - a curious phrase this - 'speak the private truth'. (10)
There is a sense of serendipity in all this. Had the programme
been produced by light entertainment as was originally intended,
transformation of the rather vague notions of Greene and then Baverstock into the programme that was 'TW3', would presumably have been
noticeably different. The point remains though, that the sense of
purpose and identity embodied by 'TW3' was essentially developed by
those involved in its day-to-day funning, rather than derived from
on high.
In the present context, one is tempted to formulate a law that
programmes which are not specifically recognized by broadcasters as
political are more likely to have a developed rather than a derived
identity; that the less the manifest political content, the greater
the latitude for developing particular programme features. A discussion programme in the sample was produced from neither a news
or a current affairs department, and indeed, was only included
because on the weeks in which the sample of programmes was drawn up,
the subject matter happened to be political. When asked about the
programme, the producer declared:

'They said "You will produce a programme in that slot". It was a
twenty-five-minute slot, it was studio based, it had very little

money. I happen to have a general theory that the notion of balance
inside television programmes is pretty sterile. Exchanging worked-
out points of view one with the other doesn't get anywhere beyond a
statement of first principles. Mary Whitehouse will say "I believe
so and so", and Ken Tynan will say "I don't, I believe so and so".
I work from the general principle that ideas are best expressed
unchallenged if you want to understand them. So we, first of all,
gave the programme the vaguest title we could think of, "Opinion",
since this clearly could cover anything. We pulled out of the
"Dictionary of Quotations" an Oscar Wilde quote which identified the
key constituent of an opinion as being prejudice. We said that the
programme was basically going to be talking heads and would consist
of people who had got positive ideas on things, and generally we
decided to let them go unchallenged.
    'So we shopped around first of all for big general areas: we
said "football season's starting, what shall we do about football?"
So we found a footballer, Eamon Dumphy, and let him express his
opinion in the company of people who could be expected at the very
most to qualify his ideas. The only concession we made to balance
was to say "We are not therefore, going to take up a political
stance that belongs to the programme and field teams of people
pushing points of view that correspond with that." We consciously
did the opposite sometimes. One week, we got a copy of the "Spectator", read through the whole thing, found the three most extreme
right-wing points of view and said "Put these people up against
Anthony Howard and they would all disappear, put them into the
studio together and you would get a much clearer idea in twenty-five
minutes of how the right-wing man thinks." So we did that, and it
was quite fruitful.'

    The situation was not quite as stark as implied here; there are
obviously a number of mechanisms which would be employed to distance
the views of the participants from possibly appearing as official
programme policy. The two most central are the billing - that this
is an opinion, and the audience is expected to understand and appreciate the point - and the presence of the detached chairman putting
questions to the participants. At the same time, the programme would
not be identified as mainstream political television, and, therefore, not only would the intellectual ground rules vary, the whole
perspective of the programme's style and development would vary also
also.
    Why this should be the case is less easy to state than the fact
that it is the case. It seems to stem from the structural position
of the department within which it was produced, presentation, which
does not have as clearly overt a role as do the other departments
whose programmes figure in this study. The external political
awareness of politicians is much more tightly focused on the television produced by the main political departments, and this in
itself creates a more 'liberal' atmosphere from the presentation
programme-makers' viewpoint. The programme was also a part of a
minority channel's output with an audience small even by the limited
standards of that channel. Its assumed significance, and therefore
its potential to generate anxiety, will reflect this perspective.
The position was ably described by another producer in the presen-

tation department, during a discussion of a late-night programme
which had featured, among other things, a quite vicious cartoon of
Edward Heath, who was at the time prime minister. It was pointed
out that one always assumed that politicians were highly sensitive
to their portrayal on television and that television controllers
were sensitive to those sensitivities. He declared: 'Context; you
have got to see it in terms of context. We can do things from this
department which you could never do from other departments.'

IDENTITY FROM OTHER MEDIA

The traditional current-affairs programme is clearly geared to the
mainstream of political life, focusing as it does on the activities
of the political elite. The attachment of these programmes to the
world of the dominant political culture does not follow just from
the statutory or ideological link to that world - though such links
are clearly important - but also from an attachment to a number of
that culture's dominant journalistic forms. What I have in mind are
the 'New Statesman'/'Spectator' and 'Sunday Times'/'Observer'
formats. (11) Implied within each model is a sense of the subject
matter, the audience for that subject matter and the way the audience wishes to have that subject matter treated. The point was
described in the following by an ITV current affairs producer:

'On Monday night, before I come in, I sit down with the papers from
the weekend and I just think for an hour. I don't look to the
papers just for stories. I suppose most items can be subdivided
into three: one is the sort of political ideas, trying to plot current events not so much from a journalistic news sense, but trying
to isolate the ideas that are behind something like incomes policy.
The idea is not just to put the government's point of view, but to
pose the real issues which it forced the unions to come to terms
with.
   'There are issues in the air like Northern Ireland. Political
ideas, which one tries not to cover in a news way. I don't like to
grab Gerry Fitt and say "What are you going to do?" Rather I like
to say "Look at the White Paper on this subject ...". We have very
long talks about it and take things like that very seriously. We
endeavour to be different from other current affairs programmes,
because we have the time to think for about three or four days or
something like that, rather than a couple of hours or a couple of
weeks. In three or four days you have got time to really get to
grips with the White Paper on Northern Ireland, to read it with a
number of people who know a lot about Ireland and work out what the
important questions to isolate are, and then say, if that's the
important question, how can we go about presenting that interestingly on television. Now that's what I'd count as the sort of
ideas section.
   'The next section is just pure "Insight" type journalism. For
example, the boat that was caught this morning off the coast of
Southern Ireland: where did it come from; where was it going to; who
paid for the arms? All those kinds of questions. That is just pure
journalism. We are, for example, mounting an investigation at the

moment into the (Wakefield) mine disaster and have two people up
there at the moment. I've been trying to decide whether to do a
twenty-minute documentary into what the causes of the disaster were.
If something like this disaster happens, then you respond immediately, and if you are a daily newspaper, you respond in one way, but
if you are "Panorama", it's just not the sort of story that you are
interested in. We are, however, interested in it as much in the
same way that the "Sunday Times" or the "Observer" would be. We as
a programme, though not current-affairs programmes in general, try
when a major story like that breaks to do an analysis. It is not a
political event, but we do try to do a news analysis.
    'And the third item is that each week, out of four or five items,
we have a short final piece on something which is not news or current affairs. It is very difficult to describe what we are looking
for, but to some extent, we try to make the last item entertaining.
Last week, we interviewed (a well-known film star) and we have done
one with (a well-known footballer). They are more digestible, more
palatable than the other items. They are not necessarily not
serious, but are general interest for a current affairs audience.
They are ideas which you come across in the paper or hear about.'

    The quality press and periodicals act not only as sources of
items and background reading on items, but also provide the working
model for the programme. His description of the types of stories
they will have is a pastiche of the diverse contents of dominant
press sources. The effect is amplified by the use of working
reporters from these papers as contributors, broadcast journalists
or linkmen in the studio. The necessity of producing something, the
feeding off and in a sense imitation of the currently available collective wisdom of the world of print means that the consideration of
certain forms of political material - 'oppositional politics' is
one that is often cited - is difficult, quite simply because they
don't seem relevant to or compatible with that programme's intent.
The point is suitably made in the following description of the origination of the ideas for a current affairs programme:

*'But are there any particular criteria you would employ to make the
final decision? If you are being fed ideas from various sources at
any one time, on what basis do you accept and reject?'*

'Does the idea attract me? - that's important. You can't please
everyone, so you may as well please yourself. I think that's a
fairly good rough and ready rule of thumb. Is it something that is
sociological or political in essence, or economic? I say "No, don't
bring me the sociology, give me the economics". I want to hear cash
registers ring; narrows it down a bit. I say, "Will I learn something about the economy in watching this programme, or will it
simply be a lot of politicians arguing or sociological information
that we can't understand." In other words, a poor man's "Panorama"
or a poor man's "Midweek", which we are not. Let them do that -
it's easier. We do something that is much better and more specialist.
    'So we have a lot of politicians arguing anyway, but you want to
have certain facts and figures to establish the parameters of the

the story. We did a story, say, on tourism about six or seven month
months ago, and we explained with two or three films, and a couple
of big discussions, how it is that tourism is our greatest dollar
earner or something like that, it's a very big industry. It's a
cottage industry at the same time. Should there be a Ministry of
Tourism, or should we let it go along as it always has done, in the
great informal ad hoc English way?

'Now, in the course of that, we tackled hotel prices in much the
same way as the "Sunday Times Business News" did six weeks later.
It's always my joy to think of something that, say, the "Business
News" will do afterwards, not before. One of my immediate questions
is, "How came you by this intelligence?" And if they say "I read
it in a newspaper," I say "Yuck!" because so did everyone else. I
am wrong of course, because more people may see us than read the
newspaper, and may not be the same people. But I have a horror of
being regarded as the younger brother of Fleet Street.'

His standards, then, are set by his differentiating himself from
'Panorama' and 'Midweek', and associating with the parameters established by the 'Business News'. The distinction between the two
areas is of more than metaphorical significance; it exemplifies the
functional code of identity from which programmes emerge.

Slowly, numbers of forces - what is happening in the news media
generally, what they can actually do, given available resources,
what would be suitable for their programme with their sorts of
audience, what they are supposed to be doing given their programme
brief - crystallize, so that eventually, a code is established which
the producer utilizes in constructing the programme. Every producer
operates such a code, though its precise nature may be poorly articulated. In the following account, its nature was clearly and
intelligently articulated:

'At one's disposal was an average of about forty minutes per night,
in which, with a particular array of reportorial skills, one could
do anything. There were no obligations in the way that a news bulletin has obligations - it must obviously cover that which is generally determined by the various evaluative processes to be the big
news of the day. Nor was it really like "Panorama", in the sense
that that programme has periodic obligations, although it's similarly free to do the set-piece interview with the Prime Minister or
the Leader of the Opposition on current major events. Its freedom
was greater than that, but its freedom was to use the qualities and
the skills that it possessed. So, I gradually worked out a series
of criteria for what constituted an item. If I can remember them
all, they were:

'First, a kind of story which told you what really went on - you
have to use the word "really" in most of these criteria. It's not
what was the news, but what had really happened. These are all
ideals. So one of the things of judging "is that an item?" was "is
it the kind of item that tells you not so much what happened, but
what really happened?" In other words, if the news is telling you
about the sacking of various ministers for misdemeanours, a "really"
item could be the degree to which British society believes sexual
morality is no longer important; or an examination of integrity in

high office, what is the meaning and what is the expectation, a discussion about that for instance; or the historical (treatment) of
that is in a sense telling you what the news story was really about.
   'Secondly, there is the extension and elaboration of a news
story. There's a simple means by which you can tell people far
more, even in the forty minutes available, than the news, and that
is in itself valuable. There would be an event, let's take the same
event, you can take all these five criteria to the same events, you
could by simply doing forty minutes on one of these particular political scandals, through just using factual presentation of "this is
where it happened" and "this is where they ...", just telling the
story in pure narrative terms with a far greater accumulation of
fact and picture and narrative content (achieve this end).
   'Third criterion is personality. There you take an important
figure involved in a news event and you just do a portrait of that
person, anything from a day in his (her) life to his (her) life
story. Told narratively. A subsection of that criterion can be a
major interview with a personality which is simply a skilfully conducted interview of twenty minutes in length, which itself was a
particular skill of the programme.
   'Fourthly, there was the story that wasn't in the news at all,
but ought to have been. That is to say, perhaps I ought not to have
used the word "ought" in there, but which could have been or should
have been if one focused sufficient attention to that particular
story. You could say that a story that had simply been ignored -
anything from the scoop, like the "Washington Post" having Watergate
when nobody else had; just getting information which wasn't formally
news yet, but by breaking it, it became news. Or something in a
slightly more moralistic way, but a story about a scandal in housing
or a fantastic good deed done by somebody, something, it needn't
necessarily be negative. It could be, and usually was, something
quite positive about something very important or very interesting
that had happened, that no one else had paid attention to and wasn't
worth paying attention to, unless you could do it at length.
   'Now the next criterion. Well, there's a subsection of that
which is investigative reporting, where you have built, not by process of discovery, but by a process of painstaking and elaborate
research which you very seldom do thoroughly enough to fulfil this
criterion. But by doing it, you produce a major investigative and
important thing. Now I think the best of these was the story of the
propaganda campaign behind Biafra. At a time when everyone else was
being pro-Biafra we showed, just by doing academic research and some
historical research and a certain amount of daredevil digging around
around, the most amazing story of how the propaganda campaign was
put together around the world. So these are five major ones.
   'But there is a sixth one. This is a story which justified
itself, because someone who happened to be working on the programme
could do it particularly well. In other words, it fitted no criterion at all beyond the fact that one happened to have someone who
was particularly good at that, or that particular thing, and therefore one could do it, through technical skill rather than through
any formulable criterion of newsworthiness. Through sheer technical
skill, something was validated which otherwise would not have been
validated.'

I have been arguing, that producers, when making programmes, employ a 'code', the constituents of which provide programmes with a workable identity. Put simply, producers operate with a blueprint or a framework, and in this sense their work is structured and inhibited. Their work is in many ways more a feat of engineering than of architecture (Sigelman, 1973). Yet there is clearly no absolute imperative about employing particular identities for pro-gramme-making, and yet equally, experimentation, the development of new formulae, is not the order of the day in political television. It is not unreasonable to ask why this state of affairs obtains. To answer this, one has to look more closely at the derivation, persistence, and petrification of programme formulae and in this way begin to tap a distinctive aspect of the social origins of political television.

When producers say of their programmes, 'It's what the audience wants', the judgment implied within that statement is based on audience figures. This, at least, is the clear message of any dis-cussion of the audience. The producer holds no precise details of his audience but he does have a crude awareness of the audience figures for his programme, and so do his superiors.

In a recent article, Mitchell (1973) describes the 'decline of current affairs television'. He shows that over a period of time various current affairs programmes have suffered a decline in their audience (Table 4.1). There is obviously something in Mitchell's

TABLE 4.1 Viewing figures as a percentage of total audience over 5

	1965	1966	1967	1969	1971	1972
'24 Hours'/'Midweek'	-	12	12	8	7	4
'Panorama'	20	-	17	13	10	8
'This Week'	-	-	10	10	9	7
'World in Action'	-	-	15	14	13	13

(Source: Mitchell, 1973)

argument that the declining figures reflect not only an increasing avoidance of political material, but also the impact of the new news programmes and their increased length - he posits 'a "Gresham" law of television' in which 'the topical drives out the analytical', and 'an undigested deluge of facts curtails the scope for depth, dis-cussion and interpretation' (Mitchell, 1973, pp.133-4). This is no place to become involved in the argument about how necessary current affairs programmes are, but it does seem to me that Mitchell touches on an important point, though I think inadvertently, when he says that: 'Television's responsibility to serious discussion is not ful-filled through programmes late at night or by serious items buried with an air of trivia' (Mitchell, 1973, p.134).

From the point of view of this discussion, the most interesting feature is that these programmes were relatively successful in their early years - 'Panorama' and 'This Week' were both developed and successful in the mid-1950s and 'World In Action' began broadcasting in 1963. It was their early success which led to their subsequent

transformation into a persistent formula for current affairs broadcasting. It is also the success of the news magazine 'Tonight' in
the 1957-62 period which has led to the persistent presence of the
news magazine in any sample of political television.

The irony is that it becomes rather difficult to say just what
the news magazine is: it is news, political and non-political
interviewing, economics, sociology, entertainment; film report and
studio report, and group discussion. It is a programme which can
contain both a serious political interview with the Prime Minister
and a film about clog-dancers, an investigation into striking car
workers and a 'Nurse of the Year' Award. From this morass, however,
we can begin to detect three components to the overall identity: a
public affairs component; a magazine component; and a view of the
audience. Any cultural form owes much to a number of antecedents,
and the origins of this rather curious form of political television
lie in the immense success of 'Tonight'.

THE ROLE OF SEMINALITY

A description of 'Tonight' written in 1961 could readily apply to
any news magazine programme now on the air (Hill, 1961):

'One night it may concentrate on three items as immediately topical
and serious as the situation in Paris before the expected invasion
by paratroops, the plans for a teachers' strike, and American and
Cuban exiles clamouring for another invasion of Cuba; with only an
interview with Annigoni and a song thrown in as lightweight at the
end. Another night the programme will start with a fox-hunting
debate, press on to the mystery of an apparently suicidal crow
repeatedly dashing itself against a window pane and follow up with
a tame mink.'

'Tonight' began transmission from a tiny studio in Kensington on
18 February 1957. It is now part of holy writ that this was a
momentous event not only in the development of television, but in
the career of a new post-war generation of programme-makers. In
particular, its producer and then editor, Donald Baverstock, was
regarded as the new age incarnate. There is no purpose here in discussing the validity of such a view of Baverstock, nor do I wish to
discuss whether 'Tonight' and its people did represent a new social
mood which dragged, as the saying goes, Aunty BBC kicking and
screaming into the new era of the 60s. (12) My purpose in mentioning 'Tonight' is much simpler - though I believe that the point is a
an important one for understanding the present state of political
television. Its emergence exemplified the response by the BBC to
the challenge of ITV, which had begun transmission only two years
previously. The effect on the BBC's audience figures was tremendous. The mood this induced was described by Hugh Greene, who was
director of administration when 'Tonight' began, director of news
and current affairs in 1958 and was appointed director general in
1959:

'There was a very serious competitive situation. The figures were

down to, I think, the lowest point reached towards the end of the
50s - 27 per cent to the BBC and 73 per cent to ITV. With Pilkington coming along, and with the knowledge that one of the main decisions to be made as a result of the enquiry was who should be given
a second channel, the BBC or ITV, it seemed to me quite clear that
whatever the enquiry might recommend, if the BBC still had an audience as small as that, it would be politically impossible for any
government to allot the third channel to the BBC. So the BBC had
to become more competitive and had to shake off a lot of its old
fashioned ways.' (13)

The 'Tonight' programme was broadcast nationally, as is 'Nationwide'. Its significance was apparent within the very first year of
its appearance, as was that of 'Panorama' which began two years
earlier. The Annual Report and Accounts of the BBC for 1957-8 stated:

'In recent years, BBC television has greatly developed its capacity
for reporting on current affairs and controversies and, more
broadly, for illuminating the most significant aspects of our life
and times. Programmes of this description now form the largest
single category of the BBC's output. 'Panorama', which has been
broadcast in its present form since 1955, has continued to open its
weekly 'window on the world' to an audience which now averages
nearly ten million. Its reputation for independent and impartial
enquiry into topical matters of national and international concern
has been fully maintained. The new topical magazine 'Tonight' has
been remarkably successful and, with its blend of serious and light
and its ability to appeal directly to the viewer, has firmly established itself as a novel and popular form of television. Its
average nightly audience increased in one year from 2¼ million to
nearly 8 million.'

These were, however, very much islands of success in a landscape
swamped by the rivals of ITV. (14) The figures presented to Pilkington are conclusive:
'At present the average evening audience for ITV programmes is
running at about 12½ million people. In homes able to receive both
BBC and ITV transmissions, the time spent viewing ITV programmes in
the country as a whole, measured as a proportion of the total time
spent viewing television, has never in any month during the past
year fallen below 62 per cent and has been as high as 71 per cent...'
The TAM figures for the early years of ITV were:

		ITV %	BBC %
1955	October - December	57	43
1956	January - March	64	36
	April - June	65	35
	July - September	69	31
	October - December	71	29
1957	January - March	75	25
	April - June	75	25
	July - September	76	24
	October - December	73	27

		ITV %	BBC %
1958	January - March	71	29
	April - June	71	29
	July - September	74	26
	October - December	74	26
1959	January - March	71	29
	April - June	72	28
	July - September	71	29
	October - December	68	32
1960	January - March	67	33
	April - June	67	33
	July	66	34
	August	67	33
	September (first week)	51	49} Olympic Games
	September (second week)	57	43} period
	September (third week)	71	29
	September (fourth week)	70	30
	September (fifth week)	72	28
	October (first week)	69	31
	October (second week)	72	28

(Source: ITA Memo (Review Paper XI), October 1960: in 'Pilkington 1960', vol 1, Appendix E, Paper No. 77)

   The BBC's response to this was to point to the difficulties of sustaining a 'balance' between 'light' and 'serious' programmes, particularly at peak viewing hours (Pilkington 1960, vol 1, Appendix E, pp.210 ff). The dismal viewing figures, it implied, were the result of the BBC's trying to do its duty to public service broad-casting by providing a diet of serious as well as light programmes at peak hours, a duty it noted that the ITV companies had singularly avoided. The BBC memorandum declared ('Pilkington, 1960', vol 1, Appendix E, pp.211-12),

'It is the core of the BBC's programme policy that its more impor-tant serious programmes should for the most part be offered when the largest audiences are available.... It is important not only to satisfy the knowledgable viewer, but also to attract "new" viewers to such programmes. Resources and facilities are directed to this purpose to the maximum extent. Many of the BBC's serious programmes have been successful in drawing audiences numbered in millions.'

It was then able to produce figures which showed that the two poli-tical programmes, 'Panorama' and 'Tonight', were the top of a league table of serious programmes: 'During December 1960 (the most recent month for which particulars were available) the following audience for "more important serious programmes" were recorded.'

Title	Time (p.m.)	% Pop	Approx. no. of viewers (millions)
Panorama (Mon)	8	19 - 20	9 - 9½
Tonight (Mon - Fri)	6.45	18 - 20	8½ - 9½
Safari to Asia (Wed)	7.55	20	9½
This is the BBC (film)	6.20	17	8
Music for You	8.30	13	6
Face to Face (Adam Faith)	10.25	9	4¼
Great Captains (Oliver Cromwell)	8.30	99	4¼
Asian Club	9.30	9	4¼
Insight (Tues)	9.15	7 - 9	3¼ - 4¼
International Concert Hall (Barbarolli)	9.15	8	3¾
Challenge to Prosperity (4-part enquiry)	9.30-10.15	6 - 7	2¾ - 3¼
Meeting Point (Sun)	7.00	6 - 7	2¾ - 3¼
Brains Trust (Thurs)	10.00-10.30	4 - 7	2 - 3¼
Monitor (fortnightly)	10.10	4 - 6	2 - 3¾
The Cinema Today: Japan	10.15	5	2½
The Coming of Christ (film)	10.15	5	2½
Replacements for Life	10.25	4	2

(Source: BBC Memo No 10 in 'Pilkington 1960', vol 1, Appendix E,
p.212)

    'Tonight', 'Panorama' and their descendants thrived because in a
potentially hostile environment they created substantial audience
figures and in helping to solve one dilemma, the lack of an audience
for BBC, established a format of political television which could
successfully be taken up by other and later producers. The close
identification with the 'Tonight' tradition and format was described
by the then head of local programmes at Granada; we were discussing
Granada's coverage of the Rochdale by-election, which was the first
ever coverage of an election, other than the party political broadcasts, by television. The context of the discussion was the origination of programme policy, during which he declared:

'I don't think one can talk about local election policies in relation to the Rochdale by-election. I think one has got to go back as
far as Granada is concerned to the BBC's "Tonight" programme in
order to trace a thread in Granada's local programming. Like most
other companies, Granada had done a form of late afternoon or early
evening programme more or less from its start. They were really
adequate for the time but didn't really thrill anybody very much -
it was cookery and middle class ladies talking about knitting patterns, and all that sort of rubbish. (15) Granada was pretty jealous
of "Tonight" and in 1963 we started a magazine programme proper with
"Scene at 6.30", which was a good programme and attracted a lot of
bright people. Historically it was right for its time and there
were all sorts of reasons why it was good. There was, for example,
a limited market for people to get jobs in. There was only

"Tonight" which was good or us doing "Scene at 6.30", therefore,
over the whole country people who were attracted to that sort of
programme were available to us for "Scene at 6.30": not like now
where every company has got a moderate magazine programme, so that
a man can go to several. And if you remember it was the time of the
Beatles and the Mersey Sound so the whole thing was jumping anyway.'

    Every region is served by two news magazines, one provided by the
BBC the other provided by ITV. The problem of talking to producers
of news magazines, as with other producers, is their tendency to
slip into loose and vague descriptions, cliches which make analysis
difficult. Nevertheless, certain themes about the audience emerge,
and the programme producer of a BBC news magazine declared,

'It's a news magazine, so what goes in it ought to be new. Right,
you often haven't got a new topic because the morning papers have
been at it, but you ought to develop it so that there is some nov-
elty about it even for somebody who has read the morning papers
quite thoroughly. It should be of interest as far as possible to
everybody in the region and that means I suppose it should be of
interest to a casual visitor to the region as well as the people who
are immersed in its life.'

The news magazine is characterized by its being central to political
television - in the sense that for large sections of the population
it is the only experience of political material that they actually
have, and also in the sense that they are an important part of the
activity of news and current affairs departments. It is a form of
political television which is also characterized by the fact that
it is intended to entertain rather than inform. When Alasdaire
Milne, a former editor of 'Tonight', argued that the programme set
out to entertain in order to inform, he assumed that a balance was
possible. In a competitive age, increasing emphasis is laid on the
entertaining aspect, and therefore on the incorporation of a number
of audience-holding techniques and material:

'How is subject matter for a news magazine programme based in London
decided on? How do you decide what items to cover in the programme?'

'Given the criteria of the programme which are basically that it is
a daily magazine programme which to some extent reflects the things
that happen in London and outside London and outside this country,
and given that it's a magazine programme so it's supposed to have a
bit of film in it, a bit of studio, to be partly political, partly
entertaining, partly social, partly to deal with the arts - it's
supposed to do a whole range of things and it's supposed to be balanced in that way, i.e. the areas you deal with should be balanced
geographically, balanced in the types of story you do and the
weights they have, and it's balanced in the length of time each has,
so you work with those criteria. There are certain things you ought
to do: when they blow up London you feel you ought to do something
about that. When a nose-playing pianist phones up you think that's
very funny and should be done. In the end you use those criteria

and the things that you find interesting. I mean I can only operate
on the principle that if I find it interesting then maybe somebody
else will. One cannot worry about the viewer because he doesn't
really exist.

'In conjunction with that you are very much in the hands of what
you can get. So your news sense might tell you that what's happening in the States vis-a-vis Watergate is very important, but it's no
good just sitting there twiddling your thumbs saying "this is des-
perately important, wouldn't it be marvellous if we could get Nixon
in and ask him a few questions". You are not going to get that, and
there's a limit to the number of times you can wheel in the same
hack "Washington Post" London correspondent for his view of the
thing. So a lot of things you just physically can't do. You then
come down to the second division of things that you can do. And it
is the balance between the two. You know that the ideal programme
to put out would be very different from the one you actually end up
producing because you just can't get it together.'

One producer in ITV described the position in the following way:

'I suppose basically you're looking for a major news story, if
there's one about, to lead off the programme. You're then looking
for a major discussion item, though we don't pursue items at any
great length on this programme, we have a lot of items which are run
fairly briefly. Tonight, for instance, I'm going to have to have an
eight-minute discussion, I think on drinking and driving. I suppose
you are also looking for a particularly unusual item which might be
funny or music of some description.'

In some instances programmes might be influenced by quite extraneous factors. The need for example to satisfy everyone within a
particular transmission area:

'We could do our programme every night on Devon stories, but we are
donscious of the fact that we've got viewers in Somerset, in Corn-
wall and in Dorset, who really want to know what's going on in their
area, and although the story may be less important in Portland than
a story in Plymouth, we would probably opt for the Portland story so
that we could get a balanced look about our programme.'

There is, then, a component created by the perceived needs of a
diverse audience. A particularly interesting example of this is
provided by broadcasting in Scotland, notably from Glasgow. Rivalry
between Catholics and Protestants in Glasgow has been a feature of
that city's life for many years. With the post-1969 strife in
Ulster, the sectarian split against a general background of economic
decay, the parallels with Glasgow have not been lost on the ruling
political groups in that city. The idea that Glasgow might well be
the 'next Belfast' is not something taken lightly by producers of
political television in the area.

When asked if there were any particular organizational rulings
which affected his work, one of the producers said that there
weren't but that the question of covering affairs in Ulster did present a number of problems and difficulties. He felt that caution in
this area was

'a fairly responsible attitude. I'm not saying that you ignore it completely, clearly you can't, but we've to be very careful what we do though. We have to think perhaps that we are a bit more potent than the "Daily Express" or the "Daily Record". It would be wrong to stir up troubles by sensational treatment of Ulster.'

The same basic position was described by another Glasgow producer, though in more depth. What is particularly interesting in this reply is the way his integration within a wide programme network, and the search for particular stories happened to clash with his own peculiar situation. It also displays the extreme sensitivity which is felt over the question of covering Ulster:

'I would say we are on our guard. We of course accept all Northern Ireland material through the BBC national network. We don't have any independent coverage ourselves. Nevertheless, there is the problem that it could happen in Glasgow. There have been several court cases and incidents, such as the two gentlemen who very fool-ishly left some gelignite in a stove; and the ones who tried to hide or planted explosives in the grounds of a Roman Catholic church. There have been a number of cases like this and we have covered them them. We also covered troubles at Orange walks, but we've never really gone looking for it. Occasionally we have come under slight pressure from the south from programmes like "Nationwide", but I'm not all that keen to get involved in this.'

'Are they trying to pressure you to do more items in this area?'

'They would like to do something all round the country along the lines of "what real support is there among the Irish immigrant popu-lation in areas like Birmingham, Liverpool, Glasgow, for the IRA and the Provisionals?" Really all we would have to do is to go down to Derry Tree and one or two other places and we'd see them selling the magazine, and on a Saturday night they'd all sit and sing the songs, but how real all this is I don't know. Our inhibitions, if any, are self-imposed. We will cover anything that is out in the open but we are not really going to go looking for Provisionals around the place.
    'One of the things I wouldn't mind doing if it was possible is the special group in the Glasgow Police one of whose more recent concerns has been the activities of extremists on both sides. Now there is a case of pressure having been put on a BBC drama unit to drop a dramatized documentary. They came up here, phoned us and asked one of our reporters how to get to grips with some Orange Lodge people. They photographed the Black Lodge march. It was discovered afterwards by the controller that in spite of their well-meaning prescriptions in advance, what they really wanted to do was to send up Orangism in a big way. Then various other people started to intervene and the idea for the play has now been crushed ... it could have caused trouble.'

This is an unusual situation for the producer of a news magazine to be in, though as we have seen from previous statements it is one that is often faced by current affairs producers. A number of

factors combined to produce this situation.   Northern Ireland politics is an intrinsically sensitive subject and coverage of the situation in Glasgow would anyway be inhibited by the lack of available
resources.   A vital additional factor, however, was that there would
be no point in becoming involved in that sort of subject matter
since though you might satisfy journalistic criteria you would not
satisfy the overall programme criteria which is the sustaining of an
audience - this producer concluded by saying that 'the bulk of the
people in Glasgow, even those who are first or second generation
Scots and are Protestant or Catholic, are not all that bothered
about that kind of content'. (16)   It would be felt by many that
this argument on the part of the producer was a mere rationalization
of a situation in which discussion of contentious issues had to be
suppressed.   This is not the explanation if it is presented with the
implication of conscious suppression.   Clearly suppression was a
factor in one instance, but in terms of the overall treatment of the
issues of that city over a period of time one must look to the
incompatibility of such subject matter with the standard formulae
for news magazines.   If one wanted to argue that there was a conspiracy against the raising of certain issues by political television then one would have to point to the conspiracy implicit in
the forms of political television, in this case the news magazine.
 This gets to the root of the discussion about the other factors
which, along with the operation of stylistic paradigms, shape political television.   The inhibitions lie in existing structures rather
than in decision-making processes.   It would on the whole be impossible to actually control political television by overt decisions
about all content - unless of course we had an overtly political
control of the broadcasting institutions, and we clearly do not have
that.   It is on this basis that one turns to a discussion of a
number of other structures within which political television is
framed and which provide the other constituents of the internal context.

Chapter 5

RESOURCES

There has been some renewed discussion of late of the economies of
the media in, for example, Schiller's treatment of an international
media network, based on the United States (1970) and the attempt by
Murdock and Golding (1974) to throw some theoretical light into the
dark corners of the debate. There has, however, been little detailed discussion of what precisely the broad abstractions of economic policy actually mean in real terms for the production of mass-
media messages in general and political messages in particular. The
first and general conclusion one can draw is that in programme-
making terms economic control is translated into a trilogy of resources with which the producer has to function: a budget, a technology, and a time component.

The total amount of political material made available by British
television is not insignificant, as the categories 1 and 8 in Table
5.1 make clear.

TABLE 5.1 Analysis of programme content at BBC, 1970-73

		BBC 1/2 - % of total output			
		1970	1971	1972	1973
1	Talks, documentaries, and other information programmes	16.5	16.5	16.0	23.2
2	British and foreign feature films and series	16.0	15.5	15.7	13.8
3	Outside broadcasts	12.6	14.0	12.8	-
4	Presentation material	9.5	9.6	10.2	4.9
5	Drama	8.0	8.0	7.2	6.4
6	Light entertainment	7.1	6.9	6.6	6.6
7	Children's programmes	6.7	6.6	7.1	7.8
8	News, weather and other news programmes	6.1	6.4	6.1	5.3
9	School broadcasts	5.7	5.7	5.3	4.7

		1970	1971	1972	1973
10	Further education	5.7	4.7	4.5	3.9
11	Sports news and reports	3.2	1.6	1.3	13.2
12	Religious programmes	2.3	2.2	2.1	1.8
13	Music	1.4	1.6	1.8	1.5
14	Open University	-	-	3.3	6.9
		100.00	100.00	100.00	100.00

(Source: BBC Annual Reports: 1970-1, 1971-2, 1972-3, 1973-4)

The figures for ITV are produced on a weekly average and the following figures (Table 5.2) are drawn from the ITA Annual Report:

TABLE 5.2   Programme output: weekly average - year ended 5 April 1970

| | Proportion total output | | |
	%	1972	1973
News and news magazines	10	10	10
Documentaries and news features	6	7	8
Religion	3	7	2
Adult Education (including repeats)	3	3	2
School programmes (including repeats)	7	7	7
Children's programmes:			
(a) informative	2	2	2
(b) entertainment	7	8	8
Plays, drama series and serials	22	20	22
Feature films	12	13	12
Entertainment and music	14	13	14
Sport	13	12	11
Other outside broadcasts	1	1	1
	100	100	100

What I have broadly described as political television forms a
large part of the total output of television, accounting for approximately 20 per cent of all broadcast material.   Norman Swallow
(1966) argues that one needs to assess the degree of importance that
media organizations attach to news and current affairs by considering 'the number of transmissions, the amount of money spent on
them and the time of day or night when they are shown'.   Accepting
for the sake or argument that the total amount of transmission time
is a substantial proportion of overall broadcast time, it is still
clear that news and news magazines now hold centre stage, while with

the notable exceptions of 'World in Action', 'Panorama' and 'This Week', the more full-blooded presentations of current affairs and features languish in the nether reaches of the schedule or on the minority channel, BBC2.

The point about the length of programmes has been made by numerous people, usually in the context of the cliche that the number of words in a broadcast news programme wouldn't even fill the front page of most newspapers. The consideration of time, how-ever, is a little more complex than this. The time made available to the programme (1) is a reflection of the priorities of the orga-nization and presents the producer with a number of formidable pro-blems. It is difficult to isolate discussion of this factor from discussion of the consequences of the technology and the nature of the medium. A number of writers have observed that developments in technology have favoured the development of news and news magazines (Kumar, 1974; Smith, 1973; Swallow, 1966). It remains true, how-ever, that television is not the most appropriate medium for poli-tical discussion - an ironical comment in view of the emphasis placed on it by many theorists as being a key element in political communication.

Why this should be so is closely tied up with the discussion of resources. The producer is forced to employ short and/or visual material which fails to delineate the depths of a political process so that, for example, international relations are reduced to the arrivals and departures at international airports of Henry Kissinger. He must also introduce the dreaded 'talking heads' - if Professor Milton Friedman has views on the nature of inflation there really is only one way to transmit those and that is to have Friedman or an interlocuter actually telling you what they are. The search is for a way round this dilemma, as in the Welfare State programme des-cribed earlier, which tried to symbolize a rather abstract process in graphically human terms. As I argued, the programme's deter-mining identity allowed it to develop the story in just this way. Other programmes would find it difficult to do this because: (a) they would have insufficient time to develop this idea - to do the background research, etc; (b) their focus would be on discussion of more immediate events; (c) they would not have sufficient screen time to develop a theme. The lack of time in which to prepare an item means that the production team is thrown back on to visible sources (i.e. ones that they know of) - newspapers, magazines, other programmes - and thus is thrown back once more into the general whirl of media-defined events.

In this context it is instructive to look at the early-morning activity on a regional news desk. Avid interest is paid to the early-morning papers, and, particularly, to local papers. These are a readily available source of stories, easily translated into the sorts of material that sustains a news magazine. Similarly, the current affairs programme which goes out nightly also finds itself dependent on readily available subject matter - though clearly cur-rent affairs programmes do generate their own subject matter on occasions. Such programmes also find themselves dependent on read-ily available people to discuss that subject matter. The stage army of British political television derives not from a desire by pro-ducers to perpetuate the ruling social and political elites, but by the fact that members of the ruling elite are the only ones who they know can talk, and before all else you have to have someone who is seen to be talking.

The implications of the amount of time available to prepare a programme and the length of time the programme is actually on the air can be discussed in the context of an item on Concorde. The producer's argument on this began with the observation that on some stories the production team had not only to become familiar with the vast amount of material available but would also need to involve outside 'experts'. Their ability to do this depended on their having time and money to do it and having the time available in which to present a programme item. He noted various people they would contact for the Concorde story: other journalists who worked in the field of aeronautics, authors of relevant books, BAC, the Ministry, politicians who had been involved in decision-making related to Concorde. His ability to contact these people he felt was a considerable strength, and he made an interesting observation:

'When you run a programme like "Nationwide" or even "Midweek", you are bound to live hand to mouth, you are bound to restrict the number of your sources because you don't have very much time. If at 4 o'clock in the afternoon you suddenly decide to do Concorde you've got to say "let's get in Andrew Wilson" because you don't have very much choice. If you have the kind of time we have then you can succeed in not using the stage army. These are the people you see all the time, the Hugh Scanlons, the Norman St John Stevas's, that tiny group of people, who are designed for television and move from one programme to another, and the instant pundits like Peregrine Worsthorne. We try to avoid these like the plague. We'd be wrong never to use Hugh Scanlon because he's a very important man, but it's also wrong to think of him as the instant trade unionist/left winger who can be brought in at the drop of a hat.'

'Do other programmes only use him because he is available?'

'Well, I'll defend why they do it on the grounds of time. If you've only got a couple of hours - if you asked me here and now to mount a debate and I had a couple of days to do it then I would find out the right way of doing it. Firstly, by finding the story and then, finding the people to get on film or in the studio to try and make the story live. The chances are that it's not going to come down to that stage if you've done it properly, it very rarely does in our case. There won't, for example, be too many people who you would recognize on our show on mortgages because we will be finding people who are expert in the different sectors rather than looking for a Des Wilson figure. Although we may have him on the show he will be among seven or eight other people who will have clearly defined functions. It's fairly obvious, the more time you spend on it the more certain you are of the range of the arguments and the more precise you are about the people you want.'

If this producer is correct, and I think that he is substantially correct, it still needs to be pointed out that many programmes are not in this situation in terms of resources. The effect on a

regional news magazine programme in a very different situation was
described by its producer:

'Any magazine I've seen, from the worst to the best, is a bit of a
rag bag because it has to be done for twenty to twenty-five minutes
every night of the week, five nights a week and I defy any organization, even with the whole of the UK at their beck and call, to do
that without it becoming at times a rag bag.'

In a slightly different area, it is no startling discovery to
find that television news is dogged by various limitations - its
dependence on film, the shortness of its stories, the distillation
of quite complex political and economic processes into a few short
paragraphs. Donald Edwards (1962) who was ENCA in the early 1960s
in the BBC pointed to all these and more. His correspondingly
senior counterpart at ITN stated similar views (Swallow, 1966, p.46).
Such arguments are usually based on the assumption that the limitations on news are perfectly acceptable so long as there is the backdrop of other current affairs and features programmes. What we can
see, however, if we look at these is that they are themselves structured and limited by a number of factors. The tyranny of the clock,
the paucity of the funds and the mediations of the technology are
frequent themes in any conversation with producers. There was a
strong sense in many of the interviews that these were the only
things that they really thought one should talk about and certainly
the only factors which they themselves thought were important. The
operation of news values, the functioning of power and ideology,
clashes with political structures - all are in the producer's mind's
eye the dross of an abstracted and dull academic argument that pales
into insignificance before the impact of the formulation of resources available to any one producer in any one context. (2) I have,
of course, agreed with this argument in a limited way be seeing
resources as one formative factor in the making of political television. It is certainly the most visible for the producer.
    The actual resources available vary from programme to programme.
There are in fact tremendous disparities in the financial resources,
though it was not particularly easy to obtain the precise budgets
for many programmes. The figures I did obtain, however, are sufficient to support this point and also give some indication of the
kind of money available. For two regional news magazine programmes,
I saw figures of £1,550 p.w. and £1,300 p.w., and for two current
affairs programmes, figures of £300,000 and £338,000 p.a., which
would be for a season of approximately thirty one-hour shows. (3)
There is a difficulty here, however, particularly in the context of
the BBC, where often the cost of an item is taken off a budget other
than the one officially assigned to the programme. So it is difficult sometimes to arrive at any exact figure. The two weekly figures were also based on regional stations which are generally
agreed, certainly within the BBC, to be somewhat impoverished. One
might conclude that a programme like 'Nationwide' (without its
regional components) or a news magazine emanating from one of the
more affluent ITV companies possesses a somewhat larger budget.
    There was a sense of accommodation among some producers to the
restrictions imposed by limited resources:

'In London you have every facility and so you don't think about it.
Here we have minimal facilities and so you do think about it, but
after a while you get so used to working with these facilities that
you don't think about it. You've got two colour cameras, a slide
scanner, a colour telecine, no VT at all, and you work out a way of
working with these facilities. We don't find them particularly
inhibiting, although in fact I'm sure anyone coming from London to
work here would find them terribly inhibiting.'

One way of detecting the actual as opposed to supposed significance
of limited resources is to discuss the question of how the programme
would be different if the producer had more resources available.
This led to the interesting conclusion, notably in the news magazine
area, that even if more facilities were available they wouldn't have
much impact on the programme content: 'We perhaps would occasionally have studio groups in more than we do. We tend to have single
interviewees now, but on the whole it wouldn't be very different.'
And yet the same producer, in response to another question, said he
thought that they lagged behind other media in the discussion of
public affairs because they didn't carry a core of specialist reporters: 'In other words there's nobody keeping an eye on education,
nobody keeping an eye on local politics, on local shipbuilding, or
whatever, in a way that you'd expect a local or national paper to
be doing. Very often good discussion items come out of follow-ups
to newspapersstories rather than being generated by us.'
    The further implications of the time people had to prepare a
programme, the dependence on the stage army and the implications of
the time available within the programme were outlined by another
producer:

'The journalist and the academic, but especially the journalist, has
this global view of the situation. You can stop a journalist in the
street, or get him into a TV or radio studio and ask him to prog-
nosticate on "Whither Nixon?" or something like that. If he's any
good, you'll get something quite reasonable, unless he's doing the
sports page on the "Sun". But if you want to have a considered
discussion or series of discussions leading from one side of a topic
to another and now the same thing but from the other point of view,
like incomes policy from the trade union, from the employers' and
from the consumers' point of view. You'd get four people - not Vic
Feather and Campbell Adamson - they are too obvious, they are the
Shakespearean stage army turning up again, but they exist because
they are good and Campbell Adamson will always turn it out. Now a
newspaper can do this. "The Economist" is marvellous, they can just
write down those four points of view, with a pretty picture on the
cover and that's it. You are sold on that, you think what a wonder-
ful newspaper.
    'I have to find people. Not Campbell Adamson for God's sake, we
had him last week; somebody as good as if not better than. And to
find a good trade unionist. Not Vic Feather, not Alan Fisher from
NUPE - Now who's in the second rank? Trouble is he's either a communist or a Trotskyite or something like that, so how do we balance
him? Immediately we are filling up our studio, we are getting to
the point where, like the British climate, we are overcast perpetu-

ally. It's quite true, we are always thinking that we ought to have
another point of view. In a newspaper nobody cares about this. If
the Town Clerks' Society don't have their comments in the story, the
they'll probably ring the "Telegraph" and say "We gave it to you but
it was subbed out". If we don't have the man from the Town Clerks'
Association "the views of Town Clerks were not represented in the
programme on local government" Very bad deal. And in the end you
have fifty people in the studio, which is unworkable because no one
gets a chance to say anything.'

Another producer complained about the use of more than one item
in an hour-long programme:

'First, there's the exhaustion of the viewer after twenty minutes
and then after forty minutes. He begins to think, "Oh Christ, and
now for something completely different.... They've done the banking
system of the world, I couldn't understand it but at least it was
done; now they are doing something about tourism in Switzerland,
that is interesting, pretty pictures; now another thing." The
modules are all wrong. If you have three twenty minute modules or
six ten-minute modules or ten six-minute modules, or any variation
of these, at the end of the show you can't remember what was in the
programme and that is very confusing. It becomes a hotch-potch, a
medley of impressions that is too much for the feeble mind to take,
or at least my feeble mind.
'So I said that we would experiment with a solid programme where
we say "Tonight, folks, we will tell you all about inflation, or
tourism, or steel, or industrial relations, but not all of them".
In this way you can avoid the problem of having the anchor man
having to say "I'm sorry folks, that's all we've got time for", and
moving on to the next thing.
'The man in the gallery, the editor upstairs, will not say during
a programme discussion "Give them a stretch, let them carry on and
we'll scrub the film we were going on to", because he's not sure
that the anchor man, the chairman of the discussion, will be able to
cope with another fifteen or ten minutes. This is a great problem
where the discussion may have dragged for the first few minutes but
then takes off just before it's due to end. The discussants find
their feet, they are going marvellously and then bang, the guillo-
tine, and we are into a story on topless waitresses, which is nice
but all wrong because it breaks up the viewer's train of thought.'

There is also a sense in which producers pursue a particular
point of style and feel able to do so because they have time in
which to develop whatever ideas they might happen to have. The
obverse to this is, of course, the situation of producers who do not
have time for this. In the following discussion there is a consciousness of fighting certain dominant formats. The response
emerged from a discussion of the advantages and disadvantages of
television when compared to print journalism, which proved to be a
particularly interesting and fruitful area in that it led producers
into thinking about and discussing their medium as a medium:

'Television imposes certain limitations. We have to write in dis-

tinctive style, this is why I always argue about house style. The
style for TV writing must be totally different: we can't recapitulate, so we've got to be writing in very short sentences, short
words; people run out of breath so we've got to give them plenty
of full stops; people can't take in a great deal through the eyes,
graphics can't be too fussy, like in print. I wouldn't say I long
for the day when everybody is illiterate and they will have to rely
upon TV, but it would be nice if people could cut themselves off
from print journalism. I'm not the young brother of print journalism. I'm a cousin, standing up on my own.

   'If one of my people suggests a montage of headlines or something
like that, or press clippings and things of this sort, that they
photograph, I say "No, never do that. Other programmes may - I
don't, because we have to do it the hard way. We have to show
moving film." If you want to say "the last eight Chancellors have
been in favour of inflation", it's easy to get from our press clippings library all the evidence you want: "Maudling says, 'let's go
for growth'" or something like that. "Gaitskell says, 'Boom round
the corner'" or something like that. It takes longer to sort it
out, to find it and to process it and to then put it on the air, and
write the commentary when you have moving pictures or even stills
of eight Chancellors of the Exchequer, but it's more fun because it
makes us live in our own right.'

   Working with film has built into it an important limitation,
often summed up in descriptions of the cumbersome nature of filming,
which the increasing use of video equipment has lessened only to a
limited extent. If, for example, a story breaks a particular distance away from the studio at a particular time of day it may mean
that it is impossible to cover the story adequately. It may be
impossible to get a crew to the story or even to contact one of the
various stringer cameramen which any television news organization
has on its lists. There may be insufficient time to get to the
event, film it, get the film back to the studio, have it processed
and ready for the transmission time. Effectively then, to appear
on a programme, an item has to occur within a critical distance in
terms of time and geographical location. The shorter the time
available, the shallower the treatment will be: as one approaches
the temporal and geographical critical point, the type of coverage
is reduced from a reporter to camera/interviewing witnesses, etc.,
to the presenter in the studio reading to camera a brief report.
It goes without saying that the closer to the critical point an item
is, the less likely it is to appear at all. We have already seen
that current-affairs programmes also operate within a critical hori-
zon, i.e. the less time there is the more likely it is to be 'Hugh
Scanlon' discussing whatever there is to be discussed.

   At the same time though, the point must be stressed that the producer very often refuses to make the most of his resources, in the
sense that even where he has, in theory at least, sufficient time
to develop a story or approach it with a degree of originality, he
will often not do so because such moves are unlikely to pay divi-
dends in terms of the audience. During the period of the local
council elections of 1973, I spent time with one of the commercial
companies which mounted a special late-night coverage of the elec-

tion results. They used a panel of three - two sitting MPs and a
Liberal candidate for Parliament - to discuss the results as they
came in. What was particularly interesting was that the two MPs
had been used by the producer of the programme on many occasions in
the past. When asked why they were using the same people again,
particularly in the situation where these were national figures,
the elections were local and therefore it might have been more
appropriate to use local figures, the replies were somewhat vague.
Reduced to its basic elements, the reasoning was as follows: they
were both experienced politicians and therefore able to generalize
out to the national level - and, after all, the interest in the
local elections was only in so far as they reflected national attitudes to the government; they were both seasoned television performers, who knew each other well and who were about evenly matched
and who therefore wouldn't produce the embarrassing spectacle of
the Labour party 'being slaughtered' by the Tory party (or vice
versa) in a televised contest; and they both represented the middle
ground of their respective parties and were therefore not controversial within the context of the internal politics of the two
parties.
    Time is not everything, however; the money and technology avail-
able, as has been mentioned, are also vital. One producer declared:

'The whole game is played within very tight rules imposed by the
finance and the facilities. With our budget it's very difficult
to manage, and the quality of the programme undoubtedly suffers.
If I could, for instance, say to the reporter "Right, I'll pay you
more for the story but you'll only do one that day", and I could say
to the cameraman, "I'll only get one story out of you today but it's
going to be good one", it would obviously be a better story than the
usual one which the reporter probably only has half a day on because
I've got to overwork him - I hire him by the day - and so I'll ask
him to shoot supplementary material for a story we are building up
or for the day after's programme. The game we are playing is to
let the cracks and the thin plaster show as little as possible.'

Another stated about the limited facilities:

'It does mean that we don't even think about doing some stories in a
certain way because "Christ, we can't afford to send a cameraman
that far for a relatively minor story that might not come off very
well anyway". So it affects your judgment in that sense. It means
another set of ground rules in which we have to build our programme.'

    The picture is not always so bleak, and numbers of programmes
have 'healthy' budgets, though I think the following extract indicates that it is impossible to divorce one form of resource from
another:

'Financial factors are always important because you cannot in my
view continue to make good television if your budget is low - though
you might have a flash in the pan, you couldn't do it every night.
Ultimately, what's important is a good staff, time and enough money

to do the programme the way you want to do it. That means you can
do it on film if you want or hire a studio in Washington if you
want. For example, we've been talking about Watergate just now.
If you were the producer of "Midweek" and I told you to do Watergate
tonight, you wouldn't do it very interestingly or very well. I have
the money to hire a studio in Washington or occasionally send a film
crew there, and we would do it in the proper way. I think probably
you don't have to say more than that. Financial considerations are
all-important in my view. When I'm setting up a programme it's
probably the only thing I'm really interested in. Of course there
are things like the Television Act, but I put that sort of thing
out of the way and the thing that I fight hardest for is the
budget.'

Commentators have been keen to point to the dependence of much
political television - the context is usually that of news - on
visual material. (4) There are a number of points to be made here.
The visual component is what distinguishes television from radio,
and yet there was a feeling among some respondents - one which I now
share - that radio was a more appropriate medium for politics. Not
only is political television encumbered by the persistent need to
be visually appealing, it has the added disadvantage that built into
this is the use of what is, despite many recent developments, a
cumbersome technology. The political-television producer is in a
sense doubly cursed. The meaning of this problem - along with one
or two others - was elaborated in the following statement:

'There is no doubt that one cannot write a very colourful piece from
the heart of Saigon without showing some pictures. It's no good
saying "There is a civil war raging in the middle of Beirut" unless
there are some pictures to show it.
    'Television is also a very cumbersome way of gaining news. When
you think that there are seven people employed on providing half an
hour's television a week - and that's only on the spot; when it
comes back here there are probably another seven or eight people
employed, it takes a long time. Ideally the programme should take
about three weeks for planning, execution, editing and everything
else. The point is that if you are a newspaper reporter you're on
your own, you write your stuff and file it. Television, however, is
a group activity and if one of the parts of the group is weak then
this can cause serious problems.
    'The other thing, of course, is that off-the-record stuff never
goes on television. Nobody is going to say "I will give an interview to you off the record" because by being filmed they are on the
record. Therefore my own feeling is that things like "Insight",
financial matters, Poulson, are all very difficult to get over in
visual terms. So although you shouldn't say "I can't do it because
of that" they are not ideal subjects for television.'

There is much sense then in the argument that the presence of the
technology leads to its use in particular ways even though the usage
may be gratuitous or may soak up resources that might be more fruit-
fully employed. But pictures are ultimately the be all and end all
of television; they are what the audience wants, and therefore they

are what the producer must provide, even though that provision
detracts from the central purpose, which is the depiction of the
political process and the communication of political information.
    Producers are excited by the medium's potential to reach enormous
audiences (5) but dismayed by the medium's transient nature and the
difficulty with which the abstractions of politics are translated
into televisual terms, 'How do you film a process?' You can show its
visible manifestations, its leading personalities, its comings and
goings; you can employ visual and metaphorical representation but
you can't show an abstraction in visual form. The usual solution
has been the use of 'talking heads' who fit the prescriptions of
good television - a further factor leading to this dependence on the
'stage army'. Such individuals obviously tend to become more and
more competent performers and therefore more and more usable. They
are particularly conscious of the format within which 'talking
heads' can talk; they will know what to say and when to say it,
what not to say, what is possibly too contentious, etc. The whole
discussion-programme format, which as we have seen stemmed from
the very nature of the medium, takes on a standard appearance - it
in effect becomes ritualized. The difficulties of reproducing
abstract political and economic processes into a suitably televisual
form, the subsequent dependence on a limited range of participants,
the 'stage army', and their integration within the established
routines of talk programmes - their transformation, in other words,
from spokesmen and discussants into performers, are candidly described by a producer who had worked on both news magazines and current affairs programmes:

'I've been involved in a lot of discussion programmes and I know
how they operate and what the ground rules are and the sheer arti-
ficiality, to say nothing of banality, of a great many of them.
Even in programmes where I'm deeply interested in the subject matter
matter, I simply will very reluctantly accept a studio chat programme as information.'

'When you say "ground rules", what do you have in mind?'

'Normally when a studio discussion programme is held, the organizer,
whether he be producer, assistant to the producer, or researcher,
or the interviewer/chairman takes trouble to find out what everybody's standpoint is, of course, before they come on. He then tends
to frame the programme in a way that they will get across the
strongest points. He allows a certain amount of time for denial,
contradiction, argument, etc. and then tries to wheel everything
round to a good closing point - which is not necessarily a summation
or clarification of what was being discussed earlier. Quite often
it's just a good dramatic out, that's all they are looking for. In
lots of these programmes there are so many complex bits of human
chemistry; for example, in the programme for which the chairman of
the governors of the BBC apologized for involving the MPs (the programme was 'A Question of Confidence'). I must admit that I sym-
pathize with the sort of people who were at the receiving end
because I know the way certain producers' minds work - "Did you see
her on women's lib? Marvellous, never stops talking, liable to

throw something, lovely woman."

'Again, studio discussion programmes are mostly convened by people whose means of outside contact is fairly limited, who are getting their names out of newspaper cuttings and magazines, or more likely they are filed because they've already been on. It's a standard reaction, I've discovered. "We'd dearly love to have Marcus Lipton on, but he's not available. We might settle for Greville Jarr - he did us a very nice turn the last time he was in." That way, though, you start perpetuating a little establishment. In Scotland that's a particular problem. The quotient of informed and available people on all subjects is in most subjects narrow, therefore you tend to get the same old faces coming back expounding the same old ideologies, theories, opinions. You see, one of the drawbacks is that the limitations on contacts throws you open to the temptation of accepting information from acknowledged bodies, and particularly bodies who have got something to say anyway.

'In the current affairs field, which incorporates the studio discussion programme and other programmes, the limitations tend to produce those people who are willing to come on and talk, and who therefore get to know the ground rules. You get awfully sophisticated tele-performers - (name of MP). I've never seen him on a programme when he didn't have the last word; he knows the rules, he reads the signals. I'm quite sure he cocks an ear, for example, if the studio manager has noisy cans (earphones) so that he can hear what is said by the director. "Two minutes now, get into so and so ..." and the MP will hear him and get the last word in. He knows exactly how to get the last word in. There's only a minute to go and he's talking and he'll hang on for a whole minute, and he won't be shut out. He'll keep saying "Hold on, let me say one thing more ..." If somebody else is talking, he will butt in and say "All very well, but I think the really important point we must make before the discussion finishes is ..." Frankly it's all a mandarin game ...'

'But you will still use him?'

'On some things, yes. I'm very much getting charier and charier in my old age about these kinds of people who turn up in these kinds of programmes, because the persons who arrange for them to be there in the first place have a very limited range of contacts. And frankly there has to be some kind of system whereby we get out into the big wide world and encounter for the first time certain new and interesting people who have things to say.'

The difficulties and problems of distortion lie both in the use of film, which tends to present the mere surface of a subject, or by the use of particular individuals who represent the interests and views of a particular social group, notably the middle and upper classes. Why this situation occurs is not, as some would believe, because of the intended representation of the views of the dominant social class, or a willing trivialization of events. Rather it follows from the peculiar circumstances of a visual medium, a particular concept of audience tastes, and the often difficult dynamics of putting a programme together. As I have shown, the kind of

issues which can be discussed, the depth and manner in which they
can be discussed, and the people who will discuss them are heavily
structured by the kinds of resources employed in political television. There is a problem, and one which producers were aware of
and concerned about. It is not just a problem that elite figures
are more visible, are in the proverbial book of contacts, but that
the elite figure is very often a better performer than many individuals. The interesting thing is that not all elite figures are
used - even very senior politicians, trade unionists or industrialists are ignored. So the selection is not just between elite and
non-elite; it also operates within elites. It is an unfortunate
fact of television life that people do very often tend to 'dry up'.
The problem, however, is not with the people who dry up on a programme, but with the internal programme prescription that drying up,
inarticulateness, is bad - and it is 'bad' because the audience
doesn't like it. The problem, if one may for the sake of argument
see it as a problem, is not insurmountable, but would require money
and time, which are often not available. At the same time, when the
central concern is sustaining the interest of an audience, the possibility of changing the 'entrance qualifications' for appearing is
unlikely to appeal to programme controllers. Most people are very
nervous before performances - even experienced interviewers and presenters. The problems which this does present were described in the
following way:

'I'm interested in how you deal with people. Programmes are about
people and it seems to me important to get the people as right as
you can. For example, at the moment there's an ASLEF go-slow. You
want to know what the people in ASLEF think about the strike. We
can do one of two things. We can ask them to the studio or we can
go out filming. If we ask them to the studio, first of all we are
likely to get the professional spokesmen who, whatever their origins
or loyalties, have a sort of middle-class communicating function.
If we ask these guys into the studio we get a pretty good performance and statement of their point of view. If we say no, we don't
want the official spokesman, we want to know what the lads really
think, you just have to think what you are putting them through: you
are telling them that you want them to come to London and the BBC.
Their families are saying "You going to be on telly?" So immediately you are putting them in their best suits, you're taking them
off their own territory into a wholly alien, hostile environment
and, consequently, they are not going to do themselves any good at
all. So one of two things happens: either you use them and you
portray them to a direct disadvantage - that applies to the majority
of the population, not just your general prole, it includes your
local GP and local academics - or you take the easy option of
getting in the professional spokesman. In a film situation the
technology is explainable: you're on his territory, he's in his own
clothes, he isn't built up, he isn't made to travel, he doesn't
have foreign drinks like whisky. You go into his pub, you drink his
bitter. Clearly, it's an artificial situation because if you walk
into somebody's pub with lights you are destroying something, but
at least it's more manageable.'

The opportunity to employ techniques of this sort if open to few producers, but one can see by this description the way in which the peculiarities of the medium, the difficulty with which most people use it, the limited resources available, can all create a situation which excludes vast sections of the population from ever being represented. There is no conspiracy about much television, one is merely faced with the unfortunate logic of TV's technology and resources, a subtle but powerful organizing principal.

The explanation proffered here is not just that the hidden hand of television is that of a machine, rather that that is but one part of the explanation. The particular direction, style and focus of political television is not only subject to a number of resource limitations and the operation of stylistic paradigms that serve the audience more than the political process. There are also a number of ground rules which affect the course of production - the implication being that the 'hidden hand' may become all too visible.

Chapter 6

THE GROUND RULES

Political television is festooned with rulings as to what it can and cannot do. (1) The actual operation of these 'ground rules' and their impact in the actual making of programmes needs to be considered. Rulings derive from both the legal and political structure, and from the broadcasting organizations themselves. Three distinct areas of ruling can be seen as particularly important:

1 those relating to the coverage of politics;
2 those relating to libel and contempt;
3 those relating to the commitment to objectivity, impartiality and balance.

It is clearly the case that interest in this area has principally focused on the question of balance, etc., and it is certainly the case that these concepts are vitally important. Indeed they are so important, and have been for so long that they operate at the level of commonsense understandings. Thus what one finds in looking at the role of 'ground rules' in political television is not only the prescriptive nature of the concepts involved, such as impartiality, but also their normative status within the profession of broadcast journalism.

The net effect of the ground rules of political broadcasting is that television is heavily tied to the presentation of points of view that derive from particular sections of the social and political structure. (2) The rulings ensure that dominant interests are represented. This is, of course, hardly surprising and indeed it would not be unduly perverse to argue that if the centre of political life in Britain was formed by the government, the CBI and the TUC, then programme-makers are only right in relating their point of view. The point of the impact of the rulings that relate to political broadcasting is, however, not of this nature. What is important is that the manner in which these points of view are presented prevents the achievement of one of the objectives of broadcast journalism. The purpose of broadcast journalism is noble, the reality less so. Broadcast journalism is a curious hybrid of the declarations of Delane that the journalist 'seek out truth above all things and ... present to his reader not such things as state craft would want them to know but the truth as near as he can attain it', and the stark realities of the relationship with the State, and with the

ethics and resources that derive from a competitive situation. That
rulings are restrictive is in no doubt, and the overall effect is to
transform what should be an inspection of the political process and
a transmission of information into the transmission of largely official viewpoints. The impression is of the whole of political television being transformed into a party political broadcast.

As will become evident, the rulings that political coverage be
balanced were readily held by many producers to be worthwhile, and
one stated that 'I wouldn't conceive of doing an item without balancing it. It would be just totally foreign. This isn't because one
is afraid of the IBA particularly, it's just that it seems to make
such enormous sense, you gain so much more credibility by presenting
both sides.' Credibility or not, the requirements to balance, that
one point of view be seen to be weighed against another, one Tory
equals one Labour man, combines with the laws relating to libel and
contempt of court to inhibit serious, detailed observation of the
political process and it is these with which I wish to deal first.

There was more or less uniform agreement that the laws of libel
and contempt were vital, that any producer bucked them at his peril,
but that on the whole they were worthwhile in that they sought to
protect the rights of the individual. A description of the consequences of libel and contempt was put in the following way by the
producer of a regional news magazine who stated:

'(They) stop us doing things.... As well as libel and contempt of
court, the other big problem is political broadcasting, the restrictions on what you can do during an election period which makes doing
political stories at that time a very unwieldy operation. As far
as libel and contempt of court go, I assume that I am the person who
would be up in court, and so I keep a fairly close eye on things.
All the editorial staff who work for me are aware of the general
rules.

'Libel is much worse. We ran with a lot of effort a story about
a group of local 'businessmen' who were trying to take over a
biscuit factory which had gone through a series of vicissitudes and
had eventually closed down. The workers were kept hanging on for
many many weeks in the hope that this group were going to reopen the
factory. They might have reopened the factory but all they were
really interested in was property speculation. The leader of the
group was ultimately interviewed. We grilled him and ran it very
long, but everything we were doing had to be very much implied. We
knew at the time we interviewed him that he was having to report to
the police every day and that he was due in court in London on fraud
charges, but we couldn't say it. OK, it would have been prejudicial
to his London Trial and so on to have said so. Whether it would
have been libellous to say that he was having to report to the
police every day on some other matter I don't know, but it does make
it very difficult to present the underlying truth and facts of a
really good local story.'

The last comment that the restrictions inhibit the presentation of a
'truth' goes to the very heart of what is a very serious dilemma,
the conflict between the legal rights of the individual and the ill-
defined purpose of the broadcast journalist, or indeed any journa-

list, to present a 'truthful' view of reality. Even more restrictive than libel is contempt of court, cited by producers as the
single most important restriction: 'In practice libel and contempt
are much more of a worry than the Television Act.' When asked how
they would actually affect programme-making, one producer provided
an interesting illustrative example:

'A thalidomide item that we did, if done another way would have been
contempt. When Distillers made their offer of £20 million, you
weren't allowed to say "Is this offer enough?" What you could say
if you knew about the law was "What does this offer mean to the
children?" We got a lot of actuaries and things in the studio and
did a very careful piece and a very illustrative piece, and worked
out what it meant on a weekly basis per child. It's not at all a
simple matter. It's very complicated. You didn't have to say in
the programme "Is this offer enough?" You never had to go anywhere
near asking the question because as soon as you start going into an
area like that in detail, although you do get an area of facts, you
don't have to present opinions, your audience can form their own
opinions from an impartial statement of the facts. In the abstract,
it was possible to say "Should they offer more?" but it was much
more interesting to work out precisely what the offer meant, and
doing it that way is more intellectually appealing, more factual and
less opinionated. In the end, after a long process, you're much
more likely to end up with a firm solid opinion, but that is not
your starting point.'

What he is arguing is that contempt is serious and forces you into
employing strategies by which to avoid it. There was an interesting
tendency for producers to say that laws of libel and contempt are
important, they are so important that you just take them for granted
and therefore they don't actually loom large in your mind except on
those occasions when a specific problem arises:

'the rulings are extremely important. They provide a kind of professional inhibition which you acquire and retain and develop over
the years. With all these things you develop both individually, and
as a group, a series of early-warning systems for all these things
so that people quickly report things that are going to involve any
of these matters, and increasingly every important issue does
involve one of these matters.'

A frequently used word was 'fair', that what all the rulings actually meant was that they should always treat people fairly and if
they did that then they were fulfilling their statutory obligations.
Clearly the situation moves between a pragmatic response to a legal
requirement and commitment to a particular journalistic style. In
Scotland, for example, though producers felt that the distinctive
character of the Scottish legal system made life for the working
journalist even more difficult over the question of contempt, libel
and the need for 'due impartiality' were seen as workable rulings
since all that was required was that 'you be fair and do an honest
job of work'. Contempt, however, was regarded as very difficult
since 'you are very much at the mercy of the judges'. The Lord

Justice General's ruling that no publishing organization was
entitled to conduct its own investigation into crime or alleged
crime, and that they could do nothing which could be alleged to be
interfering with the course of justice,'that the river of justice
can be polluted before it starts to flow', was thought to be particularly restrictive. Because of the nature of the subject matter
that this affected, mainly criminal proceedings, the rulings applied
particularly to news programmes, and it is certainly possible, and
this was in fact argued, that a story such as the biscuit factory
item related previously would not be done in Scotland, at least not
in the same way.

One of the ironies of the legal underpinnings is the vagueness
of their formulation and meaning. A persistent problem is not that
the law seeks to sustain the due process of law - those producers
with whom this was discussed overwhelmingly welcomed this as a necessary protection of the rights of the individual - but rather that
it is often difficult to know what the due process is with any
degree of clarity and certitude. The enormity of the problem, but
at the same time the difficulty of its operation, was exemplified
by the case of Emile Savundra who appealed against his conviction
in 1967 on the grounds of the pre-trial publicity which he claimed
prejudiced a fair trial. A central feature was an interview with
David Frost on ITV in what was widely regarded as a 'television
trial'. (3) The practice was savagely condemned by the appeal
judge, Lord Justice Salmon, who concluded his summing up by saying
that

'The court has no doubt that the television authorities and all
those producing and appearing in televised programmes are conscious
of their public responsibility and know also of the peril in which
they would all stand if any such interview were ever to be televised
in future. Trial by television is not to be tolerated in a civi-
lised society.'

This had a rather profound impact on the broadcasting institutions,
who since have had a highly developed respect for laws of contempt.
Even where it was acknowledged that the existing situation was not
quite so difficult as it had been immediately following the Savundra
case, the point was still made that 'even now I would not be in-
clined to say that there had been a major change. Very, very slight
and only if you are clearly referring to the facts of the case, if
your intention is clearly not to prejudice.'

Lawyers are always available for consultation and advice, but
editorial responsibility remains with the producer:

'It's easy within the BBC and I suppose the ITV, too, to have a
relevant lawyer come along and look at things, and then give you
advice on whether or not to take a risk. And then you are on your
own really. You are not obliged to take their advice, but very
rarely do you not - even in the heat of the moment when it's a
matter of minutes before transmission, you always refer it upwards
to the BBC if you want to take a risk, and if it's an important
political question and you want to reject the advice of the lawyer,
you have the whole BBC hierarchy to refer it up to, and at some

stage the Director General or someone will take the decision to go
ahead despite the lawyer's advice.'

It is usual that if a decision for referral has to be made at the
very highest levels in the BBC, it will be made by the ENCA,
(editor, news and current affairs), though there was not much evidence that this was a particularly frequent occurrence, nor in most
cases a contentious one.
   Of obvious importance for political television are the regulations relating to election coverage; it is here that one comes into
contact most obviously with the rulings that apply specifically to
political broadcasting. In the context of an election, broadcasters
are highly sensitive to the to-and-fro of the party battle. The
distinction between election and non-election broadcasting was described by one producer who was presented with a dilemma by the presence of a National Front candidate in a by-election taking place
within his transmission area. The date of the election had not been
announced, nor had the writ for the election been issued, which
effectively meant that the stiff restrictions on elections did not
yet apply.

'We've interviewed the Liberal candidate and we feel obliged to
interview the Conservative candidate when he's nominated. We were
going to interview the Labour candidate because we feel we ought to
balance even before the pending period. We won't now because
there's an NF candidate and so we are wondering whether we need to
do anyone more than the Conservative candidate at this stage.'

'Why do you baulk at the NF candidate,'

'I don't baulk at him, but we are not obliged to give parity to candidates at this stage. We are carrying things on their news value.
What I was going to do was interview the Labour candidate because I
had interviewed the other two. He is, however, very boring with
nothing to say, but if we interviewed him then I would still further
feel obliged to interview the NF candidate. I don't want to feel
under that sort of obligation that I must at this stage interview
every candidate in the by-election. I may well do it during the
election period but that's a different thing. But at this period
when we are reporting news of the election rather than setting out
to balance as required by law then I don't want to feel obliged to.

   The requirements for balanced, objective and impartial coverage
of any subject, but particularly political subjects, were widely
accepted as being valid, as was the notion that the operational
framework implied within the rulings applied to a representation of
the legitimately established components of the British political
structure, which, in effect, meant the representation of the points
of view of the three main political parties. The centrality of
balanced reportage of political affairs is one of the basic rulings
that underpin broadcasting and the beliefs of political broadcasters. The 'reality' behind the 'appearance' of this structure
of balanced and impartial coverage has been a persistent theme of
public comment on the workings of the rulings. Of particular

interest are the vitriolic statements by individuals who have themselves worked, not only as producers but also as senior administra-
tors, in the broadcasting organizations. Stuart Hood declared that
both the BBC and ITV run least risk of annoying politicians when
they interpret 'impartiality to be the duty to reflect that middle
of the road consensus in political matters which is spanned by the
two-party system and acceptable to the whips on either side' (Hood,
1972, p.417). Norman Swallow, formerly assistant head of films at
the BBC, and assistant editor of 'Panorama', openly attacked the
concept of impartiality (1963, p.227) noting that, 'TV's impartiality tends to stop at Calais, where wogs traditionally begin'. The
position adopted by these writers is that 'impartiality' is limited
in scope, and is used as a strategy of defence to fend off the possibility of actual interference from governments. The implication
is that because of a parallel employment of two concepts of impartiality - one derived from journalism and one derived from the
political needs of the organization - conflict is inevitable when
discussing political matter. Subdued when there is a good deal of
consensus on what is and is not 'correct' in terms of policy in the
public sphere, the operation of an 'impartial' view becomes more
acute when no such agreement exists, and where the purpose of the
journalistic model of broadcasting to pursue the 'truth wherever it
may lead' comes into sharp conflict with the view of the model of
broadcasting which reflects the needs of the institution to preserve
itself and the needs of the centres of power within society to
remain undisturbed. An example frequently cited of this kind of
situation has been the coverage of Northern Ireland affairs.

For fifty years the needs of the Ulster establishment, the
Unionist party, were a permanent and significant feature of the
policy of broadcasters towards the province. There was, in effect,
a specific avoidance of serious discussion of the nature of the community power structure. Where attempts were made to address the
'problems' of the province strenuous efforts were made to either
prevent the programme being broadcast or to make sure that the incident was not repeated - the focus for such pressure being the office
of the ·Controller, Northern Ireland.

Smith, in a lengthy article in 'Index' (1972) argues that the
events of the summer of 1969 effectively ruptured the profound sil-
ence which had pervaded coverage of the province's affairs since
the founding of broadcasting in 1924. In so doing, they threw into
stark relief two different and effectively opposed concepts of the
role of the broadcast journalist: a view from the State that the
broadcaster should merely reflect events; a view from an increasing
number of broadcasters working in Northern Ireland that their role
was to investigate and enquire. In the context of a social structure, dominated to a quite extraordinary degree by a Protestant
establishment, the operation of the second role would inevitably
generate conflict. As the crisis heightened from 1969 to 1971 a
complicated system of referral developed within the BBC, paralleled
by an increasingly careful scrutiny by the ITA of ITV's coverage of
events. This was particularly relevant in the case of interviews
with, and items about the IRA. The item had to be cleared by the
news editor in Belfast and the editor in Belfast and the editors of
current affairs for television and radio in London. If approved,

the item could be recorded and then submitted once again for approval by London and Belfast, and often by ENCA in London. What was
happening during these two stormy years was that editorial control
shifted sharply not only from Belfast to London, but also from the
producer level to the very highest levels of the Corporation, a
development which was summed up in Charles Curran's observation that
he was editor-in-chief.

   The tight system of referral was viewed by some, though as Smith
points out by no means all, broadcasters in the province to be
excessively restrictive. He makes an interesting point in saying
that there emerged an increasing use of secondhand reporting, a
situation which placed the standards and style of reporting back in
the dull years of Tahu Hole when the BBC 'never had a scoop'. There
was a gradual formulation of the parameters of impartial reportage
which received its starkest description in the now famous words of
Lord Hill that 'as between the government and the opposition, as
between the two communities in Northern Ireland, the BBC has a duty
to be impartial not less than in the rest of the UK. But as between
the British army and the gunmen the BBC is not and cannot be impartial' (Hill, 1974, p.209). The context of these words was made
clear in the memoirs when Hill stated that what his critics didn't
seem to realize was that the hierarchy in the BBC are fighting a
battle against censorship, control, regulation, intervention from
outside. The claim of programme-makers in news, current affairs
or in any other field that they should decide what goes on the
screen or emerges from the microphone without guidance or instruc-
tion from above, is just the sort of claim that brings external control nearer (Hill, 1974, pp.210-11).

   This development over the coverage of Ulster can be seen as one
part in the overall development of broadcasting in the late sixties
in which the appointment of Lord Hill played an important role.
These developments were serious, but I think there is much to be
said for Smith's final point that the whole nature of broadcasting
was impinging on the development of the broadcast reporter's role.
A further point was that, owing to the multiple factors outlined
previously in this book, it was in many ways not within the capacity of television adequately to approach the questions posed by the
crisis. (4)

   Professor Rex Cathcart, former IBA representative in Northern
Ireland, in a recent programme on the difficulties of covering
affairs in Northern Ireland stated:

'inherently in the nature of the state set up here in 1920 there
were potentially problems for any broadcasting organization which
would move in. Those problems relate to the fact that there is no
consensus, no agreement that the State should be set up.... When
the BBC came to Northern Ireland the decision which had to be made
was what kind of an operation would they run there, and that decision became one of running what was essentially a broadcasting
system supporting the State, so that for the greater part of its
history the BBC has, of necessity, supported the State here.' (5)

The ideology of broadcasting, impartiality, etc. does not embody a
series of absolute definitions. In the context of Ulster, balanced

reportage is discreetly circumscribed and limited, actively defined
by the organizational and state elites. The parameters of accep-
tability are determined not by the philosophy of broadcast journalism, but rather by the needs of the State to maintain its hegemony
in Ulster. The coverage of political crises, because such events
necessarily are at the borders of 'legitimate' political action,
force the point at which day-to-day decisions are made higher and
higher within the institutional hierarchy.

There is a temptation to leave the description at this level, and
indeed many commentators on media affairs have tended to present a
version of the above process as an absolute and all-inclusive description of the situation of broadcasting. This is not, however,
the whole story, and one is really talking about quite specific
programmes in specific historical situations. Not all producers
interpret their situation in the same way, and not all would describe the concepts of objectivity, impartiality, balance as being
particularly inhibiting. What others describe as infringements
and restraints are, for some, useful guidelines. For example, when
asked about the requirement for balance, impartiality, objectivity,
one news editor of one of the smaller ITV companies stated:'They
are obviously important. More than anything else it is a help to
have guidelines. So they are obviously important and essential.'
It is significant that this comment came from the news editor of a
company which by virtue of its location, available resources and
defined area of interest would be unlikely to delve into contentious
areas on a national level. There is, if you like, both a 'geographical' and 'political' distance from the concerns of the State.
The dominant ideology of broadcast journalism is for him a relevant
set of beliefs, readily applicable to his situation. He operates
with a set of definitions which define the 'area of interest' and
'focus of attention' for his programme-making, and which tend to
remove him from the situation where the possible contradictions of
his role as journalist as well as broadcaster are teased out by
force of circumstances.

Even for a nationally networked current affairs programme the
concepts may seem adequate and workable:

'IBA pressure? If you are talking about outside pressures like the
law and everything, IBA pressure nil.... But Northern Ireland, I'm
very much aware myself, is a very problematical field. Personally,
having worked in Northern Ireland, I'm always worried about Northern
Ireland, but unfortunately the situation has become so serious that
almost anything you put out cannot be inflammatory any longer,
because everything inflammatory has been said. That used to be a
thing I used to worry about. I still worry about it myself in the
sense that I wouldn't do four Catholic programmes and no Protestant
programmes. I personally feel objectivity is very crucial, really.
This is not a "One Pair of Eyes" series where you can hire a man
from the "New Statesman" to say capitalism is wicked. It could come
out in the programme, by the way, that capitalism is wicked, but
that wouldn't be by setting out with a thesis, it would just happen
to be in this particular situation capitalism was wicked ... That
could come out, but that would be as part of an enquiry into a particular subject.'

'Are there any organizational rules that you have to contend with?'

'I think none except the legal ones. Occasionally, in the past,
people have said "What are you doing? We are a bit worried about
that", for example, over a programme on commercial radio in the
United States, saying it's a rather appalling thing. People were a
bit worried about that but nobody is going to stop it. I mean, I
just don't like commercial radio too much. The point is, it wasn't
a programme that said it is a bad thing, but said this is what it's
like in practice ... So I've never had anybody leaning on me and
telling me "For Chrissake leave off the trade unions" or "For
Chrissake lay off the prime minister" or "Lay off Harold Wilson",
because that hasn't come into it. But that may be, of course,
because one has exercised a certain kind of self-censorship. I'm
not aware of it but I suppose everybody does choose things here
and there.... The last thing I would want to do would be to put on
a piece that would tell people what to think about someone.
Although, you might say, the way you have chosen the images, the
way you've edited the interview would make people think this way.
I don't think that I've consciously edited this way.'

What is being described here is almost a model of 'message-by-
accident', where in order to comply with the necessary strictures
of political broadcasting the programmes are so constituted as to
not take an overt stance; that a 'stance' might emerge is a secondary, perhaps fortunate, event. Clearly though, for this producer of
a leading current affairs programme the concepts of impartiality
had a good deal of validity and were ones which he tried to respect.
At the same time he was arguing that there was little or no pressure
on him to make sure that he followed the implied guidelines of the
rulings - he was genuinely worried about Northern Ireland and
created the impression that the greatest restraint on his action was
his own feelings of the possible consequences of provocative broadcasting.
    Another producer within ITV, also working on a networked pro-
gramme, developed the proposition that while he recognized the
implicit restrictions of the rulings, there are distinct ways in
which these can be circumvented. In response to the question 'How
important would you say the law is in your type of programming?' he
declared:

'It is something you learn to live with quite quickly. To say you
get round it is misleading, but you soon learn how to do proper
journalism within the confines of, particularly, the Television Act.
The Television Act, as it is now interpreted, is not, frankly, a
great restriction and arguably has produced quite interesting journalism, and the IBA won't now interpret a Television Act terribly
literally. So, if you were doing a programme about defence, there
was a time when they would count minutes and say "Why don't you give
half the time to the Minister of Defence and half the time to those
who say he is wrong?" They are now much more sophisticated in the
way they interpret it and they are now prepared to look at it in the
way that a journalist does and say "Have you fairly represented all
relevant opinions on this subject?" Now it may be that it is incon-

venient or you don't want to fairly represent every view on a particular subject.... There are rare occasions when you have disagreement - there was a time when they would say that if you were
going to examine Protestant opinion then you'd got to have Catholic
opinion in the same programme, or you'd got to have Catholic opinion
in the next programme. They now would allow you to say "Why are
Protestants resorting to violence in the street?", or to ask "Who
are the Protestant para-military leaders?" Now they are acknowledged - that it's journalistically reasonable to ask those sorts
of questions. As long as you are seen to be fair and not particularly seen to side with any (side) over the run of a programme, not
seen to go out of your way to defend a particular point of view,
then they will leave you alone. I don't personally often suffer
from the Television Act, although I am aware of it.'

There is a clear implication here of the broad restraints imposed
by the legal rulings, though it is interesting that he, like many
other producers, returns to the Irish situation as an exemplary
focus for the process of operating within the law. It is also
interesting in the way he discusses 'proper journalism' from other
output which takes full account of the restrictions. There is again
this sense that you have to follow the ruling, not because of any
particular threat of sanction if you don't, but because it constitutes the essence of good 'journalism'.
A strict balance is maintained on the appearances of politicians,
as was indicated by the following statement:

'In politics there aren't restrictions but there is the set of built
in inhibitions, for example, the need to create balance. We, in
fact, solemnly count up every month the MPs and politicians who
appear on our programmes, and if we are four Conservatives short by
the end of the year, we are going to have to start looking for four
Conservatives to get on, quite literally. One has to be very
cautious. For example, at the moment we have three Liberal MPs in
our area who are all on good causes: Russell Johnston is knocking
the Scottish Transport Group, David Steel is causing a great furore
about maternity services in the Borders, Jo Grimond going for the
throat of oil developers up in Shetland. These are good stories
and you may feel the need to cover them, but, if you find yourself
trucking along with these three, people will start howling.'

'Who will start howling?'

'Members of the public, members of other political parties.'

'And they will get on to who?'

'Probably me.'

'Not the controller?'

'Possibly the controller, depending on their personal knowledge. On
the political side there are certain inhibitions but I haven't found
them all that oppressive.'

There is no real consensus of opinion on the significance and
nature of the requirements of the law, and for example over the
question of Ulster there is disagreement over their ability to
report in what they would consider to be an adequate manner and as
to whether their organizational superiors take a restrictive or
liberal view of what they can and cannot do. The differential responses to the situation of the journalist vis-a-vis the rulings
reflect differential positions, in both structural terms and in
ideological terms, occupied by producers working particularly within
current affairs. There is no blanket, absolute situation into which
all broadcast journalists fit, and for the person who produces a
major network programme for the BBC the implications and necessities
of his position are drastically different from the man who is responsible for producing news and current affairs in the Highlands of
Scotland. Their perceived area of programme material, their importance in the eyes of particular elites, their significance for
organizational elites, their essential purpose, all are factors that
together imply a different programme experience. There will also be
a difference over time in the situation of the broadcast journalist,
and periods of intense political activity will necessarily imply a
response by the state elite that will be felt within the organization. The BBC's current affairs group at Lime Grove is indeed the
battle front, the prime interface between the structures of the
State and the structures of broadcasting, both because of the centrality of the BBC to British national life, and also because it is
the single most visible physical representation of political television. If I might extend this analogy, if Lime Grove is the main
battlefield and the members of the current affairs group of the BBC
are its shock troops, then the current affairs and news personnel
of the regional ITV clearly form its home guard.

Nevertheless, organizational and external restraint is a real
feature of much production within the sphere of political broadcasting. What are the mechanisms of this restraint and on whom do
they operate? As we have seen in some instances there may be little
or no need to 'restrain' since there is already a disposition to
acknowledge the organizational line. Where that inclination is
missing, however, or where an action is taken which creates the
anxiety among the state or regulatory agencies responsible for
broadcasting, then other means must be sought and employed. These
may vary from the oblique suggestion to the direct order, from the
withdrawal of resources to the control of career patterns. There
are the obvious examples of control - there is the blunt refusal to
allow a broadcast, the refusal to give the go ahead for a project,
etc. These are, however, rather fierce examples and occur infre-
quently. A vital mechanism in the control procedure is the close
control over career that the organization has. In one interview, I
discussed the BBC's ending of the graduate traineeship, and made the
point that:

'I get the impression that what you are saying about the general
traineeship and the cutting off of entry to the BBC at source is
that they will have more control over who is coming in (to the
organization) and so are able to manipulate career patterns in order
to allow people to survive who they want to survive.'

To which the producer replied:

'Yes, well, by cutting off the general trainees, they have in fact
said that there is no structured career pattern for those people who
are going to become producers and above. The only career patterns
that are still systematically available are those of the technical
grades, the engineers, the studio managers and so on. To become a
producer now, in a way, you've got to either work your way up inter-
nally through these technical grades and apply for the jobs as they
come up and go on attachment. What's becoming more and more common
is that if you are a person on attachment - these are studio managers - you apply for an attachment and you get six months as a producer, and if you do well and they like you, you then apply for a
job and if it comes up in the department you may get it. So that's
one way, although in fact there's not much mobility.
    'The other way is of outsiders applying directly for production
jobs and then usually getting short-term contracts, which means that
the BBC can renew them if they want to, or get rid of them if they
don't want to. And that's really the thing, that's the great power
they've had since they abolished the general traineeship, they don't
have to give anybody a job which lasts more than, say, a year or
two. And they are going in increasingly for short-term contracts
in both radio and television, and that of course gives them enormous
control, because if a man's a nuisance he's only a nuisance for a
year.'

Another important mechanism is the development of particular images
of the purpose of broadcasting which reflect the perceived possibility of the situation at that time. This is not necessarily a process where there is a clear articulation of the position that
receives official sanction, but rather is a more oblique, subtle
process:

'How do you know what senior executives are thinking? Is it done
in terms of memos, directives, conversations?'

'Well, it's really made known when you put up an idea the first time
and you get a discussion. What's very interesting is that programme
ideas, no matter what future they may have, do generate quite interesting policy discussions at ... meetings, and one gets a sense of
policy mostly, I think, at the meetings with the controllers because
they are the closest we get to the very top of the hierarchy, that
is the managing director and above him the director general. So we
get a quite clear indication from the controllers of what's going
on, in some senses, by their response to ideas. So really you get
the directives by bouncing these proposals of them and finding which
ones work and which ones don't.'

'So it actually depends on the internal political climate?'

'Yes.'

'Would the ramifications of this strategy be more important for
particular departments?'

'Yes. Oh **yes**. I think that's so. In light entertainment, drama
and music there are internal political arguments which will affect
what they are doing, but the sensitivity of what they can show is
very much a political and social sensitivity, so it's the area of
language, morality and attitude which they feel that society is not
certain about, so the best thing is to keep careful about that....
In politics and the area of social morality they think that society
itself hasn't given any clear directives so the best thing is to
steer clear from them yourself. And those are the difficult ones.'

Finally, the most obvious mechanism of restraint is the direct
order. We have seen how this might be exercised in the kind of
public statement of what is and is not to be braodcast: the various
rulings over the coverage of Ireland by both the IBA and the BBC
being the most notable example of recent years. The direct order
may however be couched in very distinct terms, as was suggested by
one very well-known current-affairs broadcaster.

*'In current affairs, how much do you come up against particular
organizational restrictions - say the attitude of ENCA, the board of
governors or the director general?'*

'Very much, very much. Very important. But very much in the back
of one's mind because all these things become absorbed and they
become part of the structure of news and they're particularly dangerous because of that because they become hard to identify....
What happens is that a pressure is exerted and is not passed directly, very rarely passed directly, to anybody. Very rarely made
explicit even, because it's felt that if it's passed directly it can
be publicized and it can be challenged. If it's made explicit it
can be avoided by obeying the letter but not the spirit of the rule.
So it doesn't work on the whole as formal restraint except for some
legal things about law of libel or something. But the things that
really matter like the coverage of Northern Ireland or the way you
treat a PM on the air, those are things that are really important.
It doesn't work by any simple rules. I couldn't tell you this is
how we have to cover Northern Ireland, but what will happen is that
somebody at the top will say something like: "Er, feel that we've
had rather a lot of rough interviews with the leader of the opposition. There's a bit of a feeling around at Transport House, I
gather, that old Richard might have got it in for them a bit. I,
er, leave it to you, or course. It might not be a bad thing if we
laid off him for a bit, er, just until things quieten down a bit.
Maybe, er, I gather there's an interview with the leader of the
opposition next week. Well, maybe whoever you decide to do it, you
will remind them to be polite when doing the interview. I rely on
you, I know you'll sort something out. Well, jolly good, thanks
very much ..."
'Now that is an example of control at its most extreme in the
BBC, because what happens is that the man who's been told that has
been given an order (a) to keep an interviewer off the screen, (b)
to soften down an interview that the person who might do the interview does. Yet none of that can be found, it's not written in
minutes, it's not written down in rules, it doesn't exist on an

agenda of a paper, this is an informal conversation. But woe-betide the head of department if that person appeared on the screen a week later ... crash, out he goes. He does not understand how the system works by the most gentlemanly vice-like grip ...'

There is a fourth important aspect which needs to be considered, and this is the role of the audience in programme-making. What becomes clear from an analysis of the producer-audience relationship is that a number of features deriving from the internal context of production militate against the producer developing any real concept of his audience. The net effect is that the audience is treated as an abstraction and as an homogeneous whole, and is absent from the overall framework of production.

Chapter 7

THE ABSENT FRAMEWORK
The audience-communicator relationship

The producer of political television is never really aware of who it is that he is communicating with, a fact which implies a vital flaw in the whole concept of television as an agent of political communication. Not only is there no basis for communication but the very existence of such a linkage break lays the whole process of production open to a number of extraneous influences.

A number of experimental studies have looked at the way in which, it is alleged, communicators internalize pictures of their audience and produce material in accordance with those conceptions (Pool and Shulman, 1959; Bauer, 1958). McQuail (1969, p.76-7), employing a perspective drawn from the work of George Herbert Mead, argues that not only do images of the audience develop but that their existence is a prior necessity for any act of communication to take place. The communicator, in response to this necessity, develops a number of internalized 'others' with whom he 'converses', thus resolving the problem of 'knowing' the audience. The problem, McQuail argues, is that a number of intervening structures inhibit the development of this 'imaginary interlocutor' and thus engender serious problems for the organization. He detects three 'sources of difficulty'. First, the sheer scale of the operations of a mass communications organization; second, the difficulty with which particular audiences can be addressed; and third, the limited nature of the feedback. The central problem for the communicator is the inability of the communicator to establish the requisite 'imaginary interlocuter'. He states, 'The normal mechanisms of adjustment open to the communicator would seem to be thwarted since the formulation of a satisfactory reference group to represent the anticipated audience is almost impossible' (1969, p.79). Thus, as one moves from interpersonal communication to mass communication, the possibility of communicating decreases.

There is, however, another view of the audience-communicator relationship which holds that the problem of developing an internalized image of the audience 'out there' does not present itself since broadcasting in general but political broadcasting in particular is a closed world, a distinctive social milieu upon whose terrain the outside world rarely trespasses. The characteristics of the audience, its requirements in terms of information are not, in this view, of central importance to the broadcaster. The most biting elaboration of this proposition was provided by Austin Mitchell, a former BBC current affairs presenter (1973):

'Producers and presenters in current affairs, and particularly in the BBC, too often assume that they are doing programmes for people very much like themselves. This has always been the section of television which made the fewest concessions to the audience partly because Lord Reith still stalks the corridors of BBC Current Affairs Group but more because the other denizens are drawn fairly uniformly from Oxbridge backgrounds. They tend to deal with the subjects they took at university. They are hardly forced to question the elitist attitude and assumptions they absorbed there by frequent interaction with the mass audience they serve.... Clearly, in so far as news and current affairs programmes accept the assumptions and the linguistic shorthand of the elite who produce them, and in so far as they take background knowledge for granted, they will not get through to a mass audience. This may not concern the PPE graduates who prepare the programmes as a means of earning the esteem of the history graduates higher up the hierarchy.'

THE PRODUCER AND HIS AUDIENCE: A CONCEPTUAL VACUUM

Mitchell is, no doubt because of the path his own career has taken, somewhat narrow in his perspective of the bases of political television. There is more to it than Lime Grove, though that building does loom large in this area of broadcasting. What I think will become clear, however, from the evidence to be presented here is that Mitchell's emphasis on the inner orientation of the producer, what Burns (1969, p.72) has described as 'the safe enclosure of the artistic world', is a more relevant description than that of producers somehow pursuing an imaginary interlocutor. In the face-to-face or group situation the substance of what is communicated, the message-content, rests on a number of assumptions and understandings that the communicator derives from his audience. He can see whether they are young or old, intellectual or non-intellectual, he can see them laugh or scowl, applaud or jeer. More than likely his addressing them follows from an invitation to speak on a particular area and so to that extent his content is defined for him. In other words the linkages in the communication chain are clear. No such clarity exists for the producer of political television. But nor as a general proposition does that present problems for them. In studying the producers' perceptions of their audience, their attitudes to their role in the making of programmes, in influencing content, one gains no sense of viewing individuals frustrated by their inability to communicate. Rather the manifestation is of a relatively closed world festooned with a number of vaguely formulated, unsubstantiated assumptions about the audience, but vitally aware of its success or lack of success in overall ratings. There was, however, no precise idea of actual figures, rather of vague impressions haphazardly gathered. To begin with a very broad conclusion: there is little or no qualitative evaluation of the audience, but there is an important quantitative evaluation, thus reflecting the focus on the internal features of programme-making rather than the external features of the audience. Elliott (1972) notes in a similar vein that 'in many ways isolation and autonomy were the most striking characteristics of the production team's situation'.

When asking producers about the sorts of people who watched their programme one was often presented with a rather quizzical look and a heavy implication that the question was not the most appropriate one to ask. And yet when responses were goaded out they were revealing of the prevalent attitudes among communicators to the idea of communication. From my reading of the transcripts of interviews there was no situation in which a producer felt he either held a precise view of the audience, even at a general level, or indeed that this was possible or desirable. The producer of a current affairs programme on BBC declared that 'I don't think about the audience', and another stated:

'I really don't know very much about the audience actually. What I suspect and what I'm told is that its very high A-B. The viewing has pretty much doubled since the start of the programme, and we seem to have built a fairly constant audience who appear to want to watch us.'

One found similar statements in almost every interview, usually combined with an assertion that 'it's everybody', 'a cross section', 'all sorts'.

Grace Wyndham Goldie, a former head of the BBC's CAG is alleged once to have stated that the audience consists of 'mature people who are not informed but who wish to be informed'. Now this is a naively classless proposition of the audience as an homogenized whole, but its sense lingers on, as was reflected in the statement by an ITV current affairs producer that

'I'm very aware of saying "Christ nobody will understand that part of the programme" or "you've got to take that argument more slowly". I think most producers see as one of their primary roles, in the presentation of programmes, is being aware of how ignorant people are. A catch-phrase is that "people are more ignorant than you realize, but far more intelligent than you expect them to be". You can't assume that they know who the prime minister of Southern Ireland is, but don't preach at them because they will be able to understand a quite highbrow discussion of what workers' participation, for example, really means.'

A number of producers working on programmes in the regions outlined general assessments of their audience from which they drew a understanding of the 'programme needs' of that audience. There was an inclination, however, to conclude with a recognition that the 'assessment' was really only guessing:

'Basically we've got a rural audience and rural audiences tend to be, to use a good Scots word, coothy. They're very largely a farming community ... so they are all very well spread out and they've got their own funny little lives down on the farm. They

are fairly simple folk - I'm talking about the majority now, though
I'm not talking down to them - they've got fairly simple, straightforward, agricultural lives. Life in the country is very different
from life in the city. It affects the kind of things they like, and
they go for the women's institute meetings and the candlemaking and
the cookery. It's very difficult to gauge exactly what that simple
majority actually do like. They like the simple things in life, you
know, they like to see a local lad coming on for three minutes to
sing. They prefer that to you doing a twelve-minute close-up on
some big art exhibition. And then you get the candlemaking
instances where they write in about the most ridiculous topics that
we've covered. You tell me what the audience is like, I don't know,
there's no way of gauging it.'
It was interesting that one theme of the interviews in the regions
was that the audience was not what one would describe as sophisticated, and yet this wasn't in any way a theme of the national programmes. Presumably one can only explain it in terms of the different programmes which were studied. The regional programmes were
predominantly the 6 p.m. news magazine programmes, which are deliberately low-key and lowbrow productions, in contrast to the current
affairs and features programmes, broadcast at a later hour and more
earnestly serious. Even allowing for the distinctions implied here,
the dominant theme of the interviews was that the audience for a
programme reflected the innate diversity of a heterogeneous society
consisting of all social types, all social groupings. The producer
of a BBC feature programme declared:

'To start with it was a very middle-class audience because BBC2
meant getting a new set. But now there's a hell of a lot of people
who live in council flats where they can't have aerials and so they
get it piped in and therefore get all three channels. We've not got
a very good mixed-bag audience from what we can judge.'

What, then, can we say about the argument that communicators
develop an imaginary interlocutor? One clearly wouldn't expect the
formulation to be in precisely those terms, but one might reasonably
have expected reference to some representative entity, if not an
internalized 'other' then at least some 'average' figure. In fact,
this is very far from being the case. The nearest to it was a
producer who argued that it is 'impossible to have an image of a
very large audience. It's two or three people sat in front of the
television set.' When asked to elaborate on what these 'two or
three' were like, he replied, 'Infinitely variable, though I suppose
older rather than younger, richer rather than poorer. It's very
difficult to say. There's all sorts of research done but I'm never
quite sure what to make of it.' Three producers expressly denied
the presence of representative figures at whom their programmes were
directed. The producer of an ITV news magazine stated:

'I don't have a "Mr Viewer" image. One knows that the BBC goes for
A-B audiences, and we go for C-D-E, with a few As and a few Bs, sort
of thing. But that doesn't bother me at all because we are dealing
with a majority audience and that's more important to me.'

Thus, not only is there an abstracted view of his audience, but
also a qualitative assessment is superseded by satisfaction at
having a majority audience - which, in effect, meant that his
audience was larger than the rival news magazine on BBC. The only
concession he claimed to make for a more specific evaluation or
assessment of the audience was not in the area of a need for precise
forms of political information, but rather rested on his assertion
that he occasionally put on items which would appeal to women
(fashion) and 'teenyboppers' ('if David Bowie were up in the area
I'd have him in the studio if I could'). Another producer, in
arguing that he didn't hold an image of a 'Mr Average' in his head,
held that life was patterned, criss-crossed by distinguishing
characteristics, and that the audience for his programme would
reflect this in all its diversity. He stated:

'It's a fairly obvious audience in a sense. It's people who come
home early from work. It's kids and teenagers who come home from
school, it's mums who are already there, old age pensioners who
watch it all the time. It's everyone really. But you can't start
saying what type of person, because you have no idea.
  'I assume that the person watching this programme is the sort of
person who likes that type of programme. He hasn't got much alternative because if he switches over to BBC he sees a similar type
of programme. So you basically aim at the widest possible audience.
You assume a measure of intelligence on the part of the viewer and
you also see him as someone who is interested in the same sorts of
things you are interested in. I really will not create, and reject
the idea that you have to create Mr Average Citizen in his back
parlour and say "Would he like it?" It's much easier to say "Would
I like it?"'

There are a number of points to be made here. This particular producer affirms the familiar proposition that he doesn't know what
the audience 'is like'; he specifically rejects the idea that he
has to develop an interlocutor; and indicates the centrality of
the ratings. The really interesting feature, though, is the emphasis at the end on the reference that he would tend to make to his
own standards for decisions about content. This particular producer went on to add about the role of the audience:

'The audience is important if it's there. If it starts dwindling
then it's a sign that something is wrong. You don't really spend
the time worrying about the audience except producing for them the
best programme that you can, and if it's not what they want you've
got to produce a different type of programme.'

A typical response was that audiences are widely based, that
there is no representative viewer held in mind when making the
programme. As one producer, in Wales, stated, 'I don't see a Tom
Jones worried about his mortgage and living in Cardiff.' The use
of themselves as a basis for judgment was only aligned to a wider
view of the audience in those situations where the producer could
say 'The sort of viewers we have tend to be largely middle-class
people like ourselves. We've no way of knowing this, we just think

that.'   This was the producer of a BBC programme, and one did hear
the argument that ITV audiences were more working class than those
of the BBC, which were predominantly middle class.   A similar point
about affinity with the audience was made rather glibly by a BBC
current affairs producer:

'I argue (to his staff) that I'm old enough now to make programmes
for me.   But because I'm in the prime of life and have become middle
class, a bit elitist I suppose, I try to compensate for that by not
being too elitist, not too middle class.   But I would consciously
accept that I'm nearer to the age group that I'm broadcasting to
than my team are.... I have an affinity with (the kind of audience)
who wear hats and drive Morris Minors in the middle of the road very
slowly and either live in Yorkshire or Kent or Dorset and have a
fairly solid attitude towards life.'

Thus, the closest he came to a concept of the audience was the identification of a level of affinity based on generational proximity
to the viewers who watched his programme.   The reference point was
himself, but the focus remained legitimate, because the audience
was like himself.

It is significant for the discussion of the audience-communicator
relationship that not only were the images of the audience so
broadly drawn as to be meaningless, but that this was widely recognized by those interviewed.   It is possible to explain a situation
where in qualitiative terms the audience is not a central feature
of the producer's working life.   There is the difficulty of the
scale of the audience.   The smallest audience of any programme
involved in this study would be several hundred thousands and the
largest would, on occasion, reach perhaps fifteen million people.
The evaluation of the tastes and standards of such an enormous
number of people would present difficulties under any circumstances.
Yet there are clearly a number of mechanisms by which the producer
could impose on his view of the audience a sense of shape and order.
The argument that the communicators develop an interlocutory figure
does not necessarily entail that the figure derives from any considered assessment of the audience.   However, as I have tried to
indicate, the whole argument about the 'imaginary interlocution'
does not stand up particularly well to the evidence and so becomes
rather academic.

The problem of the audience nevertheless does present itself,
so long as one is talking about communication and so long as a
number of feedback sources are available.   What happens to these
sources of information about the audience?   It would be curious
indeed if one could show an attention to feedback sources and at the
same time the persistent absence of an 'audience' image.   What one
found in the interviews and also in the observation was at best a
crude awareness of feedback, a general distrust of these sources,
combined with an occasional strategic use of their content.   One
would understand the purpose of feedback - to distinguish it from
ratings - to be an in-depth evaluation of audience needs and
response to the programme content with a view to its integration
within the programme-making process.   Such a description remains,
however, hopelessly naive and of no relevance to the actual nature
of programme-making.

Three main sources of feedback are readily available to the producer: audience research carried out by the broadcasting organization; letters and phone calls in response to a particular programme; personal contacts.

A number of things stand out about the producer's attitude to audience research (AR): he does not see much; what he does see he doesn't think very much of; and in a number of situations there is actually no research at all carried out which could possibly be seen by him. The response of a producer of a news magazine was that 'We pay a bit of attention to audience research, but really I'm not too convinced of how scientific they are.' It was, in fact, rather difficult to get producers to say anything about audience research. In looking through the transcription one is struck by the general paucity of the answers to questions in this area. In a number of instances questions about audience research as a source of feedback from the audience indicated either the ineffectiveness or absence of research. One producer noted:

'Across the country we have a fairly good viewing figure, although audience measurement by the BBC in the regions tends not to be done unless specially commissioned for the regional programmes. They do it for national network programmes, but they don't necessarily do it for regional programmes. We had a survey done in the last quarter of last year. That postulated that in December of last year – and these were the last figures that I've ever seen for a television programme in the evening, we were doing about 22-23 per cent of the population over 5 years old.... The breakdown of the figures I wouldn't be too sure about, but I think we get a pretty fair cross-section.'

This statement was made in September 1973, and so for a period of nine months the producer had not only not seen any in-depth audience research, he hadn't seen any research at all, including his rating figures. This was by no means an unusual situation, and another producer declared:

'We've never carried out specific AR because as you know there's a separate BBC AR department and that carries out research on regional figures, so that we know roughly what the size of the audience is. But we've never carried out detailed research. The reason for this is that, first of all, it costs money and secondly, we were supposed to have colour for quite some time and it kept getting postponed and so we decided to postpone any detailed audience research until we were in colour and colour had been going for some time. Then we would be able to get some idea of the audience. But as far as I can tell the only way that we've got of knowing what the audience is like for our programme is obviously from the people who ring us up and write letters to us.'

The limitations on the use of audience research is no peculiarity of the regional television stations of the BBC. Producers in ITV regional stations, ITN, and BBC and ITV current affairs and feature programmes all made more or less the same point about the relative absence of AR. In network programmes, notably in the BBC, a good deal of AR is actually available to the programme-maker, (1) but I can find no evidence from my study that the fruits of the scientific evaluation of audience tastes, standards and needs plays any important part in the occupational life of the producers of political television.

This would seem to throw a good deal of importance in feedback terms on to a source already mentioned in these statements, that is letters and phone calls from viewers. The number of letters which programmes receive obviously varies with their scheduling and subject matter. According to current affairs producers, the number of letters which their programmes would receive varies between about fifteen and fifty per week. (2) One somehow expected far more than this: for example, one producer of a current affairs programme on ITV talked about the low level of letter writing both in terms of quantity and quality:

'I guess I get around ten to twenty letters a week.'

'Only ten to twenty?'

'Does that sound very low to you? (Yes) You don't get many. On other programmes like "World in Action" you get far less. I must add that most of the letters we get are really not very well-considered letters, to put it politely. they are mostly invective, or "why doesn't that cow wear proper lipstick?" (a reference to a female presenter) or "why doesn't that cow talk about God and why does she always look so left wing?" Those kind of letters are really not ones that challenge one intellectually. Occasionally, however, perhaps 2 per cent of letters make you sit down and think "God, this guy has thought it out, I've got to write a proper reply".'

Programmes always get a large amount of PR material, and some programmes, notably news magazines, get far more letters than a current affairs programme. This reflects the positive encouragement of letters by this type of programme, for example, through increasing the use of consumer items which clearly encourage people to write. (34) During observation at ATV the morning post averaged thirty letters which came directly from individuals rather than from organizations and firms.

There was some evidence that producers did try to assess their audience by reference to the letters. One producer, discussing the relative lack of importance of his colleagues in terms of feedback, referred to his experience on a previous programme which had a very high level of letters - it was a 'consumer' programme. Referring to the volume of letters he declared:

'That's what really mattered to me; if you're making a programme for a general audience you learn a lot from the letter. I obviously didnpt read all the letters, but from going through them you see what they liked, what they didn't like, what they didn't understand, what we'd done too fast, what hadn't been funny. I find that much more useful than colleagues who often have an axe to grind.'

This was on the whole an unusual response, a more typical one being
that 'We get letters that, I'm sorry to say, tend to be more about
people appearing rather than the content of the item or the story.
Certain people object to certain presenters and reporters on television. They object to the way they speak, they object to the way
in which questions are phrased.' There was a sense of despondency
that the letters weren't more articulate or pertinent. (4) A number
of producers argued that not only were letters often not particularly relevant or informative, but also stated that experience in
reading viewers' letters led to certain skills in graphology!

'I would hope that I was attracting a general audience with as Cs
as A-Bs there. I know that I am because I get letters in immaculate
typescript from people who've got good typewriters or secretaries in
their office, and I also get spidery handwriting on lined notepaper
from old age pensioners.'

Another producer of a programme which received quite a high level of
mail (150 letters per day on average - though this included PR
material) made the point that there tend to be many people who write
regularly to the programme (a point made by a number of other producers). He added,

'You start to recognize handwriting. You get a high proportion of
nuts and eccentrics. There is a certain style of handwriting, you
recognize it immediately - it's sort of both hands, heavy print,
capital 'i's' with dots and a rather bad biro. Lots of words are
underlined. Every current affairs producer becomes a sort of mini-
amateur graphologist. You can recognize a nut at a hundred yards.
    'The other category of people who write are the ones who want
help. You get an awful lot of people who write or ring and think
you're actually Parliament or a citizens' advice bureau.'

There was also some indication that letters may be used strategi-
cally within the organization - letters thus becoming important in
those situations where it was in the interests of, say, a senior
executive to make them important. I was also told that quite senior
personnel would occasionally become involved in a lengthy correspondence with a letter writer who happened to engage his interest,
and there was also some indication that letters would occasionally
lead to items for programmes. On the whole though, letters provided
either a very general impression of the audience (being employed to
support notions that, for example, 'we have a broad cross-section
of viewers', etc.) or were felt to be too few to be representative,
or were on the whole written by individuals who were in some respect
unusual and therefore were definitely unrepresentative. (5) There
is no way in which letters can be seen as a significant part of a
communication chain, and one is led to conclude that, in fact, the
concept of feedback is not particularly appropriate.
    If letters were not strikingly relevant in the development of a
concept of the audience for a number of reasons, telephone calls
were positively distrusted. Though some live programmes did take
up phone calls during the programme, 'We've just received two phone
calls saying that what the MP said about housing is nonsense, what

do you say to that MP...?' and though logs are kept of phone calls,
there is, to say the least, a rather aloof attitude to the people
who do phone. Reference was frequently made to the fact that only
those with complaints tended to phone, and this was felt to be
unfair on the programme-makers and also unrepresentative. Let me
refer to just two statements by producers which, from the evidence
I have been able to gather, sum up the relevant attitudes in this
area: 'Letters and phone calls? We take note of them but tend to
think they come from cranks.' This was a rather blunt representation of the position on calls, though the second statement by
another producer, while taking account of the complexities of discussing the role of phone calls, made a broadly similar point.

'I honestly don't receive many phone calls immediately after or
during a programme, although some people will phone me during a
programme immediately after an item.'

'What sort of people?'

'I would say the bulk of them tend to be, from the calls I've had,
the ordinary working-class people who've taken umbrage at something.
A great many tend to be extremists on one point or another: rather
than left and right, however, I would say that angry phone calls
tend to come from people who are involved in the Roman Catholic and
Protestant religious feeling in central Scotland. Sometimes people
just phone in and go screaming mad. Occasionally you get people
who phone up and say they like something, though these are few in
number. When it happens, though, it can be quite touching – for
example a story of a blind girl in need of an operation which she
could only get in America led to a lot of phone calls from people
wishing to help and saying they were touched by the story and
thanking us for putting it on. But these occasions tend to be fewer
than those where somebody says something controversial, or somebody
omits to say something that somebody of an extremist standpoint
thinks should have been said. And occasionally we get downright
lunatics – and I use the phrase lunatic advisedly, really scatty
people who say that they want to phone the man in the studio so that
they can tell him to take back what he's just said. He's probably
said something totally harmless and well within journalistic impartiality. For example, a lady phoned up and said "Phone him and tell
him," and I said "I'm sorry the programme is on the air," and she
said "Don't tell me that, they've got a telephone at the side: I've
seen him use it before now, just phone him up".'

Golding (1974) has noted: 'Relations, friends, taxi-drivers, doormen
and secretaries serve as functional microcosms of the unknown
audience, and are frequently mentioned in defence against the accusation that communicators are too isolated from and unresponsive to
their audience.' Certainly one source which was referred to by a
number of producers as a possible means of assessing the audience
was personal contacts with the audience, 'family and friends',
'what I hear in the pub'. However, this was nowhere stressed as
being in any way a significant source of audience information.
  In trying to explain the absence of an 'audience image' I have

pointed not only to sheer scale but also to the overall paucity and
inadequacy of the possible mechanisms by which knowledge of the
audience could have been established. The problem of feedback is a
difficult one to assess. The levels of wariness which exist towards
audience research, letters, phone calls, which do not on that basis
constitute part of the communications process, can be seen from a
number of different perspectives. The question which needs to be
addressed is does the attitude to feedback lead to the absence of
an audience image, or does it reflect an already existing lack of
concern with the audience thus reflecting an ideological stance
vis-a-vis the audience.

As a general proposition producers see much of the feedback as
irrational and/or negative and therefore to be rejected. That the
nature of the available feedback is dubious is undoubtedly true,
and would on the whole present very serious intellectual problems
for the producer in attributing any significance to them - anyone
who has read through many of the letters that are received can
attest to this. The conceptual vacuum thus represents a very real
problem. However, while this may be the case, the attitude to the
audience - or rather, if the drift of this argument is correct,
the lack of an attitude - reflects the subordination of the
producer's professional commitment as a communicator to his commitment to the wider goals of the organization, the most relevant of
which is an emphasis on audience maximization. The assessment by
producers of the audience may thus be seen as ideological in the
sense that it is consonant with their real interests. The attitude
towards the audience, the great depreciation of the feedback sources
sources, the establishment of a gulf between the production and the
viewer stem to a large extent from organizational practice. This
presents a view of the forces sustaining the internal world of the
producer and his production, a world cut off from the audience
because there is no organizational emphasis on knowing the audience,
only on having one. To clarify the notion that an important factor
in generating and sustaining the 'absent framework' one has briefly
to leave the discussion of the data gathered in the interviews with
the producers and look at certain problems and inconsistencies in
the public rhetoric of administrative personnel in BBC and ITV.

PUBLIC RHETORIC AND PRIVATE PRACTICE

There is a gulf between the public representations of senior broadcasters and the realities of their occupational world. At the level
of public statement the main proposition is that broadcasting in
Britain is about 'public service'. Charles Curran, director general
of the BBC can state that, 'Our only stated obligation in the
Charter, and therefore our central responsibility, is to serve the
public ,' (6) and Sir Robert Fraser of the then ITA can state on
24 September 1970 at a dinner given by the Authority to mark his
retirement:

'And so, with an audience of members, I have said nothing about the
one feature of Independent Television with which they will be
equally familiar: the great political compromise, the successful

political compromise, on which the whole Act rests, of creating a
system of private enterprise under public control.'

The public is a central point of reference in these statements, but
according to Curran the broadcaster cannot accept as given the level
of popular taste, he must seek to influence it, raise it and thus
fulfil the proper role of public service broadcasting by serving
'intelligently', leading as well as following. The chairman of the
then ITA refers to the benefits of improving standards which accrue
from competition: '... in the years of controlled competition
between the two broadcasting bodies, the scope and quality of
British television have been vastly improved.(7) Kenneth Lamb
(1970), speaking of the licence-fee system, declares,

'It reinforces a frame of mind in the BBC which impels us constantly
to ask ourselves the question: "What ought we to be doing to serve
the public better?" But if the BBC is to seek to serve the public
it must listen to what the public says.'

He then proceeds to list the various means by which 'the BBC
conducts this essential dialogue': programme correspondence, AR, the
advisory councils etc. He states, 'we try to make proper use of the
information we receive. Audience figures and indications of reactions are made available to programme departments and to planners
in a variety of charts and reports issued at daily, weekly and
quarterly intervals.' A kind of theoretical footnote was made by
Robert Silvey, then head of audience research at the BBC, in another
lunchtime lecture in 1963, when he declared that '"Communication"
cannot be said to have taken place unless there is a recipient as
well as a communicator and the part played by the recipient is anything but passive' (Silvey, 1963, p.6). What such accounts fail to
take note of is the tendency of the relationship between the two
broadcasting organizations to undermine these pretensions to public
service in assessment of taste and their placing of an emphasis on
the audience as a series of statistics. Other statements by senior
personnel do begin to indicate a slightly less righteous but more
realistic posture. The whole argument of the BBC to the Pilkington
Committee was that the competition for audience had a debilitating
effect on standards. Indeed this was the basis of their demand to
be allocated the second channel. Aylestone, in an address to the
Royal Television Society in Birmingham in October 1968, declared,
'Other things happened with the coming of Independent Television.
The first and most obvious, was the struggle for big audiences.
All television calls for big audiences - that is the nature of the
beast, and I know of no public television service in any country
which is not keen to get as big an audience as it can for its programmes.'

Howard Newby a senior BBC Radio administrator wrote in 'The Listener'
on 3 December 1970 (8):

'I have been using the word "competition" to mean rivalry for large
audiences. In talking about radio and television it can have little
other meaning.... In the public debate about broadcasting, and more

particularly that part of the debate that has to do with the appor-
tioning of funds, the only hard facts are about the listening and
viewing habits of licence-payers. Everything else is opinion.'

Given this kind of explanatory framework it is not difficult to see
why there is an apparent de-emphasis on substantial in-depth audience research as opposed to what can only be termed head counting.
As Wedell (1968, p.235) notes, there has always been an ambivalence
within the BBC rowards the audience - a tension between a willing-
ness to accommodate the information about the audience emanating
from AR and a refusal to be drawn into programme-making by plebi-
scite. This was the position at the time of the Beveridge Report.
The emphasis was changed somewhat by the Pilkington Committee, a
position which was later summed up in a BBC document: 'The conduct
of AR, and the communication of its results to the rest of the Corporation, constitute the limit of the (Audience Research) Department's responsibilities: its findings are never mandatory.' (9)
The Pilkington Report did not deal extensively with audience
research, whereas the Beveridge Committee had heavily criticized
the prevalent attitudes as 'irresponsible'. The prevalent attitude,
which does not appear to have changed since 1966, is that the
rogramme-maker need only take account of the audience as reflected
in the AR findings in those situations in which he chooses to do so.
There is, as Lamb states in the extract quoted previously, a formal
distribution on the findings of AR. Within that, though, there
appears to be an emphasis on quantitative data. It is, however,
difficult to obtain any indication as to the measures which are
taken to implement the findings at programme-making level, other
than that they are 'never mandatory'.

    The position vis-a-vis audience research was perhaps most suc-
cinctly summed up in a speech by Charles Curran at an international
seminar on 'Broadcaster/Researcher' co-operation held in Leicester
on 17-21 December 1970. He stated that (10):

'If there has been a single discernible thread running through what
I have said I hope it will have been this: the BBC is in the programme-making business and its overriding concern must always be
with those who make programmes and those who watch and listen to
them. We reject the idea that we should contribute financially to
research because it is not part of our proper function to redistri-
bute public money in this particular way. We have no right to pick
the pocket of the viewer to find out what is in his head....
Research must always be subservient to programmes.'

    It is this general background of organizational practice which
can be seen to provide a third process sustaining the absence of an
adequate and meaningful conception of the audience. It is in light
of these three factors - scale, feedback, organizational practice -
that one can begin to explain not only the absence of any understanding of the audience but also the facility with which producers
are able to deny the significance of the audience. As a general
proposition one can argue that producers declare that the audience
does not figure in the programme-making process in any substantial
way, and that this leads to a dependence on themselves as points of
reference.

The producer of a current affairs programme on ITV, making a virtue of necessity, made the point that he was the one who was responsible for the programme, that one couldn't distil the necessary creativity from the audience and that this was what successful programme-making was all about. He was an advocate of a state of creative autocracy:

'I don't think you can plan a programme for an audience, and I don't know quite who you would plan it for. As I said before, when you make a decision as the producer of a programme, you can't be democratic, because you have to make them very quickly. In the end ... I never say to myself in a blatant way that I will construct a programme for any audience, and I really don't know anybody who does that in any programme. I think if you get to the stage, which you see on television all the time, where you say "I will construct a situation comedy for them" and it's usually awful. It's only guys who are writing things like "Steptoe and Son" or "Till Death Us Do Part", those who are writing because they personally believe in the idea, who are doing anything worthwhile. This is not to say that they ignore the audience because I'm sure they don't, they are aware of their audience, but not primarily aware - they keep the audience somewhere to the left of their vision but not straight ahead and that's the same with me.... I back my own judgment because I've seen how my own judgment works out in practice. I have a broad sense of how successful my programmes have been, and I actually like to think that they've been very successful in terms of audience as well as critics. I'm not all that interested in making programmes for very small minorities, but I'd also recognize that I never really set out to make a programme for a mass audience because I never believe that it's either possible or particularly worthwhile.'

The 'I'm responsible' argument was argued more forcibly by the producer of a BBC current-affairs programme who stated 'I try to use myself as arbiter for the simple reason that in the end I'm responsible for it. They'll fire me if they get fed up with it. So in the end I have to say "I don't like this" or "my preference is for so and so". One can reproduce similar statements from different producers in different situations:

'I think the audience is very unimportant. It's a pity, but they just don't come up with massive suggestions. We have an advisory council that meets here three times a year, lay people who are interested in broadcasting, who are asked to make suggestions for programmes and even they don't come up with very many. We are just left to get on with it really.'

There is a strong sense in this statement of the professional distance, the broadcasting clergy possessing the knowledge and expertise, and the 'lay' audience, unable to contribute, there to be spoken to rather than communicated with, a passive rather than active audience. The producer of a BBC features programme did, however, feel that the lack of an audience image signified an absence of professionalism:

*'You didn't have a particular audience in mind when you were doing
the programme?'*

'No. In fact the thing that makes us a pretty unprofessional outfit
I'm sad to say is that we tend to make the programmes for ourselves.
I was really just making programmes for myself which is bad.'

An interesting feature which emerged was that the producers,
having said that the audience wasn't important and that they used
themselves as a kind of gauge of programme content, tended to add
that they did try to sustain 'a level of interest' among the
audience, tried not to 'bore' them. This became closely tied up
with the attitudes to the ratings, 'interest' being confirmed in
viewing figures. The producer of a current-affairs programme on
ITV in declaring that the ratings weren't particularly important,
only served to make the point that they were, to the extent that
their centrality is very much taken for granted:

'I don't think one could say how much store one puts in the audience
ratings. they are not the be all and end all. No one in ITV, the
managing director or the programme controller, has ever said to me
"Your ratings are bad". I don't think they've been that bad anyway.
The only thing I'm interested in is whether they fall from the
previous programme. My feeling is that if you can hold an audience
within a few points of the previous programme then it's a lot,
because after all the previous programme is always an entertainment
or something. If you can hold them - it obviously depends what is
on the other side - but if you can hold them then I think you are
doing it well. Look, it's a fantasy to expect people who have been
working and are tired and everything else, to think that they want
to sit down to an undiluted diet of catastrophe, news, trade figures
and everything else. It's absolutely silly to think that.... Why
should we expect the audience to dot around from news to current
affairs to documentary. They'd be a fantastic audience if they did.
They'd also be mad.'

The problem is one of sustaining a level of interest and therefore
viewing figures against the natural tendencies of the audience to
drift off into other, less demanding areas. A similar position was
adopted by a producer working in a completely different context,
that of producing a BBC news magazine programme:

'in a television programme of twenty minutes at night you are trying
to hold audience attention by not having too many solid items at the
beginning. For example, we always try to orchestrate our headlines.
For this we usually have three subjects in the headline: Nos 1 and 2
tend to be more important stories, No. 3 tends to be usually a
feature-type subject that will probably be about four minutes on
film.'

And a Scottish producer tied up the different threads of depending
on their own tastes and perceptions and seeking to blend that with
audience interest and thus sustaining an audience. When asked about
the importance of the audience he stated:

'Totally, in the sense that there's no point in making a programme
that nobody watches. I don't think they can influence the programme, though. What we are aiming to do, and it happens to be our
privilege, is to produce the best programme we are able to do and
the best general interest programme that we are able to do. We
would very rarely say "there's not much point in doing that because
who's interested?" But at the same time if we thought there was a
general interest in an item and we thought we could do it, we would
do it.'

In other words, the audience is important so long as they are there,
but as people with specific interests and needs they are encapsu-
lated within a concept of 'general interest' that only occasionally
is allowed to intervene in programme decisions.

Producers do not have an obsession with the ratings in the sense
of avidly following them for every programme that is produced.
Rather they develop what one might term a sense of well-being, an
ill-defined feeling that their programme is able to maintain a level
of interest among the audience. As previously indicated, producers
may in fact have no idea about the precise audience figures for
their programme, may even depreciate ratings, but they nevertheless
retain a residual sense of the state of play:

'I don't think you can manage to work anything out from the ratings.
I mean, on some of the programmes which I thought had been absolutely fantastic, the ratings have dropped and on some of them in
which you think the programme is absolutely diabolical the ratings
have gone up. (11) There is no way of reading anything into the
ratings, and it's a terrible danger to try and do so because you
get trapped in the ratings game. since the ratings are fairly
reasonable and they don't vary that much I don't really worry about
them. It's somebody else's problem really. They'll tell me if they
drop.'

What points can we make from all this; what themes emerge from
the numerous statements already referred to? I think one can make
a number of fairly conclusive statements about the nature of the
relationship between the producer and the audience.
  1 Producers do not 'know' their audience in terms of their having
either detailed knowledge or a clearly worked out impression. That
is, the audience has neither an objective nor subjective presence
for the producer.
  2 Producers do have very general, loosely formed, vague impressions of the audience. This tends to be of the order, 'it's everybody', 'a cross-section' or 'we get a lot of women/elderly people/
middle class, etc'.
  3 This can be explained at a number of levels. There is the
sheer scale of the audience - ranging from several hundred thousands
to several million. There is a lack of meaningful 'feedback', so
much so that the implications of that concept do not fit the reality
of the communications process as exemplified by political television. The organizational practices of the broadcasting organizations in emphasizing the competitive basis of broadcasting in
Britain inhibit attempts at the development of any in-depth concepts

of the audience. The emphasis is on a quantified view of the
audience rather than a qualitative one.

4 The general effect of this situation is to emphasize the inner
world of the programme setting rather than the linkage with the
audience which would be an essential prerequisite of any adequate
political communications system. There could be no communication
in situations in which the audience represents a series of ciphers
and percentages.

This is what the absent framework means. It means, however, that
there is not only a vital 'missing link' in the communications process but also that this engenders an environment in which a number
of processes are able to operate. These are the processes which
operate on the production, shape it and fashion it, so that in
large part the content of political television derives from internal
requirements and propositions rather than from the conscious desire
by programme-makers to relate to the information needs of the
audience-electorate. The absence of a framework which embodies
both the communicator and the audience is therefore an important
flaw in the whole notion of communication and a cause and consequence of the distinctive internal social milieu from which political television emerges.

Part three

THE EXTERNAL CONTEXT OF POLITICAL BROADCASTING

That there is a perpetual battle between the worlds of politics and broadcasting is frequently heard and read. (Because of the breadth of the issues under discussion here, it is necessary to employ the more inclusive term of broadcasting rather than just television.) A key proposition is that broadcasters are subordinate to the political institutions in society and that therefore programme content made available by the broadcasting institutions reflects the nature of the pressure flowing from one to the other. It is certainly the case that a discussion of the internal consequences of external institutions must be an integral part of the discussion of the nature of the production of political television. Two points need to be made, however, one relating to method, the other to analysis. In terms of method there is always the danger of failing to distinguish between a pressure applied and a response made, an internal procedure and the exercise and operation of power. There is also the difficulty of taking as given 'facts' which are at best dubious. For example, a popular version of the BBC in the Suez crisis is that the BBC successfully warded off immense pressure from the government which, at one point, was planning to take over the corporation. The story was aired in Harman Grisewood's autobiographical 'One Thing at a Time' (1968) and was repeated wholesale by Smith (1973, p.142) and in Hood's review of the book in 'The Listener' (1968). The picture is not, however, quite so clear as these accounts would imply and, in an interesting article, F.R. MacKenzie (1969) has a rather thorough critique of this prevailing orthodoxy, and even goes so far as to imply that the problem with the BBC has always been that of too much immunity from external scrutiny rather than too much pressure. Analytically, it is important to consider the view that while political institutions may hold centre stage in any i discussion, account must be taken of the interlocking of production within organizations that themselves are but constituents of industrial and commercial corporations.

The whole question of this interaction between an external environment of political and commercial institutions and the internal programme-making processes needs detailed examination, not in terms of statements of assumed causal connections between external interest and internal process; rather in terms of detailed study of particular instances of those interests and processes actually interacting. In short, the elucidation of the mechanics of these implied relationships. It would be naive to assume that one could begin such a discussion without some kind of latent view of the significance of that external context. For example, there have been a number of major rows in the history of political broadcasting, 'Suez' and the programme 'The Question of Ulster' being prominent examples. It would be reasonable to assume some kind of connection between the existence of the 'row' and a submissive response from programme-makers or their organizational superiors. The question of the validity of such assumptions is, as it were, the point of the following discussions.

Two central components provide the external context of political broadcasting: the political institutions of the State and the commercial institutions, which in the case of large sections of ITV provide the 'parent' company.

THE STATE

The notion of a central and dominant political structure within society is a familiar feature of many discussions of the political process and is usually couched in terms of 'the State'. It is not so familiar to find that term defined so that one knows just what the writer has in mind. Indeed the terminology is so familiar that one is almost tempted to assume an understanding, and yet the details of the definition are important in the context of the discussion of political broadcasting.

One can begin with an acknowledgment of Weber's proposition of the need to distinguish between the State, as one form of political association within society, and the innumerable other political associations by attention not to ends but to the means available to it to achieve those ends, and that the specific characteristics of those means is that they consist of the monopoly of the legitimate use of physical force within any given territory. This seems to me ultimately to be one of the more useful formulations, but it does still leave the need to root that monopoly within its institutional form: within what or whom does such power reside? From a fairly elaborate definition of the institutions of the State as 'the government, the administration, the military and the police, the judicial branch, sub-central government and parliamentary assemblies' (Miliband, 1973, p.50), one can extract what are the central political institutions for broadcasting: namely, the structure of government (with the governing party and the administrative agencies), the parliamentary structure, the legal structure. Resting on the assumption that these three structures form part of the wider network, it does seem clear that, on available evidence, they form the main points of connection between broadcasting and the State.

THE COMMERCIAL CONTEXT

One has to make the rather obvious point that much of political television is produced within organizations that are themselves only constituents of larger industrial enterprises, the central function of which is the pursuit of profit (Murdock and Golding, 1974). The logical proposition here is that the micro-goal of political communication is subsumed within the wider goal of the pursuit of profit.

In short, then, these political associations within the State and the spirit of commercialism provided by a location within industrial corporations, provide the context of political broadcasting. To illustrate the impact of this context on programme-making, four case studies are presented which confront empirically the main dimensions of the framework outlined above: the governmental structure, the parliamentary structure (notably in the form of a leader of the main opposition party in Parliament), the legal structure and the commercial environment. the case studies are dealt with chronologically and a general conclusion is drawn at the end of the book bringing together the main themes and observations. The choice of case studies was, of course, not solely based on an assessment of the theoretical questions raised by considerations of the role of 'environment' in broadcasting today. The choice was also based on their intrinsic interest and their availability for study. Nevertheless, they do allow consideration of the very important question of the extent to which the making of programmes is influenced by outside processes and interests.

Chapter 8

THE BBC AND THE GENERAL STRIKE
May 1926

'(Reith) put his native guile to good use at the time of the General
Strike of 1926, when he had to walk as delicately as Agag between
asserting the independence of the BBC too strongly (and perhaps
losing it for ever) and surrendering it on the spot. The compro-
mises which he then accepted made it possible for his successors
to be much more firm and uncompromising when they faced the anger
of governments about the BBC's treatment of such crises as Suez 16
years ago and Northern Ireland today.' (Greene, 1972)

'In time of national crisis the Government, as it did during the
Strike, rightly takes over the conduct of broadcasting.' ('Morning
Post', 26 May 1926)

The historical treatment of the concept of 'impartiality' - its
initial formulation and subsequent utilization - provides an insight
into the precise meaning the social environment can have for the
process of production. At no time was this more apparent than in
the period of the General Strike in May 1926. At that time the
fledgling British Broadcasting Company and its dominant and iras-
cible general manager, John Reith, made it clear to parliamentarians
that their interpretation of 'impartiality' in 'controversial'
broadcasting would not offend the established political orders.
     Times of severe political crises - the General Strike, Suez,
Northern Ireland after 1969 - have created considerable problems
for broadcasting in defining its position vis-a-vis the crisis,
and have thrown into sharp relief the nature of the relationship
with the State (Smith, 1972; Hill, 1974). The previous chapters
indicated the continued importance, and difficulties of interpretation, of impartiality in the production activities of programme-
makers. As will become apparent from the present discussion, the
precise nature and elements of the concept of 'impartial broadcasting' were argued over and established in the very earliest days
of broadcasting, but the importance for this discussion was the way
in which the precise meaning of impartiality was clarified by the
looming presence of Baldwin's government during the days of the
Strike - most notably in the shape of Churchill (1).
     When the British Broadcasting Company was formed in 1922, one

of the main concerns was the possible danger of 'controversial broadcasting', though there is actually no specific reference to 'controversy' or to 'controversial broadcasting' in the original licence of January 1923. There is, in fact, a good deal of obscurity about the veto on controversial broadcasts and on the attitudes of different governments to it during the early years, and yet it was always assumed to exist during the period leading up to the General Strike of 1926. The director of telecommunications of the GPO told the Ullswater Committee in 1935 that from 1922 onwards, a general veto had been imposed by the Cabinet on all subjects of political and religious controversy. (2) Despite protestations to the contrary by the postmaster-general in the period 1923-6, the BBC was wise to act with circumspection, even though, as far as can be detected, there were no specific instructions on the matter: 'foolishness would be followed by withdrawal of the Licence' (Briggs, 1961, p.170). The BBC's attitude was that a 'broadcasting service which contained no reference to politics could not claim to be a balanced service, or an informative or educative one'

Equally difficult in this period before the Strike was the question of news broadcasting. The licence granted to the BBC on 18 January 1923 included a clause which said that the BBC should not broadcast any news or information except that obtained and paid for from the news agencies (Briggs, 1961, p.133). It was the major newspaper interests in the shape of the Newspaper Proprietors' Association which were to be the severest baulk to the BBC's developing any kind of news organization. From the beginning of the negotiations with the companies which were eventually to form the BBC, the PMG had made it perfectly clear that the press interest should in no way be alienated (Briggs, 1961) or financially embarrassed by the new organization. Despite protracted negotiations during the 1923-6 period, and despite one or two minor concessions by the press interests (see Briggs, 1961, p.263), it was possible for Briggs (1961, p.267) to sum up the situation by saying that 'throughout the whole period when the BBC was a company ... it was subject to such severe restrictions on the broadcasting of news and outside events that the ordinary listener had only the remotest idea of what the shape of future broadcasting would be.'

The subject of controversial broadcasting was first brought to a head in April 1923 when a question was raised in the House concerning a broadcast by the Editor of 'Building News' in which he had asked that a threatened building strike be called off, appealing to the parties involved to accept arbitration. In reply to the concerned questions of various Labour MPs, the PMG, Sir William Joynson-Hicks, stated: 'I think it is undesirable that the broadcasting services should be used for the dissemination of speeches on controversial matters, and I have had the attention of the BBC called to the incident' (Quoted in BP5) - something which Reith interpreted as a direct order. Nineteen twenty-three saw several attempts by the BBC to have controversial programmes broadcast: for example, a request was made for the BBC to be allowed to broadcast the King's speech at the opening of Parliament and for the leaders of the three main parties to broadcast during the forthcoming election. Both requests were refused by the PMG.

The restrictions imposed on broadcasting in the years up to the

General Strike were severe and wide ranging, news, for example, effectively being limited to a 7 p.m. bulletin (when all the papers were deemed to have been sold) with material provided by the news agencies. (3) The restrictions reflected both the economic anxieties of the newspaper publishers and the political anxieties of the government. As Briggs (1961, p.267) puts it: 'the Derby and political speeches alike were taboo'. The BBC was pressed on both sides by the newspaper owners and the politicians, and it was in this context of a badly underdeveloped news service that the BBC found itself in the May of 1926, as the major national source of news.

Prior to that, however, there were a number of events which were to highlight the position of the BBC: a sense of growing confidence in some circles that the BBC could to an extent be trusted politi- cally even though it still could not be allowed to infringe the economic interests of the newspaper and news agency owners. In 1923 a committee of enquiry had been set up by the government under the chairmanship of Sir Frederick Sykes to examine all the issues of finance, organization and control which remained unresolved. It reported on the question of controversial broadcasting and declared that the BBC should be allowed to broadcast on controversial affairs, particularly since there was really no subject on which controversy would not arise at some point. (4)

Following the committee report, a broadcasting board was esta- blished to 'advise the Postmaster-General on matters connected with broadcasting' (Briggs, 1961, p.247), and at the meeting of 14 May 1924 the question of the broadcasting of speeches on controversial matters was raised. Reith suggested that the exclusion of such matters tended to reduce the interest and value of broadcasting (BP5). He proposed that the BBC should be allowed to broadcast speeches by members of each of the three main parties during impor- tant debates in the House or at the time of elections. The choice of the speakers was to be entirely a matter for the parties. Other members of the Board argued that this would create difficulties in that there would be too many requests to broadcast and that it would be difficult to know what should and should not be broadcast, impartiality would be difficult to sustain and the great danger would be the misuse of broadcasting by the party in power. In June 1924, the Board reported to the PMG, Vernon Hartshorn, that while the restrictions on political speeches should be retained, in other areas previously thought of as 'controversial' a more liberal atti- tude should be adopted (BP5)

The initial breach had been made then in the restrictions on con- tent, but at the same time, the basic elements of the whole dis- cussion about political broadcasting were also being developed. What I want to suggest is that the essence of the restrictive con- cern was rooted in the fact that no one quite understood how things would work out in practice; they were politically unsure as to the consequences of granting permission to the BBC for 'controversial broadcasting', though it has to be added that among most MPs there was a remarkable lack of concern with the new medium (Briggs, 1961, pp.350-1).

In 1924, Reith entered the fray once more by seeking permission to broadcast a debate between the party leaders. Permission was not

forthcoming, although Ramsay Macdonald, Baldwin and Asquith did, in
fact, broadcast during the election of October 1924. In 1925 the
government, as intransigent as ever, employed the excuse that, as
the Crawford Committee was to consider the whole issue, the making
of a premature decision would be wrong. The BBC's memorandum to
the committee declared in passionate terms (5) that the restrictions
on talks and political broadcasts be reduced. The memorandum argued
that the BBC should be allowed to broadcast 'controversial matters'
always under the 'adequate safeguards for impartiality' and added
that 'naturally there are certain subjects which the broadcasting
authority would not desire to handle at all, but it is not difficult
to draw the line'.

Apart from the central argument of Reith that the BBC should be
transformed from a commercially based enterprise to a publicly owned
body (Briggs, 1961, pp.331-2), he was pressing for an expanded news
service and greater freedom to cover controversial matters, and it
was on these matters that the bulk of the opposition to the BBC
rested. When the Crawford Committee reported on 5 March 1926, its
major recommendation was that the BBC become a public corporation,
but it also recommended that there be a 'moderate amount of controversial matter'. (6) The attitude in Parliament to 'controversial
broadcasting' was that 'each "side" complained of the advantage
given to the other, and both parties had to be reassured by the PMG
(with only a few members expressing uneasiness) that all kinds of
political broadcasting were being prohibited' (Briggs, 1961, p.352).
(7) On the 14 July 1926, the postmaster-general announced that the
main recommendations of Crawford were being accepted by the government. He was later to add, on the 15 November 1926, in response
to the expressed anxieties of many MPs, that 'he had instructed the
Corporation that, when it began its operations, it was not to broadcast its own opinions on matters of public policy nor was it to
broadcast on matters of political, industrial or religious controversy' (Briggs, 1961, p.359). To soothe the disappointed Reith
some of the restrictions on news programming were removed. In the
debate of 15 November on the BBC's new charter, Lord Wolmer, the
assistant postmaster general declared: 'I want to make this service
not a Department of State, and still less a creature of the Executive, but as far as is consistent with ministerial responsibility,
I wish to create an independent body of trustees operating the service in the interests of the public as a whole' (Quoted in Briggs,
1961, p.360). That, however, was said in November 1926, nine
months after the publication of the Crawford Report. In the meantime, the BBC had been through the events of May. It is perhaps
important to note that the inhibitions imposed on the broadcasting
of political material seem to have derived not from a concept of
the possible threat this would pose to State power but rather
because of the touchy sensibilities of politicians concerning party
advantage. It would be made clear, however, during the period 3-12
May that the central question in crises of that order would be the
relationship of the BBC to the State and therefore to the political
and moral order which that structure was deemed to represent. The
BBC entered these events with a severely limited scope in what it
could do, no experience of the news process and no proper news
organization. Nevertheless, Reith saw the Strike as a 'stupendous

opportunity to show what broadcasting could do in an emergency'
(Reith, 1963).

Developments were not only afoot in the legislation of broadcasting; drastic developments were taking place in the economics of
mining, which were to have almost as significant an effect on broadcasting as they were on the mining industry. From 1924 Britain had
been governed by Baldwin's Conservative government. In the face of
mounting economic difficulty the government had revalued the pound
sterling. The coal industry had been particularly hard hit by this,
since the increase in the value of sterling increased the price of
exports, unless the producer was willing deliberately to cut the
price of his goods. Since the cost of labour was such a large part
of the production of coal, the only way the owners saw of cutting
prices was by reducing the wage bill and increasing the number of
hours spent earning the smaller wage (Symon, 1957; Lloyd, 1970).
On 31 July 1925 a commission had been established under the chairmanship of Sir Herbert Samuel which reported on 11 March 1926.
The report satisfied neither the owners nor the miners. In April
1926 negotiations within the industry broke down completely and led
to renewed calls for the General Council of the TUC to organize a
general strike. During that month and into May, the government and
the TUC were locked in negotiations over the dispute but when, on
1 May, the government subsidy which had underpinned the miners'
wages ended, the Strike effectively began. The actual spark or
signal that the General Strike was on was provided by the printers
of the 'Daily Mail' who, on the evening of 2-3 May, refused to
print an anti-Strike editorial. On hearing the news in the early
hours of 3 May, Reith sent a message to the Prime Minister asking
for a personal message to the people; 'It came quickly: "Keep
steady; remember that peace on earth comes to men of goodwill"'
(Reith, 1963).

Though the collapse of the newspapers was by no means as total as
is sometimes imagined, particularly in the provinces where many
papers operated almost as normal (symons, 1957), the BBC became
overnight the single most important source of national news. On
3 May, Reith arranged with the Home Office that BBC property would
be protected and got authorization from Davidson (8) for bulletins
to be broadcast at any time; (9) he also arranged with the news
agencies that for the duration of the emergency copyright could be
suspended. Reith also arranged for all official news to come from
the headquarters of the chief civil commissioner and from the ten
government centres around the country. He states: 'I had the Chief
Civil Commissioner and the Home Secretary and Davidson agree that
the BBC should not be commandeered, meaning that it or I should be
trusted to do what was right' (Reith, 1963). Reith's self-assurance
that he could do what was right was aided by his overall view of the
pros and cons of the Strike. Symons (1957) states:

'Four years earlier he had written to Clynes, feeling that in the
Labour Party there was most chance of finding the essence of his
own beliefs about a practical application of Christian principle to
national and international affairs. But although, like many other
liberals, he might have supported the miners against the coal
owners, he was certainly not prepared to support the strikers
against the government.'

Reith's position was in tune with that of Baldwin - the strike was a threat to constitutional government and therefore had to be defeated.

A three-shift system of BBC personnel was organized so that the newsroom, receiving most of its information from Reuters and from Davidson's office at the Admiralty, was manned round the clock. The real question facing the BBC was not, however, whether it could function adequately during the Strike but rather on whose side it would function. The position adopted was that they were 'impartial' and 'objective'. For example, in the first news bulletin on 4 May, having pointed to the difficulties which people would experience in turning from newspapers to the limited radio bulletin, the bulletin declared:

'The BBC fully realize the gravity of its responsibility to all sections of the public and will do its best to discharge it in the most impartial spirit that circumstances permit. In the last issue of the newspapers, allusion is principally made to the possibility of wholesale oscillations. (10)   As to that we express no opinion, but we would ask the public to take as serious a view as we do ourselves of the necessity of plain objective news being audible to everybody.... We shall do our best to maintain our tradition of fairness, and we ask for fair play in return.' (11)

The question of the actual status and role of the BBC was, however, posed in the sharpest possible form and illuminates the details of the relationship with the State. Constitutionally the BBC's position was quite clear. Not only could the minister order the BBC to broadcast particular messages; he could, if he so desired, take over the running of the organization. There was a continuous debate within the Cabinet as to whether they should in fact commandeer the BBC for the duration of the Strike, Churchill, then chancellor of the exchequer, being the main advocate of such a move, Baldwin arguing that this would not be necessary. Reith first heard of Churchill's desire to take over the Company on 5 May, and on 6 May he sought a clarification from Baldwin who agreed to 'leave the BBC with maximum autonomy and independence' (Reith, 1963). He might well leave the affairs of the BBC in capable hands of Reith since the clarity with which Reith and his senior personnel saw their position vis-a-vis the government is vividly portrayed in the internal documents of the period. A memo dated 6 May was entitled 'Suggestions for the Policy of the Broadcasting Service during the Emergency'. (12)   It states that the BBC has a 'duty' to broadcast anything that the civil commissioners or the government require, that they should 'maintain an objective news service' and that 'we should make a particular point of emphasizing statements calculated to diminish the spirit of violence and hostility'. The memorandum made three main points: that consultations should be the basis for the relationship between the government and the BBC; that if the BBC were overtly partisan then the strikers could cripple the service; and that the BBC had a 'positive' conciliatory role to play (Briggs, 1961, pp.362-3). It is ridiculous to suggest that the BBC had no opinions in the Strike, apart from the obvious point that the very notion of conciliation is itself an opinion. The 6 May memo declared that they should

'try to convey to the minds of the people generally that the prolongation of the general stoppage is the one sure process calculated
to reduce wages and the standards of living which it is the avowed
endeavour of the Trade Unions to maintain and improve; and to try
to make it clear that the sooner the General Strike is satisfactor-
ily terminated the better for wage earners in all parts of the
country.'

The memo concluded with the famous argument that:

'As the Government are sure that they are right both on the facts
of the dispute and on the constitutional issues, any steps which we
may take to communicate the truth dispassionately should be to the
advantage of the Government.'

    Similar sentiments were echoed in a 'Note for Mr. Davidson: the
BBC and the Emergency'. (13) In this Reith argues that the value
and virtue of the BBC lay in its being seen to be 'independent'
from the Government and continues: 'Assuming the BBC is for the
people, and that the Government is for the people, it follows that
the BBC must be for the Government in this crisis too.' The rest of
the memo was of the same order as the 6 May memo, and it was clearly
the case that the overall policy, albeit in a sophisticated and
oblique manner, was one with Baldwin's, though its general tone may
have been slightly more conciliatory than the prime minister's.
The position was made even clearer in the 'Managing Director's
Report to the Board of Directors' dated 18 May. In this, Reith
declared:

'Under the Emergency Regulations Act the Government could have commandeered the BBC, but definite action of this kind was actually
not necessary since a clause in our Licence made it obligatory on us
to broadcast official announcements at any time. They could therefore use us to a considerable extent without definitely comman-
deering.'

He continues (14):

'There could be no question about our supporting the Government
generally, particularly since the General Strike had been declared
illegal.... We could not therefore permit anything which was contrary to the spirit of that judgement, which might have prolonged
or sought to justify the strike, but we were able to give authentic
impartial news of the situation throughout. Apart from the clause
in our Licence the broadcasting of official communiques would have
been demanded irrespective of the political complexions of the
Government.'

This was similar in content and tone to a memo Reith sent to senior
members of his staff on 15 May 1926. (15) Reith's fervent accep-
tance of the 'illegality' ruling was rather hasty since it was subsequently shown that the precise validity of the ruling was in some

doubt. At this stage, Reith felt that the BBC's position was one of
being 'neither commandeered nor free' but was adamant that the BBC
could do nothing which would support the Strike (Reith, 1963).

By 6 May the connection between the BBC and the government had
become a physical one in the sense that Reith and other staff, at
Davidson's request, moved into the Admiralty building on 4 May.
Gladstone Murray, deputy managing director of the BBC, shared an
office with Captain Gordon Munro, one of the assistants to Davidson,
where together they drafted news bulletins (James, 1969, p.246).

What one can see in these internal documents is Reith-as-the-BBC
defining quite clearly what he understands to be the bounds of
legitimate political activity within which the impartiality of the
BBC must fit. Given competing definitions of the situation offered
by the strikers and the State, the Reithian logic was to acknowledge the latter. The rationale behind that logic derived partly
from the perilous position of the BBC and partly from a genuine
attachment by Reith and his senior personnel to the government's
course.

There was a quite clear institutional imperative for the actions
taken by Reith, which effectively meant that the ability of the
company to fulfil its function was only as great as Davidson (for
the government) was willing to allow. This resulted in the remarkable situation where the leader of the official opposition in
Parliament and the Archbishop of Canterbury were refused permission
to broadcast during the Strike.

On the morning of 5 May, Reith had met a deputation of the Parliamentary Labour party and on 7 May was approached by the Labour
MP, William Graham, who had served on the Crawford Committee, with
a request that a Labour member be allowed to broadcast (Briggs,
1961, p.376). The Labour party became more adamant when on 9 May
Viscount Grey broadcast on behalf of the Asquithian Liberals and
'included some bitter strictures on the action of the trade unions'
(ibid, p.376). Ramsay MacDonald, the Labour leader, approached
Reith personally on 10 May and even sent a copy of the transcript
of his proposed text. Reith's inclination was to allow the broadcast but Davidson and Baldwin refused the request, ostensibly on
the grounds that it would set Churchill off again. Reith's diary
indicates that he was rather disturbed at this, particularly since
the BBC was 'to a certain extent controlled' and following Government policy and decisions, while Reith had the unsavoury task of
implementing the policy: 'I do not think that they treat me
altogether fairly'. (16)

On 7 May Reith received the text of a proposed broadcast by the
Archbishop of Canterbury. The gist of the speech was conciliatory,
proposing that the Strike be cancelled, the government subsidy be
renewed for a period and the mine-owners withdraw their suggested
wage-scales. In other words, all the points of contention should
be removed so that negotiations could then take place. Gainford,
the BBC's chairman, replied to the Archbishop that various changes
might be made but added that the decision was ultimately Reith's.
(17) This was not true: Reith showed the text of the speech to
Davidson who told him that it could not be broadcast, again arguing
that this would set Churchill off on his attempts to commandeer the
BBC. Reith informed the Archbishop of the decision and told him

that they could broadcast nothing that would embarrass the government. On 8 May Reith received a letter from the Archbishop expressing surprise at the decision. On the letter Reith has pencilled:
'I made it quite clear that (the broadcast) was dependent on what
the message was' and that whatever the bishops and clergy wished to
say, 'it must not embarrass the government. The greater the authority the more the embarrassment' (Archbishop of Canterbury file).
In his letter of 8 May to the Archbishop, part of which is quoted
in Briggs (1961, p.279), Reith makes the point that he felt justified in his decision not to permit the broadcast because 'it was a
great relief to me to find from you that he (Baldwin) had said that
he would prefer the message not to be broadcast' on the basis of a
respect for Baldwin's judgment 'not *qua* Prime Minister but *qua*
himself.' (18)

   Reith was later to write that both men should have been allowed
to broadcast - 'neither of them would have done the slightest harm
to the position of the government'. His rationale for arguing that
they should have been allowed to speak was on the grounds that their
speeches would have made no difference to the situation. Thus his
apparent liberality on this question rested on pragmatic considerations rather than on principle. He added (Reith, 1963):

'I was justified in not letting them speak, in terms of what would
have happened, or anyhow was likely to have happened, if I had.
The BBC could not say, nor permit to be said, anything that might
have helped to continue the General Strike, neither could it operate
as a strike breaker. It was on the side of the Government, and
should have been, and should be to the extent of supporting the
cause of law and order, and helping in the maintenance of essential
services.'

   It seems likely that the actual reason for the refusal of the
request by the Archbishop was that he was arguing that a compromise
was necessary between the two sides, whereas Baldwin's policy,
despite its later more conciliatory tones, demanded nothing less
than the total surrender by the TUC (Hyde, 1973, p.269):

'"The issue is really quite simple," (Baldwin) remarked to Davidson
... "This is an attempt to take over the function of the Government
by a body that has not been elected. If they succeed it will be
the end of parliamentary democracy which we have taken centuries
to build. There can be no negotiations. It can only end in a
complete surrender".'

   Briggs (1961, p.379) describes this as the 'low-water mark' of
the BBC because it was so clearly existing by 'sufferance'. It
might be more correct to view it as exemplary, the starkest evidence
of the general situation of the BBC vis-a-vis the government. Basic
decisions on content were in effect being made by the deputy chief
civil commissioner, Davidson, rather than by Reith. In later explaining his decisions, Davidson was to write that (James, 1969, p.249):

'The publication of the Archbishop's statement was not in line
either with the general view of the public or the policy of the

Government.... When the Archbishop suggested that negotiations should be started, I think he failed to realise that the contest was fundamentally a Constitutional struggle.'

The commitment of the BBC to the government side was not just a function of the preservation of the 'organization' - there was another dimension altogether. There was in effect a distinct ideological imperative to support the government - a genuinely held belief by Reith that the General Strike could under no circumstances be justified. Reith was a neighbour of Davidson's not only in their residences (19) but also in their thinking about the Strike and the political crisis that it induced. Davidson wrote in a memorandum after the events (James, 1969, p.232):

'It has got to be made absolutely clear, in everything which is written about Baldwin and the General Strike, that his vision and his judgement were clear and decisive, and that he didn't waffle. The idea was always put about that he was under pressure. But there was no question of pressure; he saw the thing as clear as crystal. The decision he took was that there should be no parley ... the Constitution would not be safe until we had won the victory, and the victory depended on the surrender of the TUC. There were many people ... running about the streets like dogs, trying to do something about it, but nothing deflected the simple man - he was simple in this, having come to a decision on principle; he just said "No, I will not accept anything but the surrender of the TUC and the calling off of the strike".'

In the memo of 15 May, quoted in Briggs (1961, p.365), Reith states:

'since the BBC was a national institution, and since the Government in this crisis was acting for the people, apart from any Emergency Powers or clause in our Licence, the BBC was for the government in the crisis too; and that we had to assist in maintaining the essential services of the country, the preservation of law and order, and of the life and liberty of the individual and the community.... Had we been commandeered we could have done nothing in the nature of impartial news, nor could we have in any way helped inspire appreciation of the fact that a prolongation of the stoppage was a sure means of reducing the standard of living, which it was the avowed intention of the Trade Unions to improve. Nor could we have initiated or emphasized statements likely to counteract a spirit of violence and hostility. We felt we might contribute, perhaps decisively, to the attitude of understanding without which goodwill could not be restored.'

What Reith was doing was defining the BBC as an 'organization within the Constitution' (2) and thereby effectively defining impartiality - for specific institutional and ideological reasons - in such a way as to make it synonymous not with a particular party line but with a particular political and moral order within which that line rested and which for the duration of the Strike was deemed to coexist with the Baldwin government. He was clear as to the overall political implications of the situation (Reith, 1963):

'if there had been broadcasting at the time of the French Revolution, there would have been no French Revolution; the Revolution
came from Marseilles to Paris as a rumour. The function of the BBC
was fully as much to kill falsehood as to announce truth; and the
former can derive automatically from the latter.'

The observation of the events of May 1926 by Reith and the BBC
involved a distinction between the national interest as represented
by the government, and the 'threatening forces' of the strikers as
represented by the TUC. Some would observe that that situation is
not dissimilar from the situation today in which the general inflection of, for example, industrial coverage, is couched in an amor-
phous notion of the 'national interest' which operates as an absolute value in relation to which all else is subordinate.
    At one level the subservience to the wishes and needs of one side
was far from total. Messages from both sides were broadcast:
reference was made to the 'British Worker' as well as to the
'British Gazette'; a conscious effort was made to distinguish
between agency copy and government copy, and many of the items
broadcast were objective in the sense that they were accurate
reports of verifiable events. As Hood (1972, p.417) points out,
though, '... accuracy is not in itself proof of objectivity or
neutrality', and what was left out was often more important than
what was included. There was the refusal to allow certain broadcasts, most notably the MacDonald and Canterbury ones, the failure
to rectify factual errors, (21) the broadcasting of requests for
volunteers (i.e. strike breakers, Symons, 1957), and the general
line of the news programmes as characterized, for instance, in a
quite unique form of content, the editorials, which were to lead to
a description of the BBC as '2 LO-quacious'. On 26 April, Nicholls,
the organizer of programmes, wrote a memo to Reith and the director
of educational broadcasting suggesting that 'if the strike comes
off we should make arrangements for some public person to give a
short message each night, just three or four minutes, after the
second general news, on the usual lines of appealing to people to
keep their heads and so on, quite non-political'. (22) On 4 May,
the news announcer was to state:

'Many of you will be missing the editorial chat in your favourite
newspapers, and I hope you will not think we are presuming if we
venture to supply in its place a few words of advice to the ordinary
good citizen. You will not expect from us any comments on the
merits of the present controversy.'

During the Strike they were bland and non-controversial but, after
12 May, they were to be continued in a far more politicized form.
The editorial broadcasts during the days of the Strike were 'designed to have a soothing effect on the nation's nerves and to
reassure them' (Archives), and they dealt with such subjects as
transport arrangements, how to keep calm, how to behave, and so on.
They were largely written by Major Atkinson in his capacity of
assistant director of publicity and head of the emergency news
service.
    Whether the view that the effect of the BBC's broadcasts during

the Strike was actually to dispel rumours, spread intelligence and
good cheer is correct is necessarily in some doubt. What is beyond
doubt is that this was the intended role of the BBC, the consequence
of its relationship with the government. This was highlighted by
the use of the editorials during the period immediately following
the end of the Strike when the miners were still out. There was
detailed co-operation between the government and the BBC to get the
miners back to work. The interests served in this relationship
worked both ways. While it was clearly necessary from the government's point of view to get the miners back by whatever means was
available, it was also in the overall institutional interests of
the BBC to have this new form of programme content developed. This
was noted in a memo on 19 May from Murray to Atkinson in which
Murray stated that the idea of having an identifiable editorial
form was 'to develop the new machinery gradually' which would help
to sustain the influences which the BBC had developed during the
Strike. (23) Reith certainly saw the editorials as a means of
furthering the BBC's interests, and in a letter on 28 May to one of
the governors, Binyon, he said that press criticism of the editorials was 'jealousy of the position we had to occupy during the
Strike' and that the press 'object to anything which would seem to
indicate an increasing importance on the part of Broadcasting'. (24)
On 25 May, the PMG complained about the editorials whose title was
therefore changed, first to 'Editorial Reviews' and then to just
'Reviews'. The objections remained, however, and the PMG demanded
to see the scripts before they were broadcast. As these then had a
habit of piling up in his wastepaper basket the BBC took the hint
and abandoned the whole idea of editorials.

Nevertheless, they were used by the government to 'get at' the
miners. In a memo to Reith on 21 May, Gladstone Murray outlined
the details of a meeting he had had with Davidson who had requested
that the BBC do an editorial on the miners' dispute. He wrote that
Davidson had suggested that the BBC,

'might do a valuable service in the holiday period by using our
editorials to give an accurate and authoritative account of the
exact position, explaining for instance that the present position
in the mines is neither a strike nor a lock-out and also giving
some account of the statistics of the actual amount of wages paid
in the mining industry, emphasising the very small proportion of
miners who are on the lower scale. He thought that we might also
go so far as to call attention to the sort of creeping paralysis
effect which the continued mining deadlock had on the whole of the
industry in the country.'

He added that (25):

'(the) government want to get at the miners over the heads of their
leaders. We would only be justified in countenancing this kind of
thing if we are convinced that the national interest demanded the
short-circuiting of the miners' leaders.... They (the government
and Davidson) feel that we might do some good now by preaching the
doctrine of cooperation, even ad nauseum.'

In a quite remarkably explicit document written about this meeting
with the deputy chief civil commissioner and the implementation of
his suggestions, Murray wrote on 25 May (26):

'I took away from my interview with Mr. Davidson a very strong
feeling that while we were to keep clear of controversy over
Whitsun, we were nonetheless to establish the status of our editorial reviews and to get people into the habit of listening to
them.... I agreed to a series of editorials commencing on Friday and
including last night, which may be summarised as follows: *Friday
21 May*. Lockout or Strike - A simple definition of the position
for general information following the lines of my interview with
Mr. Davidson. It should also be noted that Friday's editorial
concluded with the following sentence: "The cold fact that we must
deal with is the fact that somehow our basic industry has been a
allowed to come to a standstill and must be restarted." Then on
Saturday our editorial was entitled "Coal and Countryside". Herein
we stressed the creeping paralysis point which I called attention
to in the account of my interview with Mr. Davidson....
    'On Saturday night we linked our editorial with the topical
spirit of the Feast of the Church of Whit Sunday. The whole idea
in this was to convey the "bring together" conception and to get
people thinking of fundamental issues such as: "More results for
given coal, and more comfort for given wates". It should be noted
that we keep constantly to the text of the Sammuel Report, a point
specifically emphasised by Mr. Davidson. Then we come to the
editorial last night, May 24. The underlying idea of this was to
stimulate confidence in the miners. *We definitely set out so to
construe the recent utterances of the leaders of the miners to give
the impression that they were moving in the direction of settlement*
.... In pursuance of the atmosphere of restoring confidence, we
camouflaged the interpretation of the miners' leaders utterances by
suggesting on purely humanitarian grounds and apart from the
immediate issues, a Government declaration of goodwill towards
family allowances and both.' (emphasis added)

    The General Strike certainly left the BBC as a major news source,
and it was during this period that the first significant definitions
began to emerge from politicians of the power of the broadcast
media. In his diary of 4 May, Reith notes (Reith, 1963):

'I went with the Admiralty Deputy Secretary to lunch at the Travel-
lers Club ... the Prime Minister was there and immediately he saw
me he left the people he had been talking with and came over. I
mention this because it showed that he knew what was what, and who
was who, at this time of crisis.'

As we have seen in some detail Baldwin was not the only one who knew
what was what and who was who. Reith further recognized that the
crisis was a unique opportunity to make significant and irredeemable
excursions into the news monopoly of the press and into the realm
of 'controversial broadcasting' - it was an opportunity he did not
let slip by. More than anything the May events of 1926 clarified
the context within which 'impartiality' functions - involving an

almost total, if oblique, accommodation to government needs and interests.

When the end of the Strike was announced on 12 May, Reith read a message from the King and then the traditional hymn 'Jerusalem' was played. Nothing was more appropriate to the role of the BBC in the Strike than the manner of this announcement. To turn to such established features of an established order was a metaphorical sigh that the crisis had passed and that the political and moral order with which the BBC had identified throughout remained intact. (27)

Appreciation of the BBC's role was quick to follow. There was much appreciation within government circles for the efforts of the BBC. On 17 May, Reith received a letter from the prime minister which thanked him for his help during the Emergency and added: 'you and all the members of your staff may rest assured that your loyal service has earned the warm appreciation of the government'. (28) Davidson, the civil commissioner, wrote to Gladstone Murray that: 'For myself I can only thank you again for your help without which our department could not have stood the strain that was imposed upon it throughout the Strike.' (29) To which Murray replied: 'I feel very strongly that in the national interest it is more than desirable that your contact with our service, both official and unofficial, should become permanent.' (30) Numerous newspapers expressed their own appreciation of the BBC: 'For our news, for the dispelling of false rumour and for the pronouncements of great public men upon the situations we thank the Voice from the Air' 'Herts and Essex Observer', 15 May 1926. There were, one might add, no such appreciations from the TUC side.

The overall conclusion to be drawn from the General Strike as a case study is looked at in the light of the general conclusions to this discussion of the external context of broadcasting. There is, however, a very important point to be made about the role of the BBC. The BBC's claim was, and indeed still is, that it was impartial because it only related news and ipso facto told the 'truth'. This claim was, anyhow, overstated with, for example, the failure to correct errors, the refusal to allow particular personalities to broadcast and the general line of the broadcasts and the editorials. It is also true, however, that telling 'the truth' via the straight-forward relating of facts can have an important propaganda role to play. There is no doubt from reading through the various memos and numerous expressions of intent that the BBC's coverage was specifically aimed toward a particular end, which was the defeat of the Strike. Hugh Greene (1969, p.20) once defined propaganda as 'an attempt to impose your own way of thinking, your own views of the situation, on the (opponents) ... and then, this having been achieved, lead them to behave in the way you desire'. Greene was connected with propaganda against Germany, the Malayan communists and the Arabs. Crusically he adds: 'There would not be much doubt either about the means to be used: to tell the truth within the limits of the information at our disposal and to tell it consistently and frankly' (Greene, 1969, p.21). Illusions and allusions to concepts of truth and impartiality, far from indivisible concepts concepts, have always figured prominently in British political propaganda. (31)

It is clearly wrong, however, to move from the appearance of impartial or balanced coverage to the argument that this somehow 'proves' that the organization and the programmes it produces are pristine and unpolluted by the views and needs of particular interests within society. Clearly in wartime it would not be denied that the intent of broadcasting, whatever its form, was to serve a specific interest, that is, the national interest. Yet in the context not of international peace but intranational strife the purpose and function of broadcasting was also to serve particular interests; those of the State, and therefore the interests which identified with or were represented by that structure. I think it is clear from the preceding account that the actual relationships of power and commitments of ideology in a crisis throw into sharp relief the actual as opposed to the assumed meaning of broadcasting's 'impartiality'. The potential for partiality within the broad framework of apparent impartiality was ably summed up by R.H.S. Crossman, one of Britain's foremost propagandists during the War:(Crossman, 1952):

'We discovered, after many experiments in Dr. Goebbels' technique, that the truth pays. It is a complete delusion to think of the brilliant propagandist as being a professional liar. The brilliant propagandist is the man who tells the truth, or that selection of the truth which is requisite for his purpose, and tells it in such a way that the recipient does not realise that he is receiving any propaganda.... From what I am saying there arises this conclusion - if the art of propaganda is to conceal that you are doing propaganda then the central substance of propaganda is hard, correct information.'

Chapter 9

THE RETIRING OF HUGH GREENE

A PROLOGUE TO DECLINE

When Hugh Greene was appointed director general (DG) of the BBC in
July 1959 and again when he announced his decision to leave that
post in July 1968 there was a quite remarkable level of praise and
goodwill extended towards him. To many it seemed that the personification of the BBC's independence and new-found creativity had been
destroyed and that, as Sir Robert Lusty was later to say, with his
eclipse by Hill a curtain had fallen across the past. Harold
Wilson's understanding of the concept of impartiality and that exercised by those under the tutelage of Greene did not, it seemed,
correspond. The fact that one had vanquished the other seemed,to
Greene's fellow journalists and broadcasters to bode ill for the
future of broadcasting.
    In a fascinating piece in the 'Sunday Pictorial' (26 May, 1959)
about Greene's appointment, Malcolm Muggeridge pays glowing tribute
to 'our man in the BBC'. Greene, Muggeridge declares, 'is on any
showing a capital choice. He is a man of unusual intelligence and
perception ... tall, whimsical, adventurous and kindly. His attitude towards the established social order is well this side of
idolatry.' He wishes that Greene rid the BBC of 'the many mandarins
who have lingered on from the monopolistic sound broadcasting time'
for their repressive, irritating and muffling effect on the BBC.
Also, that he not 'bother himself about the abounding protests which
inevitably fall round his head'. Greene, he claims, can be indif-
ferent to commercial and political pressures, needn't pursue a
mass audience, needn't accept criticisms about programmes. 'What
a chance for Greene! How devoutly I hope that he makes a great
success of it.' 'The Star' said that Greene 'does suggest the best
kind of uncle - the kind who isn't stuffy, prefers chuckles to a
frown; wants his nephews and nieces to treat serious things seriously, but doesn't wish to spoil anybody's fun.' And soon the
response to the appointment was uniform, an almost total enthusiasm
for his accession to the director generalship.
    When his retirement was announced, press comment was principally
absorbed in the question 'why?', summed up in the 'Guardian' leader
of 16 July 1968, 'Did he jump or was he pushed?' Most of the copy

made much of the statement at the press conference announcing his
retirement in which Greene had said that 'it is my personal
decision. I do not regard myself as being kicked upstairs but
rather as walking upstairs with pleasure'. However, it was widely
believed that since Hill's appointment in 1967 there had been a good
deal of conflict between the two men and the events of July 1968
were the culmination of a long-drawn-out battle.

    Later discussion of these events has been dominated by the
observation that Greene as DG had an enormous effect on the whole
style and content of BBC programming. Worsley (1970, p.247) states
that Greene 'carried the BBC struggling and kicking out of its
Auntie image into something much more relevant to the decade'.
Black (1972, p.210) talks about the 'Death of Aunty' and describes
the period 1956-66 as the golden era of BBC TV, and Bridson (1971,
p.288), in his autobiography, declares 'for the first time, under
his leadership, broadcasting seemed to have caught up with the
times; on occasion it even managed to pull slightly ahead of them'.
Shulman (1973, p.102), speaking of the position in 1967 when he
feels that pressure began to build up on Greene, states, 'after
7 years as DG, Sir Hugh Greene could feel that he had helped push
the BBC right into the centre of the swirling forces that were
changing life in Britain, and that by its activities the BBC was not
merely reflecting and recording these changes but was helping to
agitate them as well.' In a discussion of 'the end of an era' Hood
('Spectator', 19 July 1968) argues that 'only the enemies of
enlightenment, the narrow puritan, the grass roots censors, the
petty minded (among them some politicians) will celebrate the end of
his period in office'. Bernard Levin (1972) in his review of the
whole decade of the sixties states that Hugh Carleton Greene,
'sensed much earlier than most figures in positions of comparable
responsibility which way the wind of the times was blowing, probably
did more than any other individual in the BBC, before or since, to
bury Auntie's Presbyterian ethic for ever' and that under 'the wily
and on the whole most courageous leadership of Hugh Carleton Greene
(the BBC) had right at the start of the decade struck out for the
shores of the future.'

    The admiration in the 'obituaries' which flooded forth from col-
leagues and chroniclers is clear. Others, however, did not see him
in quite the same light and it was to be the crystallizing of the
views of these oppositional forces within the person of Harold
Wilson that was ultimately to lie behind Greene's retirement. A
recent edition of 'The Viewer and Listener' (1974, vol. 10, no. 2),
the paper of Mary Whitehouse's National Viewers and Listeners
Association, quotes from Robert Dougall's recent autobiography
(1974):

'If there were any one man who more than any other helped to shape
and influence opinion in Britain in the sixties it must surely have
been Hugh Greene.... It may not be just a coincidence that by the
end of his nine and a half years in power this country was riven
with doubts and anarchy was in the air.'

Throughout the eleven years of her work for NVALA Mary Whitehouse
has castigated the role played by Greene, and the inclusion of this

quote five years after Greene ceased to have any kind of editorial
connection with the BBC is evidence enough of the pervasive hostility felt towards him. Whitehouse is only the most persistent of
his critics. The whole period of his director generalship was
marked by a persistent carping from political circles. In January
1964 the political establishment awarded Greene a knighthood, but
by March 1964 sections of that establishment were making serious
attempts to effectively dethrone the new knight. In January 1964
the chairman of the BBC, Sir Arthur Fforde, resigned for health
reasons, and Sir James Duff was appointed chairman until July of
that year. The search for a new chairman provided Greene's opponents with an opportunity to devalue his apparently dominating role
within the corporation. On the 7 March an item in the 'Daily
Express' spoke of the government's efforts to find a hard-line
chairman who would stem the excesses of Greene's BBC. Other reports
spoke of 'curbing Greene's power' and 'Chairman of stature for the
BBC sought'. Support for Greene came from among others, the
'Express', the 'Observer', from MacLachlan, a member of the general
advisory council, in an article in the 'Sunday Telegraph', and from
Harold Wilson. Bevins, in his account of his years in political
life, does not expressly relate to the 'curb Greene' campaign,
though he does detail his own 'analysis' of what was wrong during
Greene's time. He declares (1965, p.116):

'The Chairman and the Governors are appointed by the Prime Minister
with the consent of the Queen. They ought to be the governing body.
It always seemed to me that they were governed by the professionals.
In my time and before I am sure that the real power was wielded by
the Director General, Sir Hugh Greene, and the top professionals.
They knew all the answers. The Director General is of course
appointed not by the Government but by the BBC and for all practical
purposes the other top men and women are recommended and appointed
by the Director General. In the result the traditional independence
of the BBC is stretched too far because the professionals are not
really responsible to anyone but themselves.'

Greene himself denies that the 'curb Greene' campaign was in any way
significant (1):

'How influential was the 'curb Greene' campaign of Tory Ministers?
Was it an important feature of your life and did it have any bearing
on what you did?'

'No, I learnt all about it. It was run at a low level in the Conservative government by the then PMG and even more by the assistant
PMG, who talked to newspapers and so on. But it had no support
higher up in the government at all. Macmillan was always very easy
going in these matters, and I was on very good terms with Butler.
So I never really felt threatened by it. Macmillan didn't mind all
these satirical programmes and so on in the least. It wasn't in
any way really serious. I had my sources of information and know
that it was not a high level affair.'

In March 1965 calls for Greene's resignation from two MPs, James

Dance (2) and Sir Leslie Thomas, followed a sketch on the satire
programme 'Not So Much a Programme' dealing with the question of
Roman Catholic attitudes to birth control, though support for Greene
came from a number of Labour MPs including Tom Driberg. In April
1965 the Church of Scotland attacked the BBC's coverage of religion
and morals, attacked a speech by Greene in which he said that the
BBC should be ahead of public opinion, and called for a viewers
council. (3) May 1965 saw another attack by James Dance, supported
this time by Stratton Mills, and in the same month Whitehouse called
yet again for his resignation. On 1 June 1965 there was a headline
in the 'Telegraph', 'BBC attacked by "Fed Up" Tory MPs'.

There was an assessment of Greene's role not only by other professional communicators, but also by a number of politicians and by
moral reformists who argued that Greene was having an adverse effect
on programme standards and therefore on the whole moral climate of
the community. These attacks on Greene made not the slightest bit
of difference to his attitudes. Indeed he quite forcefully counter-
attacked, and in a speech in Rome in February 1965 - this was the
speech which received the rebuke from the Church of Scotland - he
placed his opponents in the context of a discussion on the 'delicate
balance' between 'freedom and responsibility'. He stated to the
assembled clergy (Greene, 1969, pp.100-1):

'We have to resist attempts at censorship. As Professor Hoggart ...
has noted recently, these attempts at censorship come not merely
from what he describes as the "old Guardians" (senior clergy,
writers of leading articles in newspapers, presidents of national
voluntary organizations) who like to think of themselves as uphol-
ders of cultural standards, although, in many cases, they lack the
qualities of intellect and imagination to justify that claim. They
come nowadays also from groups - Hoggart calls them the "new
Populists" - which do not claim to be "Guardians" but claim to
speak for "ordinary decent people" and to be "forced to take a stand
against" *unnecessary* dirt, *gratuitous* sex, *excessive* violence, and
so on. These "new Populists" will attack whatever does not under-
write a set of prior assumptions, assumptions which are anti-intel-
lectual and unimaginative. Superficially this seems like a "grass-
roots" movement. In practice it can threaten a dangerous form of
censorship - censorship which works by causing artists and writers
not to take risks, not to undertake those adventures of the spirit
which must be at the heart of every truly new creative work.'

While Greene always remained personally adamant in his hostility to
cries for moral reform what was probably significant is that such
opinions were never located within the main body of political life-
in other words, they were never possessing of power. They were not
only beyond the mainstream of Greene's thought but were also beyond
that of the ruling councils within the main parties. However, with
the emergence of Harold Wilson's second administration in 1966 there
began a period in which hostility to the BBC in general, and Greene
in particular, crystallized in the Labour leader's mind. (4) It is
the intellectual perspectives of Harold Wilson, his response to the
BBC's coverage of politics, particularly during the 1966 election,
that lie behind the events of July 1967 and behind the retirement
of Hugh Greene.

Relations between Greene and Wilson during the period 1963 (when Wilson became leader) to 1966 were described by Greene as 'rather friendly' and it is certainly the case that Wilson had defended Greene against the onslaughts of Tory MPs. Williams (1972, p.233) states:

'There is no doubt that Harold has been extremely angry with the BBC on a number of occasions over the years of the Labour Government and since. Before 1964 his relations were very amicable with all levels within the BBC.'

In his memoirs, Hill (1974, p.100) refers to a meeting with Wilson in which he gave 'examples of the Corporation's wickedness, many of which went back long before my time'. In the 1966 election the BBC hired a whole carriage of Wilson's train from Liverpool to London and built a whole studio in the carriage, anticipating a 'victory interview'. Wilson refused to be interviewed by the BBC, despite their lavish preparations and instead granted an interview to ITN. Marcia Williams (1972, p.232) describes ITN as the epitome of impartiality and fairness. 'What there was (at ITN) that was missing elsewhere was the implicit protection against untrue bias, and where bias occurred, machinery for appeal.' She contrasts this with the iniquities of the BBC coverage of elections (Williams, 1972, p.233):

'anyone who watched the BBC coverage of the last election campaign with a fair eye can really be in little doubt over the selective editing of films, and the placing of coverage within a programme. The Tory case seemed to be put over clearly and successfully with Edward Heath's own personal coverage of the highest quality. Labour coverage was scrappy and uneven.'

And the problem as she and Wilson see it lies in the stupefaction of an oversized bureaucracy (Williams, 1972, p.234):

'just as in the Civil Service ... there is always a top tier of special people who appoint the same sort of special people to follow them, while just below there is a second tier of extremely imagin- ative competent people, who if only they could break through would alter the whole complexion and character of the Corporation.'

It is unclear as to just who she means by 'special people' (though one might reasonably assume that Greene is one). It is necessary to point out, however, that if Greene did anything at all he sought to give the 'extremely imaginative' their head: that he did so, that there was no control over zealous producers, was in fact one of the charges laid against him. It may well be that the abilities of the producers working under him, particularly in the period 1962-4, were the very stuff upon which Greene's reputation and career fed. At the same time one can only draw the conclusion, as will become clear as this argument develops, that the events of July 1967 were speci- fically aimed at strengthening one section of the top tier within the BBC (i.e. the governors) at the expense of another section (i.e. the executive). That this was to be the specific intention, and that Williams realized this is made clear (Williams, 1972, pp. 197-8):

'Before we went off for our holiday that year, Harold appointed Lord Hill Chairman of the BBC. This was greeted with some bewilderment, though Harold had gone to great pains to consider all the people who were qualified to take on the job from within the organization itself. If one was going to have a Conservative, he felt it was best to have the real thing, and a man who had already presided over an organization where impartiality had to be observed because of the Act under which the ITA operates. He felt Lord Hill might even be able to educate the BBC in how to operate a broadcasting system on these terms, rather than in the spirit of the independent empire the they had preserved for themselves.'

It is certainly the case that there is a relatively widespread feeling within sections of the Labour party that the BBC is a bastion of Conservative rule: consider for example the writings and speeches of Benn and Crossman. It therefore remains ironic that a former Conservative minister was chosen to dull the impact of the corporation's partiality.

There is a persistent attribution of a relationship between the presence of Hugh Greene in the BBC and the state of being of social and political life in the nation. It is at this level in the first instance that one can situate the events surrounding his retirement. What one needs to consider here is the precise meaning the events of July 1967 have for programme content in political television: do they tell us much about the nature of 'control' exercised by the State on the broadcasting organization and therefore on the making of political programmes. As I think will become clear, one can in fact begin to detect certain influences and processes, but the picture that emerges is not of a State machine riding roughshod over the broadcasting structure, rather it is one in which a redefinition of the overall purpose of the BBC was intended to flow from a marginal readjustment of the distribution of power and control at the very highest levels of the Corporation.

ARRIVAL AND DEPARTURE: THE NARRATIVE OF DECLINE

On the early morning of 15 June 1967, Lord Normanbrook, chairman of the BBC board of governors since 1964, died. A month later on the evening of 25 July Lord Hill, chairman of the ITA, was contacted at his home by Philip Philips, television correspondent of the 'Sun'. Philips wanted to know if it was true that Hill was to become the director general of the BBC. Hill was surprised by this suggestion - as well the head of the BBC's competitor might be - and described it as 'a load of nonsense'. Hill, perplexed by the suggestion, contacted the postmaster general, Edward Short, to be informed that he had only heard a rumour 'from a Daily Mirror executive'. Shortly afterwards, however, Short returned the call, asking Hill to meet Wilson at the House of Commons at 2.30 p.m. the following day. Hill describes the meeting (1974, pp.69-70):

'Punctually at 2.30 p.m. I was called in to find the Prime Minister
in a relaxed mood and smoking a big cigar. Accompanied by Edward
Short, the Postmaster General, he opened by saying that I had done
a good job at Independent Television. The post of Chairman of the
BBC was, as I knew, vacant following Lord Normanbrook's death.
Would I go to the BBC in the office of the chairman of the governors? The press had got wind of what was in his mind and it would be
convenient if I could give my answer forthwith with a view to an
announcement at midnight.'

Hill then refers to a number of stories which appeared in the press
over the next few days, the gist of which were that his appointment
was motivated by a desire to get rid of Hugh Greene. Hill, as one
might imagine, was vehement in his denial of this and eagerly
accepted the appointment since 'the invitation was irresistible'.
(5) This was to cause complete incredulity among many sections of
the BBC since they could not understand how anyone could make such
a move, could go over to the opposition at only a moment's notice.
Hill informed Robert Fraser, the director general of the ITA,
immediately upon leaving Wilson, and informed the governors of the
ITA that evening. Wilson and Short must have discussed the appointment, if only in the period immediately before Hill was summoned
into the prime minister's room. Wilson was certainly aware that the
appointment would cause a furore, and made it perfectly clear that
he was so aware at an 'Economist' function the evening before.
     On the same day, 26 July, Sir Robert Lusty, acting chairman of
the BBC, received two phone calls from the postmaster general. The
first asked if he could call upon him at the Post Office on the
afternoon of the following day. Shortly after, the PMG called again
(Lusty, 1974):

'this time with a note of urgency. Mr. Short was extremely sorry
but an emergency had arisen. It was imperative that he should see
me that Wednesday afternoon. Would I kindly be at the Post Office
at half-past four?'

He was told by the PMG that their future plans for the BBC had
'leaked' and this was what had necessitated the urgent meeting.
Lusty was informed that the name of the new chairman was Charles
Hill, that the announcement would be made that evening at 8.10 p.m.
and that he would take up the post on 1 September. Lusty's response
to this information was perhaps predictable (1974):

'The full horror of the situation numbed my mind. All I could
wonder was how to break the news to Hugh Greene and the others. It
was the end of the BBC as I knew it and the end of Hugh Greene too.
After 8 years I knew what was thought of Charles Hill by the BBC...'

Lusty returned straight to Broadcasting House and Hugh Greene's room
and in the doom-laden terms which were beginning to characterize
these events told him of the appointment:

'I'm sorry but I bring you the worst possible news. Charles Hill is
being switched over to us. He is to be our next Chairman. I might
just as well have shot the DG.'

Greene's immediate response was that he would phone Short and then resign. He did phone but was persuaded from resigning by his assistant, Oliver Whitley, and by Lusty.

At 11 o'clock on the following day, Thursday 27 July, the board of governors of the BBC met, by now aware of the appointment from the morning papers. Lusty describes the meeting, 'a shocked and numbed assembly met me there. The resentment and mystification was towards an apparent act of political malice.... As a Board we had not been impressed by Lord Hill's chairmanship of the ITA' (Lusty, 1974).

The reaction within the BBC was a mixture of sadness and anger. The dominant impression was that the end of a golden age had been heralded, that Greene was bound to go, 'that the curtain had fallen on the past'. Hill himself was very clear as to this mood and sought to explain it (1974, p.141)

'Greene had seen that during my spell at Brompton Road I had streng- thened the role of the Authority at the expense of the Director General and no doubt he feared that I would seek to do the same at Portland Place and as a result lose something of his public standing. Bearing in mind also that the Authority had actually lunched with and listened to Mrs Whitehouse, he was wary of my approach to controversial programmes. This was part of the back- ground of suspicion and animosity against which I began at the BBC. Not unnaturally I resented the mood of courteous hostility that greeted me and it was some time before my resentment died.'

In his account of the period, Lusty (1974) describes the corporation prior to Hill as being in 'good heart' under the direction of the 'brilliantly contentious' Greene. With the latter working in harmony with Normanbrook, 'The sixties had seen public service broadcasting in its finest hour of liberation and only a few were aware that distant signals were faintly ominous.' He tells us that there 'existed in Normanbrook's mind some anxieties that the forces aligning against the Director General were becoming more formidable, and that they derived from sources of much greater consequence than Mrs Mary Whitehouse.' But precisely what were these forces and how did they perceive their connections with the appointment of Hill?

'In the introductory paragraph to your article in the "New States- man" you state "the sixties had seen public service broadcasting in its finest hour of liberation and only a few were aware that distant signals were faintly ominous". Who exactly were "the few"?

'Well I don't think I was referring to any specific number of people. I think it was simply an impression one began to get that there were doubting voices being raised as to whether the BBC was going too far in Hugh Greene's policy of opening windows and so on. It all seemed to be going very well and it engendered an excitement in broadcasting, particularly within the BBC. But part of the operation of the governors so to speak is to pick up the climate outside, and I think that one was becoming aware that there were doubts being expressed by rather wider areas than Mary Whitehouse.'

'What were the particular signals that you picked up?'

'You can simply say that there was a general air about it, and of course they were nearly always engendered unfortunately by accidents and such programmes as 'TW3' and the Wednesday Play. It was nothing one could put one's finger on.'

'You also mention a conversation with Normanbrook in which you suggest that he began to appreciate that difficulties would arise and you refer to his anxieties about forces of greater consequence than Mrs Whitehouse. What were the anxieties and difficulties?'

'Well that was part of a lunchtime discussion we had. I was vice-chairman and he was chairman and we were covering the general scene and wondering what might happen if anything happened to Hugh Greene, if he were to walk under the proverbial bus, who might take over and so on. I think Lord Normanbrook was becoming a little worried by some of the complaints which were reaching him about what people regarded as BBC blunders in the field of religion and good taste and all the rest of it.'

'Presumably though, the reference to people more significant than Mary Whitehouse refers to senior politicians, people of that stature?'

'Well I don't know about politicians, no I wouldn't say it was particularly politicians, but the BBC is always news to an extent that the IBA certainly isn't. Anything at all sensational, or less than sensational, with a BBC programme would be commented upon far in excess of any comment on any IBA programme. You just sense that there are certain anxieties or a certain lack of confidence, whatever it might be. Part of the chariman's job is to wonder about these things and to see whether the director general is going in the right direction.' (6)

The formulation of just what these pressures, anxieties etc., actually consisted of is not particularly well articulated, to an extent that might lead one to believe that their formulation in the article was perhaps informed by post hoc reasoning. One must of course allow for the fading of memory over time and the protection of confidences, but Greene himself doubts the wisdom of placing too much emphasis on Normanbrook's signals:

' Sir Robert states that Normanbrook began to pick up signals, danger signals. Did Normanbrook ever intimate to you that things were happening, or that there were possible difficulties ahead? Did he ever discuss the dangers, the "signals"?'

'My own feeling is that Bob Lusty is perhaps exaggerating a bit there. (7) I can remember one talk which you could regard as along those lines. You remember there was a White Paper under the Labour government - it must have been in late 66 or early 67 - in which the decision was made about the BBC starting Radio One to deal with the pirates, and also to start local radio. I think there was some

decision on the licence fee in the same White Paper. (8)   In a way
it was everything that one had been fighting for, everything had
gone one's way. I remember Lord Normanbrook saying to me rather
gloomily, this is going to turn people against us, it's too good.
And I said to him, however that may be, when one's fighting for
something, when one's trying to achieve victory, one can't try to
achieve half a victory. I think he may have felt that we had done
too well and that was in my mind too, that somehow the BBC had done
too well out of Pilkington for its own good.'

*'Did Normanbrook specify at all? Throughout your career as DG
there were calls for your resignation. Was there something apart
from that, pressure from a very high level which Normanbrook was
beginning to pick up?'*

'I don't think so because I was on very good terms with Ted Short
and he was an enormous improvement on Wedgy Benn as PMG. I don't
know. I find it difficult to understand these signals.'

   There does not appear to be any clear sense in which one could
point to events and personalities which would logically entail the
feeling that the appointment was the logical culmination of a long
process of incursion upon the 'independence' of the broadcasting
organization. With the appointment of Hill, though, ill-formed and
little-articulated notions crystallized into an assumption that
Wilson's motive was to destroy the confidence of the BBC and to
force Greene to resign. David Haworth in the 'Observer' (30 July
1967) wrote a piece with the title 'The Feud that brings Hill to the
BBC': 'the Prime Minister with this appointment has given notice to
the BBC that henceforward things cannot be the same again, and that
the Corporation and the somewhat free-wheeling policies it has
enjoyed under Sir Hugh will have to change.'
   On hearing of the appointment Greene and Lusty wrote a 'short
formal letter' to the postmaster general 'acquainting him with the
BBC's anxieties in the matter'. Following this, on 9 August, Lusty
had written to all the governors stating that following an amicable
lunch with Hill on 8 August he now felt that 'many of the anxieties
which we have been feeling become much less substantial and my own
fears for the future are to an encouraging extent diminished'. He
sent a copy of this 'new situation' letter to the PMG to balance
the earlier 'anxiety' letter, only to receive a rebuke from Short
for having had the anxieties in the first place, 'There is no clear
implication that something was not right about Lord Hill's appointment' (Short, in Lusty, 1974). Lusty in turn replied to the rebuke
using the argument that the apprehension did not arise from personal
hostility to Lord Hill but rather from the fact that people in the
BBC were aghast at the fact that the chief of their main broadcasting rival was suddenly transformed into their chief. What he
did not mention in his letter to Short but what he certainly implies
in his article was that the move was seen as a definite attempt to
force Greene into resignation, and that this was Harold Wilson's
main motive. (9) In his article Lusty (1974) states: 'The appointment was certainly no act of charity or goodwill on Wilson's part.
But many continue to think that it was an act of premeditated

malice.   This I accepted for a while but later grew to doubt.'   And
what made him doubt it was the revelation that Wilson had first
offered the post to Lord Aylestone (then Herbert Bowden).   He had
been told about this by sources in Ireland and having checked it he
believes it to be the case, 'For various reasons I now believe it to
be true and it demolishes the theory that Harold Wilson acted in
pursuit of any long, deep laid plan.'   Some of the confusion over
this stems from the 'missing evidence', though Wilson does imply in
his brief account that there was nothing unnatural in the appointment, though he does not mention the offer to Aylestone.   In a
later interview, when asked how he viewed Wilson's motives in light
of the new evidence, Lusty was not as definite as he had been in
the article:

'Well, I don't quite know, I've never been able to discover really
what Wilson's motives were.   I think Hugh Greene and Aylestone
would probably have got along quite well, but I certainly believe
that it was the appointment of Hill which capsized Greene.   You've
met him and he will say that it made no difference to his direction
of the BBC, but I think it took the spirit out of him, I think he
simply couldn't understand it and at that point he became bored.
There were other things going on in his life too, it upset him.
The association between himself and Hill could never be other than
difficult because he had absolutely no respect for him, and the one
thing that the BBC director general must have for his chairman, or
Hugh Greene must have, is respect.'

He added, however,

'There was complete bewilderment as to why the Government, and in
particular Harold Wilson, had done this.   What was the point, what
was behind it all.   If there was nothing behind it it was still a
most extraordinary appointment, and I'm quite convinced in my own
mind that a purpose was to dislodge Greene.'

   Subjective perceptions of what was happening and why, were more
important throughout this period than were any objectively accurate
assessment of the underlying motives.   From the point of view of
understanding the relationship between the political and broadcasting spheres as exemplified by Hill's appointment, one cannot,
however, discuss only subjective perceptions.   Greene's own perception of the motives is clear, and does provide enough evidence for
one to believe that it is substantially accurate.   He was interviewed for this book both before and after the publication of the
Hill memoir and the Lusty article.   During the first interview he
was asked about the circumstances and motivations of the appointment:

'It really revolves around the strange character of Harold Wilson,
with whom I'd been on rather friendly terms when he was leader of
the opposition, during his first administration between 1964 and
1966 - his touchiness, his belief that people are conspiring against
him all the time.   This reached its height during the 1966 election
when he felt that the BBC was slighting him and what not - and

indeed the BBC did not behave in every way very sensibly in following protocol and making arrangements in the proper way for things
like an interview by Harold Wilson on his way back to London after
the results were out. So we brought this period of difficulty on
ourselves to some extent.

'Harold Wilson did not have the tolerance of Macmillan about
being made even gentle fun of. And I think it's quite clear that
in his mind I became associated with all that he disliked. This
was a long process. After all, Harold Wilson became prime minister
in the autumn of 64, there was the spring election of 66. Normanbrook and I discussed these things quite frankly with Harold Wilson
and though one wasn't always able to persuade him that he was wrong,
one could talk to him.

'Then came the death of Normanbrook in the spring of 67, and then
in the late summer of that year the appointment of Charles Hill as
chairman. I think there is good reason to believe that one of
Harold Wilson's motives was the expectation that I would resign
immediately. It was not a direct attack on the output of the BBC
or an attempt at political influence, because whatever one may say
about Charles Hill's record as chairman, so far as resisting political attempts at exerting influence from outside he was perfectly
good at helping to resist those. Dick Crossman put it in a piece in
the "New Statesman" that Wilson had two objectives: one, to get rid
of me, and two, to break the self-confidence of the BBC.'

'Were they the same thing?'

'Well not quite the same thing. I think Dick said that one was
achieved fairly quickly and the other took rather longer. You know
these things are awfully difficult to handle with exactness and
therefore tend to be oversimplified. I wouldn't say that I knew the
full background to this development myself.'

'What was your initial reaction upon hearing that Hill was to become
the chairman?'

'Of such a rage as I have never experienced about any other event
in my life. I very nearly decided to resign but then I thought to
myself, that's what Harold Wilson wants, so I decided not to.'

When the Aylestone revelation was mentioned during the course of
a second interview, he still affirmed his belief that the motive was
his removal. He had been informed the morning after the appointment
by a member of the BBC's political staff that 'excellent sources'
revealed that one of the motives was the expectation that Greene
would resign immediately. (10) While there is some confusion over
the precise details of the appointment, it is widely believed that
the intention was to force Greene's resignation, to weaken the post
of the director general and to strengthen that of the chairman.

Hill had his first meeting with Lusty (at the latter's suggestion) at lunch on the 8 August 1967, and with Greene (at Hill's
instigation) on the afternoon of the same day. (11) At the lunch
with Lusty a number of issues were raised, Lusty suggesting that a
social gathering be held with the board of management and an

informal meeting with the board of governors, both of which Hill
declined. Lusty then offered to take the chair at the first board
of governors meeting attended by Hill, which he also declined. Hill
describes Lusty's demeanour in this meeting as 'sadly contemptuous'
(Hill, 1974, p.75). At this meeting Hill had also mentioned his
wish that he had his own secretary rather than having to share a
secretarial pool with the director general - which had always been
the convention within Broadcasting House. He tells us in his
memoirs that prior to the 8 August lunch he had had something of a
running battle with BBC officials over the question of his secre-ary
tary, over his use of a car other than that provided by the BBC, and
over the use of a colour television set installed in his home (rent
paid for a year) by the ITA only a few weeks previously. The
pettiness of these squabbles was superseded by a later request that
he have a new room in Broadcasting House. This has come to hold
tremendous symbolic and real significance in the view of those
involved and needs to be detailed.

Hill states that soon after his arrival he raised the matter of
the office (1974, pp.80-1):

'The office traditionally used by the chairman was on the third
floor separated from the director general's office by the room
occupied by his secretaries. My secretary was a flight of stairs
away on the fourth floor on the grounds that there was no room for
her on the third floor. My office I thought resembled an oak-lined
coffin, airless and sunless, and after an hour or so the atmosphere
became heavy and stuffy. I asked for another and more cheerful
office, preferably one with an adjacent room for my secretary. I
did not ask for an office on another floor, for I did not mind where
it was, provided it was light and airy, with my secretary's room
close at hand. Nothing happened for some time, as is the way in big
organizations, and I asked that the search for a new office should
be intensified. Once it was clear that I was serious, the Central
Services Department got cracking and eventually I was offered two
small offices, adjacent to my secretary's office on the fourth floor
floor, which could be knocked into one.... Those who have visited
me at Broadcasting House know the modest but adequate office that
resulted, but this did not prevent the press describing it as a
penthouse on the top floor. I read too that I had deliberately
moved to another floor to set up a chairman's establishment in competition with that of the director general. This was not my last
experience of a pastime indulged in by some BBC staff of feeding
the press with malicious tit-bits. The fact is that I would have
stayed on the third floor if someone had been willing to move to
give me houseroom.'

The words of a bitter man, and it is certainly true that the interpretation placed on the move to the fourth floor by Greene and other
members of the BBC was that this was a conscious attempt to signify
the changed relationship between the DG and the chairman. Lusty
told Hill that the question of the car and secretary weren't really
important, but he did feel that the question of the room, when he
heard of it, was immensely important:

'What did seem to me to matter was the setting up of a chairman's department, and on the pretence of not liking the smell of wood - my wife was the first person to be told about this because she sat next to Hill at some function and he told her that he was going to move out of his office because he didn't like the smell of wood and it was a panelled office. When she told me this afterwards I was horrified, this was going to explode the BBC. I mean secretaries, cars, anything else, are minor matters but to blow up this arrangement which had gone on since the beginning of Broadcasting House and was very important, ought not to have been done, and he never consulted the Board at all, it was just done. Whether he realized what he was doing I don't know, I suspect he probably did, but this in a curious way blew up the traditional relationship between the chairman and the DG. It destroyed a delicate set up which had worked, because instead of being able to to and fro and just chat to each other it had to be a formal thing between one floor and another, and one set of secretaries and another and so on. I think this was a deliberate, clever step in which to establish his authority.'

Greene's response to the change of rooms, the administrative and ultimately policy implications of a structural change, is in a similar vein:

'How do you view the changing of the rooms? Was it an incident that was blown up out of all proportion or was it of very significant, symbolic importance?'

'Very significant, not just symbolic, but also of practical importance because one could no longer have this informal relationship. With Hill it wasn't a case of walking in and out of each other's offices. If you had the same group of secretaries it meant that each knew what the other was doing, one saw copies of letters and so on, and so there was no chance of going off at a tangent, in different directions. I don't think that Hill liked that arrangement. The way he complained that he didn't like the smell of wood, well, that seemed to me at the time to be pretty petty. He didn't give the real reason, he just gave this silly reason. And as for the office being small, it was smaller than the DG's but it was for a part-time chairman and Hill remained a part-time chairman. It had been used by all the previous chairmen before him. In fact Normanbrook when he became chairman asked me if I'd mind if he regarded his office in the BBC as his headquarters - he'd got various other directorships - and used it as such. I said of course not. Well, Hill would have never asked a question like that, but if it was big enough for a big man like Normanbrook it ought to have been all right for Hill.'

For those working within Broadcasting House these events seemed to clarify everything, it was as if this one move to a different room provided the final evidence of Hill's intentions. Wilson had installed Hill in order to force Greene to resign, thereby creating a power vacuum in which Hill could easily function in his task of strengthening the governors and thus ensuring for Wilson's peace of mind the future 'scrupulous fairness' (12) of the BBC. So went the scenario, and as with many scenarios there would seem to be both truth and myth encased within it. What does begin to become clear when studying the Hill appointment is the actual subtlety of the relationships between the broadcasting and political spheres. Even acknowledging the crudity of the original appointment, there was no sense in which quick and harsh decisions were taken by Hill, riding roughshod over the wishes and policies of the BBC executive. When, at the end of his discussion of the 'shock' of his arrival at the BBC, Hill indulges in a little self-pity, listing the possible fears of the BBC personnel which have accounted for the hostility he faced, he is perfectly correct when he asks rhetorically, 'Did I yield to lobbies, political, libertarian or other? Did I turn over the BBC professionals to the mercies of the layman? Did I argue for advertising on the BBC? The answers are to be found in the records' (1974, p.81).

Greene (1974) in his review of Hill and in an interview, Lusty in article and interview both concur with Hill that he preserved the 'independence' of the BBC and sustained its form of finance (the twin pillars upon which, it is believed, the BBC and its reputation are founded). What they argue, however, is that Hill's points are irrelevant to their critique.

Hill took up his post in September 1967, and Greene announced his retirement on 15 July 1968, though his decision to retire was effectively made two months earlier. Charles Curran was appointed DG designate on 8 August 1968, and Greene finally left his post on 31 March 1969. He became a governor on 11 July 1969 and told Hill of his decision to leave that post on 5 August 1971. The crucial period from the point of view of this discussion is, then, September 1967 to July 1968. Two points are central: the nature of the working relationship between the DG and the chairman, and particularly the question of whether Hill fostered and nurtured a distinctive chairman's department, and a distinctive chairman's identity, counterposed in public and private to that of the director general; and the precise reasons why Greene chose to retire.

The initial meeting of 8 August was felt to have been a notable success, but between that date and the first board of governors meeting in September, doubts began to set in. If nothing else, Hill set about his job with a great deal of energy and quickly established that he intended to be not only a dominant force within the BBC but the dominant force . Lusty noted:

'You said that you came away feeling much happier than you did when you went to the lunch.'

'Well, then I began to have my doubts as to whether I should be quite as happy as that. This happened during a period between Hill coming in on the 1 September and the first board meeting he had which was towards the end of September. Of course the BBC was very much on edge at that time to see what was going to happen. It was just little things that I picked up, the rather underhand way, well not underhand exactly, the quite different way in which Hill approached the job compared to what previous chairmen had done - seeing executives without telling the DG, and burrowing around on

his own and so on in a way which was utterly alien.   I was there
when Normanbrook came in so I knew how a traditional BBC chairman
would operate.'

   Hill believes that the board of governors aré on the horns of a
dilemma, being both responsible to the public and for the programmes
transmitted.   Greene sees no dilemma so long as the former responsibility is taken by the governors and the latter is taken by the
full-time executives, particularly the DG.   Hill's diary for 18
January 1972 declares (1974, p.216):

'How long it has taken to strengthen the role of the Governors:
Wilson and Short may have expected that my appointment would briskly
lead to a more effective Board.   If they did, they have had to wait
an awful long time for it.'

In a conversation with Harman Grisewood, chief assistant to the DG,
Hill made his position very clear: Grisewood (Hill, 1974, p.106):

'talked about anxieties within the BBC since my appointment.   Was
I really a dedicated BBC man?   Was I assuming a new and strengthened
chairman's role at the expense of the management?   Was this not
creating tension?   I told him that those who assumed that I sought
to strengthen the Governors' role in overall policy were right in
their assumption.   I did.   But this did not involve taking over the
proper role of management.   This would be as undesirable as it would
be difficult.   Since Reith's days the Governors had for the most
part been ciphers.'

In line with his policy of de-ciphering the governors, Hill instigated a number of changes and a number of new procedures.   He introduced the use of voting on a frequent basis at board meetings, a
practice rarely used previously.   He introduced a committee system
for the governors, placing particular emphasis on the finance sub-
committee chaired by Sir Robert Bellinger.   There was close scrutiny
of the discussions and decisions of the board of management - Hill
even has a chapter entitled 'Clashes with Management' which really
involves a theme he develops throughout the book that the board of
management dislikes the board of governors' arriving at its own
decisions.   Hill carped at the limitations on discussion of
editorial matters and on the inability of the governors to affect
programme policy (1974, p.94):

'On one occasion a governor raised the matter of reports of the
party conferences.   Why had it been decided, as he had read in the
press, that there would be less reporting of the next conferences
than in the previous year?   That, said Greene, is an editorial
matter.   I intervened to point out that the governors could raise
any question that they liked although I would always advise them
not to raise questions of management.
   'The range of subjects discussed at the board were wide.   There
was the usual emphasis on current affairs, their balance, the obser-
vance of the requirement that there should be no editorializing, the
methods of the interviewers, and so on.   The "Wednesday Play" came

up again and again for scrutiny, for both praise and criticism. Bad
language, emphasis on sex, all these matters came up frequently in
one form or another. But there the matter seemed to end. We could
talk but that was all. Policy was made by management.'

What Hill was doing, and what one might have expected him to do was
to ask the question, like Mrs Snowden and Lord Clarendon in Reith's
day, and Beveridge and Lord Simon in later years, of just 'who is
the BBC?'. (13)   The answer he came up with was the constitutional
one that the governors are the BBC. Hill's premiss was that prior
to his arrival the governors had played only a nominal role, that
they had been 'ciphers'. This Greene (1974) passionately denies,
saying that Hill had 'fantasies of greatness', that he misrepresents
the historical role of the chairman and the governors, that the
habit of head counting introduced by Hill was mistaken and that the
institution of the governors committee was 'a plain piece of administrative nonsense'. Greene's affirmation that the board played a
much greater part in the history of the BBC is not particularly well
supported in the literature, though he may be correct in establishing a degree of perspective by indicating that past boards were
not quite the ineffectual dullards which Hill implies.
     In the closing pages of his memoir, Hill poses two opposite
views, the Normanbrook position (governors need to be dominant), and
the Whitley position (the DG is effectively dominant), making perfectly clear that he identifies with the former position. He was,
he says, 'an active chairman and not a stooge' (1974, p.266). In
adopting this position he transgressed a dearly held view of the
relationship between chairman and director general and in the eyes
of the latter compromised the whole position of the BBC. Greene
was asked about this:

*'In the review you did of Hill's book you argue that the governors
were never ciphers as Hill claims. In saying that are you not going
against a popular description, a belief that ever since Reith's day
the DG has in fact dominated the BBC, and that while the word
'cipher' may be inappropriate, nevertheless the director general is
and always has been the dominant character in the BBC?'*

'I agree that that is the popular impression. I wouldn't put it
like that, that the DG is the dominant character, the way I'd put it
is that since Reith's day it had been the tradition that the DG was
the main spokesman of the BBC, that he was the person known to the
public as the personification of the BBC. 'Reith's BBC', 'Greene's
BBC'. When there were quieter men like Haley and Jacob, it wasn't
perhaps - well, no, I think 'Haley's BBC' would have been a fairly
clear phrase. Jacob was a quieter man and didn't appear so much in
public. Even so he would be, when necessary, the main spokesman.
But it doesn't mean that the governors and particularly the chairman
didn't play a very important role behind the scenes, even in Reith's
day. And there are some remarks of Reith's which are quoted I think
in Asa Briggs' second volume, indicating that he felt in the same
way, that he was responsible to the board, the board were in the end
the masters, that he was the public figure. It doesn't mean that
the DG so dominated the board that he always got his own way. It

didn't mean that one didn't have to be very persuasive, argue
strongly with the board about one's attitudes and sometimes the
board wouldn't accept the things one wanted to do.'

Greene then identified with the Reithian position seeking,
however, to imbue it with a liberal imagination. In his history,
Briggs refers to Reith's attitudes to the board as follows (Briggs,
1965, p.424):

'All de jure authority lay with them, while, by contrast, the
Director General's power was de facto. Their role, he thought,
should be that of 'trustees' exercising neither executive nor administrative functions. They should not seek to be 'experts' certainly
not experts in particular departments of broadcasting business.
Their value lay in their 'general experience of men and affairs'.
The Director General had to manage the BBC, to coordinate the
various activities of broadcasting and take responsibility for the
daily conduct of affairs.'

Greene is clearly cast in this mould, but it is also true that on
the occasions to which he refers in the interview he did not get
his own immediately. These two issues which he has quoted on a n
number of occasions were in fact the question of advertising
alcoholic drinks in the 'Radio Times', and the question of giving
the starting prices for horse racing. It was on the basis of its
obscuring the traditional board-DG relationship that Greene regarded
the emergence of the governors committee system not just as 'administrative nonsense' but also as a 'mixing up of the functions of a
non-executive and an executive'. The curious thing is, however,
that when one looks carefully at the events, the tensions of the
working relationship of Hill and Greene derived not from Hill's
becoming the overtly chief executive of the BBC but from Greene
calls a 'lack of confidence' in the chairman:

'You compare Hill unfavourably with Fforde and Duff and Normanbrook.
In what way was your job made easier or did you function better
under those three than you did under Hill?'

'Well, the main thing was confidence. Fforde, Duff for a short
period and Normanbrook were all men in whom one could have absolute
and complete confidence. One would know that in no circumstances
would they ever go behind one's back, that they would always be
completely frank with me and I would always be completely frank with
them. That there was a genuine friendship, an informal way of
dealing with things, that they would walk into my office and I would
walk into theirs because we were only separated by the secretaries'
office. So there was a complete sharing of minds even though, you
know, not always complete agreement. But if I had something which
I wanted to do which had to go before the board of governors, if I
wasn't able to persuade the chairman I would never go any further.
And I don't think the chairman, if he knew that I violently objected
to something that he thought would be a good thing, would carry it
further either. It was a consensus way of conducting things. With
Hill all the informality and walking in and out of each other's

offices went immediately. Partly through Hill moving his office,
but even before he'd done that I think he only came into my office
once, and you knew that he was acting behind your back all the time.
I know from what was told to me when he was first chairman he was
going around the Regional centres talking to everybody, talking to
producers and so on and saying "I'm going to show who's master: Hill
not Greene".

'He would see members of the staff without telling one that he
was going to, or what had happened. He would see politicians and
give them undertakings without telling one in advance. So that is
the fundamental thing. Bob Lusty says, and I suppose one says it
out of politeness, that the objection to Hill was that he came from
the ITA, not to him as a person. Really the fundamental objection
was to Hill as a person.'

Which came first, the hostility to Hill at the personal level or
the awareness that he was going to disturb the orthodoxy of the
relationship between DG and chairman? Greene is a man who likes to
establish the intellectual calibre of individuals - Lusty, for
example, describes Greene as being 'intellectually contemptuous' of
Hill and it was stated in another context that Greene did not want
Mary Whitehouse to broadcast, not through fear of her capacities
but because he was 'intellectually contemptuous' of her. Clearly
one can't be definite on this, but it does need to be discussed in
the sense that it is very clear that Greene's reaction at least in
part was hostility to Hill as Hill. It is not unreasonable to argue
that Wilson clearly 'knew his men' - he was certainly well known to
Greene - and detected the incompatibility which would eventually
drive Greene from the BBC. It was not, however, just a question of
the usurping of the DG's power and command of the organization:
Greene made an interesting point on this:

'*Did Hill at any point articulate his feelings to you on the role of
the Chairman, the role of the DG? Did he ever say "I want to be an
executive chairman"?*'

'Oh no. In fact, to do Hill justice, I think that Kenneth Adam has
put around a lot of misleading stuff about Hill in the articles in
the "Sunday Times" and in one or two reviews and things that he's
written. (14) The objection to Hill is not that he becomes an
executive chairman, he didn't spend enough time on it to be an
executive chairman. The DG remained the chief executive, but he
destroyed the right sort of relationship between the chairman and
the DG. He wanted to appear in public to be the man running the
BBC, but he didn't ever say it to one, or indeed do it. It comes
back really to this question of confidence and the setting up of a
separate centre of power.

It is terribly difficult to pin down the precise nature of 'the
right sort of relationship' and one can only conclude that what he
means is the position described by Briggs as the position articulated by Keith, and given form in the Whitley document. Hill claims
that once he and Hugh Greene began to work with each other the
latter's fears were gradually allayed; Greene commented:

'He said that we behaved in a civilized way I think and part of the
way of behaving in a civilized way is not to be quarrelling all the
time. My fears were allayed to the extent that I saw he was not
going to give way on political issues, and that he was not going to
try to lead the BBC towards taking advertising. In that way my
fears were allayed, not that they'd been very serious fears on
either count. But it was his general influence on the relationship
between DG and board, on that my fears were not allayed at all.
I thought that all the time he was doing damage that might be
irreparable.'

What were the circumstances surrounding the actual decision by
Greene to retire? In his account of this, Hill makes much of
Greene's divorce, which was raised by Greene in December 1967, 'a
matter which was to have important repercussions' (Hill, 1974,
p.85). He then refers to a 'remarkable letter' which he received
from Hugh Greene, (15) 'asking that the governors should publish
forthwith that he would stay until the age of 60 and possibly there-
after and that his successor should come from inside the Corporation
(1974, p.85). He detected, he says, a changing 'demeanour' and
the impression that he was 'clearly concerned about his future',
Greene does not regard this as in any way a remarkable letter, and
argues that he only wished to allay press speculation and that it
was routine anyway for a member of the BBC on reaching fifty-eight
to discuss the future, whether they should retire earlier than sixty
or stay on after sixty. In May 1968, Hill and Greene discussed
possible future senior appointments and the question of succession
to him, 'Naturally we got round to his own future. Greene, Hill
felt, 'seemed to want to go early' though he detected also a
'nagging doubt' in his mind which derived from his fear that if he
resigned and was divorced at the same time it would be assumed that
he had been made to go because of his divorce. It was at this
point, Hill says, that he thought of offering Greene a seat on the
board since this would mean that he could retire 'with honour'.
Hill put this to Greene, who eventually accepted, and Hill obtained
Wilson's agreement to the 'deal', for deal it was. Greene was
delighted, Hill states, because it solved the problem of retiring
at the time of the divorce, because he would be the only governor
ever to have been DG, and because it would mean less contact with
Hill (1974, p.88). Lusty emphasizes that Greene was particularly
attracted to the thought of being 'one, if not two, up on Reith'.
   It is always difficult, if not impossible, to say why something
happens at a particular moment, why this moment was the time chosen
for Greene to retire. One cannot, I think, place too much emphasis
on the question of the divorce, nor on Greene's desire to better
Reith. It does seem clear that the underlying force was the reali-
zation by Greene that Hill's star was more firmly in the ascendant
than his own, that he had in a sense been beaten and that the offer
of the governorship was a shrewdly placed peg upon which to hang his
retirement. He was asked why he retired then:

'Now let me try to get this clear in my own mind as well. I wasn't
happy at that time, as you can imagine. My divorce really played no
part whatsoever. It wasn't in my mind in the way that Hill suggests

at all. I regarded it as private and nothing to do with one's
business life.'

*'So Hill would be wrong in saying that you were wary about the
coincidence of your divorce and the resignation?'*

'Yes, as far as I remember I don't think it ever entered my head.'
He then referred to the discussion in May about possible successors,
and states:

'one day Hill said to me "would you like to become a Governor?"
Whether Hill had already discussed it with Wilson at that time I do
not know. I said that I'd like to think about this but the next
time I saw him I said "Yes". I must say that it was a bribe, so to
speak, well attuned to my character, because it had never happened
before.'

'Your being one up on Reith?'

I think Bob Lusty exaggerates that a little bit, but I would put it
certainly in the way of making history. It had never happened
before, whether to Reith or anybody else. So I took that bait,
being quite clear in my own mind that it was bait, but still, why
not take it? But again whether it had been fixed with Wilson before
or after I just do not know and I don't suppose we will ever know.'

*'At the time did you see this as the culmination of a long process
that had been taking place since Hill was appointed?'*

'No I didn't. It was the culmination of a series of conversations
over a few weeks. I'd just imagined myself soldiering on till 60
and conceivably longer if they thought there wasn't a successor
ready. But I must say that a lot of the pleasure of the job had
gone.'

THE MEANING OF IT ALL

In a rather percipient remark in March 1964, Greene, in response to
a question by Kenneth Harris as to what makes a good director
general, replied (1969, p.84) (16):

'God alone knows.... But I can tell you one thing which makes a good
BBC - it's a good relationship between the DG and the chairman of
the governors. However able and well intentioned a DG was, or a
chairman, if they couldn't work together, the BBC would be in
trouble.'

Descriptions of the relationship between the DG and the board of
governors are, to say the least, abstract. There is much talk of a
'delicate balance' between roles but the hard details are rarely
spelled out. Yet it was the nature of this relationship which Hill,
and through him Wilson, sought to change. The logic can only have
been that in this way the whole 'tone' of BBC political coverage

would change. In his Granada Lecture (1972) Greene argued that the
amicable relationship between himself, as DG, and Fforde, Duff,
Normanbrook and Lusty was disturbed by Hill because the latter
'blurred' the division of functions which for the governors, Greene
states, is the 'right to reprove and restrain'. Lusty (1974)
declares that 'there disappeared in the time of Lord Hill elements
of extreme importance to the relationship between the chairman and
the DG and between the Governors and the management...' but as to
what those elements are, no word.

In law, the governors are the BBC, paragraph 1 of the Charter
states this clearly. Therefore, strictly speaking, the whole discussion of the DG-chairman relationship is one of the merits or
otherwise of a series of informal working arrangements. These
arrangements were first given definition in 1931, following a
struggle between Reith, the first director general, and Clarendon,
the first chairman, over the very questions discussed here. As
Boyle (1972) describes it, the battle between Reith and Clarendon
revolved around the question of the relationship of the DG to the
governors: were the latter the 'commander in chief' or did the
former occupy that role? The 'problem' was resolved as far as Reith
was concerned when in February 1930 the prime minister, Ramsay
Macdonald, appointed Clarendon governor general of South Africa, and
subsequently appointed John Whitley, a former speaker of the
commons, as chairman of the governors.

In response to the difficulties between Reith and Clarendon,
Whitley, the new chairman, and Reith worked together on a document
detailing the relationships which were to exist between the governors, the DG and the public. The Whitley document as it became
known, effectively defined the governors as trustees or representatives of the public interest functioning within the corporation.
Their functions, the document states 'are not executive, their responsibilities are general and not particular'. (17) The document
goes on:

'With the DG they discuss and then decide upon major matters of
policy and finance, but they leave the execution of that policy and
the general administration of the service in all its branches to the
DG and his competent officers.'

The position outlined here, with the emphasis on the centrality of
the DG, was not challenged by the chairman or the governors until
the appointment of Simon as chairman in 1947. Simon took the view
that Reith's overpowering personality had fashioned not only his own
career in the BBC, but had also generated the institutional impo-
tence of the governors. Simon expressly denied the validity of the
position adopted by the Whitley document and told the Beveridge
Committee so. The latter was in accord with Simon and reinterpreted
the role of the governors from being analogous to trustees, as
implied in Whitley, to being analogous to ministers of the crown.
The Committee Report (1949) stated that the governors must:

'themselves undertake the function of the Minister, that of bringing
outside opinion to bear upon all the activities of the permanent
staff, of causing change where change is necessary, of preventing

broadcasting from falling in any way whatsoever into the hands of
a bureaucracy which is not controlled.'

The Whitley document was 'tacitly abolished when the revised
charter of 1952 was granted' (Smith, 1974, p.60). A memorandum from
the Labour government in 1951, in response to the recommendations
of the Beveridge Committee stated (quoted in Smith, 1974, p.99):

'They (the Government) see no reason to dissent from the views of
the Committee that the Whitley document should disappear and that
the position of the Governors in future should be defined only by
the charter ... the Government have no doubt that the Governors will
regulate their procedure so as to preserve, on the one hand, the
recognised right of the Chairman to take emergency decisions subject
to report to the Board, and, on the other, the day to day executive
responsibility of the Director General of the Corporation. In
regard to this office, the Committee suggest that there is no need
to specify a Director General in the Charter. While the government
agree that the administrative and executive form of organization
most suited to the Corporation should be decided by the Governors,
they think it desirable to continue in the Charter the requirement
that there should be a chief executive officer with the title of
Director General.'

Thus, as early as 1951 there is a serious attempt to redefine the
role of the governors, but there is a definite reluctance to do this
by directly deposing the stature of the DG, hence the insistence
that the DG be specified in the charter as the chief executive
officer. It is, therefore, not surprising that despite the implicit
attempt to reduce it, the 'executive supremacy' (Smith, 1973, p.144)
of the DG remained and was inherited by Greene. Wedell (1968,
p.113) describes it in the following way: 'Although, over the years
since 1952 the balance of power between the Governors and the
officials has varied according to the personalities concerned, there
is little doubt that the ghost of the Whitley document lingers on.'
As I have shown, Greene in fact denies the extent of the supremacy,
arguing that such a view ignores the operation of a consensus prior
to Hill - implying that the DG was only the foremost figure because
the chairman and governors had been in accord on the whole with him,
and because this was the way things were done.
    In 1965, Normanbrook, chairman of the governors, took up the
question once more of the 'functions of the BBC governors', an
interpretation of which Hill was later to make great play: 'I unhes-
itatingly accepted the Normanbrook definition of the Board's role
...' (Hill, 1974, p.263). He quotes with approval an extract from
Normanbrook's paper in which he states,

'within the BBC the ultimate level of decision, even executive
decision on matters of first importance, lies in the Board of Governors or, in a matter of urgency, the chairman acting under the
authority delegated to him by the Board.'

But Normanbrook does also add that this is the ultimate point of
decision and that in practice it is very difficult to say where the

making of policy ends and its execution begins. He also adds, as
Hill would have known had he read Wedell (1968), for it is quoted
there, that the control which the governors exercise (Normanbrook,
1965, p.15):

'is mainly by retrospective review - by comment, whether praise or
blame, after the event. It is of course easy to say that this is
not enough, that there ought to be tighter control and a more strict
enforcement of the views and attitudes of the Board. This is a
matter to which I have myself given a good deal of thought, as I
imagine my predecessors did before me. But I have come to the conclusion that, if one is speaking in terms of systems, there is no
other system which could be operated successfully in relation to
the enormous volume of programme output handled by the BBC.'

It is by no means the case then that Normanbrook took the line which
Hill claims for him.
    Hill did seek, and he acknowledges this, an actively interven-
tionist role for his chairmanship, and sought to foster the relationship of governors as 'ministers' and the full-time professionals
as 'civil servants'. (18) Such developments - though perfectly
correct in law, and only in keeping with a number of suggestions
over the years - were guaranteed to make Greene bridle. Since
Reith, the relationship had been more of headmaster to school governors than permanent secretary to minister. The intended reactiva-
tion of the role of the chairmen of both broadcasting authorities
was pointed to as being a desirable development in the White Paper
on Broadcasting of December 1966. (19) When Hill chose to extend
and develop the role of chairman he was both reducing Greene's
power, if only by undermining his sense of purpose, and also laying
the seeds of future difficulty by establishing a contradiction
within the BBC's ruling body which would create more, not less,
trouble.
    It was clear that Hill did not, and indeed could not, affect pro-
gramming on a day-by-day basis, no more than could the DG. The
volume of programme output is simply too great. Greene always 'led'
by focusing on one or two particular programmes and programme-
makers, and shaped overall policy through their impact. His reputation among BBC employees was always that of someone who would be
receptive to ideas, always open to suggestions from his 'young
Turks'. His essential identity was the central feature of a number
of speeches dotted throughout the years of the early 1960s, and in
this way developed a distinctive presence which implied, if it
didn't state, a liberal, progressive programming philosophy.
    One has, then, to look to the ways in which Hill, and through him
Wilson, by exerting the power of the governors - that is, by denying
the validity of the Whitley document - sought to dismantle this
'presence' and to impose another, more inhibiting and less lively.
In this way we can begin to understand the significance of the
appointment, rather than in looking for specific acts of malice or
overt political control, since it remains the case that Hill did
sustain a modicum of independence and did not threaten the method of
financing the BBC - which was always regarded by friends of the corporation to be the foundation for their independence. The presence

implied by Greene, ill-defined, only loosely articulated but nevertheless critical, was that broadcasting was to be a force shaping
and leading social events. Given such a perspective, broadcasting
would necessarily transgress dominant social codes, since it could
not lead otherwise. Greene's was a liberal imagination not shared
by Hill. Hill's purpose was to reorient the programming policy back
from the vanguard of the social process, into the position where it
was keeping pace with orthodoxy whatever it might be. There was
nothing sharp or drastic about this, but it was crucially underpinned by the structural change in the moving of the office (which
served notice that things would not be in the future as they had
been in the past), by a strict constitutional reading of the charter
charter, and by Hill's own idiosyncratic approach to chairmanship.
These sustained Hill's position, allowed it to develop and ultimately undermine that of Greene.

There remained, however, a vital contradiction not perceived by
Wilson and Hill: there was a basic incompatibility between the two
roles of 'minister' and 'trustee' which Hill was trying to integrate
within the same body. As is shown in the discussion of 'Yesterday's
Men' the working out of this was to undermine in many eyes the whole
cridibility of the BBC.

Greene clearly embodied in the Labour leader's mind the rather
rabid independence of the BBC, an overblown institution which he
felt to be in need of deflation. The logical relationship is
between the removal of its embodiment, Greene, and a change in its
rabid independence, or as Wilson puts it, the restoration of a
'scrupulous fairness ... in respect to comment on public affairs'.
It was clearly the intention that the readjustment of roles which
followed Hill's appointment would induce change from one view of
broadcasting to another, Greene's view was (and indeed remained)
that programmes should flow from his own, and his subordinates',
imagination, born out of their intellectual perspectives, which
should not be a pale reflection of popular morality or political
orthodoxy. (20) He crucially states that their purpose as broadcasters was 'to be ahead of public opinion rather than always to
await upon it' (1969, p.101). Greene sought the critical impact of
the liberal conscience of the convinced journalist. Hill sought the
domination of the conservative imagination as reflected in a document for which he was largely responsible, 'Broadcasting and the
Public Mood' (July 1968), and in which he steers a careful line
between being too restrictive and too progressive.

Greene felt that broadcasters should lead public opinion, should
be able to cast a critical eye over the political orthodoxies and
institutions of the time, should in other words fulfil the role of
the political journalist. Hill sought the comfortable pastures of
a 'middle ground', neither ahead nor behind but comfortably
entrenched within, more responsible than journalistic. Though he
did not, and could not, find comfort in that role, this was the real
purpose and, to an extent, consequence of the appointment of July
1967.

Chapter 10

YESTERDAY'S MEN

The only occasion when Harold was extremely angry was after the
1970 election. It was the now famous David Dimbleby interview
for a programme called 'Yesterday's Men' which sparked it off.
(Marcia Williams, 1972, pp.234-5)

It ill behoves those who live by the sword to bleat when they
cut themselves shaving. ('Guardian' leader, 19 June 1971)

The events surrounding 'Yesterday's Men' - broadcast on 17 June 1971
- are difficult to disentangle, but once unravelled they throw into
sharp relief the intentions of programme-makers and the considerations of programme-making, the effect of political pressure on programming, and the curiously ambivalent attitude of the Labour party
to the media in general and to the BBC in particular.

A NARRATIVE

On the day of Harold Wilson's defeat, 19 June 1970, David Dimbleby
did an interview at 10 Downing Street with the deposed and surprised
prime minister. It was at this time that the idea for 'Yesterday's
Men' began to crystallize in Dimbleby's mind: 'the loss of power,
what does it actually mean?' He describes how he was 'struck by the
general air of dismay and by the speed of dismissal', and how he
couldn't quite see 'how people could readjust. I assumed there
would be a very painful period of readjustment, which indeed there
was, Mrs. Healey for instance saying that Dennis Healey was like
having a sportscar in the garage and no petrol.' (1)
    The idea for the programme occurred to Dimbleby in June 1970, but
he did not prepare a programme synopsis until October. The original
idea had been that they 'quite simply make a film by following the
opposition around for a few weeks and see how they were getting on
and settling down'. By the time Dimbleby's proposal had been presented to Paul Fox (controller BBC1) and John Grist (head of current
affairs group), several months had elapsed since the election and
so the original intent of looking at the immediate impact of the
loss of power was no longer attainable. No work could begin on
making the programme until the idea had been accepted, a budget
allocated and a producer (Angela Pope) appointed, by which time it

was Christmas 1970, six months after the election and the loss of power.

Dimbleby's synopsis of the programme - incidentally presented under the title of 'Yesterday's Men' - indicated that the film would describe the impact of defeat on the senior members of the Labour government; would consider the role of the opposition as seen by the ex-ministers; would 'cover inquiries as to what it was like to lose high office with its rewards suddenly and unexpectedly, and would include their comments on the "secrets" that were being made public in memoirs' (Governors, 1971). The appeal of such a programme, the synopsis argued, would be in showing the response of former public figures to a period of enforced relative anonymity. Having been granted permission to go ahead on this basis, letters were sent by Dimbleby to Wilson, Callaghan, Crossman, Healey, Jenkins and Castle explaining that he was 'preparing a documentary film for the BBC on the Opposition. It would be about the political and personal nature of the job of Opposition.' Crosland was approached in exactly the same terms on 8 December by Angela Pope, who also wrote to Castle on 14 January - a letter which is reproduced here (2):

'We are planning a documentary film about some of the leading members of the last Labour government during their first year in Opposition. We will want to talk to them about their view of the job of Opposition and what they consider will be the important issues in the next four years. The film will also deal with their reactions to defeat in the short term, ii.e. how they felt immedi- ately afterwards, and how it has affected them personally in the long term: for example, what it is like to have power to make decisions withdrawn, the kind of facilities they now have in terms of research, secretaries and office space, how a cut in salary affects them and whether they need to find work outside their job as an MP. To do this we need both to film an interview with you and to film you in various situations which illustrate something of the life you now lead. For instance, we might like to film you in your home surroundings, or perhaps preparing single handed the debate on the Industrial Relations Bill. The tape recorded inter- view which I mentioned to you on the telephone would fill in areas which we have not discussed on film and would be used where we need only your voice. In the finished version of the film you voice would be used to run over pictures of yourself or events to which you have referred in the interview. We may, for example, ask you what you do, or do not, miss about the DEP, and use your tape- recorded replies over pictures of you walking through St. James's Square.'

An important consideration is that over the period of months which had elapsed since the idea was first broached the to and fro of party politics had been firmly re-established, and in particular the producers perceived two significant developments in the affairs of the Labour party: the appearance of a schism over the Common Market, and a possible challenge to Harold Wilson as leader of the party. So, gradually, the passage of time and the movement of events implied a constant flux in the perspectives of what would be discussed, a fact which is implied in a letter from Grist to

Crossman saying that he was pleased Crossman had agreed to take part and adding that

'Since the producer first discussed this item with me we have been able to fix a transmission date in the middle of June.... This, as you probably realise, means that we will postpone filming, although we may be doing some odd events we won't be doing it over the whole year. I hope this will not change your plans to participate in the programme.'

Having been given notice in January that the programme would not be broadcast until June, Dimbleby and Pope decided to leave the idea for two or three months, both being involved in other programmes in the meantime. So initial contact had been made in the November 1970 to January 1971 period, and there was a lull in the programme until March 1971. During this initial period there was a vital development which throws considerable light on the later events. Dimbleby's original idea had been that the programme would fill a 'Tuesday Documentary' slot, but he would not be given permission to explore the possibilities for such a programme until the whole idea had been ratified by his superiors in CAG. Having been given permission and having talked to the intended participants, he and Pope 'decided we didn't want to do it, too dull, too difficult, too boring'. The producer argued that there was simply insufficient interesting material to sustain fifty minutes, though she felt that there was a possibility of producing a shorter item for inclusion within another programme. Informing the BBC of this, they were told in return that 'you can't not do it, because now you've been and talked to them they'll think it's the BBC being hostile to the Labour party if we don't put it out. So you've got to do it, no question of dropping it.' Eventually, late in the programme's development, a compromise solution was arrived at. It would no longer be a distinct documentary but would be broadcast under the aegis of '24 Hours', though the editor of this programme, Anthony Smith, was recognized by the BBC as not having the normal editorial control. Dimbleby and Pope had then been effectively locked into a process from which a programme had to emerge and, a supreme irony, the final turning of the key in the lock had been the conceptions held by senior BBC personnel of the sensitivity of the Labour party.

Dimbleby and Pope resumed work on the programme, assisted by one secretary, in March 1971, paying particular attention to the interviews with Wilson and the other Labour leaders which they regarded as the 'absolute core of the film' and on which they worked 'absolutely together'. The organization and shooting of additional film was done principally under the direction of Angela Pope in her role as producer. The circumstances dictated by the passage of time were indicated in a letter to Wilson from Dimbleby written in April, in which he said that the film was

'still conceived as it was when we talked about it in your office earlier this year. It will be both about the defeat and its impact in political and personal terms and about the problems Opposition poses.... Obviously the Opposition's handling of events in recent months now plays a bigger part than if the film had been made at the turn of the year.'

The particular formulation of this letter and of earlier ones is
important in the light of the later accusations about 'deception'.
In April 1971 Dimbleby and Pope decided that the original synopsis
title, 'Yesterday's Men', would be used and also contacted the
Scaffold, with a view to their writing and singing a song for the
film soundtrack. A contract was negotiated with them during May.
The governors' report states that the title 'was known and accepted
by their superiors', but was never, in subsequent correspondence,
communicated to the Labour party people.

In the process of making this programme, as with any other programme, editorial control could have been exercised at two points:
during the making of the programme, and after the film had been
completed but prior to transmission. Three possible levels of
editorial control were immediately relevant: the editor of '24
Hours' (though as we have seen, informally this was waived in this
instance), the assistant to the head of CAG, and the head of CAG.
In April 1971 Pope submitted to the assistant head of CAG a draft
of a detailed account of the topics which they were going to discuss
with the politicians, and details of the song which the Scaffold
were being commissioned to do. To those who wished to know, it was
clear that a 'satirical, funny' song had been commissioned for the
programme by May 1971. This much the governors' report acknowledged; what it did not acknowledge was the question of editorial
control once the programme was being cut and put together in its
final form. Three internal views of this predominate: one view is
that the troika of editorial control knew about the content of the
programme, but failed to take into account, indeed could not have
known, the reactions of the Labour leaders over the period 16-18
June. A second version has it that the editorial control was lax
because of the commitment of Grist and Smith, the editor of '24
Hours', to other concerns during this period which effectively meant
that they weren't familiar with what was happening until it was too
late. A third version is that they knew what was happening but
refused to take responsibility for it. This latter is rather difficult to accept if only because they would clearly realize that any
serious consequences would be bound to reflect back on to them.
The role they adopted is much more understandable if the premiss is
that they did not perceive the serious consequences of the programme, since all that is called into question then is their judgment, and not their integrity.

There is an important divergence of opinion here between Dimbleby
and Pope. The former argues that there was in fact very little
editorial control, whereas the latter argues that there was much
more control than usual with constant office discussions between
herself and either the head of CAG, Grist, or his assistant,
Tisdall, about ideas and content, vetting of correspondence,
viewing of the rough-cut and so on. There is a possible explanation for this in that Pope did seem to be more permanently located
within the walls of Lime Grove than did Dimbleby, so that any control which took place would be more likely to happen through her
than through Dimbleby. Whatever is the truth about the control, it
is almost certain that no one foresaw the reactions of the Labour
party.

Arrangements were made to film an interview between Wilson and

Dimbleby at 6 p.m. on 11 May in the rooms of the leader of the
opposition at the Commons. The interview covered numerous areas but
when Dimbleby referred to the amount of money which Wilson received
for his memoirs, the Labour leader became rather agitated, and then
extremely angry, demanding that all references to the memoirs be cut
from the recording (the full text of the row is available in Hill
(1974)). On the following day, 12 May, a telephone conversation
took place between Joe Haines, Wilson's press secretary, and John
Crawley, ENCA (3), which covered, as Lord Hill describes it and is
confirmed by a number of other sources, 'the extent of the deletion
promised to Mr. Wilson by David Dimbleby and Angela Pope' (Hill,
1974, p.181). In fact the promise of a deletion seems to have been
made by Pope (though she denies this), and Dimbleby promises that
he will not leak the details of the extractions to the press. The
central bone of contention is whether Crawley promised Haines that
he would cut out the whole of the reference to the memoirs, or
whether he only promised to delete part of it. The governors'
report states (para 7)

'Following a disagreement on the appropriateness of certain questions, an undertaking was given to Mr. Wilson on behalf of the BBC
that a part of the film would be destroyed and all that was possible
to be done to see that the story of the disagreement did not leak.
There was a lack of agreement between the parties to this undertaking about the extent of the film which it covered.'

Lord Hill claims that 'John Crawley ... had no doubt that the assurance related only to the third question' (Hill, 1974, p.181).
Dimbleby and Pope are unclear as to the precise implication of the
statement in the transcript that an extraction would be made, though
they do admit to fighting very hard to keep in what they felt to be
the legitimate question of the earnings from the memoirs and to keep
in Wilson saying that 'I'm not going to answer that' because they
'thought it was revealing and quite important that it should be
seen'. Haines, in a piece in the 'Guardian' (15 July 1971), wrote
that

'On May 12, Mr. John Crawley, special assistant to Mr. Charles
Curran, The Director General, telephoned me to say that he had "no
hesitation in saying that the whole of that section will be destroyed formally, lost sight of and forgotten'. I still possess my
original shorthand note of that conversation.'

Reading this extract from Haines's article, it would still be possible to argue that the reference was to the second part of the conversation. When asked about this in an interview, Haines declared:

'There is no doubt in my mind, there is no doubt I am sure in John
Crawley's mind, there was no doubt in Angela Pope's mind, there was
no doubt in David Dimbleby's mind, what the objection was. You have
to keep coming back to the point that this was a programme, a
serious Tuesday Documentary about the workings of Her Majesty's
loyal Opposition, and the whole of that section (in the "Guardian")
means simply that. He (Dimbleby) had gone from discussing visits

to America, relations with the Common Market, Africa and all that suddenly to the question of Mr. Wilson's money. There can be no doubt what we are objecting to. the conversations that I had with Curran, with John Grist subsequently, with Crawley, with Dimbleby, with Pope, they had no doubt, none of them. If they try afterwards to justify a bad programme, that I understand. They may feel compelled to do so because the alternative is to admit that they were wholly in the wrong and I wouldn't expect them to do that. But there's no ambiguity, there was no doubt, none at all. In all the conversations we had with them I don't think there was ever any real possibility of doubt. They knew what I meant and I knew what John Crawley meant.'

For a month, then, from 23 May to 16 June, there was an apparent understanding between Wilson (via Haines) and the BBC (via Crawley). Even this, however, is not totally clear since Lord Hill, quoting from his diary of 17 June, declares (1974, p.181):

'When the incident in the programme, "Yesterday's Men", concerning Harold Wilson's income from his memoirs was reported to me by the Director General two or three weeks ago, he told me that the questions on this subject were to come out, Wilson having been so assured. Today he said that the assurance given to Wilson - in fact it was given by John Crawley to Wilson's press adviser, Joe Haines, - was that it was only the third question that should come out, and that the television people proposed to include the first two questions and the answers.'

What seems to have happened is that a precise interpretation of the Crawley-Haines conversation was established at this high administrative level, was in line with Haines's understanding as to the nature of the agreement, but that this was never transmitted to the 'television people'. When these latter were preparing a rough-cut of the film they decided to leave the questions in:

'We decided to put in this much of the question, "Mr. Wilson, it has been said that you earned several figures (sic) from your book, is that true?" and he answered "I don't know why that should be of any interest to the BBC", and then he went on. We realised obviously that the row could not be in, so we cut on "It's no interest to the BBC".'

One source argues that everyone in the hierarchy, effectively meaning the troika previously described, knew that the question and answer were left in and thought nothing of it, 'None of us knew that it was going to blow like that', and they could not have known because the behaviour of the Labour people was 'totally irrational and unpredictable'. Thus, not only was no clear picture of the 'pledge' transmitted to Pope and Dimbleby, but also those in direct editorial control did not have a clear understanding of the extent of deletion promised to Wilson. Curran is adamant that John Crawley only promised a partial deletion. (4)

What is crucial is that until Wednesday 16 June, Wilson and Haines believed that the whole of the extract would be erased. On

10 June news of the 11 May row was made public for the first time in
the 'Londoner's Diary' of the 'Evening Standard', and was repeated
over the next three days in the rest of the press. By the 16 June,
Wilson, and particularly Haines, became aware that all was not as
they thought it would be. Haines states:

'The first thing that alerted us was when we discovered that the
programme was called 'Yesterday's Men', and we discovered that by
looking in the 'Radio Times'. I protested about this.... I had
spoken to John Grist about this and almost in passing I said "I take
it that these other points, the house and more particularly this
conversation, would not be in" and to my astonishment John Grist,
who I knew very well, said that he could not help me on that, he
would have to refer me to higher authority, and just went all stiff
and formal, and when I questioned him he kept repeating that he
couldn't help me. By this time we were getting alert. I think that
what then happened was that I did refer it to Curran and then Curran
told me, or told Wilson, that this part of the conversation was
still in.'

   This was the making of the second major row, which did not just
revolve around the questions having been kept in, but also involved
the fact that photographs had been included of Wilson's Buckingham-
shire farm, and a dislike of the tone of the title, 'Yesterday's
Men'. The history of the photographs was basically that Pope had
wished to include film of the new farm but this had been rejected on
the grounds of security. Instead of film, a number of photographs
had been included which was felt by Haines to have been another
broken 'promise'. By the night of the 16 June the question of the
programme had been taken out of the hands of Dinbleby and Pope, and
was being dealt with at the very highest levels of the BBC. The
central question was what assurance had been made to Wilson about
the deletions from the programme. Hill's diary for 17 June notes:
'Last evening there were further talks between the Director General,
Huw Wheldon and Wilson's advisers, including Lord Goodman.' The
meeting had taken place at Lord Goodman's flat. A particular point
of contention was to be that in late May Charles Curran had sent
Wilson what he described as the only copy of the tape in existence,
along with a memo from Angela Pope to John Grist stating that this
was indeed the contentious part of the conversation. On the 16th
Wilson and Haines discovered that not only was it not the sole
record but that part of it was to be broadcast nationally the following evening. The point was compounded on the 18 June when the
whole of the conversation was leaked to the press.
   Following the meeting of the evening of 16/17 June, during which
Goodman had hinted that an injunction might be sought to prevent the
programme being broadcast, there followed a night in which Hill
tried to avoid talking to the representatives of Wilson (1974,
p.182):

'I was staying at the flat at the BBC following a dinner and Mrs.
Marcia Williams tried to get me so that Wilson, accompanied by his
solicitors, could speak with me. The telephone girl had already
informed Mrs. Williams that I was on the telephone to Charles Curran

and would ring her when I had finished. I had to indulge in the
subterfuge of getting her to tell Mrs. Williams that I had gone
home, whereupon Mrs. Williams said she would ring me at home in
about an hour's time, which would have been about 1 a.m. I rang
my wife straightaway and told her not to answer the telephone during
the night. My purpose in all this was to avoid being put in the
position of having pressure applied to me.'

During the same night at some point Hill and Curran agreed that the
governors should see the film, but had great difficulty in obtaining
it since the producer had the film reel and was not contacted until
6 a.m. on the morning of 17 June, transmission day. The demands of
the Wilson camp had crystallized into three: the title should be
changed; the photographs of Grange Farm should be removed; the
question and answer about the memoirs should be excluded. A press
showing of the programme had been scheduled for 11 a.m. on the 17th,
but since the governors were to see the film this was delayed until
noon. The governors' meeting (5) concentrated on two issues: the
legitimacy of Dimbleby's question about the memoirs; the nature of
the pledge made to Haines about the extent of the deletion. The
question of the Grange Farm photograph and the title were also
raised. The decision was made to delete all of the references to
the memoirs but to retain the title and the still photographs of
Grange Farm.
   Haines had initially intended to boycott the press showing on the
grounds that they had been promised a separate showing of the film
so that they could comment on it but had then had their request for
the separate showing turned down. Following the revelations of the
night of the 16th, their discovery of the title and a telephone call
to Transport House from someone within the BBC 'warning how bad this
was', Haines decided to attend. The press reaction was to be mixed
but Haines's immediate reaction was that the whole programme was a
send up and that, given the fact that they had been assured that it
would be a 'serious documentary', there had been a 'carefully calculated, deliberate, continuous deceit over a period of months'.
This then brings us to the third and perhaps most significant controversy, the question of the programme's intent - which was rapidly
followed by two further points of contention: a statement in the
film about Wilson having 'privileged access' to government papers
for writing his memoirs (which brought an immediate threat of
libel); and then the leaking of the deletions by an anonymous caller
to a number of newspapers. The press on 18 June was full of the
substance of the deletions. The Labour people were further annoyed
when on the night of 18 June, the same spot in '24 Hours' carried
a rather celebratory review of Heath's first year in office.
Entitled 'The Quiet Revolution' it was described by Greene, among
others, as a 'programme of a very different character' from 'Yesterday's Men' (Greene, 1972). Following the governors' decision about
the content of the programme, the final decision about its actual
transmission at 10 p.m. that night seems to have been made by Grist,
head of CAG. He had another production team preparing an alternative programme in case the decision was not to broadcast 'Yesterday's Men', and it was only a very short time before the programme
that the decision was finally made to go ahead.

Press comment on the programme dealt with both the details of the row and the critical appraisal of the programme. The accounts of the row were, as one might expect, shallow and unclear. Having gone through all the press copy which sought to assess the merits of the programme, I estimate that there was 3:2 favourable comment ratio. The programme was variously described as 'fascinating television' and 'one of the most interesting (programmes on politics) ever shown on British television' ('Telegraph'). It was lauded for turning 'yesterday's people of power into real people' ('Express') and for refusing to 'look on the touchy untouchables as stuffed penguins.... It was human, lively and interesting ... an entertaining and professional job' ('Mirror'). But it was also criticized for being '45 minutes of television gossip column' ('Guardian'). 'The Times' editorial (19 June 1971) attacked the programme for trivialization, the 'Telegraph' editorial felt that both sides had cause for complaint and the 'Guardian' thought it was a 'night worth forgetting'.

Following the transmission of the programme the controversy revolved around four main questions: had the Labour leaders been deceived; had the film been cut in such a way as to present a distorted view of the lives of the Labour leaders; had there been a breach of faith by the BBC; who had leaked the extracts to the press (Hill, 1974, p.185)? These were to provide the central focus of the enquiry which was instituted by Lord Hill on 21 June, and conducted by Maurice Tinniswood, the director of personnel, and Desmond Taylor, ENCA. The investigators' report was delivered to a special meeting of the governors on 7 July, along with a draft of a possible governors' statement prepared by Hill. Published in 'The Listener' on 15 July, the governors' report consisted of an amalgam of the investigators' report and the Hill draft.

Between 17 June and 20 June a large volume of press copy, stemming mainly from the Labour party's briefing of the lobby, indicated that the party was extremely annoyed and felt its representative had been deceived. This culminated in a speech by a senior Labour party man, Bob Mellish, in which he stated that there was 'a limit to how much democracy can abuse, insult, sneer and jeer.... If the BBC go on with this type of campaign, we must counter it by whatever activities we have at our disposal within the party publicity machine.' It was in the context of this furore, particularly over the question of deceit, that the enquiry was instituted. It was amplified when Crossman, in his other role as editor of the 'New Statesman', made a scathing attack (25 June 1971) on the programme-makers, sparking off a further wave of press comment and publicity.

The governors' report ('Listener', 15 July 1971) was a detailed refutation of the principal charges. It poured forth facts, and in doing so sought to swamp the Labour arguments. It showed that the ratio of transcript available to transcript used was for each of the participants on average 12:1. It provided details of the time (minutes and seconds) spent on the different areas, 'Defeat and adapting to the idea of being an Opposition: 4 minutes 48 seconds, Financial consequences: 4 minutes ...' etc. It argues that of the seven main areas of questioning 'all the participants were questioned on nearly all of these matters'. The report then proceeded to 'comment' on the programme and on this factual analysis. It argued that the question about the memoirs and the money were per-

missible, but that given the misunderstanding on the scope of the
deletion it was only right to delete that area. The report argued
that on the whole the area of questioning 'conformed to the description that the programme would be about the "political and personal
nature of the job of Opposition"' and that no major area of interviewing was omitted. In any journalistic exercise, it argued, there
is a need to edit and cut material down to a manageable size and
that given their analysis (paras 5 and 6) 'the material finally
selected from the interviews for use in the transmitted programme
was on the whole representative and fair', 'there was no improper
or inadequate intercutting'. The title should have been transmitted
to the participants, and the programme-makers should have realized
that the song used 'represented a substantial change in the atmosphere in which the film would be interpreted by the participants
from that which they might have expected from earlier descriptions
of the programme.' Certain aspects of the treatment were 'too
frivolous'. The leaks are condemned but, the report adds, there
was no conclusive evidence as to where in the BBC they originated,
but that there was some evidence that the BBC was not the only
source of the leaks. The nature of the placing of 'Yesterday's
Men' and the Heath programme on the following night was an error.
The report ended on a flourish of principles about the fair and
impartial nature of BBC news and current affairs coverage, embodied
in a 'case law' of 'principles and practices'.

The report was seen by the press as a defence by the governors
of their own staff, with only a mild rebuke for one or two misdemeanours, and there were such headlines as 'BBC defends Dimbleby',
'BBC Rejects Charges', 'New Labour Fury', 'Carry On Dimbleby'.
There is little doubt that in many ways the whole report was a
defensive exercise. Dimbleby thought it a 'very shrewdly devised
political exercise by Lord Hill to recover from a disastrous position'. There is also a strong feeling that the firmness of the
support for the programme-makers in the report was because (a) the
governors had cleared the film for transmission on 17 June and
therefore could not, without severe loss of face, condemn the programme; (b) to have condemned the programme would have been to imply
that Pope and Dimbleby were without adequate supervision; (c) to
have argued that there was full editorial control would have made it
even more difficult to take the programme to task since the whole
editorial structure of the BBC current affairs would have been
implicated.

In mid-July Hill was sent a letter from Wilson's solicitors
'demanding an abject apology, trailed on the air and in the Radio
Times, plus the payment of his costs and a contribution to a charity
named by him. In short we were asked to grovel ...' (Hill, 1974,
p.190). The legal question was still over the use of the phrase
'access to privileged documents'. The BBC publicly apologized on
Friday 6 August, for the use of 'certain words (which) might suggest
that he had made advantageous use of privileged or secret documents
in an unjustifiable fashion'. The controversy of 'Yesterday's Men'
was ostensibly at an end.

A number of questions need to be considered, not the least of
which is the possible light which the controversy throws on the
nature of the relationships, and the consequences of the relation-

ships, between broadcasters and politicians. We need to consider
this in terms of the overall consequences of 'Yesterday's Men' for
programme-making since 1971. There is, however, a third point which
needs to be considered, and it is, on reflection, perhaps the most
profound and significant of the three. This is the insight that
the making of the programme provides into the situation and intentions of the programme-maker, and the way in which this is generated, not by political malice or bias but by a competitive institutional structure and a limited technology. Ironically an analysis
of the consequences of external structures leads back into the
previous discussion of the internal processes of programme-making.

Hardcastle (1971) argued that conflict between broadcasters and
politicians has been a recurring theme throughout the fifty-year
history of the medium, and that the first and most important consequence of the 'Yesterday's Men' controversy was a 'strong assertion by the BBC of its right of independent editorial judgement'.
Rejecting Labour party notions that the programme exemplifies a
general state of malaise and anti-Labour opinion within the BBC,
Hardcastle's view is that there was, on this occasion, 'an obvious
lack of consistent editorial supervision'. It was, he implies, an
anomaly, a mistake. This view was put by a number of other individuals obliquely connected with the programme: that the editor of
'24 Hours' had been away for some of the time, that it wasn't
'really' part of '24 Hours', that Grist was more concerned with programmes about the Common Market, and so on. There is ample evidence, however, that throughout they were made aware of what the
programme would be about: they knew of the song, for example, and
even saw rough-cuts of the actual programme.

If Hardcastle's tone was pro-BBC, anti-programme-makers, support
for the latter came from Kee (1971) who argued that the programme
was a 'vulgarly brilliant equivalent of the newspaper cartoon - a
concentration on one point of truth to a near grotesque extreme, as
is the way of cartoons'. In his only full-length public discussion
of the programme to date, Dimbleby (1972) takes up this point.
Detailing the problems of looking at the 'political and personal',
problems of the new Opposition, he describes it as an ambitious aim
which could only be achieved by using all 'the facilities television
afforded us'. 'In addition to interviews and commentary, there was
to be music, cartoon and even a hint of satire. In this respect we
took less liberty than the press does daily with its choice of headlines, its cartoons, its speculations, its editorials and its
satirical comment.' The initial spark to the controversy he states
was an 'extraordinary outburst' following a 'question to the Leader
of the Opposition ... put in a bantering fashion in full expectation
of an equally bantering reply' (Dimbleby, 1972). In similar terms
Smith (1972) states that the problem arose because of 'the smile
which Mr. Wilson failed to see'. Broadcasting, Dimbleby argues, has
been characterized by a tradition in which not only has the professional broadcaster been excluded from the formulation of general
policy, but is also excluded from the formulation of policy in areas
where he is specifically and directly concerned, as for example over
'Yesterday's Men' where 'At no point during the "Yesterday's Men"
affair did the Chairman or the Governors talk directly with the
programme-makers', and it is this 'failure to consult', not only

in the context of 'Yesterday's Men' but 'right across the board in
current affairs broadcasting' which irks Dimbleby greatly. Essentially, Dimbleby wishes the heirarchy firmly to identify with the
professional broadcaster, and harks back to a golden age of Greene
when a unity of interest between broadcaster and administration was
deemed to exist. From this unity, the argument goes, there emerged
a forthright and aggressive use of the medium. From that, however,
emerged contention and so slowly that the sharp edge of television
journalism has been blunted and the world of broadcasting gone into
retreat. Dimbleby's is an interesting piece in that 'Yesterday's
Men' becomes not a cause of events, not a unique example of pressure
and its consequences, but rather exemplifies an already existing
process. The walls, as it were, had already begun to crumble;
'Yesterday's Men' merely served to weaken them further.

   'The Times' editorial thought the programme 'utterly trivial',
'the attitude of the gossip column or the political novelette', the
view of 'immature young people' (Crossman was to describe Dimbleby a
as a 'cub reporter promoted above his station'). The 'Guardian'
(19 July 1971) pitched in with a similar theme, saying that

'Pope and her jump cutters produced a giggly, gossipy documentary
full of snide visuals and engagingly crass questions of the would-
you-stab-Harold-in-the-back-or-front variety. Sometimes it looked
like a breakfast food commercial, sometimes it echoed Butch Cassidy;
always it steered away from issues or real problems or fundamental
political judgements. Like so much other TV "reportage", it was,
in fact, a technical entertainment job - a skilled blending of
interview snippets and scenes from life and lilting soundtracks by
a team whose commitment was to the blend and not necessarily to the
issues involved. Mr. Wilson chanting "Through the Night of Doubt and
Sorrow", fumbling with his golf clubs or parading against the sunset
to a sardonic score may make a splendid collage of emptily symbolic
photographs, but are the judgements they conveyed worth anything?
Were they picked because they make a slick little ... jab or a
point?'

Contrasting the artificially slick 'Wizard Wilson' of a Labour party
broadcast, with the equally artificial 'stumbling derisory Wilson'
of 'Yesterday's Men', the 'Guardian' concludes that the problem
faced by the BBC is not the sustaining of its independence but
whether 'the independence it seeks to defend is being used seriously
by production teams who care about getting it true and gritty. Is
Miss Pope's Wilson any more life-like than Transport Houses's? If
not, why not?' In a perceptive piece of writing in the 'Guardian'
(22 June 1971) Peter Jenkins argued that the Labour Party did have
cause for complaint, that the treatment was trivial and superficial
but that this flowed from the nature of the medium, 'film in current
affairs is all too frequently the enemy of content, and visuality
is itself inimical to the treatment of most serious subjects'. The
problem, it is argued, lies in a contradiction between the use of
the medium to entertain and inform in a competitive situation.
   There are a number of themes in the public discourse over the
programme. The lack of editorial control; the impropriety of the
questions; the trivialization of the subject matter; the bias of

the BBC against the Labour party; the contradictions in the position
occupied by the governors. The central theme of the attack by the
Labour party on the programme was that they had been misled into
expecting a serious programme and been served with a send-up. The
most forthright presentation of the Labour party case came from one
of the participants, Crossman. Arguing that they had been invited
to do a serious programme, the participants, Crossman states, were
interviewed at length on a number of issues, and no one doubted for
'a moment that while the programme in which he was due to participate would provide lively television entertainment, its main concern
would be to present a fair and objective picture of how the Labour
Party ... had settled down to its role as Her Majesty's Opposition'
(Crossman, 1971). The actual programme 'was grotesquely and
indecently different' from the programme the ex-ministers expected.
The interview material was chopped away to leave only the 'spicy
trimmings', 'distorted' impressions were created of what had been
said, and apparently contradictory extracts were juxtaposed:

'the effect was achieved first through the deliberate fraud by which
the politicians were persuaded to take part and, secondly, by the
even greater fraud by which fragments were snipped out of the interviews they gave and juxtaposed in order to convey a false impression
of what they had meant and even of what they had actually said.'

The whole programme, Crossman states, was 'shallow and trivial', a
'fraud' perpetrated by individuals with inadequate editorial supervision. Broadcasting House, through its negligence, effectively
granted them 'a licence to distort and misrepresent'. Haines described the programme as disgraceful:

'It was never any attempt to be a serious film about the Opposition.
It was a send up. I remember that Dennis Healey's contribution was
cut in such a way as to make it appear as though he was bemoaning
his loss of income; he said that his income had dropped from whatever it was, £10,000 to £9,000 p.a., to £3,000, and there it
stopped, whereas what Dennis had in fact gone on to say was "but
I am not complaining - most of my constituents in Leeds are far
worse off". It was that sort of cutting ... the thing was generally
a send up ... the intention all along was a send up. This was
really our principal complaint - it was not the question that was
asked but the deceit....'

These various charges appear to be refuted by the governors'
report. The 'facts' however do not speak as loudly as they were
made to seem since 'tone' does not lend itself to the type of quan-
tification carried out in the report: one can produce details of
the distribution of question areas, etc. but that tells one nothing
about the overall character of the programme. The principal view
which emerges from press comment on the programme is that it was a
send up, though there was disagreement over the suitability of such
a send up. Difficulty, of course, lies in assessing the impressions
created in the minds of the participants by the programme-makers,
and in assessing the particular motives of the programme-makers.
Two questions linger: did Dimbleby and Pope create the impression

that it would be a 'serious documentary' as would be understood by
seasoned politicians raised amid the conventional forms of 'Panorama' et al.; did they intend to create that impression or indeed to
make such a programme? All the evidence points to 'yes' for the
first question; a qualified 'no' to the second question. 'Yesterday's Men' employed a number of unusual techniques which created the
adverse reaction of the participants, but their employment did not
flow from any commitment to an anti-Labour line. Indeed, it is
possible to argue that the problem lay in a profound disinterest in
the more traditional forms of politics and political television
which led the programme-makers to develop new ideas of presentation,
and this was to be the spring for the controversy.

A major feature of 'Yesterday's Men' was the ambiguous and ultimately contradictory position adopted by the governors of the BBC.
To whom do the governors owe their loyalty and responsibility, to
the public interest or to the programme-makers? The problem arose
from the governors not only vetting the programme, and therefore
acting in an editorial role (the 17 June role), but also sitting in
judgment on that editorial decision (the 15 July role). Hill is
aware of the problems involved (1974, pp.189-90):

'Reflecting on the sequence of events, a nagging question kept
recurring in my mind. Whose role was it to protect those who
believe they have been unfairly treated by the BBC? Strictly
speaking, the answer is the Governors, for they represent the
public. But, as in this case, it is often necessary and right for
the Governors to defend the staff of the BBC when they have been
unfairly attacked. The more we were seen in this defensive role,
the more difficult it was to be seen to be, if not actually to be,
the trustees for the public.'

Smith (1972) puts the point succinctly: 'What right had the Governors of the BBC to sit in judgement on a matter of editorial content
which they had themselves viewed and sanctioned on the day of the
transmission?' Given the inability of the governors, the argument
goes, to exert any authority over the broadcasters, then somebody
must be instituted to exert control and authority, viz. a Broad-.
casting Council. The chairman and governors could not occupy twin
roles of senior executive and public guardian. The supreme irony
in this debacle is that the initial step towards the establishment
of an executive board was made first of all by Wilson who, through
the appointment of Lord Hill, sought to supplant the authority of
Greene. The process had in a sense begun with Normanbrook, and
certainly at the time of his appointment as chairman in April 1964,
Normanbrook was thought to have been a 'tough' appointment. As
Greene indicates, however, in his role as chairman, Normanbrook
always refused requests for the governors to vet programmes before
transmission, deeming this an executive role and therefore not
appropriate to them. Hill clearly pursued an executive role as was
indicated in the account of his appointment and Greene's subsequent
retirement. On this most important executive action by a non-
executive board the result was not to Wilson's liking.

POLITICS AND PROGRAMME PRACTICES: INNOVATION AND INHIBITION

To understand why 'Yesterday's Men' turned out as it did, and to see
the interaction between the political sphere and the act of making
programmes, one has to consider very carefully the particular conceptions of current affairs television possessed by the programme-
makers. As described in the preceding narrative, Dimbleby and Pope,
following their initial research for the programme, had doubts about
the possibilities of the programme but, having informed the Labour
people of their intentions, were forced to go ahead and produce a
programme. Both wished to avoid what they regarded as the more
boring aspects of current affairs television, and the producer
declared 'I certainly wasn't going to make a film about the constitutional position of the opposition'. From the early stages of the
programme the producer had in fact felt that the views of the Labour
leaders on their political role, as the official opposition would
not provide fifty minutes of television, and this in itself led to
a focus on the more personal realm of individual adjustments to a
new role:

'In my experience a programme emerges through the following process.
A general idea for a programme is researched thoroughly in various
ways, and during research the idea gets sharpened and focussed, and
the structure of the programme is decided upon. In the case of YM,
this was partly done by talking to the participants to see whether
they were interested in talking about the topics we had in mind.
We found that a few months after defeat, the political and personal
impact of that shock was still fresh in their minds. We also found
that with the exception of one or two limited areas, they had not
yet had time to formulate their policies for the next five years
and none of them really wanted to talk about this.'

In other words, Pope is arguing that because of the difficulties of
discussing the more overtly political questions, they were thrown
back onto discussing the more personal questions of the adjustment
to the loss of power and status. It is, however, possible to argue
that this developing perspective was never transmitted to the participants and, for example, the letter from Dimbleby to Wilson could
be interpreted as meaning that there would be more, not less, attention paid to political questions. What must be added though, in
fairness to the producer is that from the inception of the programme
the interviewees had been informed that there would be at least some
discussion of the more personal objects of opposition life.
   At the time of 'Yesterday's Men' Pope had a clear conception of
herself as a producer who though interested in the machinations of
political life was more concerned with the problems of translating
politics into televisually appealing programme content. This was
initially based on her critique of existing political television,
whose conventions and forms seemed inadequate for dealing with the
idea of 'Yesterday's Men'. She notes:

'I remember that when I was first asked to make "Yesterday's Men",
I felt rather daunted and wondered how I would make people watch.
I didn't think that seven long interviews would work. There were

certain things that David Dimbleby and I wanted to say about the
nature of political life - its motives, prizes, privations and so
on - as seen through the eyes of seven prominent politicians at a
certain traumatic point in their political lives. We decided to
use a variety of television techniques to say those things. I was
very interested in learning the techniques of film and TV and in
mastering them sufficiently to be able to say what I want to say as
engagingly as possible.'

The task as seen by Pope was then to deal with a serious subject in
an entertaining way: 'I wanted to ask some serious questions but I
wanted to do it in an edgy, biting and I hoped engaging way.' The
earlier discussion of the internal context of programme-making
indicated the way in which different definitions of programming and
stylistic criteria derived from different departmental structures.
The whole experience of 'Yesterday's Men' was based on the exclusi-
vity of form within CAG and therefore the presuppositions of politicians about the nature of programmes to emerge from the group.
Anomaly was the keynote of 'Yesterday's Men' and embedded in differential expectations of what the programme would look like; the
result was controversy.
    The conceptions of the producer were allied to the very similar
views held by Dimbleby. Discussing the way that 'Panorama' tends
to focus on subjects such as Willy Brandt's policy of Ostpolitik,
he observed:

'Now, Ostpolitik is (a) extremely important, (b) very complicated,
(c) not very televisual in the sense that there is nothing to look
at very much except the faces of German politicians rabbiting on,
(d) is therefore pretty dull on the screen. But some people believe
that television has a duty to do these dull things because that is
what life is like and all the rest of it.
    'I find that admirable but I'm not sure myself that it is a sen-
sible view. I don't take the view that it's all got to be froth,
at all, but I do think that one of the merits of the machine (TV) is
that it can make subjects, which people otherwise would not be
interested in, interesting and worth watching. You are involved
with a constant, almost paternalistic, activity of coaxing people
to come and see, come and find out, come and watch.'

The challenge in Dimbleby's mind is to take a subject which, though
serious, has been done many times previously in a rather boring
manner and to make that subject televisually appealing. He chose
the example of trade unions to illuminate the point.

'To most people in the audience trade unionism is something they've
heard so much about, and they are so used to the same old union
leaders rabbiting on, that if you are coming to make a film about
how trade unionism works, one's first thing is to say "Well, look,
we all know what those people are going to say and the audience
knows, let's not do that again," let's try and find some way, for
instance, of explaining the grass roots strength, explaining the
role of the shop steward. Now one way of doing it is we can do a
sort of university of the air type programme about it, where you

interview some shop stewards in a fairly solemn way and explain
where they stand on the shop floor. That's one way.
'The other thing you can try to do is to make a film which was
about them as individuals as well as about them in their political
role and which would become something which at an individual level
was interesting. People, you see, work very well on television.
Institutions, abstract concepts, don't work so well. And what
people like about television - and in a way they are sensible
because the abstract concepts come across better in print - what
they like is this feeling that you are actually being shown the man
who's in this situation. Take the trade unionists, of course you
can spend time explaining what the shop steward's role is, of course
you can talk to the union or the management about the shop stewards
and all that sort of thing. But in a funny way, unless you can
also make the shop steward come alive as a person, it won't amount
to much more than an awful lot of stuff that's been done already.'

Dimbleby's proposition is that by focusing on the more personal
aspects of a man's life you can in a sense 'make him come alive'
and, in doing so, throw light on the motivations of his political
self as opposed to his private self. A key factor in this view of
broadcasting and a key to the nature of 'Yesterday's Men' was a
belief that

'television is not the same kind of medium as books or newspapers,
and it's not at heart an intellectual medium, though the process
demands intellect of course, but it's not at heart something that
appeals to the intellect. It's something that works on all sorts of
different levels, much more emotional than intellectual.'

The premiss is that the political broadcaster is 'an entertainer as
well as a political journalist. And people who aren't become very
quickly not watched.' And, of the relevance of all this to the programme: 'the idea of the song and the idea of the music and the idea
of the cartoon weren't in our minds in the beginning. Those things
gradually came in as you try to make a potentially very boring film
into something that's watchable.'
The most significant feature in all this and the most relevant to
the accusations of the Labour party was that in making the film the
programme-makers adopted and developed techniques which were incompatible with the more traditional political formulae of '24 Hours'
and 'Panorama' which at the time of 'Yesterday's Men' were the
centre pieces of CAG output. This clearly did not fit with the
expectations of the Labour politicians taking part who were used to
the more ritualized aspects of the Robin Day-type interview.
Whether they were deceived is difficult to say. The problem was
described in the following way: 'They may in a sense have felt that
their expectations weren't fulfilled. Certainly their expectations
weren't fulfilled but those expectations were based on their own
assumptions and not on anything that we had told them.' The fact
also remains that at least two of the participants sent friendly,
but secret, notes saying that they weren't particularly bothered
about the programme.
Much acrimony was caused by the fact that the Labour leaders were

not told of the programme title. Part of the problem was that they
did not care to ask the title since in the normal course of events a
title like 'Yesterday's Men' would not have been used. The programme-makers argue that at no point were the participants led to
believe that the programme would be called 'Her Majesty's Opposition' or the 'Loyal Opposition' or the 'Labour Opposition'. The
Labour leaders argue that the term 'Her Majesty's Opposition' was
used in their correspondence and that they quite naturally assmed
that this would be the title of the programme. However, the two
programme-makers were clearly aware of the possible difficulties
which such a title might engender. They argue that it is not journalistic practice to disclose 'headlines', 'we treated the title as
a headline in a sense and had we communicated the title they wouldn't
have accepted it'. Pope's notes from the time state:

'The second point raised in arguments about the title is that even
if the participants did not raise the question of the title, I
should have done. I have never been required to do this in the
past, nor have I ever heard of any producer being required to do so.
As I understand it, it is standard and accepted practice for a producer to choose his title.'

There is then another ambiguity or twist in that the programme-
makers, having moved from the world of 'straight' broadcast journalism, on this point are firmly employing the principles and practices as laid down, albeit informally, within that world. They are
commuting between two different explanations of current affairs
television in accordance with particular circumstances and it is
therefore not too surprising that problems would be induced by such
an ambivalent position.
    One might expect a clash between broadcasters and politicians of
the scale of 'Yesterday's Men' to have enormous consequences, at
least at the level of the careers of those involved. The two
directly involved, Pope and Dimbleby, aare both still functioning,
and Dimbleby has become the presenter of the programme which epito-
mized the formal, boring current affairs television that he opposed,
'Panorama'. Angela Pope faced a number of difficulties when preparing a programme requiring the co-operation of members of local
authorities and it seems unlikely that she would be allowed near
Wilson again. The principal casualty was undoubtedly the head of
CAG, who was transferred to controller, English Regions. In his
book Hill described a meeting of the governors on 14 July 1971, at
which Curran proposed (Hill, 1974, p.190):

'a change in the headship of current affairs in television. He had
had this in mind for some time in order to give John Grist a new
area of activity after a long spell in current affairs. He also
proposed to strengthen the control exercised by the editor of news
and current affairs and to add to the team someone with recent knowledge and experience in the parliamentary field.'

In September Curran informed another board meeting of the 'fruits'
of the changes, with Desmond Taylor, ENCA, 'having a closer and
fuller responsibility for all current affairs programmes, *spending*

more of his time at Line Grove' (my emphasis). (5) Curran 'thought
that the new appointments and the redrawing of the lines of responsibility would have a visible and significant effect on '24 Hours'
(Hill, 1974, p.190).

A clearer statement of the tightening of organization and editorial control would be difficult to imagine. In fact the civil tones
of this piece hide a considerable furore over these events. Contrasted with the placid description by Hill, I was told that at a
meeting between Curran and Wilson in May 1971 'Curran said to Mr.
Wilson when we met him at a party, "Heads will roll for this", and
I guess the heads that rolled was just John Grist's head.' Curran
denies emphatically ever having said this. Asked who did say it
and whether it could have been Hill for example, he replied, 'Maybe,
I don't know.' 'Would you have liked to have said it?' 'No, but
even if I had privately to have done so would have been political
nonsense and a sign of great weakness.'

Mistakes of a diplomatic nature were undoubtedly made by the programme-makers, and one would certainly wish to question their judgment on certain issues. The events of 'Yesterday's Men', however,
derive principally from their attempt to integrate a number of
original practices into the making of political television. Why
this was so and how it relates to a general situation in broadcasting are discussed in the general conclusions to these case
studies. What is significant is that they sought to embed new seeds
in an institutional and political environment which was far from
ready to accept them. One can't explain the actions of the programme-makers in the rather strident tones, involving imputations
of conspiracy employed by the Labour party at the time. The change
and effects induced by Wilson's response to 'Yesterday's Men',
while subtle though profound, probably only represented an acceler-
ation of a retrenchment which had been gathering pace over the previous four years. An interesting parallel is 'TW3', which had a
relatively brief and successful life within CAG but which was
removed by Greene in the light of what he felt to be its declining
standards, the increasing problems posed by its style in an election
year (1964) and the increasing disquiet among the board of governors
about its content. The conception by those involved of what .the
impact has been, the consequences for programming, are clear and
Dimbleby states:

'Under Hugh Greene we were still in a stage of trying to discover
what television can do. Now I think we are on the retreat in that
I don't think you can expect any fireworks for some time. I think
everybody is too much aware now of the kind of trouble like this
that you get into to allow it to happen. But I think that is allied
in many people's minds to a genuine doubt about what the role of
television is, and a genuine feeling that perhaps all that was perhaps the wrong way to use it and that you shouldn't be challenging,
investigating in quite that way. I don't myself subscribe to this.
I think that it is the right way of using it and I think it's a
great pity that it hasn't really had a chance. But these new
audience participation programmes, for instance. In theory they are
an attempt at enlarging the access to the BBC, in practice they are
as disciplined as any other sort of programme.... So I detect a

rather hideous softening. It's not got very bad yet, it's true,
and you can still see fairly straightforward reports on 'Panorama'
and 'Midweek'. You still have very hard interviews with politicians, but somehow the feeling that it was a medium with which one
could experiment has gone. The feeling, for instance, we had with
'Yesterday's Men', there was a chance to really try and do something
different with a political film, try and make it different so that
it explained things in an entertaining way. All that's gone.'

   The impact of the Labour party protests on the process of production within the BBC current affairs department was part of a much
wider process, tied up with the appointment of Hill, then the
retirement of Greene, threats of broadcasting councils and the
break-up of the existing broadcasting institutions. Perhaps the
most interesting perception of the impact of the 'Yesterday's Men'
affair lies in Pope's own conception of the new parameters of the
permissible, of how her own programming will be affected. "Yesterday's Men', she states, was 'sharp and entertaining,'

'and the kind of telly that politicians have never been part of.
In retrospect I can see this much more strongly than I could then.
I think that to an extent I have learned an awful lot about that
from the whole episode and one of the worst things is that I would
never try to do it again. I have had my fingers burnt. I wouldn't
try it and no one else would try it for a very long time.... Nobody
must do "Yesterday's Men" again. You mustn't. Better be safe than
be imaginative.'

Chapter 11

TELEVISION IN THE GENERAL ELECTION
A 1974 case study

The supreme event in the to and fro of party politics is the calling
of a General Election. Massive efforts are made, both by the parties involved and by the media, to present to 'people' a 'full
account' of 'what is happening' and what the 'whole thing is all
about'. Few events in the broadcaster's calendar match in importance the coverage of the results of an election - perhaps a royal
wedding, the death of a president, the peril of an astronaut or the
fate and fortunes of 'our' representatives in the Olympics or the
World Cup, evoke a similar kind of response from the broadcasting
organization in terms of their allocation of broadcasting time,
man-hours and financial resources. It becomes a massive logistical
exercise, characterized by large doses of computerology and pundi-
try, 'latest news' and 'in-depth analysis'. The expressed commitment is to a 'full and exhaustive' coverage of the 'event', broadcasting displaying to the full its public service wares. This is
an account of one piece of the overall mosaic of that process, a
case study of the coverage of the election of 1974 by one commercial
television station, Associated Television (ATV). The main part of
the election campaign was spent in the company's news and current
affairs department, observing newsroom activity, holding informal
interviews and noting as much as possible - decisions, discussions,
conversations, jokes, phone calls (who to, what for, etc?) - everything. This is an account of those notes, digested over the months
that passed since then, and, while it clearly cannot hope to tap
the whole logic of the television process, the final result does
provide at least an insight into the 'logic' within which broadcasting is encased and throws some light on the nature of the relationship between television and the world of politics.

Walter Gieber may have been a little severe in his observation
that news consists of 'a series of related symbols that can be mani-
pulated in the damnedest sort of ways by the damnedest type of
people...' (1964), but anyone who has spent time in a newsroom will
surely acknowledge that it is the damnedest type of process to try
and describe. That what happens in the newsroom is important is
argued profusely by many, that what happens during the course of an
election campaign is even more important is reflected both in the
plethora of regulations and agreements that ostensibly control the

whole affair, and also in the rigorous attempts by the parties to
gear their campaign to the requirements of the broadcast media (the
'walkabout' and Mr Wilson's pipe are both part of the battery of
campaign techniques, both blend with the need for 'pictures' the
central fact of life in the TV process).

How did this particular news organization approach the election?
What issues did they see as important, how did they cover these
issues, and why did they cover them in the way they did? To these
basic questions were attached a series of sub-questions: what decisions were made, by whom, for what reasons, with what effect on
their interpretation and selection of the issues of the election
campaign?

POLITICAL IMAGES FROM ATV: THE COVERAGE

ATV's actual 'election coverage' began on Monday 18 February, the
beginning of the second week of the election campaign.   The centre-
piece of the coverage was 'Midday Report', a twenty-minute programme
that went out at 12 p.m. each lunchtime Monday to Friday. The
format for each 'Report' was a discussion between the members of a
panel formed from candidates, or particular interests (unions,
business, etc.) or 'ordinary' voters, and varying in number from
three to six members. Candidates might also appear as spokesmen
for their party rather than as 'the candidates from X constituency'.
The panel discussion was never mixed, in the sense that candidates
were always 'pitted' against candidates, spokesmen against spokesmen, and voters against voters, and the panel was always formed from
adherents of the three main parties (in Britain), and of the major
interests in the industrial sector. Strenuous efforts were made to
maintain a 'balance' within each individual programme, and on the
one occasion when that balance couldn't be maintained the programme
was abandoned. Where the discussion was with candidates they were
always from the same constituency, the introduction by the inter-
viewer/presenter taking the form of 'And today we have the candidates from Constituency X, who are Mr A, Mr B, and Mr C ...' Where
candidates were appearing as spokesmen representing the general
interest of their party rather than their own particular candida-
cies, they were named along with their party, but no mention was
made of their constituency. So, for example, one particular MP
could appear on the 'Report' even though the three other candidates
from his constituency did not appear.

In addition to the time allocated to the main parties, time was
also allocated to the two main 'minority' parties, the Communist
party (CP) and the National Front (NF), each being interviewed for a
few minutes during one of the 'Report' programmes. Prior to this
there had been some discussion over what to do with the various
small parties that were putting up candidates in the Midland region.
The editor decided that they must distinguish between the CP and NF,
and other parties such as the Workers Revolutionary party, the
English National party and Dick Tavernes' Social Democrats. He felt
that while they might be able to make time available to the first
two, who were putting up a number of candidates, they could not
allow time to the other three who were putting up only one or two

candidates each. He was well aware of the kind of anomalies
implicit in the equation 'number of candidates = time allocated',
and pointed to the fact that if one allocated time strictly according to number of candidates and overall electoral strength, the
Liberal party in the region would not receive equal time with the
Conservative and Labour parties, 'It all comes down in the end to
using your common sense, there are no easy answers'.

Within the actual newsroom the literature from the minor parties
was not taken particularly seriously, though this was not the criteria by which the right of access to time was judged. This was
done solely on the grounds that they had not enough candidates to
warrant time. There was, for example, a good deal of antipathy
towards the policies of the National Front and the Communist party,
but it was felt by the editor that they were sufficiently important
to warrant at least some time on the screen to put their views
forward, whereas the various other minnows of the electoral battle
could not, it was felt, be given any time.

The actual interviewing of the representatives of the two
minority parties was carried out by the more experienced of the two
political reporters, mainly because of an ill-defined feeling that
the interviews would 'prove difficult'. As an added 'safeguard'
the interviews were pre-recorded since no one was quite sure what
the National Front and Communist party spokesmen would actually say,
and so as long as the interviews were pre-recorded control remained
firmly in editorial hands. Another argument used was that 'We don't
want to associate the Conservative and Labour parties with the NF
and CP by putting them on live together in the same programme.' (1)
There was this feeling that while they must take account of these
two minority groups, it would be wrong to taint the purity of the
prevailing orthodoxy by bringing them into too close a contact with
the major parties. Another 'problem' with the minority parties was
the difficulty of getting hold of someone 'good' to represent them
in the interview. This was particularly the case with the National
Front from whom they were particularly keen to have Martin Webster,
their National Organizer and only acknowledged media figure. Interestingly enough, this was not just a problem for the minority party,
since the inability of the Liberals to produce anyone of broadcast-
able quality for the programmes was referred to frequently. The
senior reporter felt that the Liberals had done very badly in all
the 'candidate contests', and during the preparation for the final
programme of the coverage he declared that he had been on to them to
'pull out the stops in getting someone good for the final programme'
which was to be a debate between spokesmen for the leading parties.
'I'm hoping' he declared, 'to get someone really good.'

The amount of time that the two minority parties were given was,
in the end, felt to be about right, '... seven or eight minutes with
the National Front and the Communist party will give them about a
third of that programme, which is about right for the rightful pro-
portional representation for the whole series.' Thus, while the
minority parties were not thought to be particularly relevant to
the election, two of them had, by their putting up a number of
candidates, laid a claim to broadcast time.

The election coverage also consisted of three 'Election
Specials': three 45-minute programmes going out at about 11 p.m. on

the three Mondays of the election campaign. These consisted of a
panel of politicians, facing an audience of on the first programme
young voters, on the second old age pensioners and on the final
programme women voters. The intention originally had been to have
this format of panel and audience every day at lunchtime, but as
that slot was only twenty minutes long it was felt impossible to
involve an audience in such a short time. The executive producer
and the editor therefore decided that they would have only the three
programmes.

These two programmes, the 'Report' and the 'Election Specials'
together constituted the election coverage offered by ATV during
the 1974 General Election. There was also the main news magazine
programme that went out at 6 p.m. each weekday for thirty minutes,
'ATV Today', but this, for quite specific reasons, contained little
or no political material during the period of the whole election.
The only other major unit of election coverage was the actual
results coverage on the morning of Friday 29 February when there was
approximately 150 minutes of election news and panel discussion.

THE SETTING OF ELECTION TELEVISION

Any television production emerges from a complex organizational network which is itself rooted in a series of economic, political and
cultural systems. The election coverage was organized as part of
the activity of the news and current affairs department - henceforth
'newsroom' - of ATV, the franchise holders for independent television broadcasting for the Midland region. While ATV is one of the
five major companies of the ITV network, the output of the newsroom
was strictly Midlands oriented, a geographical boundary that pro-
ided one of the essential news values underpinning the main news
magazine programme.

The editorial staff of the newsroom hovered around the figure of
twenty, an indefinite figure since it allows for one or two reporters
who, while being technically freelance, are employed almost wholly
by ATV. In addition there is a large body of technical operatives -
directors, film editors, videotape editors, camera crews, plus the
secretarial staff permanently resident in the newsroom either as
secretaries to the executive producer and the news editor, or as
facilities clerks, copytakers, autocue typists, etc. Of central
interest to this study, however, are the editorial staff, since it is
they who ultimately defined the content of the programmes produced
by ATV.

Figure 11.1 represents the formal aspects of the decision-making
structure - the theoretical flow of authority from the editor and
executive producer down to the rest of the editorial staff. Direct
editorial control was the same for both processes, but the actual
work for the election coverage was done solely by just two reporters, a much smaller staff than were working on the news magazine
programme. The acknowledged political correspondent for ATV over
the years had been responsible for the political content of their
programmes, carrying out the main political interviews etc. He was
assisted for the election by a younger reporter who had, prior to
the election, been concentrating on industrial stories for the

6 p.m. programmes, though not in any sense that he could be described as an 'industrial correspondent'. He did, as he stated,
'stories on the day for the day'. Which meant that when a likely
story came up he went to do a short report for the programme.

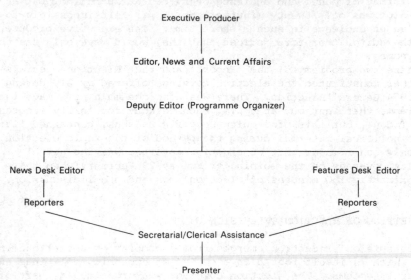

FIGURE 11.1 The structure of a newsroom: ATV

    For the duration of the election there were two 'organizations'
and 'processes' functioning within the newsroom at the same time:
that responsible for the evening news magazine programme 'ATV
Today', and that responsible for the election coverage, as in
Figure 11.2.

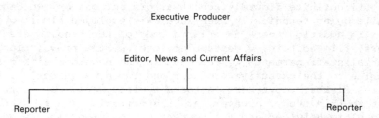

FIGURE 11.2 Organization of the election coverage

    It was rather difficult to assess why this particular reporter
had been chosen to assist in the election coverage, though it would
seem to be a combination of his industrial reportage (and at least
one of the main parties was saying that industrial affairs were what
the election was all about), his being a 'bright young man' (New
College, Oxford, etc.), and his general availability. Neither of
them, however, could be regarded as specialists, and both did non-
political stories for the 6 p.m. programme before the election.
    The political coverage was but one part of the overall activity
of the newsroom during the period of the election. Vast amounts of

A	B	C
story/idea	stringers wire service newspapers/radio (i.e. local mainly, some national) own personnel PR output	Their selection and transmission of information is a whole process itself, each part constituting a 'gate', each being part of the overall production and dissemination of the informational environment within Britain
discussion	editorial staff at morning conference	suitability relevance - to programme, to region, to 'house style' feasibility is it interesting/boring/ amusing/important
decision to do or not to do	executive producer editor general consensus	suitability, etc.
assignment of reporter	editor deputy editor news desk/features eds	availability suitability
'research'	reporter - newspaper cuttings, telephone contact with rele- vant individuals	relevance to story use of 'expert' opinion
information assembled, script written	reporter	'time' allocated for the item normative style of writing
if film is involved, loca- tion shooting	reporter crew	suitable illustrative shots
editing	reporter film editor	construction of the item style quality illustration
programme	director	house style orchestration

FIGURE 11.3

information are flowing into the newsroom all the time, from the
wire service, from stringers, from newspapers, other programmes,
calls from the public. The traditional view of the processes operating within the newsroom is that of the gatekeeper, where news is
seen to flow along 'channels' that at various points are blocked by
'gatekeepers' who filter the flow according to particular criteria
or news values. The task for the media sociologists is to define
who and what those keepers and criteria are. Figure 11.3 presents

A	B	C
resource allocation (time, budget, etc.)	director of programmes	companies 'needs': requirements of the franchise, audience 'needs', broadcaster's responsibilities, commercial requirements
programmes: format, subject areas, type of questions	executive producer editor	conception of their role in the election. The need for 'neutrality' and 'circumspection'. audience requirements. resource limitations. needs of ITN
assignment of personnel for election coverage	editor	suitability
programmes: decisions about particular contributors, organization of participants. formulation of questions	the two election reporters	brief laid down by the editor. The need to involve relevant groups/parties. house style. use of known 'performers' available resources

FIGURE 11.4

schematically the idea of news-flow and gatekeeper within the context of ATV's main news production, and Figure 11.4 applies the same schematic presentation to the election coverage. A is the basic unit for consideration (in the case of Figure 11.3 a story or an idea for a feature, in the case of Figure 11.4 the presentation of the issues of the election), B are the relevant 'decision-makers', and C are the 'criteria of decision-making'.

In essence one is here presenting the general 'decision context' of the newsroom activity. The particular context of the election coverage - what decisions were made, by who, in relation to what criteria, with what effect on the coverage - is outlined in Figure Figure 11.4. One of the key features of Figure 11.3 is the notion that concepts of particular 'styles' predominated. This emphasis on the style of items, the appearance of things, the dominance of the notions of visual and linguistic appropriateness is a significant feature of the production process. Figure 11.4 looks at the decision context of the actual election coverage, though here one is not dealing with particular stories but rather 'units' of the coverage whether at the level of a decision as to who to have on the programme or at the more fundamental level of whether to have a programme at all.

Thus, there were four levels to the organization of the election coverage and four levels of decision-making that parallel the general pattern of authority within ATV. In sheer quantitative terms the bulk of the activity took place at the fourth level, i.e. the activity of the two reporters who worked on the coverage full-

time. This was, however, activity within a tightly prescribed brief
that detailed the amount of time they would be allocated, the basic
resources they had available and the types of questions they would
ask. The four levels constitute the hierarchies of decision-making
within the organization, but the centre of control lay with the
director of programmes and the editor.

THE POLITICS OF MAKING POLITICAL IMAGES

The most immediately striking feature of the election coverage was
the very powerful belief within the newsroom that the audience
would become bored by an excessive amount of political material,
especially as the BBC and ITN were giving a good deal of coverage to
the election. It was within this context that one could begin to
explain the rather interesting and revealing timing of the programmes. The three specials went out at 11 p.m., and the 'Report'
at 12 p.m. lunchtime. These are clearly off-peak viewing hours,
when the viewing audience is likely to be relatively small. The
editor, his deputy and the reporters involved, were aware of this
and argued that politics was not something which interested large
numbers of people, and that ATV was ultimately in the business of
obtaining large audiences for their programmes,' ... when you come
down to it, television really is a question of audience figures, you
have to aim at satisfying the largest number of people possible.
The election programmes were put on when 'interested people could
watch if they liked, but (at a time when) we wouldn't be forcing
people who weren't interested into watching'. Clearly, 'interested
people' - who presumably were partly defined by their access to a
television at lunchtime and by their having the energy to stay up
until a quarter to midnight - are not the only ones who decide the
fate of governments in an election, and therefore are not the only
ones requiring the information which was the raison d'etre of the
election coverage. At the same time, in adopting the assumption
that people do not 'like' political material, one begins to deny the
possibility that such taste might conceivably develop if given the
opportunity to do so. Clearly the economic logic of ITV does not
allow for such experimentation, since the experiment would of necessity be long term, would require a good deal of subsidizing with no
guarantee of success, and this the economics of commercial television cannot allow. The principles of commercial broadcasting do not
readily marry with the principles of political communication. I am
not suggesting here that ATV was being particularly cynical about
this. Serious political material has always been pushed to the
fringe of the schedules, with one or two notable exceptions such as
'This Week' and 'World in Action' - witness the cri de coeur of the
late Kenneth Allsop over the demise of '24 Hours' (Allsop, 1972).
    In the construction of this basic framework for the election
coverage, we can see several interrelated factors - propositions
about the nature and role of broadcasting that structured these
decisions.
    1 There was the initial feeling that they must do something
during the election. It could be argued if ATV did nothing at all
in the way of serious broadcasting that they were not fulfilling
their franchise requirements. This, however, is tempered by -

2   The basic economic logic that underpins the commercial television system in Britain. This essentially requires large audience
figures; political television rarely attracts large audiences and
therefore such coverage cannot command peak viewing time.
There are, then, two goals, which tend to pull in opposite directions: a political goal which requires that the company, in tune
with the requirements of the Television Act (Section 1(4)(a)) shall
disseminate 'information, education and entertainment', and that
responsibility for observing this and the various other provisions
of the Act 'should be taken by the companies themselves as part of
their contractual obligations'; and an economic goal since ATV is a
commercial enterprise seeking to make a profit. Within this framework decisions reflected the attempt to balance the two competing
interests, i.e. responsible/serious broadcasting versus commercial
broadcasting. This had whole series of consequences for the next
level of decision-making - what 'kinds' of programmes were to fit
into the slots made available, how were they to be done, who was to
do them?

The single most important person on the organization of the
election coverage was the editor. He it was who decided who, from
those available in the newsroom, would be responsible for actually
putting the election programmes together and getting them on the
air. He it was who decided how each programme should be approached,
what kinds of questions would be asked and the types of people to
whom the questions would be put. That he held this position was not
particularly surprising. The editor is the principal figure in any
newsroom, even though he might not be responsible for every aspect
of the day-to-day activity of programme-making; at ATV the main
responsibility for getting the programme on the air every night at
6 p.m. lay with the deputy editor. Always, though, it is the editor
who has ultimate responsibility for hiring and firing, for bud-
geting, for the administration of the newsroom, for deciding in particularly difficult or contentious matters and for establishing the
whole tone and style of the output from that particular newsroom.
Decisions about the main programme's content are taken at the
morning conference, where the bulk of the editorial staff discuss
with the editor the possibilities for that day, both in terms of
possible news stories and other material for the main programme.
There are very few concrete decisions actually made at the meeting,
and indeed the actual point at which hard and fast decisions are
made is difficult to pinpoint. During the period of the election
the two reporters directly responsible for election material did not
attend the morning conference. Their days were planned well in
advance, again testifying to the duality within the newsroom, the
parallel structure of the 6 p.m. programme and the election programmes.

In the election, the editor was particularly careful to attend to
potentially controversial details of all newsroom output. He was,
for example, insistent on the need to be careful in dealing with
potentially political material in the 6 p.m. programme. There was a
suggestion at one morning meeting that they do an item about a local
screw-making factory. The work-force at this particular factory had
gone on strike and the owner had brought in members of his family to
continue the production until the strike was over. The editor

asked, 'They (the owner and his family) are not Tories are they?',
which the other members at the meeting thought was an amusing question, but to which he added, '... be very careful about election
stuff'. He was clearly aware that the general election was, for one
side at least, about the whole question of strikes and industrial
militancy, and therefore felt that any strike story had, necessarily,
political implications and was therefore to be treated with great
care.

Two major decisions were made by the editor about the content of
the election programmes. He decided on the three areas that were to
be covered in the three 45-minute election specials: these were
young voters, women voters and old age pensioners. These particular
areas were thought to be both interesting and relevant to the outcome of the election. The women-voters programme seemed to be
singled out as a particularly 'good idea', a feeling which rested
on the observation that in 1970 it was the response of women to (the
cost of) inflation which had projected Heath into Number 10, and
which might therefore be again decisive in the context of the 1974
inflationary spiral. The three areas were also chosen because it
was felt that these were areas where they would not duplicate the
national coverage offered by ITN and where they could do adequate
programmes.

The editor also decided the basic types of questions that were to
be put in the midday programmes and in the specials. A particularly
interesting and significant decision was that as far as possible
the election programmes would avoid adopting any position on the
issues of the election and would only provide a forum for the
various contestants and their supporters to state what they felt the
issues to be. There was, however, something of an ambivalence on
this. One of the two reporters informed me that the general area of
questioning 'that is, to look at their positions on the two major
issues of "who governs" and "prices" was decided by (the editor)'.
The deputy editor said, in reply to a question on how they decided
on which issues to cover, that

'We have to cover them all and ask the questions that are being put
by the parties.... Even though we may not think that they are the
issues we have to cover them and ask questions about them because
the parties are raising them and we must balance.'

The editor himself was very clear that the position he wanted
their coverage to adopt was one of asking 'What are the issues?'
rather than 'These are the issues, what do you think?' He said that
the specific aim of the programmes was to allow the parties and the
voters to define the issues, 'It's not up to us to tell them what
the issues are. They must tell us - always within, of course, the
limitations of the various restrictions imposed upon us by the Act
(the Representation of the People Act).' If they were going to ask
questions, then they would have to ask the sort of things that the
audience would ask if they were given the chance. This format for
the programmes was generally held to and, while the specific questions in the script were drawn up by the presenter (the two reporters alternated), it was always a variation of the form 'What do
you think the issues of this election are?', followed up by various

supplementary questions. This was not without its problems and
there was a clear desire by the two reporters to develop specific
lines of questions. One 'Report', for example, was to be a discussion between a panel of four non-politicians, two businessmen and
two trade unionists. (The composition of this group was interesting: they consisted of one representative of big business, one of
small business, one blue-collar trade unionist and one white-collar
trade unionist. They thus might be seen as representing one view,
a miniature, of the essential components of the non-political social
world.) Before this particular programme there was some discussion,
between the two reporters, of what questions they should put: they
were particularly keen to raise the question of nationalization and
the question of the Common Market, both issues which they felt -
from their reading of the newspapers - to be emerging as important,
and ones which were particularly relevant for this panel. The
younger of the two suggested that they did not use the opening
question 'What are the issues?', but in the event they did stick to
the prescribed formulae, and only attempted to raise these other
questions as supplementary points. That specific issues were raised
was more a function of the tendency of discussion to wander into
other areas than the result of any preconceived plan.

The tensions implicit in such a situation stems very much from
its conflict with the concept of the professional interviewer who,
in terms of the professional ideology, plays the key part in the
'construction' of an interview: for the course of the election the
brief they had to operate was such as to render any 'construction'
impossible since the course of the interview was to be determined by
the participants. For example, there was a feeling among the two
presenters that the Liberals could not be treated in the same way
as the Labour and Conservative parties since, 'whatever happens they
are not going to win the election'. It was therefore felt to be
pointless to put the question 'What do you think are the issues?'
to the Liberals, since this implied that what they said and what
they proposed in the way of policies were important in the sense
that they might, after 28 February, have to implement those
policies. It was felt that a more relevant question to put to the
Liberals was 'What will you do in the event of your holding the
balance of power in the new Parliament?' This was the question that
was increasingly posed by the newspapers. The decision was not
theirs to make, however, since the editor had ultimate say over the
lines of questioning. This is not to say that such questions
weren't put to the Liberals at all, rather that they were not the
main theme or put in ways that the two presenters might have preferred. That the editor was able to influence the questions in
this way, though perhaps unusual, reflected his possession of the
overall responsibility for the programme output of ATV's newsroom,
a responsibility he took most seriously, as one journalist commented,
'If anything goes wrong he's the one who goes to jail.' Why the
editor took these decisions in the way that he did is central to the
concerns of this chapter since it throws light on the factors that
influence and structure political television in general and election
television in particular.

Editorial decision-making within the election was rooted within
three particular structures, each of which is closely interwound

with the production of programmes: legal, professional and organizational.

  1 The legal and constitutional framework is provided by the Independent Television Act, and by the Representation of the People Act.

  2 The professional communicator possesses a series of definitions
about his situation, his role, the needs of his audience, the nature
of election television, the nature of politics, etc. In short, he
possesses a political and occupational 'ideology'.

  3 The television production is part of the general activity of a
particular organization, which has its own needs, requirements,
definitions of their purpose, resources, etc., each of which will
have a bearing on the specific production.

1 THE LAW AND THE ELECTION

The producer of political programmes has to work with a series of
rulings, legally binding, as to what he can and cannot do, and the
requirements of the law proved to be vital in influencing what ATV
did during the course of the election, not only within their election programmes but also within their other output such as the
6 p.m. news magazine programme. There was a strong feeling that the
IBA would be closely scrutinizing their programming to see that it
was 'balanced', 'fair', 'objective', 'impartial', all the qualities
that the law demands of broadcasting, and time and time again was
emphasized the need to 'be careful' and to make sure that 'ordinary
stories' had no 'political implications'.

  One of the developments in political broadcasting in recent years
has been that the maintenance of 'balance' between the parties could
be achieved over a series of programmes rather than within every
programme. In the election period no such latitude was felt to be
permissible and strenuous efforts were made to finely balance the
three main parties - whether that was in terms of the film reports,
the audience in the studio or the panellists - a political symmetry
had to be maintained and be seen to be maintained. Several incidents were particularly revealing of this process. When Enoch
Powell's ex-constituency nominated his successor there was some
discussion as to whether they could actually cover this, and if they
could, how they should do it. The deputy editor declared that,

'Had there not been an election on we would have gone and interviewed him. This time because there's an election we can mention
his name and background, and then go through all the other candidates.'

  In point of fact they could have covered his nomination in terms
of its obvious news value, without having to rigidly balance. (2)
But this, of course, led to a situation where one might be criticized for being biased. At the same time in using the 'excuse' of
news-value for not balancing it was felt that they would be offen-
ding against the spirit of the RPA. For example, when the press
secretary to William Whitelaw phoned to say that he would be on a
walk-about in the city during which he would be willing to answer
questions, there was some discussion about this and eventually the

newsdesk editor, whose responsibility it was to present about ten
minutes of news for the 6 p.m. programme, decided that they couldn't
use it. This was interesting since here was a visit by one of the
most powerful men in Britain, a senior Cabinet minister who was seen
as both the prime minister's most trusted colleague and likely
successor as leader of the Conservative party, who was offering his
services for an interview, albeit an informal one, but who the newsdesk decided that they did not want to bother with. I asked why
they decided in this way. The argument used was that if they
covered Whitelaw then they were morally obliged to balance this by
showing some equally important Labour and Liberal leaders, and this
they didn't want to commit themselves to. Thus a clear moral obligation to balance was evident, but to have followed it through to
satisfy the 'spirit' of the RPA would have created a situation where
they had to include material in their 6 p.m. programme - i.e. items
on other leading politicians - which they did not want to include
because their audience did not like such material. In order to
avoid this latter possibility, the first possibility had to be
rejected. (3)

Towards the end of the election coverage the need to 'balance'
and the legal implications of not balancing were very clear. One
edition of the 'Report' was to be a panel discussion between the
candidates from one particular constituency. The two reporters were
using as their basic guide to the election the 'Daily Telegraph'
list of candidates. There had been a typographical error and one of
the candidates from the chosen constituency had not been listed in
the 'Telegraph''s list. His mistake had not been noticed until
twenty minutes before the programme was due to go out live. The
senior of the two reporters having discovered the mistake was then
faced with the choice of pretending that it hadn't happened, going
ahead with the discussion and praying that no one noticed and complained; or he could tell the editor about the situation. Several
minutes thought led him to choose the latter course and once that
decision was made there was never any doubt that the programme as
scheduled would be cancelled. At something like 11.50 a.m., with
ten minutes to transmission they had to put together another programme. As about eight minutes of the programme was the taped
interviews with the National Front and the Communist party, they
had twelve minutes to fill with live material; a slightly extended
'election news' introduction to the programme accounted for some of
that time, and the rest was taken up by an impromptu discussion of
the difficulties of broadcasting during elections!

After the programme, the senior reporter said that he had had to
tell the editor about the mistake since 'I'd rather face his wrath
than risk possible legal proceedings and a possible rocket from the
IBA'. Later I learned that following the programme this reporter
had received something of a dressing down from the editor, not
because of the original mistake of failing to contact all the relevant people, but because they had explained this mistake to the
viewers and had apologized for it. Ironically, the various people
who had turned up for the programme but could not appear, and were
naturally somewhat peeved at this, felt that the apology was very
reasonable and all departed feeling that 'justice had been done'.

The election coverage was terminated on the Tuesday before the

Thursday polling day on the grounds of a long-established IBA rule
that 'if we had a "Report" on the Wednesday and if we made a mistake, it's too late to rectify it' (editor). From Tuesday lunchtime
until the polls closed on polling day there was effectively no
coverage or discussion of the election from ATV. In the morning
conference on Tuesday, Wednesday and Thursday, particular stress was
laid on the need to be careful in the stories that they did for the
6 p.m. programme in order to make sure that they weren't 'political'.
At the Thursday morning conference, that is, polling day, the editor
declared that 'everyone must remember that we mustn't do anything
that sounds as though we are persuading people to vote,' to which
the newsdesk editor added 'We are not even allowed to say that it's
been a light poll', since it might be thought that by saying that
they were encouraging people to go out and vote, and that, the IBA
might argue, was contrary to the meaning of the Representation of
The People Act.

The legal framework effectively defined what would and would not
be regarded as 'political'. It was 'understood' that politics was
about the activities, beliefs and fortunes of the three main parties, and that balance, objectivity and impartiality was conceived
of within the party political framework and no more; any 'extra',
the granting of time to the other groups, was a discretion within
the gift of the organization. This situation provided a rule of
thumb for the programme-makers since so long as the three main parties were represented that constituted the correct form of election
television, and so long as they were each given time to say what
they thought the election was about, then that constituted the correct content of election television. That there may have been
other definitions of what the election was about could not have been
considered particularly seriously since compliance with the basic
legal criteria was of primary importance.

Such legal considerations not only structured the overall form of
the coverage - a forum of the three parties - but also influenced
the kind of material made available within that format. The potential sensitivity of the area (combined with a lack of resources)
created the situation where it was felt that they should allow the
parties themselves to 'do the talking'. Two roles and two sets of
ideology were available to the broadcast journalists: one that they
be inquisitive, searching, questioning (to use a vogue word, investigative); or two, that they be the mere brokers or coiners of someone else's information. In the contentious context of an election,
the former was impossible to operate and therefore the latter tended
to dominate. The composite of restrictions and the implied definitions of the political process provided one important factor as to
why the election coverage could be little more than a version of the
party political broadcast.

It would, however, be wrong to create the impression that the
legal requirements were the only determinants of the election coverage. Some importance must also be attached to the professional criteria applied to the making and judging of television, and the
organizational arrangements within which these functioned. It
would, of course, be nonsense to suggest that the professional criteria were somehow distinct from or uninfluenced by the organiza-ion
tion. Occupational values and professional ideologies are deeply

influenced by the structures within which they exist.   These are
the second and third 'elements' of the production process.

2   THE PROFESSIONAL COMMUNICATOR AND THE ELECTION

It is popularly held that television in general, and news and
current affairs television in particular, are really 'about' the
dispositions and ideologies of a small group of men who control the
production of programmes.   Such a view, however, implies that broadcasters bring to the organizations a stable set of beliefs which
they are then able to translate into their work.   It avoids the
possibility that beliefs can be inherited from the organizational
hierarchy.   In a sense the central question when studying the role
of belief-structures in communications, is which way the values run
in an organization.   It would be disconcertingly easy to argue
either of two polar points: (a) programme-makers are committed individuals who inject their own values into 'messages' in a purposive
manner; (b) programme-makers are the passive receptors of an
'organizational' view of reality, determined by senior officials.
A further version placing itself somewhere along the continuum
between the two points has emerged from the academic study of the
operations of media communicators.   In this view the communications
process is about the conflict between the individual communicator
and his organizational superiors (Breed, 1955).   Recent work,
however, suggests that a more accurate description would look to
the procedures by which conflict is avoided rather than created.
In this view the key 'to understanding bias lies not in conspiracies,
not in conflict, but in cooperation and shared satisfaction'
(Sigelman, 1973), implying that there is a basic compatibility
within the media institution since newsmen tend to go to organizations with whose policies they are in agreement.   The work which led
to this formulation was carried out in the United States on newspapers which had overtly political leanings.   The question addressed
was how attachment to the institutional mythology of journalism
(what we have termed the ideology of the fourth estate) was compatible with working in a newspaper where policy clearly reflected
the political leanings of the publisher.   The answer was seen to lie
in an already existing compatibility between the publisher's 'line'
and the newsman's own belief structure.   An integrated structure in
which because publisher and reporter shared a common political ideology, the professional ideology of the reporter could operate with
apparent efficiency.
The situation within the newsroom at ATV was of course, different
in some important respects, the most important being the absence of
any explicit editorial line.   The observation did, however, provide
an opportunity to consider some of the lines of thought outlined
above, to consider the role of the individual communicator in the
context of a British media institution.   We have already seen that
control resided in the editor, and thus attention to the operation
of professional and political ideologies leads, in this case at
least, largely to an account of the dispositions of the editor.

Editorial dispositions - the practice of passivity

To the cynical ears of the academic observer there is much that
sounds hollow in the editorial professions of broadcasting credo.
Yet it would be wrong to leave the conclusion at that. Roger Brown
(1969, p.156), argued that the hollowness of public utterances by
broadcasting personnel may 'have more to do with the devitalized
language which they borrow from the world of public relations than
with an actual lack of faith in what they are doing'. He continues
(1969, p.156),

'a cynical division of mind between what is stated in public and
believed in private turns out to be an exception, rather than the
rule. It may be extremely difficult for literary intellectuals to
believe that popular journalists really consider their work to be
of social importance, yet there are grounds for suggesting that this
is indeed the case.'

    In the context of ATV's election coverage three possible roles
were open to the editor: 1. the practitioner of commercial broadcasting ('show-biz'); 2. the practitioner of political journalism
('fourth' estate'); 3. the negotiator of political reality ('oper-
ator of objectivity'). It was the interaction of these three roles
that induced a non-committal attitude to the coverage, the skeleton
of election television with none of the meat. Twin themes characterized the editor's view of the role and purpose of the election
television for which he was responsible: a strong feeling of 'give
them (the audience) what they want and don't give them what they
don't want', a core belief in any commercial broadcasting organization. He believed, for example, that the level of election coverage was 'about right' in both the time-slot allocated to it (12
noon, and 11 p.m.) and in the length of particular programmes,
'since most people are bored by politics and are avoiding political
material. You can see this if you look at the audience figures for
political programmes. The idea behind putting on our election programmes was so that we didn't force people into watching it. If no
one watches because they are bored by politics it doesn't particularly matter.' This position clearly involved a much broader
organizational policy, that is, ATV's central purpose is to make
profits, and small audiences do not produce profits. It would be
wrong though to see the editor's argument as merely a cynical rationalization of this wider economic logic. There was a firm belief
that ultimately television was about what people wanted (as reflected in the audience figures), that the people clearly didn't want
politics and that therefore you didn't give the people politics, or
at least you didn't give them politics when they might be watching.
(4)
    The other dominant theme was that 'it is not our role to say any-
thing that could be constructed as controversial or political, and
we must do everything in our power to avoid these traps'. This, put
briefly, and rather crudely, was the recurrent theme throughout the
election campaign. In meetings and general conversation, 'safety'
was encouraged and demanded.
    The editor was widely regarded within the newsroom as being 'very

safe', a phrase that was employed several times by different members
of the newsroom. One reporter said 'He and I were raised in the
same way and we have a kind of built-in caution. I think though
that his is a little more developed than mine.' The style of questioning - 'We must ask the questions the audience would want us to
ask' - was influenced, in part at least, by the general feeling that
television journalism should not preach, rather that it should be
the means by which the audience is allowed to receive information
untouched by the broadcaster's own disposition.

There was a strong sense of the passive broker. The notion
followed from the position in which the editor made decisions, a
situation that can perhaps best be described as 'structured autonomy', decisions made within conditions laid down by the wider political and resource situations. That this did not engender apparent
conflict reflected the feeling that passivity was the role of the
broadcaster. Situated as he was within a complex commercial and
political setting, the concept of 'passivity' can be seen as an
adjustment to the limitation of that setting.

Reportorial disposition - the mechanics of passivity

If the editor's situation was constrained, even more so was that of
the two reporters. They worked within a tightly prescribed brief
which left little room for individual initiative or the injection
of personal preferences and bias. They could not easily pursue, as
did Blumler's subjects (Blumler, 1969), topics which they felt
should be pursued (for example, the Common Market and nationalization), though they were by implication able to exclude or limit
topics which they felt should not be covered on the grounds that
they were not 'relevant', 'important' or 'suitable'; for example,
in the women voters 'Election Special', a member of the audience
raised the question of women's liberation, to which the presenter
said 'But surely that's not an issue in this election?' though he
did allow some discussion of the topic. They were able to develop
one or two stories and items which they felt were important; for
example, the likely importance of Enoch Powell's 'vote Labour'
speech, and also the possible consequences of a balance-of-power
situation in the Commons. These developments were, however, only a
minor part of the general approach which, as we have seen, was
strongly influenced by other considerations.

The two reporters were in an essentially mechanical role, func-
tionaries who made the programmes 'happen', but who ultimately were
not creatively responsible for that happening. Operating with a
brief over which they had had little control their main task was to
make sure that each programme (a) went on the air, and (b) when on,
went smoothly. They were responsible for contacting panellists and
participants, and for making sure that representative audiences
were assembled at the right time. Logistics were the grist in their
day-to-day activity. Two of the lunchtime programmes were to be
panel discussions between on one occasion the 'six best old age
pensioners' and the 'six best young voters', and the two reporters
were responsible for choosing the 'best'. They had some difficulty
with the OAPs since there had been only one Liberal in the original

programme whom they liked, and she wasn't available. They therefore
had to contact the Liberal party to ask for two Liberal old age
pensioners to take part in the panel discussion. The reporters were
also responsible for preparing material (much of it culled from
newspapers), the biographies and background of the candidates on
their 'patch', photographs of the candidates and other information
which it was felt might come in useful at some point.

The main source for the panels of candidates and the industrialists and trade unionists, was the proverbial list of contacts
which the senior reporter had accumulated during his years of broadcasting in the region. Many of the leading names of regional politics were known to him personally, and in particular it was his past
use of particular politicians which made them familiar participants
in ATV's output. Where doubts arose, and particularly where the
audiences of party supporters were being assembled, the parties
themselves were contacted for help. There was, however, a strong
tendency to use as participants in the programmes individuals who
were known to be good performers. This is not necessarily an
adverse comment, but it does raise certain questions about the way
in which routines of production within television tend to limit the
range of opinions that television makes a ailable. The litmus test
for judging political importance was electoral size, and three main
'types' of political groups were readily discernible: the three main
parties; the Communist party and the National Front - who were
fringe but warranted some attention; the other groups who were
either 'idiots', 'too small to bother with', or both. The significance criteria applied followed electoral size, though not that
closely since the relatively 'unimportant' Liberal vote in the
Midlands was given equal billing with the Conservatives and the
Labour party, reflecting the overall national perspective that politics has within the British political cultures, rather than a focus
on specific issues or topics. There was, however, a good deal of
circumspection in the treatment of the CP and the NF, the senior
reporter declaring that when interviewing he always tried to be perfectly objective, but with these two groups his biases became clear.
He clearly identified with the assumed middle position of the three
main parties.

His statement that he felt himself to be overtly biased when
interviewing fringe groups raised the whole question of just what
role they saw themselves as occupying when acting as an interviewer.
They did not see themselves, in this election at least, as cast in
the mould of 'the Robin-Day-type', putting hard, thought-provoking
questions to the hapless victim, the politician. They were, in
keeping with their prescribed brief, more intent on generating a
discussion between those taking part, particularly among the non-
politicians who took part in the programmes:

'We don't adopt the Robin Day-interviewing-Heath position. It would
not be on in the type of programme that we have been doing. In the
"Midday Report" what we are looking for is a discussion between the
participants, and I'm there to put in a few points and questions when
it begins to dry up. Obviously this is very different from what you
would do with politicians.'

In point of fact it wasn't so very different from what they did with politicians, though there was less likelihood of politicians 'drying up'. That they did want a lively discussion was clear, as, for example, was indicated after the lunchtime discussion between the six 'best of the young voters'. The presenter/interviewer for that particular programme, thought that it could have been better, that only three of the six were 'any good' and that they weren't lively enough. Prior to the programme he had been pleased to see that they immediately engaged in a lively, animated discussion about the election. He told them that once the programme began to forget about him and discuss among themselves, though he wanted to avoid a slanging match. Asked why he thought they were not lively enough, he reasoned that: 1. they would have been briefed to behave themselves, 2. they were nervous, 3. they were still young in their ideas, 4. the chairs were arranged in a line facing the presenter, instead of being in a semi-circle which would have been much more conducive to an animated discussion. The director of the programme and the other election reporter did not agree with him, and the director informed him that the editor and the executive producer had been very pleased with it, and thought it looked very good - 'They were especially pleased with the wide angle shots'.

The two reporters were the means by which editorial decisions - themselves reflecting more fundamental organizational and political criteria - were implemented. Their situation was akin to that of the reporters studied by Sigelman whose (1973)

'autonomy may realistically consist of little more than his freedom to manoeuvre within the constraining bounds of his assignment. But the reporter's perception of his role is sufficiently narrow and technical that he does not feel that his functional autonomy is jeopardized. His task, as he sees it, consists of writing the best story he can within a given framework: his is more a feat of engineering than of architecture.'

Theirs, then, was the professional ideology of the servant. Decisions moved from the basic questions of time, resources, areas of coverage, etc., down to detailed arrangements - making sure that a taxi is ordered to pick up an old lady who is to appear on the programme, etc. - and the two reporters came into their own in the latter rather than the former part of the process. Underpinning the early parts of the process were a series of organizational arrangements and considerations which provided the third crucial element in the decision making processes surrounding the coverage.

3   THE ORGANIZATIONAL ARRANGEMENTS

ATV is a major commercial company with both a declared public responsibility and a private motive. It was widely acknowledged within the newsrooms that ATV was essentially a 'show biz' affair that sustained a large audience through the basic formula of providing the audience with the entertainment which they required. The election coverage of ATV at the same time as being characterized by the legal limitations, the preferences and attitudes of those directly respon-

sible for the making of programmes, and by particular definitions
of politics, was also characterized by a sense of the general
'ethos' within the ATV which was that of 'show biz,' and intellectual framework of serving a mass audience with goods the way they
wanted them, entertainingly. This was reflected in: (a) the resources made available for the coverage; (b) the expectations made of
the coverage, that it be recognizable as political television, that
it be visually appealing, lively, with the right people in attendance.

The commercial ethic which underpinned ATV affected the election
coverage in two ways. As we have seen, it determined the time that
the election coverage went out and the amount of time made available.
It also influenced the standards by which programmes were made and
judged. This generally consisted of a notion of not only what their
programmes did ('what are the issues?'), but also of what their programmes actually looked like. The process was one of composition,
different parts are brought together to form a whole, 'a programme'.
The programmes had to be entertaining and informative, because all
television aims at that, and one therefore looked for animated
discussions, 'a bloody good ding-dong', between the participants.
This had to happen within a relatively short space of time, usually
twenty minutes, and therefore there was the need to make as 'good a
show as possible' within the time available. Thus each programme
had a musical introduction over the opening caption, and the same
music over the closing shots, the boundaries of the 'event',of
the 'product' demarcated by an appropriate score. Each programme
would then have a brief introduction, the latest news, and then a
formalized discussion between the panellists in the studio. The
whole, rehearsed and orchestrated by the director, is more important
than the constituent parts, and the key to the process is to keep
hidden the stitching that holds the object together - hence the
need to keep camera booms and floor staff out of shot, because if
they do appear then that becomes an indication that what is being
presented as a natural happening is in reality a manufactured event,
and that is deemed as being anathema to the audience.

What I am suggesting is that the limitations on programme-making
combined with the implicit definitions of what good television
looked like created a situation where more emphasis had to be placed
on the general appearance than on the substantive content of each
particular programme. That is not to say that nothing came out of
the programme, but it is to say that what did come out wasn't the
point: that the situation was created where something could come out
and that the situation was seen to be created, was the point. The
name of the game was form. In his book, 'The Illusion', David
Caute (1971) argues that within literature content is primary, and
form is a secondary factor, a 'vessel' to facilitate content. In
television the roles are reversed. The form is primary and content
is the medium through which the form is affirmed. Thus the communication of political information is inhibited by inadequate resources
and an emphasis on the appearance rather than the substance of programme content.

Let me illuminate these points further by giving a detailed
account of one particular programme in which I think all the tendencies and trends indicated are clearly in evidence.

'THE FEMALE VOTE': ONE PROGRAMME

On 25 February there was a 45-minute special on the female vote in
the election. The premiss was that the female vote had been crucial
in deciding the election in 1970 and might well, in the context of
an inflation-ridden economy, be crucial in this one. They therefore
decided to devote one of their forty-five-minute slots to a discussion between an audience of forty women and a panel of three
female politicians. Having a female panel seemed to be assumed as
obviously the correct type of people to have since they would best
understand the questions and problems posed by an audience of forty
women.

Once the decision had been made to do such a programme the task
of the two reporters was to decide on the panel and assemble the
audience. The responsibility for this was mainly the senior reporter's who knew the MPs and knew how to assemble an audience. For
the Conservatives he chose Sally Oppenheim, for Labour Betty Booth-
royd, and for the Liberals he had to go to the House of Lords for
Lady Sear.

The audience was assembled from two sources. The political
parties were approached and asked to send along party members to
take part in the programme. On an earlier occasion one of the
members of the editorial staff, when asked how the audience was
chosen for such programmes, said that the parties were asked to send
along 'bright sparks - well, you have to have bright sparks otherwise it makes a very bad programme with the panel dominating the
discussion'. These committed members of the audience were expected
to be the main participants in the programme. These constituted
about half the audience. The other half were contacted through
various sources that the newsroom staff use whenever they wish to
get together an audience.

On the day the programme moved through several stages. During
the morning the presenter worked on his script, the final checks
were made about the availability of people and the actual camera
shots for the programme were worked out. The programme was scheduled to be recorded at 5 p.m. for transmission at 11 p.m. Prior to
the arrival of the audience and the panel at about 3.30 p.m., the
presenter went along to the studio to test the positioning of the
panel's seating and the voice levels, he also discussed the various
opening camera shots. At about 3.30 p.m., the women began to arrive
and, having been brought up to the studio by various members of the
female staff of the newsroom, were met by the floor manager and the
presenter. Rows of raised seats had been arranged and they were
asked to sit according to their politics, the Labour women on the
left of the platform, the Conservatives on the right, and the
Liberals and Don't Knows together in the Middle, '... it's so we
have some sort of balance', though it also served the function of
allowing the presenter to know where to go to ask particular questions.

When all the women were assembled the 'warm-up' session commenced,
with the presenter talking to them very generally - about what they
had had for lunch and what they thought of dieting, etc. This warm-
up session served three functions:

1 It provided the opportunity to test voice levels and camera
positions;

2 It got the audience talking and removed nerves;
3 It allowed the presenter to outline the 'rules of the game'.
He asked them when speaking to address either him or the panel and
not the camera; to stick to the point under discussion and not to
wander off into 'irrelevant areas'. Also 'We've found in the past
that there have been no questions for the Liberal member of the
panel, and so if the Liberals among you could make sure that they
get asked a few questions we would appreciate it.' He told them
that 'my job is to keep things equal and make sure that there are
questions from all sides.' He also asked them to be reasonably
brief in their points to the panel especially if they were coming
back at a point that the panel had made - 'Don't overdo coming back
at statements from the panel. We want to be fair and get as many
questions as possible in.'

He then asked if there were any questions about the mechanics of
the programme and some of the women asked if they could use notes
they had brought along, to which he replied 'You can use them if you
really want to but we would prefer it if you didn't.' Towards the
end of the rehearsal he asked them to avoid mentioning individual
candidates 'because of the electoral laws' - that is, the panel were
present as 'experts' rather than 'candidates'. One member of the
Labour side of the audience had brought along a copy of Andrew
Roth's book on the business background of MPs and indicated that
she wanted to make a point about Sally Oppenheim's involvement with
property companies. The presenter, when he noticed the book and
discovered the intent, asked her not to refer to it as it was not
'that kind of programme. We don't want personal attacks do we?
I'm sure none of the ladies over there (the Conservative side) will
raise that sort of thing. It's not in the spirit of the programme.
Really we want to discuss issues.' After the rehearsal I asked the
presenter about this incident. He pointed out that he didn't want
the woman to use Roth information as 'it's not that kind of programme. For her to use it would constitute a personal attack which
wouldn't fit in with what the programme was about. And moreover one
would have to forewarn Sally Oppenheim if that kind of attack was
going to be made.'

There was a sense of what the programme was 'all about', and
that was 'issues' of which a statement about an MPs business interests was not one. It was also about issues as they related to the
particular 'type' of women in the audience - aged about 20 to 40, '
'housewives' who had 'decided the last election'. A very old lady
had come along to the studio with Oppenheim so that she could appear
on the television. Unfortunately for her, they had already had a
programme about old age pensioners and the election and it was felt
that her appearance among a group of younger women would not fit in
with this particular programme's intention which was to allow
younger women to have their say. The Conservatives asked if she
could just sit in the audience and take no part in the actual discussion. This was considered but eventually rejected on the grounds
that the camera would inevitably pick her up and if the presenter
appeared to be ignoring her by asking her no questions, and if she
took absolutely no part in the programme, then the viewers would
notice this and assume that he was ignoring her on purpose (which
would of course have been a perfectly accurate assumption to make)

and that this would have (a) annoyed them, and (b) defeated the whole purpose of the programme, which was to be audience participation.

Each of the programmes in the coverage employed a set of cliches laid down at the beginning of the election coverage: questions to electors about how they were going to vote, whether that involved a 'switch', and questions to electors and politicians about what they thought the issues of the election were? Systematically a 'representative' of each of the groups was asked what she thought the issues were. The plan of allowing them to define the issues for discussion was largely adhered to, even when the presenter thought that they were not in fact the issues of the election. One Liberal said that the issue was 'worker participation', to which the presenter replied 'Is that the main issue?' 'Surely not.' This particular woman, however, pursued her point and said that the media put over 'housewives' issues in terms of prices whereas in fact there were many other women's issues, such as discrimination. He took up the point and asked the panellist about anti-discrimination legislation, and added 'But surely anti-discrimination legislation is not a vote-getter?' Having allowed a discussion to take place on this area, he said 'One more point and then we are moving on to inflation' - this after all was what the programme had been all about.

It seems that two important points can be made about this programme, and, through it, about the other election programmes. What was crucial in the context of the election was that while they had to produce some sort of coverage, they could not be seen to be overly involved in the political process. The editor and his assistants were to be the brokers rather than the makers of events. It therefore became a problem of making political television, but treading very carefully, and doing so with relatively limited resources. In the context of the programme the important point was that the women and the politicians were seen to be discussing whatever they wished to discuss, and that the reporter as representative of the broadcasting organization, was seen to be a detached, neutral participant. If this formulation could be achieved then the programme would successfully affirm the much-desired news organization's broker role, and therefore display for all the world to see its 'responsibility' by having produced neutral, stingless political television. It is as if the aim, if I might return to an earlier metaphor, was to convince themselves and the world outside that they were indeed 'eunuchs in the harem of ideas'.

CONCLUSION

'although the professional communicator has gradually emerged as a new style intellectual in society, the tendency is for him to be preoccupied with the form rather than the content of communication ...' (Elliott, 1972, p.165).

The views of the election of February 1974 presented by ATV to the people of the Midlands was fashioned within a quadrangle of political, legal, professional and organizational considerations. Closely inter-related, these four influences meant that what

coverage there was had limited resources and was above all else
'safe'. Rather than employing the medium to cast a journalistic
eye over the political questions of the election, studios and facilities were effectively given over to the propagation of the ideas
and feelings of the three main parties. The central political commitment and belief during the three weeks of the election coverage
was that to be seen to be defining issues was anathema and must
therefore at all costs be avoided. By adopting the role of question
master, where the question was the same refrain 'What do you think
the issues are?', the coverage guaranteed the presence of legitimate
respondents and therefore guaranteed its own legitimacy in the context of legal and political rulings.

The central professional commitment was to work within this
severely truncated framework and present 'good television' which
was entertaining and presentable. Programmes had to be coherent
wholes, with a clear beginning, middle and end; with an opening and
closing statement, music, wide-and-tight-shots of the participants
locked in debate, an emphasis on speed and covering as many points
as possible so long as they were 'relevant'. Variability, fresh-
ness, a change of face and pace. All were criteria geared to the
very nature of the medium, and all this within a twenty-minute or
forty-five-minute slot.

The editorial conception of the role of the medium rested on an
assumption, central to the ideology of commercial braodcasting, that
'good television' is by definition that which presents the audience
with what it wants. As most people don't want politics, the assumption continues, programmes that are broadcast at peak viewing hours
will not contain political material; those that must contain political material are put on at times when the bulk of the audience will
not be watching, and are presented in such a way as to not 'bore'
those few who do watch.

If this interpretation of the events of those three weeks at ATV
is correct, the broadcast journalist in a commercial setting is
looking in two directions at the same time. He looks at, worries
about and is influenced by a number of particular audiences (the
organizational hierarchy, the IBA, the future members of the
Commons, the judiciary); and also looks to and considers the 'needs'
and 'interests' of a general audience (the bulk of the people who
watch television but who have no specific interest in the institutions of the media). Thus at one level the politics of election
broadcasting are important; at another level of transcendent importance is the need to satisfy a viewing audience, for which purpose
the cosmetics of making 'good television' take over from the politics of making safe television.

Part four

CONCLUSION

Chapter 12

DEFINING THE CONTEXT
The external determinants of political television

While many of the conclusions to be drawn from these case studies are clearly implicit within the text, a number of general points emerge which throw light on the nature of political broadcasting.

A general inference throughout Part three has been that the external context of political broadcasting involves interaction with the State. The specific purpose of the particular case studies was to examine, through the provision of detailed accounts, the nature of this relationship in what is a contentious but murky area. Can one say from these case studies that the broadcasting institutions and therefore the programmes produced by them are influenced to any extent by the various institutions subsumed within the total structure of the political and commercial exterior?

Within the political context, three themes or relationships emerged:

1 The broadcasting organizations and the governing party;
2 Programme-making and a non-governing party;
3 The legal system and programming.

Thus the relationship with the political context operates at both a high organizational level and at a programme level, and within this one can see three mechanisms functioning: the definition of impartiality, the sustaining of conventional programme forms, and the force of law - through which the State is able to retain a level of control over what is produced. A fourth theme emerged from consideration of the influence of the environment of a commercial enterprise on programme making:

4 Programming and the commercial context.

In other words, while any adequate consideration of the external context of political broadcasting must focus first and foremost on the political institutions of the State, it must also consider the impact of a parallel structure, the institutions of commerce. At the same time, the case studies illuminate a number of specific questions within broadcasting, for example, the contentious issue of who is to exert control within the organizations. Should the legally constituted bodies exert control in a quasi-executive manner, or should they indulge in a rather post-hoc control? The case studies also touched on the question of programming practices, and particularly the way these relate not only to the expectations

and anxieties of politicians, and the professional criteria of
working journalists, but also the demands which a competitive system
makes on programme content, even in the apparently non-commercial
area of news and current affairs.

1   BROADCASTING ORGANIZATIONS AND THE GOVERNING PARTY

It has often been assumed that during the General Strike the BBC was
able to sustain its independence, even though at times somewhat
shakily. The study here shows that such a view is little more than
fiction and that there was in effect a clear submission to the
wishes of the government. This is clearly of more than historical
interest since it does show the way in which a central ambition of
political broadcasting - that it be impartial - was interpreted in
the light of the anxieties and needs of other, political, institutions.
      The original decision to look at the events of the General
Strike, even though it meant leaving the specific discussion of
political television, was based on the observation that there were
striking similarities between statements made in 1926 and those made
in recent years with reference to coverage of, for example, Ulster.
      Prior to the events of May 1926, there had been a good deal of
doubt and discussion as to the permissibility of political broadcasting - either in its news form or as 'controversial' material
which broadly corresponds to what we would now understand as
'current affairs'. Following the events there was something of a
revolution in news broadcasting with, for example, a relaxation of
the restrictions on news and the development of a separate news
section under the aegis of Stobart and the education department.
What is particularly interesting is that when the restrictions on
controversial broadcasting were lifted in March 1928 this was done
on the understanding that the broadcasts were within the spirit of
the Crawford Committee Report. That 'spirit' was that the broadcasts be of 'scrupulous fairness'. This was the same phrase as that
used by Harold Wilson in explaining his rationale behind the
appointment of Hill. There was a clear understanding of Reith's
concept of 'impartiality' which was to be the embodiment of a
'scupulously fair' broadcasting system. The concept - defined
within a conventional framework, structured by constitutionally
legitimate forces - was to be the main defence of the BBC's institutional integrity and the main governmental insurance against fears
of what broadcasting might be capable of.
      At the root, however, of such a conception of an impartial broad-
casting service was a tension. This rested on the simple but all-
important fact that there would be occasions and types of coverage
which did not readily meet the rules of the game implied in the
initial formation of the concept. The meaning of impartiality as
drawn from the model of the journalistic role in the fourth estate,
implying divorce from attachments which might colour or prejudice
reportage, did not fit, and in fact would inevitably clash with, the
meaning as applied in political crises. In times of crisis the
interpretation of impartiality by the broadcasting organizations
becomes crucial in the eyes of government: the evidence from the

General Strike on this is overwhelming. The presentation of that
impartiality, again as evidenced by the General Strike, so that it
is in overall accord with government policy has historically not
been the broadcasting of manifestly propagandist pieces, rather it
has involved the presentation of abstracted 'facts' which deal with
the appearance of sections of political events rather than the complexities and depth of the total event. To illustrate this argument
I would merely point to the comparison between the views of the
General Strike contained within the news bulletins of the BBC and
the views contained within later accounts; or a more recent example,
compare the glimpses of the Ulster situation portrayed throughout
the media and the different accounts of that same situation from
the same individuals who did the reporting in the field (Simon
Winchester's book (1974) on his time in Ulster is a good example of
this). The problem is of course that the construction of those
facts is a journalistic exercise. It is at the interface of the
government's definition of what is sees as the situation (in the
General Strike, or Suez, or Ulster) and that of the broadcast journalist - whose profession is allegedly a fourth estate - that a
latent tension resides. This is not to say or claim that in every
political crisis every broadcast journalist is seeking to undermine
the State by posing alternative views of reality. Clearly this is
not the case and large sections of this work have sought to try and
explain why that is unlikely to be the case. In that sense, the
reporting of any political crisis is not just a function of the
realities and pressures of political life. It also involves the
whole gamut of inhibitions on the use of the medium. Nevertheless,
the political dimension is important and the significance is that
it would always be likely to become increasingly important as
political crisis heightened since it is clear from the available
evidence that the government is reluctant to allow the broadcast
media any latitude in the construction of 'alternative realities'.
Given the formal status of the government vis-a-vis the broadcasting
organizations it can *ultimately* ensure that opposed realities do
not arise by defining within what context impartiality will operate
and thus within what context views of reality will be constructed -
for example, to put it rather crudely, who will be quoted and who
won't, who will be given air time and who won't, and the inflection
and context of factual statement.

One can perhaps see the General Strike as exemplifying a penulti-
mate point on a sliding scale of broadcasting-State relations, where
the ultimate point is a takeover of the organizations. One might
also present it as a scale along which the latency of the formal
legal context becomes gradually manifest in relation to a heighten-
ing crisis. One is not of course here talking about the transformation of an autonomous structure into a subordinate one, rather of
the transformation from a latent to a manifest politicized structure, since broadcasting organizations as institutions within
society have no actual autonomy and in that sense they have never
possessed a legitimate membership of the 'fourth estate'; the effect
has always been illusory, in the sense that their presence on the
terrain of the press has never actually been felt in political
circles to be right and proper. That fundamental absence of legitimacy as autonomous entities has always defined the political reality
of political broadcasting.

If one can extrapolate from the General Strike, the actual linkages between the broadcasting organization and the government of the
day promote programme output which is compatible with the views of
the dominant political institutions and in particular with government. This is clearly the message of the BBC's situation in the
General Strike and its relationship with the strikers, who were seen
as threats not just to Baldwin's government but to the whole idea of
the existing constitutional framework. It was in this context that
Reith and the BBC were expected to identify with the Baldwin position, not with Baldwin as Tory prime minister but with Baldwin as
constitutional leader.

This is the crucial link between Reith's proposition that as
between the strikers and the government he could not be impartial
and almost exactly the same statement by Hill that as between the
Ulster gunmen and the army there could be no impartiality. In both
cases the strikers and the gunmen were identified as threats to a
'legitimate' order and therefore beyond the bounds of impartiality.

In the relations between the government and the broadcasting
organizations what is at stake, and this is clear from not only the
study of the General Strike but also the study of the appointment of
Hill and the retirement of Greene, is the definition of an 'impartial' broadcasting service. That is, the different emphases of the
two situations merely reflect the differential capacity and necessity to impose a government 'sponsored' line. Reith was left alone,
in a sense, by Baldwin and Davidson because it was felt that he
could be trusted to interpret impartiality in a 'responsible' manner
and, as was seen in the case study, he did just that to their great
satisfaction. Wilson, as he clearly states in his history of the
1964-70 Labour government and as Marcia Williams indicates, placed
Hill as chairman of the BBC because it was felt that he would make
the corporation 'scrupulously fair and impartial', and because he
clearly felt that Greene could not be left alone to guide the
corporation along the same lines. There was a confidence in Reith's
intellectual and political orientation; there was no such confidence
in that of Greene. The validity of Wilson's analysis notwithstanding, the point remains that definition of impartiality was his main
concern.

The clarity of the issues involved in the General Strike, however, is far greater than the events surrounding Greene's retirement. This is partly a function of the unique circumstances of the
Strike and the availability of a number of sources which are not
yet available, if indeed they exist, for Greene's retirement. It is
also undoubtedly related to the fact that in 1926 the news service,
and therefore the principles upon which it was to rest, were largely
embryonic whereas by 1967 the practices within which those principles were formed - reference to established sources, balancing of
spokesmen, detached comment, etc. - were well worked out and therefore the possible infringements which even Harold Wilson would be
likely to detect were of a far more marginal nature. Baldwin's
effort was a hefty shove to put the BBC in its place; Wilson's was
a nudge back into its place.

The point about Reith and Hill and the point of their appeal to
Baldwin and Wilson was that they both clearly recognized these
implicit limitations within which political broadcasting was to

function and both recognized an institutional and ideological ratio
nale for accepting the validity of the limitations. It is interesting to note that the present chairman of the BBC, Sir Michael
Swann, in a recent statement, identified with the necessity on
institutional and ideological grounds of a commitment to the theses
and conventions of the established social and political order.
Pointing to the increased concern of the governors under Lord
Normanbrook and under Lord Hill to exert greater control of the
output of the BBC, he states (Swann, 1974):

I look on Lord Normanbrook's analysis of what the Board shall do,
and Lord Hill's attempts to actually carry it out, not, as some
people have naively imagined, as power seeking, but as an inevitable
response to criticism, and the demands on every hand for measures to
control the BBC.... Lord Hill and his Governor colleagues had no
option but to strengthen their own hand, and it is surely to their
credit that they did so, and in the doing fended off a series of
threats to the BBC's autonomy. The fact of the matter is that
inadequate as the Governors may be, they are in the last resort the
BBC's only guarantee of autonomy ... If we move further into
national crisis, and still more if a new government arises in due
course which is further to the Left or Right than any past government, the pressures could become acute. The Governors' role will
become more crucial even that it is now, if the BBC is not to be
fettered. The trustees of the national interest look like continuing to have alarming responsibility.'

This is as clear a view of an anxious response to an external political reality as one could imagine. The phraseology - the 'trustees of the national interest' - clearly echoes Reith, and for the
reason that underlying the broadcasting organization, and therefore
indirectly the programme-making process, is the fact that they are
very much 'institutions within the constitution'. Within that context the operational feasibility of 'impartiality' is not difficult:
that is in circumstances where there is a consensus that there is a
consensus within society. The difficulty lies in situations where
the coverage of the political process takes them outside the context
of the legitimate constitutional structure. Where such situations
of extra-constitutional political conflict arise, where the clear
position of consensus becomes clouded by new circumstances, the
central difficulty of broadcast journalism is in what relationship
it stands to these circumstances. As an institution of the press it
should presumably understand and explain the historical mood; as a
citizen of the State it must give voice to the accredited definitions of reality posed by the State elite. In short, the definitions of political reality which are likely to be made available
will derive from the response of organizational elites to the
expressed concerns and wishes of the State elite, not therefore on
the basis of their membership of the press, but on the basis of
institutional and ideological commitment.
    Such is the nature of broadcasting's relationship with govern-
ment. Clearly on the evidence of these case studies the intensity
of the relationship varies such that one can locate the General
Strike and the appointment of Hill at different points along a

spectrum of - to revert to the more generic term - State-broadcast-
ing organization relations. Unlike the level of political control
achieved in the General Strike when the relationship between the
Baldwin government and the BBC was almost direct, the manner of
Greene's removal was oblique and tortuous and indicates the real
inhibitions on the power of the government to act in the contemporary environment. The 'back-door' politics of Hill's appointment not
only indicates a concern for the visible integrity of broadcasting
but by implication also raises the question of the social determination of political intervention. On what, in other words, is
the intensity of political intervention founded; why were the
relationships in 1926 more assertive of governmental power than
Wilson's rather limp efforts in the same direction in 1967?

What I wish to argue is that one really has to consider the
relationship between the intensity with which a government pursues
and ensures a broadcasting system which is 'responsibly impartial'
and the approximation of a political system to a state of crisis.
It is possible in fact to bring together the main themes of this
discussion and to schematize the system of relationships involved.
To this end it is necessary to define 'crisis', for that provides
one axis of the schema and to develop the notion of an ideal-type
of broadcasting-government relationship which forms the other axis.

I would begin by adopting Gouldner's (1971) view that the central
implication of a system in crisis is that it 'may, relatively soon,
become something quite different than it has been'. His reference
is to a crisis he sees in Western sociology but the definition
equally applies to any 'system'. The definitional distinction
between change (a constant feature of systems) and crisis (which is
not) is that a crisis 'implies that taxing changes are proceeding
at a relatively rapid rate; that they entail relatively sharp
conflict, great tensions, and heightened costs for the system may
soon find itself in a significantly different state than it had
recently been' (Gouldner, 1971, p.342). I have in the schema taken
'crisis' as a given feature of a political process and have therefore not sought to extend the point into a discussion of the social
bases of political crises. Briefly, the description offered by
Gouldner does seem to provide a useful shorthand for the conceptua-
lization of the implications of the change from one regime (say a
liberal democracy) into another regime (say an authoritarian or even
totalitarian structure).

The second axis is provided by consideration of the extent of
real political control of broadcasting. In the preceding pages I
described how the General Strike situation represented the penulti-
mate point on a scale, the logical extension of which was direct
State control of broadcasting. One can develop this and present
that point as an ideal type against which to measure other institutions. Thus by placing it at the end of a spectrum of latent to
manifest politicized broadcasting, it provides the requisite means
of orientation and enables one to consider the approximation of
contemporary relations between broadcasting and government to a
theoretical type. One is in fact tempted to present the General
Strike as the ideal type since the clarity of the relationships at
that time is such as to offer a logical and conceptually unambiguous
point of reference for discussion of existing relationships which
are far from clear, logical or unambiguous.

A simple schematic representation of what I have in mind is presented below:

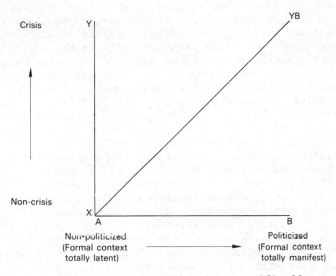

In this schema I am of course referring specifically to the
British political system and more generally to those systems characterized as industrial democracies. While one does not wish to be
unnecessarily crude in the attribution of causality in the relationships between levels of politicized broadcasting systems and political crisis, the schema does reflect the general observation that
on the evidence the greater the systemic crisis the closer the
approximation to the ideal-type structure of YB. There is a predic-
tive element implied within this and I would certainly argue that
the factor which ultimately governs the intensity of the governmental intervention is the level of political stability within the
structure of the advanced industrial societies. The question is,
of course, how would you know that a broadcasting system had been
politicized or rather manifestly politicized? What criteria would
one look for?

I do not wish to become involved in the detailed complexities
of an all-encompassing schema, but the process of a transformation
of latency into a manifestation of a government's power can be
judged by presenting the features of the theoretical ideal. Four
main factors would be crucial:

1   Direct State control - institutionalized in terms of the
creation of, for example, a Ministry of Information;

2   The direct appointment of senior personnel, not just at the
level of controlling Boards but also at the level of senior administrative personnel.

3   Direct appointment of editorial personnel: that is, those who
on a day-to-day basis are responsible for producing programmes.

4   Direct control of (3) by (2).

The politicized broadcasting organization is characterized by a
deliberate and persistent control of the production of content by
the State, and it is against this definitional point of reference
that one must place any discussion of the relationships involved in
broadcasting.

Viewing the relationships of broadcasting organizations and governments in this light, one can begin to locate the present state of relations and place them in some kind of contextual perspective. By adopting such an overall view of the varied possibilities of governmental control one can readily understand how the appointment of Hill was a pale political act that reflects the existing inhibitions on governmental control. By extension one can argue further that the lower down the schematic scale one goes the more autonomous the organizations appear and the more significant are the programme-making practices. Thus Wilson's relative 'success' in the controversy surrounding 'Yesterday's Men' derives partly at least from the fact that there he related to programme practices at a time when historically those proactices remained important.

The relationship between the broadcasting organization and the government is then important for political broadcasting in that it involves the definition of the operational concept of impartiality, not directly at programme-making level but at the level of control over senior executive appointments and ultimate control over the organization's institutional licence. Given the actual level of autonomy which is maintained at the present time, one has to refer to the details of programme-making and the success of associations within the State structure in influencing not only the interpretation of impartiality but also the persistence of conventionality within programme-making; this is shown in the capacity of a party out of power to exert considerable influences on conceptions of programme-making.

2   PROGRAMME-MAKING AND THE NON-GOVERNING PARTY

It is clear from the previous discussion of the capacity of government to act and influence broadcasting, and from the discussion in Part two that the producers of political television are left with a level of 'autonomy' or 'freedom'. Notwithstanding the clear prescriptions on impartiality, the government's holding the institutional licence and the capacity to appoint the 'controllers', producers do not work solely or mainly in response to directives from above or outside. Nevertheless the State does retain a residual power. In office Wilson sought to influence coverage of politics through appointees, and out of power he remained a central and powerful figure, evidence of the State's capacity to inject some influence into the production of programmes.

One irony of 'Yesterday's Men' was the way in which the events of the programme undermined the purposes of his appointment of Hill. This had clearly been the strengthening of the governors vis-a-vis the more 'irresponsible' programme-makers. That position was undermined by the emphasis the programme placed on the contradictions in the governors' role. In short the duality of their position – trusteeship and activism – contained inherently incompatible elements suggest the real complexity and subtlety of the general state of broadcasting: (that, after all, is what their founding documents are all about) and also institutions that aspire to a level of independent political and social observation. One can readily see the likely difficulties that follow from an attachment

to a 'national interest' which ultimately is defined by the State
(not the individual government, but the totality of Parliamentary,
administrative and judicial institutions) and also an attachment to
a defence of their employees against the potentially oppressive
effects of that 'national interest'. Thus most broadcasters would
see themselves as journalists (for example, the overwhelming percentage of my sample of producers were NUJ members - however lapsed)
for whom there is not a national interest but merely a set of competing interests in society about whom they must provide information
and description and between whom they must not choose. The problem
is of course that the luxuries of detached comment and free provision of information are not so readily doled out to the practi-
tioners of *broadcast* journalism. This, for example, is the relevance of the 'formal context' that entails the prescriptions on
practice in what I would interchangeably define as broadcast journalism and political television.

'Yesterday's Men', however, provides an interesting example of
the limitations which exist on the capacity of one part of the State
structure to intervene and influence (the governors did not after
all accept all of Wilson's demands) but at the same time to have
certain small but significant, long-term but not readily detectable
influences. Examples are changes in personnel, the structural
changes - the implications behind the observation that ENCA was to
spend more time at Lime Grove - the effective ban on producers from
producing in certain areas where they have previously trodden with
unfortunate circumstances, etc. This is the stuff of influence but
it is the marginality of the influence which is fascinating and it
reflects the full complexity and subtlety of these relationships,
the difficulties of their analysis, definition and apprehension in
the present political context, which contrasts sharply with the real
clairty and ready apprehension of the relationships in the General
Strike. In terms of the original schema it is almost as if in discussing 'Yesterday's Men' as an exemplar of current relationships one
were marking out a central point at which the pull from polar points
is relatively equal. Any move towards either extremity will then
depend on external political events. This is certainly the point of
Swann's statement quoted previously and I think his analysis is substantially correct. What one can add with certainty is that the
movement or fate is out of the hands of Swann and his associates
throughout broadcasting, and is within the control of the central
characters of political life.

If the broad meaning of 'Yesterday's Men' was the complex interaction of prescription and practice, the illumination of the present
limits on political intervention, what were the detectable consequences of the visible ire of leading State figures on programming?
When Wilson had previously sought to influence broadcasting the
political motivation was obvious, the method oblique. When he
attacked what he thought was an unjust programme the political element was oblique, the method direct - phone calls, writs, press
coverage, etc. - and the consequences significant. The visible consequences of power, the manifest relationship between the broadcasters and a key political figure such as Wilson, is not always the
most significant area for analysis since it misses the less obvious
and tangible aspects of power, what Bachrach and Baratz (1963) have

called the 'invisible face of power'. In effect it is inadequate
always to look for or only to consider the conspicuous manifestations of the impact of the political associations and personalities
within the State.

Thus the potential impact of the State as exemplified by 'Yesterday's Men' was not just on the previously mentioned structural
changes but an ill-defined feeling among programme-makers themselves
that such programmes should not be repeated, thus fashioning an
image of what in future would be the most appropriate form of programme when dealing with politics. One has therefore to consider
the way in which outside pressure was able to influence the largely
unspoken assumptions about programme-making.

The conception of the producer and the reporter on 'Yesterday's
Men' echoed a persistent discussion in broadcasting of how one produces programmes in a competitive environment with its emphasis on
entertainment and audience size using a medium which only with difficulty is able to treat and discuss the political process. The
initial problem with which the programme-maker wrestles is not political pressure but the whole meaning of the medium for political
communication. It was their attempt to solve the problem by breaking out of traditional formulae that led to the political controversy. What one can say is that programmes which stray from forms
and practices that normally govern the television coverage of politicians – that is, the formal interviews, studio discussions,
reportage of speeches, information about Parliamentary affairs,
etc. – are likely to provoke a sharp reaction. Wilson's success was
to ensure that these forms would remain intact, that there would be
no repetition of the "Yesterday's Men' programme, that recalcitrant
producers would be forced back into established production routines
and practices, and to generate concern among the hierarchy that the
boundaries of these forms not be breached again.

In summary, the interest of this case study has several dimensions:

1 It illuminates the real limitations on the ability of leading
political figures to interfere with broadcasting at the present
time.

2 It illuminates the consequences of earlier attampts by government to transcend the subtleties and complexities of the relationship with broadcasting in a relatively stable political environment
by imposing a 'political appointee'.

3 It illustrates the problems of programme-makers in political
television in particular in producing what they would regard as
meaningful content.

4 It illustrates the consequences of change from established
processes of programme-making.

5 It indicates that while a leading politician may not be capable
of direct intervention he can, simply by his hostility, engender a
number of consequences, the most significant of which is that types
of content and format with which he is familiar and which are effectively conducive to his own needs (that is the *electoral role,*
appearance being equated with popular appeal, and a *political role,*
the opportunity to put forward views, information, etc.) are in fact
maintained.

6 Since the programme was in parts reminiscent of a rather mild

satirical cartoon, its being quashed exemplifies yet again not only
the restrictions on form in television but also the perception that
particular content is politically unacceptable, the biting edge of
satire being the most notable example. I have in mind a comparable
situation: 'That Was The Week That Was', produced by CAG, was uncon-
ventional and certainly aggressive. Greene removed it not in
response to a direct order but rather in response to a loosely
defined feeling that trouble 'was brewing' and a conviction that
should he not remove it a direct order would eventually emerge.
    Wilson's ability was to mould the appearance of things, maybe
not as effectively as had he been in full political control, but
surely effectively enough for us to define his role as the impact on
programming of the external context.

3   THE LEGAL SYSTEM AND PROGRAMMING

The influence of associations and personalities within the State is
not only their capacity to, as it were, define impartiality and
ensure that the types of programme produced are to their liking, nor
is it only embedded in practices; it is also firmly rooted in the
laws relating to broadcasting. The point is straightforward, though
important, and need not be laboured or discussed at length. The
study of one department's coverage of the General Election led to a
number of conclusions about the framework for that coverage, and in
particular emphasized the tremendous concern that producers have
for the law relating to broadcasting, notably the emphasis that is
placed on the strict adherence to 'impartiality' and 'fairness'.
The simple truth of that body of law which relates to the coverage
of politics is that, rightly or wrongly, by asserting the dominance
of the main parties within British political life it ensures that
the coverage of politics is tied to the transmission of public
statements by leading representatives of the leading sectors of
British political life. However worthwhile one considers those
statements to be, they do lead one to conclude that this vital
feature of the external context provides a crucial bracket within
which discussion of political affairs has to take place.
    The focus of the study of the coverage of the General Election
was a discussion of the treatment of the issues of the election and
the way in which decisions were made about that treatment. One of
the benefits of such a perspective was that it became possible not
only to describe the legal dynamics of election television but also
to situate that coverage amid the various forces which influence it,
and to assess the extent to which the main criteria are political,
commercial or professional. From this one can begin to define the
importance of a coexistent context, the commercial, which provides a
fourth and final theme in these concluding remarks.

4   PROGRAMMING AND THE COMMERCIAL CONTEXT

One can say conclusively that as important as the political reality
of political television is the commercial reality. Where commercial
television companies are locked into the wider structure of indus-

trial and commercial activity (ATV, for example, is part of ATC Ltd) emphasis is placed on the consumption aspects of political broadcasting. The theme to emerge from the ATV study, and I have no reason to doubt its general applicability, was that the output of news and current affairs departments is as much a product for consumption as those advertised in the commercial breaks.

The effect of such an integration within an industrial enterprise does not lead one to a conspiratorial view of the processes of control involved. There is no direct pursuit of the ideals of big business or a studied support for the virtues of corporate capitalism. Rather the definition of political television as a product for consumption involves a view of what the right type of content will 'look like'.

Though the BBC is in no way a commercial organization, it does not avoid the logic of commercialism and is drawn into that logic through its competition for the same audience as commercial companies. The consequences of this structural relationship though perhaps less obvious than the would-be consequences of political pressure are just as insidious, in my view, an influence on programme content.

To summarize the impact of the commercial context:

1 There is a disposition on the part of organizational controllers to allocate limited resources to the coverage of politics.

2 A tendency by programme-makers to emphasize familiar 'symbols' with which the audience is felt to be accustomed and which therefore enable the 'correct' construction of a programme.

3 A disposition to treat with great respect the attitudes of judicial and political superiors on whom the franchise viability of the whole organization rests. That is, the sustaining of a passivity which ensures the legitimacy and therefore viability of their activity.

4 A refusal to develop the medium, an attachment to existing modes and therefore a virtual veto on experimentation.

If a political context implies a locking in of programming to one system of controls so that the formation of content is compatible with the susceptibilities and anxieties of political figures, the commercial context controls a given form through its emphasis on the tricks of technology and the formulae and cliches of production procedures. The net effect of these being a standardization across the network and a superficial glimpse of the political process.

To look at the relations between political broadcasting and the political and commercial environment in which it takes place is to view an affair of complexity, alternating moments of apparent autonomy and real subjection. There is no doubt that the external context of programme-making functions at one level (the political) as a latent 'presence', the manifestation of which could take a number of forms: for the programme-maker it could affect career, invoke close scrutiny by superiors or the sheer embarrassment of being 'carpeted'; for the organization as a whole, there is the possible non-renewal of the franchise or a refusal to raise the licence fee, threats of dismemberment, the use of political appointees and the threat of stricter external control (Broadcasting Councils, direct Parliamentary control, etc.), general, loosely defined hostility.

These provide the crucial links between the realm of broadcasting and that of politics. Thus the capacity to influence, however obliquely, rests on both sides understanding the potential reality of the powers and consequences that yet remain latent. The necessary economic logic of continuing to exist, the capturing of the BBC by that logic, merely serves to lay the basis for the smoother implementation of that influence.

The direction that that influence has taken has been the defining of impartiality, the underpinning of conventional forms and a commitment to the productive and consumptive practices of a commercial process; these seem to me to be the themes upon which one must focus when considering the role of the external context of political television. They are far more important and influential than a phone call from the chief whip or the prime minister's office.

As I have indicated at a number of points throughout this book, broadcasters, usually at a senior level because they are the acknowledged definers of the situation, frequently engage in a rather self-satisfied back-slapping as to the virtues of their independence; Hill's memoirs, for example, which have figured prominently here are dotted with such allusions to the independence from the political structure. While one might grant that there is a level of dissociation from the party structure, the preceding account has, I think, pointed to a number of linkages which do exist and which therefore tie production, in part, to the dominant political institutions. The connection with the commercial sector was also seen to be an important dilution of the 'independence' argument.

There is however another important perspective on this argument. The main parties themselves, through their political practices, their commitment to welfare capitalism, embody, reproduce and ustain the hegemony of a world of essentially bourgeois practices rooted in the ascendancy of the urban middle class, an hegemony and ascendancy which, as Thompson (1973, p.91) states, is enclosed within a number of 'fixities of concept': property, the rights of money, innate human nature, political realism, etc. It is fundamentally that world from which political television is not independent, which its practices reproduce and which its external context ensures that it reproduces. It was Hill after all who, in praising to the skies the BBC's fight for its independence, stated also of the 'Question of Ulster', 'in television terms the star was Bernadette Devlin, with her captivating flow of oratory. Sir John Foster, almost like a would-be lover, coyly demonstrated her irrelevance to the issues under discussion, save under the heading of social reform' (1974, p.226). This is a remarkably patronizing view of Devlin's argument that the solution to the Ulster question lay in deep-seated change in the social organization of British society. The adequacy or not of her arguments is unimportant here, the dismissive treatment of them, not only by Foster but also through implication by Hill, as 'irrelevant' speaks volumes as to the frame of mind which underpins large sections of broadcasting's treatment of political and social issues. That Hill adopts such a position is not particularly surprising, it merely reflects a general theme in numerous other statements by him (in 'Broadcasting and the Public Mood', in relation to Ulster, throughout his book) and by other senior braodcasters, notably Greene. This general theme is that

there exist a number of moral and political absolutes beyond which
broadcasting will not and dare not go.   In a clear exposition of
this view, Greene states (1969, p.107):

'although in the day-to-day issues of public life the BBC tries to
attain the highest standards of impartiality, there are some
respects in which it is not neutral, unbiased or impartial.   That
is, when there are clashes for and against the basic moral values -
truthfulness, justice, freedom, compassion, tolerance, for example.
Nor do I believe that we should be impartial about certain things
like racialism or extreme forms of political belief.   Being too
good 'democrats' in these matters could open the way to the destruction of our democracy itself.   I believe a healthy democracy does
not evade decisions about what it can never allow if it is to
survive.'

   This seems to me to reflect a commitment, however loosely
defined, to those moral fixities of which Thompson wrote.   What I
think is clear from the case studies is that it is not a question
of such 'fixities of concept' being articulated by senior personnel
and therefore being taken up by the lower echelons of those who
actually make the programmes.   Nor is it a function of the attachment of the lower echelons themselves to these fixities.   Rather to
understand the mechanics of their reproduction in political broadcasting - and by extension I would hypothesize, the rest of the
media - one has to consider the fixities of practices which the
programme-maker derives from the total external context, but principally the governing parties, the legal system and the necessities
of commercial life.   These provide a backcloth, a 'check-list' of
things to do, people to talk to, things to talk about: there is an
attendance to the statements and perspectives of leading figures of
the leading political institutions (and here I would include the
industrial sector).   This position is underpinned by a clear perception of the relationships between commercial interests and political needs; by attendance to the superficial and readily observed
features of politics because of the economic logic which limits
resources; and because of the attendance to the familiar and recognizable based on an assessment of audience taste.   In short the
external political and commercial context locks the programme-making
process into a cycle of dependency - in which the dependency is on
established political imagery and established political figures.

Chapter 13

PERSPECTIVE ON PRODUCTION

The central purpose of this study has been empirically to examine a number of opposed views of the situation and nature of broadcasting within British political culture by offering a sociological analysis of the actual production of programmes within political television. The initial premiss, supported by the research literature, was that one needed to consider both the internal and external context of programme-making, and the institutional and intellectual frameworks which derive from those contexts.

In these concluding remarks I want to consider how the general findings of this work relate to this wider debate and in fact to argue that there are now reasonable grounds to begin judging the various positions. We know that political broadcasting as such and political television in particular are important forms of political communication. On the evidence of this work we now know something about the processes which operate on it and shape it, and as such can begin to make a number of clarifying statements about the arguments discussed in chapter 2. There it was asked whether television serves 'the people' and the 'political process' as is implicit in the view that the broadcasting organizations are becoming more autonomous and therefore more important as agents of communication. Or does programme production, because the organization as such is not autonomous, serve dominant interests by portraying their world-view, and thereby tacitly conspiring to sustain that dominance? The conclusion must be that the resolution of the question of autonomy-subordination really depends on the breadth of the perspective one applies to the discussion, since the media institutions production of political content exhibits varying commitments: serving 'the people' some of the time, political interests most of the time, themselves all of the time.

THE VIEW FROM THE FOURTH ESTATE: THEORY AND PRACTICE

The idea of a free and healthy 'press' is, of course, an integral component of the collective imagery of the cultures of advanced capitalist societies. An intriguing example of this was the language and fervency of the fight during 1975 by editors (including

both electronic and print media) against the provisions of the
Labour government's Trade Union and Labour Relations (Amendment)
Bill.   This, they argued, would enable working journalists as member
members of a monopoly trade union to wrest control of content from
the editorial chair, have control over what other journalists write,
have control over access to the press by non-journalist contributors; in effect, have a possible controlling and censorship role
which would be anathema to the British democratic system.   A typical
statement was contained in the editorial columns of the 'Sunday
Times' (19 January 1975).   The argument is familiar and revealing:

'a union's interests are quite properly those of its members, while
a news organisation's are those of its readers and listeners and
viewers.   These two groups of interest do not necessarily coincide;
and it is the second which Parliament ought to prefer.   An intelligent electorate needs the fullest possible flow of information
from the widest possible range of sources. "A fundamental part of
the freedom of the Press" declared the International Press Institute
in Zurich last week in a comment on the Bill "is the right of access
to it of all citizens."   Amendment No. 11 deserves to be adopted.'
(1)

Such a position in the context of broadcasting, I would suggest,
ignores the reality of the inhibitions which actively hamper the
'fullest possible flow of information'.   Analysis of programme-
making leads one to conclude that political and commercial realities
undermine the arguments expressed in the 'Sunday Times'.
     The dominant mode of political broadcasting in Britain, when it
is not an obsession with the form rather than the content of programmes, an emphasis on mere appearance, or when it is not a head-
long pursuit of an audience rating at the expense of political
content, or when it is not hidebound by a straitjacket of values as
to what is and is not 'political' or 'current' or 'news', is essentially a process of discussion and critique within sanctioned areas.
This is not to posit a conspiracy theory of the production process
or to look for overt acts of repression (though these are not
unknown); it is merely to say that these facts of programme life
are the consequences of the routines and practices of programme-
making and therefore embody an historical congruence between the
development of political television and the needs and interests of
political elites.   What has been shown is that the view of an autonomous process fails to consider a number of features of the internal processes of making programmes which undermine and inhibit the
fulfilment of a fourth-estate role.   Four central mechanisms were
outlined: 1. the operation of programme 'paradigms' or historical
legacies, what was termed the 'functioning of identity'; 2. the
important resource limitations on programmes (in terms of time,
finance, technology); 3. a number of powerful legal restrictions;
4. the absence of any meaningful concept of the audience.   It also
ignores the way in which these mechanisms reflect the political
and commercial reality of political broadcasting, such that one has
greatly to temper the view of the autonomous institution and consider the significance of the linkages between the programme production, the organization and those political and commercial

institutions which provide the environment or framework within which
the production process has to fit.

The argument that structural alterations in the situation of the
media organizations have endowed them with a critical and vital
presence, an issue-defining capacity that is altering the face of
British political life, involves a somewhat abstracted, not to say
optimistic, view of the situation.

The central facts of life of political broadcasting in Britain
and the facts which one must place against the arguments of the
fourth-estate role are the emphasis placed on a large audience (with
all the attendant trivialization and inhibition on experimentation),
the inhibitions of a technology (though even here one needs to consider the social determination of a technology's potential in the
sense that, for example, there have always been economic restrictions on the development of lightweight cameras, use of videotape,
etc.) and the looming presence of a highly sensitive and potentially
all-powerful political structure. These institutional inhibitions
and the production procedures entailed by them indicate the gulf
between the theory and the practice of a 'free press'. On the
whole, the medium can be viewed not as a channel for the transmission of information and analysis but rather as a medium for the
transmission of entertainment (for example, the package-deal broadcasting of news magazines in which nuggets of political information
are submerged within a heap of popular fayre) or as a means of
satisfying certain established political necessities, of which the
ritualized interview between the leading politician and the leading
broadcaster is only the most prominent example.

It is of course impossible to begin to 'weight' influences, one
can only hope to map out the main elements of the framework, to show
the general setting of a process. In the context of this discussion, however, one can pinpoint one major influence historically and
thus locate more precisely a theme which has been a thread of explanation throughout this thesis. This was the decision to institute a
commercial and therefore competitive television service.

Criticism of the impact of the commercial television service is
far from novel, but one can now show how this broad framework of
competition underpins the programme-making process and the premisses
upon which political television rests. The use of particular types
of programme which are known to be successful, the type of resource
provision there is, the treatment of the audience as a statistic to
be added to, all derive from the impact of competition. It would
therefore be incorrect to view the inhibitions on political television as purely political. As important, and in some ways possibly
more important, is the commercial context, and the practices of
programme-making reflect commercial anxieties as much as political
anxieties.

In this context it is interesting to situate the ascendancy of
news and news magazines, both highly successful formats. From their
ascendance one might predict either an absolute decline in the more
serious, lengthy and involved political programmes or their injection with a more entertaining format and content or, and I feel this
is the most likely, the 'ghettoization' of serious political programmes. This would almost certainly be the case if ITV were to
obtain the fourth channel. And all this would happen under the
banner of cultural democracy.

The development of political television since 1954 is analogous
to that of the popular press. Williams distinguishes between the
'newspaper' as embodied in 'The Times' and the 'miscellany' embodied
by the 'Daily Mail'. What Williams argues is that the late eighteenth and early nineteenth centuries witnessed the burgeoning of a
press which tapped a different social base from that upon which the
'newspaper' thrived, that is, the urban middle class. The new tap-
root was the urban working class which wanted entertainment rather
than information or edification or share prices. This new press was
established through

'the institution of the Sunday paper, which, particularly from the
1820s took on a wholly different character and function from the
daily press. Politically these papers were radical, but their main
emphasis was not political, but a mescellany of material basically
similar in type to the older forms of popular literature: ballads,
chapbooks, almanacs, stories of murders and executions' (Williams,
1965 p.198).

The emergence of this popular press was premissed on the emergence
of a new social order - the industrial society with its industrial
mass, its increased productive forces, faster communications, etc.
The press could develop along these new lines and could therefore
establish these new content forms because the urban mass provided a
unique economic viability. The central image of the established
press was the urban middle-class reader, that of the new populars
was of an urban mass whose tastes ran to something very different
indeed.
     If one then looks at the situation in broadcasting, the pre-ITV
period in terms of political broadcast it was characterized by the
cultural ethos of the professional middle classes, and it was that
cultural context which was shattered by the emergence of ITV. I am
not saying that the changes involved were as fundamental as the
changing social base which Williams describes in his analysis of the
emergence of a popular press - he was after all referring there to
the emergence of industrial society. Rather, I am arguing that
while the social arrangements of society did not change on that kind
of scale, the social and structural arrangements of broadcasting
changed with a consequent 'rediscovery' of mass, urgan man.
     The emergence of ITV laid the basis for an enforced recognition
of the urgan mass which, though it had been watching and listening
to the refined tones of the BBC, had also been reading the 'News
of the World'. The consequences of this change of gear is of
immense importance in any discussion of political television as
political communication because the economic logic of commercial
television necessarily involved the BBC and the result in terms of
content has been remarkably similar to that involved in the change
from the 'newspaper' to the 'miscellany', the social basis of which
is the competitive broadcasting structure. It is within that situation that one can begin to explain the mechanics of the internal
context. Thus, even though one might, in more optimistic moments,
concur with the view that as institutions within the political
process broadcasting has established a degree of autonomy from the
party structure, an alternative set of restraints on 'autonomy'

derive from the changed nature of the post-1955 broadcasting environment. Television in particular, during this period, discovered not so much a political role (which was seen as the corollary to the idea of autonomy) as an increasingly depoliticized popular role rooted in perceptions of mass taste. The trend is, and I think will necessarily continue to be, popularization and not politicization, always underpinned by the real political inhibitions which do exist. If there be a conspiracy it is as much one of the social arrangements as of the political arrangements of broadcasting, and the real social basis of the formation of much political television content is the social organization of popular taste.

Thus we have the news programme with its emphasis on the style of presentation (headlines, signature tunes, pairs of newscasters, background imagery of the newsroom, use of by-lines by reporters in the field); eye-catching tricks of technology; its emphasis on the visual, exciting and the drama of conflict; the structure and flow that resembles the fictive form of beginning, middle and end; the limitations specifically imposed on the length of time which any one story can expect to have; the focus on prominent faces (in which 'the familiar' is constantly reproduced and therefore sustained in its familiarity); the limited geopolitical location of reporting (i.e. undue attention to a number of 'newsworthy' spots). The news magazine with its limited resources, its mix of serious and light, political and non-political, with the emphasis on the light and the non-political, the emphasis as with news on the manifestation of technology (what one might call the 'over to you Bristol/Edinburgh/ Newcastle, etc.' syndrome), its reproduction of the values of the news (employing the 'stage army' for example), the dependence on newspapers, particularly in the regions. Even the apparently worthwhile developments such as phone-ins, politicians on the spot, participation, increase in consumer slots largely derive not from an altruistic wish to serve the greater public good, but rather from the fact that they are cheap, are enjoyed by politicians and are good for the public relations image of the organization as such. There is also the visual and lively documentary, the 'human affairs' orientation of much political television (a 'day in the life' of a striking miner, portraits of 'larger than life' politicians/businessmen/trade union leaders). Or where these formulae cannot operate and where, for example, it is necessary to have a 'talking head' in the studio for a lengthy discussion, the timing of that type of political content coincides with low audience-ratings slots (Sunday morning, late evening or the minority channel). All these exhibit not a desire to keep political content away from the audience, nor a desire deliberately to skew the 'sample' of political actors represented within output, nor a desire to glorify established political figures, but rather to cater to 'audience requirements'. They thus exhibit what Theodore Adorno, in discussing the social basis of popular music, described as 'the congealed results of public preference'.

The emergence of 'miscellanized' political programming provides an interesting insight into the manner in which developing practices become, in the context of particular social arrangements, petrified and inhibiting. It is useful here briefly to indulge the luxury of conclusion and offer a few tentative thoughts as to how the process

of transformation of new programme forms into a rigid orthodoxy
might be conceived. There was, I would argue, a transition in the
post-commercial period from a Reithian view of the social responsibilities of broadcasting (which was basically a commitment to a
solidly traditional middle-class world-view emphasizing restraint
and institutionalized inhibition) to a view that broadcasting had a
responsibility to a more engaged, critical and lively presence
within British society: a view which was summed up by its archetypal
representative, Donald Baverstock, as the destruction of cant. (2)
Such a view rested on the assumption that the Britain in which programmes were to be made was a society in which the end of ideology,
the end of real class division and conflict, was the new social
truth (a mood forever symbolized by the success of Anthony
Crosland's belief that 'it is rather absurd to speak now of a capitalist ruling class' (1956, p.75)) and in which the remnants of a
decayed social order suffocated the potentially thriving classless
society. It would then be at least conceivable to begin to link
this strong sense of intellectual 'retooling' which does seem to
have characterized sections of broadcasting in the years of the late
50s and early 60s - most notably in the 'political' departments
of Granada and BBC Lime Grove - and the belief, summed up in
Wilson's vision of a 'white hot technological revolution', that
there was an urgent need for an economic retooling and revitali-
zation throughout the whole social fabric.

The structural alterations in broadcasting thus provided the
necessary basis for the assertion of an intellectual mood from which
emerged the kind of political television with which we are now
familiar. Structured within the political and economic context of
broadcasting, however, what was innovatory in its early stages
became petrified as a cultural form and inhibited by the economic
logic of making a programme which obtains an audience and is therefore 'entertaining' - the transition from 'Tonight' to every news
magazine which is now produced, the popularized current-affairs
programme - and the political logic which engenders sanitized political content; these provide the social background to political
television.

Looking at the formation of political television in this way is,
I would argue, a more substantial view of the nature and situation
of political television than the unreal formulations of the 'view
from the fourth estate'. By focusing on the circumstances in which
political television is made it is clear that rather than serving
the 'electorate' or the 'people' as an information-starved collective entity, and therefore acting out a role in a system of political communication, such television serves particular institutional
and political interests.

NEW PERSPECTIVES ON A RADICAL ORTHODOXY

There is an affinity between the broad conclusions of my analysis
and the view that the broadcast media rather than being separate
institutions are in fact bound by the needs and interests of institutions and groups within society. What I have tried to do,
however, is to show that one cannot look at these relationships as

consisting of the persistent imposition of interest, but rather at
the way in which the development of the making of programmes effectively, but only occasionally purposively, serves those interests.
For example, the programme-maker's limited finance and time to make
'good television' stems from the need for an economically viable
service. At the same time, the lack of those resources, combined
with a sense of political and legal sensitivites, can prevent the
programme-maker pursuing stories which are by any standards important and which the producer knows to be important. In this way different interests, however incidentally, are served: the organization
benefits by controlling its expenditure and by avoiding political
controversy, and political interests are served by leaving untouched
issues and problems which could prove embarrassing or difficult.
Within this context one can begin to explain the persistent failure
of broadcasting to explain, for example, the Poulson case at a time
when a number of small papers were pursuing the story and when many
producers in the regions knew that the activities of that ubiquitous
man required a very careful examination. Poulson, and that is but
the most obvious example, is a classic case of the way in which a
number of factors, not all political or legal, can operate to
inhibit political broadcasting.

Miliband (1973), for example, suggested four control mechanisms
through which dominant social institutions, including the State,
control the output of the mass media. The first is direct ownership
and control. One can argue that it is more accurate to look at the
kinds of perspectives and goals which the institution provides for
its members than to think of the consciously political control of
someone like Axel Springer. His second mechanism, the power of
advertisers, does not involve a direct influence on specific content
content. In the context of television in general, and to a lesser
extent political television, the significance of advertising is that
it requires popular forms of television and thus is one factor
accounting for the petrification of miscellanized forms and not, as
Miliband suggests, because their financial importance leads to business being treated with 'sympathetic understanding'. It is important to note, however, that the effect is more likely to be significant in other areas of television rather than in the area of political television. As a general rule, anyhow, the power of advertisers
to directly influence content in any area is not, on the available
evidence, an important factor at all in British broadcasting -
largely because of the system of spot rather than sponsored advertising. Miliband's third mechanism consists of pressures from the
state system and clearly there is a good deal of validity in this.
His reference is to 'news management', 'pressures and blandishments'
and 'threats'. While there is an acute sensitivity, for example to
the need to always balance representatives of the three main
parties, threats and blandishments and the capacity to manage news
successfully have tended to vary in strength historically between
the General Strike situation when the full potential of the State
structure was clearly manifested, to the frequent but not noticeably
successful basis on which they now operate. Political elites have
sought to influence the perspectives which would be used in political broadcasting by defining how the broadcasting organization
should be impartial, and that is by transmitting images of the

information which arises in the Whitehall-Westminster nexus. By
defining the operational corollaries of this, that the coverage be
balanced (the use of statements from both sides of the Commons/
industry/etc.) and objective (rendition of available statements and
information from politically established sources) it is clear that
the State can ensure to an extent that the political images made
available by broadcasting will be 'right and proper'. At another
level the State provides a specific body of law which is massively
inhibiting for the coverage of political issues. Ideological disposition of media personnel, which is Miliband's fourth factor, is
significant only in the sense that ideological prescriptions are
provided for the producer by the formal legal context and by historical practice. The proclivities of individual ideologies are
inhibited by strict adherence to the ground rules, by the concern of
the organizational hierarchy with that adherence and by the routinized mechanics of programme-making.

If the first part of this conclusion has been an act of faith in
what the book has been able to say, the second part, as a brief
statement, is a profession of humility about what it has not been
able to say and what it therefore might suggest as the possible
basis for future research.

A number of aspects of the institutional context of the making of
political television might be considered. A sharper focus on the
linkage between that context, the programme and the political structure. The focus could be either at the level of relationships
between senior executives and leading politicians ('the consequence
and meaning of dinner at Chequers' comes to mind when reading Hill's
memoirs) or the daily contact which politicians at all levels have
with producers, reporters and researchers. The role and consequence
of the upper echelons of the policy-making process on the activity
of making programmes needs a closer look than has been available
here.

One difficulty, however, would always be the problem of obtaining
adequate data. It is actually difficult, if not impossible, to
obtain any kind of access at the highest level apart from the
occasional interview. On this basis I would suggest that a second
area for development is historical research, informed by a sociological perspective. This would not only have analytic consequences
by providing a long-term perspective on the development of political
broadcasting, but would also have methodological implications in
that archival sources are more readily available, as are the reflections of past employees.

In the pursuit of an understanding of how those political images
which people receive are actually produced there is ultimately no
alternative, despite the benefits of historical and institutional
research, to detailed accounts of the actual making of programmes,
preferably based on the researcher's immersion into that process and
with access to the requisite documentary sources. At the present
time such a piece of research does not seem feasible, though one
likely area is the increasing tendency for political television to
take the form of politicized drama and dramatized politics. Given
the emphasis on visually appealing material, one area in which there
is urgent need for sociological analysis is the making and editing
of film/tape items. A focus on the role of the director, film crews

and particularly on the film editor should provide the basis for
any such discussion. In this way one could detail the technical
construction of images and then link this to a discussion of social
context of an applied technology.

These constitute three areas which, in the light of this work,
require further examination. The proposals within the three areas
are only intended as examples of the kind of work that one might
engage in and in no way exhaust the possibilities. However, while
this research can detail the formation of content, and can say what
political images and information are made available, it can only say
that. It can logically say nothing about the relationship between
political images and social consciousness of political questions.
For that a much broader and total conception of production and consumption is required, and our understanding of both components is
as yet only loosely formulated and hardly validated. It is hoped
that this has been a modest contribution to the formulation and
validation of one part of that total process, the production of
political television.

NOTES

PREFACE

1   The two weeks were 2-8 December 1972 and 13.19 January 1973
    inclusive. 'Sample' is perhaps inappropriate in that the pro-
    grammes represented in these two weeks comprised the main output
    for the whole year. For the original rationale behind the two-
    week sample, see Halloran and Croll (1971).
2   Those individuals with direct responsibility for the programme
    through their ability to allocate the resources made available
    to them, decide on subject matter and be held responsible by the
    organization for those decisions. The title varies between
    programmes.

CHAPTER 1   INTRODUCTION

1   See Emmett (1972).
2   These figures are in line with more recent figures taken from
    a survey carried out by the CMCR, Leicester, in the last three
    months of 1972: see Croll (1973).
3   For example, see Halloran et al. (1970); Hartman and Husband.
    (1973).
4   Blumler (1970).
5   See Windlesham (1966) chs 4, 5 for an interesting case study.
6   A useful review of the literature on political organizations and
    political action is contained in Dowse and Hughes (1972).
7   On this see Halloran and Croll (1971).
8   An extensive analysis along the lines presented here is to be
    found in Faulkner (1974), especially ch.1.
9   In terms of the paucity of many of the analyses offered by
    social theorists I have in mind those offered by the Social
    Morality Council (1973) and Ralph Miliband (1973).
10 For a more extensive review of the literature see: Tracey
    (1975), Elliott (1977) and Schlesinger (forthcoming).
11 White (1950).
12 See for example: (Gieber (1956), Cutlipp (1954), Breed (1955),
    Warner (1971).

13 See also Bowers (1967), Donohue (1967), Judd (1961).
14 Klapper (1948).
15 Blumler (1969).
16 Halloran et al. (1970).
17 Epstein (1973).
18 Cantor (1971), Baldwin and Lewis (1972).
19 Elliott (1972).
20 Smith (1973).
21 Smith (1972).

CHAPTER 2 THE PRODUCTION OF POLITICAL TELEVISION: A CONCEPTUAL FRAMEWORK

1 The following account is based on the work of Siebert et al. (1956).
2 There is some problem over the precise terminology, and as to whether ruling groups consist of social groupings (Domhoff, 1967), economic (Miliband, 1973) or organizational (Mills, 1967) elites. They agree, however, that power is concentrated in somebody and that therefore decision-making is controlled. Interesting analyses of these questions are contained in Crewe (1974), notably his introductory chapter, and Stanworth and Giddens (1974) especially chs 1, 3, 12.

CHAPTER 3 THE PRODUCERS: AUTONOMY OR SERVITUDE

1 While in this book I am using the term 'producer' in a generic sense, within the setting of the larger current affairs programme there will be numbers of individuals working to a senior producer (the various positions described by this interviewee). The origination of this was alluded to by a former Editor: 'I need to explain perhaps the origin of the word "editor". It was introduced by Donald Baverstock in the latter years of "Tonight" when "Tonight" had grown and had producers and senior producers, and it was clear that a new function was evolving of someone who didn't have time to make every segment of a programme because the skills had grown in number. There was a division of labour in fact, and so above all these various functions of film producers and studio producers and so on, there was a new fellow and they started using the word editor. This then became standard for someone in charge of a large team which contained many producers. Originally and indeed still, it was made analogous in some ways to the editor of a newspaper who is responsible both for the layout and the content."
2 An interesting account of the very long history of anxiety is contained in Smith (1972) and referred to below.
3 Interview with author: 28 May 1973.
4 Internal documents produced within the BBC which lay down rulings about the treatment of controversial issues. They relate in particular to the concept of impartiality.
5 The position he is referring to here is that of Regional Television Manager, the senior administrative positions in the BBC's regional stations.

CHAPTER 4   THE FUNCTIONING OF IDENTITY

1   A seminal work in this area is that by Galtung and Ruge (1965),
    reprinted in Tunstall (1970).
2   Hood (1967, 105) notes that the early years of television news
    were controlled by men who did not feel that it was the most
    appropriate medium for news. He observes, 'In Britain their
    attitude was reinforced by the extreme conservatism of this
    BBC's News Division whose upper echelons manifested an almost
    pathological fear of the new medium.'
3   For a discussion of this see Green (1969). Up until July 1954,
    British television news was cast in the cinema newsreel style,
    and radio news was the dominant form of news programme until the
    late 1950s. On this see Paulu (1961), especially ch. 5.
4   Hill (1974) has a fascinating account in ch. 3 of what he calls
    the 'Battle for News at Ten'.
5   The newsroom is not actually in the background, it is in another
    part of Television Centre. The effect, courtesy of a technolo-
    gical 'trick', is illusory. Since the manuscript was finished
    the BBC has abandoned this method.
6   The original use of the phrase 'social contract' had been called
    from what the producer described as a 'rather impressive' letter
    from a viewer.
7   Kumar (1974) has written an interesting article on the central
    importance of the presenter in broadcasting.
8   The pressures leading to the formation of 'Tonight' and 'Pebble
    Mill at One' were institutional - a logical use of resources to
    fill the extra time that was made available.
9   Interview with author.
10 Interview with author.
11 I do not pluck these names out of the air. It was astonishing
    the number of producers who made reference to them, in parti-
    cular to the 'Sunday Times'.
12 For brief discussions along these lines, see Smith (1973), Hill
    (1961), Booker (1970), Lewis (1970).
13 Interview with author.
14 An Audience Research Department Report (BBC, 1959, p.6) could
    state: 'BBC Television News enjoys greater respect than ITN
    amongst those who can view either. Nevertheless this is not
    powerful enough to prevent ITN audiences from considerably out-
    numbering the Band III audiences for the BBC-TV News.'
15 A Scottish producer described the early state of news magazines
    as being characterized by the 'Japanese flower-arranging syn-
    drome'.
16 Though news magazines are classified as political television,
    they do not contain totally or even mainly political material.
    For example, an analysis of items in regional news magazine
    programmes produced the following distribution: politics 7 per
    cent; work, economy 19 per cent; police, court, prison 23 per
    cent; environment 3 per cent; minorities, race relations 7 per
    cent; welfare, housing, poverty 21 per cent; culture, science,
    education 13 per cent; human interest 59 per cent; violence
    13 per cent (Source: Croll, 1973).

CHAPTER 5   RESOURCES

1   Time is not only of consequence in a linear sense, i.e. whether
it is a 10-minute or 70-minute programme, but is its significant
in two other ways. What time the programme is broadcast and how
frequently the programme is transmitted: is it every night or
every week? This can be of consequence for the time available
to prepare items and for the time 'perspective' of the programme:
is it a treatment of the days news or a review of the events of
the week?

2   See for example John Whale's argument in 'The Listener' (15
October 1970) that news is about accidents of time and place
rather than news values, and that it is therefore random and
fundamentally unpredictable.

3   These figures compare to the £3,300 per hour cost of television
suggested by Thorne (1970). Pratten (1970) in his analysis of
the economics of television, places a figure of £10-15,000 per
hour for a documentary programme such as 'World in Action';
£8,000 per hour for '24 Hours' and 'This Week'; £8,000 per hour
for a national news programme; and £2,000 per hour for a local
news programme. This compares to a £75,000 per hour cost for
the Englebert Humperdink programme and £25,000 per hour for
drama. A production of Robinson Crusoe by the BBC for showing
in Christmas 1974, is reputed to have cost £250,000. The
figures drawn from Pratten (1970) are now four years out of date
date. As recent events in the BBC suggest (economy measures,
etc.) costs are now substantially higher.

4   Croll (1973) shows that 53 per cent of all television news and
43 per cent of all news magazine programmes consist of filmed
reports.

5   There is much illusion and irony in this view. Not only are the
audiences for political television decreasing but also there is
evidence that as the audience for types of political TV coverage
increases the political content actually decreases, as for
example, the news magazine.

CHAPTER 6   THE GROUND RULES

1   There is no space here to go into the details of these rulings.
For a detailed account see my 'The Production of Political
Television in Britain', ch. 4, the formal context of political
television (University of Leicester, 1975). Also Seymour-Ure
(1968), Street (1972), O'Higgins (1972).

2   It is a remarkable fact that in 1964 only 61 politicians were
quoted on radio or TV during the entire election campaign of
that year; in 1966 the figure was 56 and in 1970, had dropped
to 44. The two leaders Wilson and Heath took up 53 per cent of
all news coverage of politicians in 1966 and 1970. (Source:
Seymour-Ure 1974).

3   See O'Higgins (1972) for a full account of this.

4   There is a point to be made in response to Smith's article in
relation to his observation that it took 'many years to wrest
editorial power from Broadcasting House to TV Centre and Lime

Grove in the days when television was first hit by commercial
competition ...' (Smith, 1972, p.30). I am not at all sure that
editorial power ever was wrested from Broadcasting House, and
more specifically from the director general. Rather I think one
has to see the late fifteis and early sixties as reflecting the
particular exigencies and perspectives of the Greene years.
There was, for example, no doubt who had hold of the 'reins'
when in 1964, Greene ordered that 'TW3' be taken off the air.
The real battle, of course, has been whether the director
general or the governors had ultimate control.

5 Transcript - programme broadcast 5 December 1973.

CHAPTER 7 THE ABSENT FRAMEWORK: THE AUDIENCE-COMMUNICATOR
RELATIONSHIP

1 It is estimated that between them, the BBC and ITV spend
   £1 million a year on AR: Television Research Committee, 'Second
   Progress Report and Recommendations' (Leicester University
   Press, 1969, p.28).
2 The correspondents studied by Tunstall received an average of
   fourteen letters a week. These were not, however, of any particular use in the formulation of an audience image since the
   letters were either from 'cranks', were factual enquiries or did
   not contain any information on readership (1971, p.252).
3 The producer of 'Nationwide' stated in a broadcast on 'The Communicator and the Audience' (BBC Radio, 25 January, 1973), that
   his programme received an average of 1550 letters per week.
4 Stuart Hood has made a most apposite summation of the feeling
   implied here: 'If one works in television one must reconcile
   oneself to the fact that the bulk of the audience reaction is
   from cranks, from the unstable, the hysterical and sick.... To
   form an equable judgement about one's audience from phone calls
   or correspondence is difficult, if not impossible.... The only
   positive thing the programme-maker knows about its audience is
   its size.' Hood, 'A Survey of Television' (Heinemann, 1967),
   p.38-9.
5 Elliott's study (1972, pp.141-2) led him to the conclusion that
   correspondence was 'no use to the production team in suggesting
   programme ideas for the future, because of its content, the way
   the team related to it, and because by the time most of it
   arrived the production team has disbanded and each member was
   working with another team on a new programme'.
6 'Broadcasting and Society', a speech in Edinburgh, 23 March 1971.
7 Lord Aylestone, 'TV and Public Taste', ITA notes (May, 1971),
   no.22.
8 Reprinted in: 'In the Public Interest'; a six-part explanation
   of BBC policy (January 1971), p.13.
9 'Audience Research in the United Kingdom: Method and Service',
   (BBC, 1966), p.3; quoted in Wedell (1968), p.236.
10 In Halloran and Gurevitch (1971), p.58.
11 This was a point made by a number of producers, that a difficulty with the audience was its unpredictability. This offended
   their own professional status in the sense that items they were

pleased with and which exemplified their craft went by without
any response, while a shoddy, hastily prepared item would have
a massive response.

CHAPTER 8   THE BBC AND THE GENERAL STRIKE: MAY 1926

1 The following account is based mainly on the collection of
   General Strike files which the BBC keeps at its Written Archives
   Centre at Reading, and on a number of secondary sources. The
   main file concerned at the Archives is: WAC 45567, News Arrangements.
2 BBC Archives: 'Broadcasting Policy (5): The Broadcasting of
   Controversial Matter (Excluding Religious Broadcasts): History
   and Present Practice' November 1942. Henceforward BP5.
3 News bulletins could not be broadcast before 7 p.m. but there
   was no restriction to one bulletin each day. The National Programme broadcast two news bulletins each evening, one at 7 p.m.
   and one at 10 or 10.30 p.m.
4 Cmd 1951 (1923), Broadcasting Committee Report (The Sykes
   Committee Report).
5 For example, it referred to 'the chains which now impede or
   nullify progress' in controversial broadcasting.
6 Cmd 2599 (1925), Report of the Broadcasting Committee, 14-15,
   para (o).
7 The statement to this effect was made in the Commons on 22 March
   1926.
8 J.C.C. Davidson, financial secretary to the Admiralty, appointed
   deputy chief commissioner, who not only liased with Reith to
   oversee the BBC's output but also had overall editorial control
   of the British Gazette - Churchill's propaganda sheet. He could
   and did overrule Churchill (James, 1969; Pelling, 1974).
9 They were in fact broadcast at 10 a.m., 1 p.m., 4 p.m., 7 p.m.,
   and 9.30 p.m. It is of course difficult to capture the essence
   of what the programmes were like, but a report in 'The Times' of
   19 May 1926 gives some indication: 'The bulletin began with
   special messages, followed by comments on the state of things,
   made by the BBC and official communications from government
   departments, after which a summary of the general situation of
   the country was broadcast, beginning with news from the Home
   Office and Civil Commissioners, then that received from agencies
   and winding up with information received by their own means.
   The second part of the bulletin consisted of a precis of the
   daily measures taken by Parliament, and news from home and
   abroad.'
10 Deliberate technical interference with radio reception.
11 Source: transcripts of radio broadcasts in BBC archives. In
   this situation the BBC which had previously been at the mercy of
   the newspapers was now the benevolent bestower of copy. On
   2 May, the BBC received a typical request from Northumberland
   and Berwickshire Newspapers Ltd, which asked

   'In view of the pending strike of the Printing Trade and the
   non-publication of newspapers, will you please inform us per

return by wire if we have permission to publicly broadcast all
items of news broadcast by the BBC stations. We understand that
it is with a view to suppressing propaganda as news that the TUC
has taken this step and no doubt it will prove of great use to
the country if such permission is granted.'

Permission was granted.

12 WAC 45567, News Arrangements. Both Briggs (1961) p.362 and
Boyle (1972) p.193 attribute this memo to Reith. The actual
memo is in fact signed by Gainford, chairman of the BBC.

13 WAC 45566, General Strike. Briggs dates this 6 May whereas it
is in fact dated 8 May.

14 WAC 45566, General Strike. In the House of Commons on 6 May,
Sir John Simon, a Liberal lawyer, declared that the General
Strike was illegal because the Trade Disputes Act of 1906 did
not cover it and that therefore the leaders of the strike were
liable for damages 'to the utmost farthing' of their posses-
sions. On 11 May a high court judge, Mr Justice Astbury, confirmed this opinion on the grounds that no trade dispute had
been shown to exist in any of the unions involved except the
miner's union (Hyde, 1973). This view was subsequently challenged - see Briggs (1961) p.366, n.2 and also Symons (1957).

15 WAC 45594, Staff Arrangements.

16 Reith's Diary, 10 May, quoted in Briggs (1961) p.376.

17 WAC 45587, Archbishop of Canterbury.

18 Ibid.

19 Of their physical proximity during the Strike period, Reith
stated: 'We were often on the telephone, or meeting in his house
or mine - near the Abbey and within a few yards of each other
or in his office or mine, during the next ten days and nights'
(Reith, 1963).

20 A phrase he was to use on a number of occasions: see Briggs
(1961), p.366, n.3.

21 For example, it was broadcast that enginemen and firemen were
returning to work at Oxford, that the Strike was breaking down
at Salisbury and that foodships were being discharged at Grimsby
Grimsby. Even though these reports were false and were cor-
rected by the unions, and even though the BBC was informed of
these corrections, they were not broadcast (Briggs, 1961, p.373).

22 WAC 45567, News Arrangements.

23 Ibid.

24 Ibid.

25 Ibid.

26 Ibid.

27 On 20 May 1926, a 'Service of Reconciliation' was held in the
BBC studios. The Bishop of Southwark read the text and
concluded with the thought that the 'success of the Strike would
have had quite incalculable results on the life and prosperity
of the nation'. (Report in 'The Guardian', 21 May 1926).

28 WAC 45566, General Strike.

29 Ibid.

30 Ibid.

31 In its white variety. The 'black' version is altogether more
nefarious. On this see Delmar (1962) and Bennett (1966).

CHAPTER 9 THE RETIRING OF HUGH GREENE

Note: Quotes from Greene and Lusty, unless referenced, are from
interviews with the author.

1 Robert Lusty notes, 'At this time I do not think there was any
   move to oust Greene (certainly no such move would have been
   other than rejected out of hand by the Governors). We might
   have had some anxieties (and those always exist) but we were
   united behind Greene.' Letter to author 29 October 1975.
2 Whitehouse (1972) dedicates the book to James Dance 'chairman
   of the National Viewers and Listeners Association (1966-1971)
   who died while this book was being written, in appreciation of
   his courage in 'standing up to be counted' and as a token of my
   affection and gratitude.'
3 Greene deals with this in ch.4 of his book (1969).
4 For a useful discussion of the Labour leader's relations with
   broadcasters, see Shulman (1973a).
5 Hill has subsequently acknowledged that this may not really have
   been totally accurate.
6 Interview with the author.
7 In commenting on my manuscript, Lusty took up this point:

   'I do not think, as Greene suggests, that the "pressures" to
   which I refer were exaggerated nor, as you write, "informed by
   post hoc reasoning". I would not feel able to go into further
   detail since I, in a possibly priggish way, have qualms which
   evade Hill! That the anxieties expressed by Normanbrook went a
   good deal further than I would divulge: hence the weakness of
   "articulation". I would prefer that you should detect a
   "certain reticence".'
8 The White Paper was in December 1966. It proposed the birth of
   Radio One and the establishment of local radio. The decision
   was not to increase the licence fee, though the Post Office was
   to make greater efforts to stamp out evasion.
9 Neither did he mention that much of the hostility was personal
   in the sense that Hill was regarded as not of a very high
   'calibre' either personally or intellectually.
10 I have been able to check this out and it is indeed the case
   that these sources stated that Wilson's office made it known
   that one expectation of the appointment was that Greene would
   resign.
11 Hill felt that the meeting had been a success, having told
   Greene that 'As far as I knew there was no anti-Greene motive in
   the appointment; certainly there was none in my mind. He
   appeared to accept what I said and we parted on good terms.'
   (Hill, 1974, p.74). When this quote was put to Greene, he
   stated 'I accepted it (Hill's answer) with a "Let's wait and see
   attitude".' Lusty indicates that the two meetings went well.
12 In his memoirs (1971, pp.423-4), Wilson describes Hill as having
   administered the Television Act when chairman of the ITN with
   'scrupulous fairness'.
13 The manuscript for this work was completed before the Reith
   Diaries were published. From an initial perusal while preparing
   these notes there is much in them that is relevant to this question of the role of the board of governors: see Stuart (1975).

14 This refers to a series of articles by Kenneth Adam, former
    Director of Television at the BBC. Those pieces were published
    between 16 March and 30 March 1969. Following their publication
    there was a personal rift between Greene and Adam and they have
    not spoken since.
15 The text of the letter actually read:

    'I am putting this on paper so that you can think the problem
    over at your leisure before our next talk.
    'I keep getting evidence that the stories about my impending
    departure from the BBC (the reports in the 'Observer' on Sunday
    and in the 'Daily Mirror' today are only the latest of a whole
    series) are causing some disquiet if not at the top levels in
    the BBC, at any rate at the middle and lower levels.
    'I wonder whether there might be something to be said in the
    interests of staff morale for an early public statement along
    the following lines:
        "In view of recent press speculation the Board of Governors
        of the BBC wishes it to be known that it continues to be its
        assumption that Sir Hugh Greene will remain as Director-
        General at least until his sixtieth birthday on November 15th
        1970. Any possibility of an extension beyond that date will
        be the subject of later discussion between the Board and
        Sir Hugh.
        The Board believes in principle that the eventual successor
        to Sir Hughsshould be found if possible from within the ranks
        of the BBC."
    'I have put in the second paragraph because I know that the
    speculation about an appointment from outside is bothering
    people at the top.
    'This, I know, would be an unusual step but it seems to me that
    it would clear the air once and for all.'

16 Compare this to a comment by Reith (quoted in Briggs 1965,
    p.431) about his amicable working relationship with Whitley,
    'Free from internal strife, suspicion and distrust, one was
    able, undisturbed, to get on with the job'.
17 On this see also Stuart (1975), quoted in Smith (1974), p.60.
18 Cf. Hill (1974), pp.264-5, for a list of the governor's tasks:
    these include broad policy and finance and the appointment of
    senior personnel.
19 On this see Wedell (1968), p.131.
20 See, for example, his speech in Rome printed in Greene (1969).

CHAPTER 10 YESTERDAY'S MEN

1 Unless otherwise stated, all quotes are from interviews with the
   author. I would like to thank Angela Pope for her many and
   detailed comments on the various drafts of this paper.
2 Pope was to note at the time of the controversy:

   'It is claimed that the participants are being misled as to the
   context of the programme, that they expected that the film would

only be about the. role of the opposition and about its policies. At no time did I discuss a programme of this kind verbally or in my correspondence with the interviewees. Indeed, whilst I see this as an interesting area of British politics, it was not one which I felt I could project on television.'

She refers specifically to the content of the letters which were sent to the participants to support this argument.

3 Editor, news and current affairs: in overall charge of output from the news and current affairs departments of the BBC and one of the corporation's most senior and prestigious posts.

4 Interview with author 28 May 1976.

5 This was after a meeting of the finance sub-committee of the governors. When the meeting was over Hill asked those governors present whether they would like to come along and see the film, which they did. The full board of governors did not therefore see the film. See: The dilemma of the researcher, 'Broadcast', 5 July 1976.

6 It is perhaps not insignificant that in his article in the 'New Statesman' Crossman states of Broadcasting House, 'It is here that the Director General and the Chairman, presumably following the Reithian tradition of not recobnising television, have their headquarters connected only by the Westway and the Central Line to that glass doughnut which is TV Centre and that dank tenement building which is Lime Grove.' ('New Statesman', 25 June 1971). Clearly with ENCA's increased presence in Lime Grove, Broadcasting House would have a more 'significant' presence.

CHAPTER 11 TELEVISION IN THE GENERAL ELECTION: A 1974 CASE STUDY

1 Having read my account the editor observed on this point: 'Whether we wanted to do this or not is quite immaterial. The major parties made it absolutely clear that there were no circumstances in which they would appear on the same platform as National Front, Communist or other such organizations' (Letter to author 3 November 1975). I replied that, 'Such an observation does seem to me to raise a further observation that in this situation you were in fact extending the power of veto to the main parties which, I am sure you would agree denies some of the central propositions of the journalistic ethic' (Letter to editor, news and current affairs, ATV, 25 November 1975). To this he replied, 'In theory you must be right, but from where I sit, charged with making programmes, what choice do I have?' (Letter to author, 5 January 1976).

2 In correspondence the editor argued:

'On the question of Enoch Powell's successor we were told at one time by the IBA that we could not even name him and show his photograph unless we gave a similar showing to his opponents. This we disputed but it is my view that if we had interviewed him there was no way we could have refused a similar opportunity to his constituency opponents' (Letter to author, 3 November 1975).

3 Both the editor and the two presenters argue that this was not
   the reason and that the real reason was the difficulty of
   finding people to balance Whitelaw. My field notes, however,
   make it very clear that the reason was the decision of the
   newsdesk editor who though he felt he would have liked to have
   used Whitelaw on the programme, felt that in the context of an
   election he would have had to balance by including other senior
   party politicians. This he rejected on the basis of his assessment of the audience for the programme.
4 This clearly implies a problem very much bigger than any discussion of this particular case study. It does however, reflect
   the central paradox of broadcasting in society: it seems that
   if you apply certain traditional criteria of good and bad programmes, then the bulk of the programmes watched by the bulk of
   the audience are, if not 'bad', certainly not 'good'. Given
   such a situation certain options are available: you can put
   'good' television on a separate channel - viz. BBC2, the
   'minority channel' a euphemistic description of the cultural
   ghetto aspects of that channel - or you can force the main
   channels to broadcast 'good' television, in which case there is
   a strong possibility that they will no longer be the main channels. It is an interesting but unavoidable possibility that,
   in the present set of social relationships and cultural arrangements of British society, the idea of 'good' television is
   inherently undemocratic.

CHAPTER 13   PERSPECTIVE ON PRODUCTION

1 Amendment No. 11, was proposed by the Conservative and stated
   that an employee be allowed to refuse to join a union on the
   grounds that his membership would hamper 'the discharge of any
   duties he may have in relation to the dissemination of news,
   opinion or information'.
2 Interview with author, 16 January 1974.

BIBLIOGRAPHY

ADAM, K. (1969), Decline and fall at the BBC, 'Sunday Times',
16 March, pp.49-50.
ADAM, K. (1969), How BBC TV fought back, 'Sunday Times', 25 March,
pp.49-50.
ADAM, K. (1969), The BBC in danger, 'Sunday Times', 30 March, p.49.
ADAM, K. (1974), Fifty years of fireside elections, 'Listener',
14 February.
ADAMS, A.A. (1972), Broadcasters' attitudes toward public responsi-
hility: an Ohio case study, 'Journal of Broadcasting', Fall.
ADORNO T.W. (1969), Scientific experiences of a European scholar in
America, in D. Fleming and B. Bailyn, 1969.
ALLEN, R. (1974), The electronic election, 'Broadcast', 15 February
and 22 February (2 Parts).
ALLEN, R. et al. (1973), Election special, 'Broadcast', 8 March.
ALLSOP, K. (1972), Goodbye to '24 Hours', 'Listener', vol.87,
no.2256, 22 June.
ALTHUSSER, L. (1971), 'Lenin and Philosophy and Other Essays',
London, New Left Books.
ANDERSON, P. (1965), Sir Hugh's apologia, 'Spectator', 2 July, p.16.
ANON (1963) Aunty's new image: Greene of the BBC, 'Time and Tide',
7-13 November, pp.6-7.
ANON (1970), The wronged box? television and the moral consensus,
'Times Literary Supplement', 6 November, pp.1299-1300.
ANON (1971), Who says so, 'The Economist', no.239, 26 June, p.26.
ANON (1974), Broadcasters and politicians, 'Broadcast', 9 September.
ARONS, L. and MAY, M.I. (eds.) (1963), 'Television and Human
Behaviour', New York, Appleton-Century-Crofts.
ATKIN, C.K. et al. (1971-2) The surgeon-general's research programme
on television and social behaviour: a review of empirical findings,
'Journal of Broadcasting', vol.16, pp.21-36.
ATWOOD, R.E. (1970), How newsmen and readers perceive each others
story preference, 'Journalism Quarterly', Summer.
BACHRACH, P. and BARATZ, M.S. (1963), Decisions and non-decisions:
an analytical framework, 'American Political Science Review',
vol.57, no.3, September.
BADLEY, F.S. (1972), 'Fourth symposium on broadcasting policy',
University of Manchester, February.

BAGDIKIAN, B.H. (1971), 'The Information Machines, Their Impact on Man and the Media', New York, Harper & Row.
BAGDIKIAN, B.H. (1972), The politics of American newspapers, 'Columbia Journalism Review', vol.10, March-April.
BAKEWELL, J. and GARNHAM, N. (1970), 'The New Priesthood: British Television Today', London, Allen Lane.
BALDWIN, T.F. and LEWIS, C. (1972), Violence in television: the industry looks at itself, 'Surgeon-General's Report, vol.1, pp.290-375.
BARMAN, T. and GREENE, H.C. (1969) Warsaw, September 1939 - Sir Hugh Greene in conversation with Thomas Barman, 'Listener', 24 July, pp.102-4.
BARTLEY, R.L. (1971), The press: advisory, surrogate, sovereign, or both? Paper delivered to American Political Science Association.
BASS, A.Z. (1969), Refining the 'gatekeeper' concept: a UN radio case study, 'Journalism Quarterly, Spring.
BAUER, R. (1958), The communicator and the audience, 'Journal of Conflict resolution, vol.2, pp.66-76.
BEATON, L. (1969), Who should control press and television? Journalists demand voice, 'The Times', 17 July, p.10.
BECKER, H.S. (1970), Interviewing medical students in N.K. Denzin, 'Sociological Methods: A Sourcebook', London, Butterworths.
BECKER, H.S. (1971), 'Sociological Work: Methods and Substance', London, Allen Lane.
BECKER, H.S. and GEER, B. (1960), Participant observation: the analysis of qualitative field data in R.N. Adams and J. Preiss, (eds) 'Human Organisation Research: Field Relations and Techniques' Homeswood, Ill., Dorsey Press, pp. 267-89.
BECKER, S.L. (1967), Broadcasting and politics in G.B., 'Quarterly Journal of Speech', vol.LIII, no.1.
BENDIX, R. (ed.) (1973), 'State and Society: A Reader in Comparative Political Sociology', University of California Press.
BENDIX, R. and LIPSET, S.M. (1957), Political Sociology - a trend report and bibliography, 'Current Sociology' vol.6, no.2, pp.79-169.
BENNETT, j. (1966), 'British Broadcasting and the Danish Resistance Movement 1940-1945: A Study of the Wartime Broadcasts of the BBC Danish Service', Cambridge University Press.
BENNEY, M. and HUGHES, E.C. (1970), Of sociology and the interview in N.K. Denzin, 'Sociological Methods: A Sourcebook', London, Butterworths.
BERELSON, B. (1959), The state of communications research, 'Public Opinion Quarterly' vol.23, pp.1-15.
BERREMAN, G.D. (1962), 'Behind Many Masks', Ithaca, New York, Society for Applied Anthropology. Monograph No. 4.
BETTINGHAUS, E. and PRESTON, I.L. (1964), Dogmatism and performance of the communicator under cognitive stress, 'Journalism Quarterly', vol.41, Summer, pp.399-402.
BEVINS, R. (1965), 'The Greasy Pole', Hodder & Stoughton.
BINGHAM, B. (1960), The responsibilities of a free press in R. English, (ed.) 'The Essentials of Freedom', Gombier, Ohio, Kenyon College.
BIRCH, A.H. et al. (1956) The popular press in the British general elections of 1955, 'Political Studies', vol.IV, no.3.
BLACK, P. (1972), 'The Biggest Aspidistra in the World', London, BBC.

BLACK, P. (1972), 'The Mirror in the Corner', London, Hutchinson.
BLACKBURN, R. (1972), 'Ideology in Social Science: Readings in Critical Social Theory', London, Fontana.
BLAU, P.M. (1964), The research process in the study of 'The Dynamics of Bureaucracy' in P.E. Hammond, 'Sociologists at Work', New York, Basic Books.
BLUMLER, J.G. (1969), Producers' attitudes towards television coverage of an election campaign: a case study, 'Sociological Review Monograph 13'.
BLUMLER, J.G. (1970) The political effects of television in J.D. Halloran, 1970.
BLUMLER, J.G. (1971), Reflection on his experience in J.D. Halloran and M. Gurevitch, 1971.
BLUMLER, J.G. (1974), Mass media roles and reactions in the February election in H.R. Penniman, 1974.
BLUMLER, J.G. (1974), The media and the election, 'New Society', 7 March.
BLUMLER, J.G. (1974), Review of Seymour-Ure 1974, 'New Society', 28 March, p.784.
BLUMLER, J.G. and McQuail, D. (1968), 'Television in Politics: Its Uses and Influence', London, Faber.
BLUMLER, J.G. and McQUAIL, D. (1970), The audience for election television in J. Tunstall, 1970.
BOGART, L. (1968), The overseas newsman: a 1967 profile study, 'Journalism Quarterly', Summer.
BOGART, L. (1968-9), Changing news interests and the news media, 'Public Opinion Quarterly', Winter.
BOOKER, C. (1970), 'The Neophiliacs', London, Fontana.
BOORSTIN, D. (1963), 'The Imago: Or What Happened to the American Dream', Harmondsworth, Penguin.
BOWERS, D.R. (1967), A report on activity by publishers in directing newsroom decisions, 'Journalism Quarterly', vol.44, pp.43-52.
BOYLE, A. (1972), 'Only The Wind Will Listen: Reith of the BBC', London, Hutchinson.
BRANDENBURGER, B. (1965), 'Working in Television', London, Bodley Head.
BREED, W. (1955), Newspaper 'opinion leaders' and processes of standardisation, 'Journalism Quarterly', vol.32, Summer.
BREED, W. (1955), Social control in the newsroom: A functional analysis, 'Social Forces', vol.33..
BREED, W. (1958), 'Mass communication and sociocultural integration, 'Social Forces', vol.37.
BREED, W. (1964), Mass Communication and Sociocultural Integration' in L.A. Dexter and D.M. White, 1964.
BRIDSON, D.G. (1971), 'Prospero and Ariel: The Rise and Fall of Radio. A Personal Recollection', London, Gollancz.
BRIGGS, A. (1961), 'The History of Broadcasting in the United Kingdom - Volume 1: The Birth of Broadcasting, Oxford University Press.
BRIGGS, A. (1965), 'The History of Broadcasting in the United Kingdom - Volume 2: The Golden Age of Wireless', Oxford University Press.
BRIGGS, A. (1970), 'The History of Broadcasting in the United Kingdom - Volume 3: The War of Words,' Oxford University Press.

BRIGGS, A. (1969), Prediction and control: historical perspective, in P. Halmos, 1969.

BBC (Annual), 'BBC Handbook', London, BBC Publications.

BROWN, L. (1971), 'Television: The Business Behind the Box', New York, Harcourt Brace Jovanovich.

BROWN, R.L. (1969), Some aspects of mass media ideologies, 'Sociological Review Monograph 13'.

BROWN, R.L. (1970), Approaches to the historical development of mass media studies in J. Tunstall, 1970.

BUCKALEW, J.K. (1974), The local radio news editor as gatekeeper, 'Journal of Broadcasting' vol.18, no.2, Spring.

BUNN, R.F. (1966), The Speigel affair and the West German press: the initial phase, 'Public Opinion Quarterly', vol.30, pp.54-68.

BURGELIN, O. (1972), Structural analysis and mass communications, in D. McQuail, 1972.

BURNS, T. (1963), Cultural bureaucracy: a study of occupational milieux in the BBC, Unpublished manuscript.

BURNS, T. (1969), Public service and private world, 'Sociological Review Monograph 13'.

BURNS, T. (1972), Commitment and career in the BBC in D. McQuail, 1972.

BUTLER, D. and STOKES, D. (1969), 'Political Change in Britain', London, MacMillan.

BUTLER, D. and PINTO-DUSCHINSKY, M. (1971), 'The British General Election of 1970', London, MacMillan.

CANTOR, M.G. (1971), 'The Hollywood TV Producer: His Work and His Audience', New York, Basic Books.

CANTOR, M.G. (1972), The role of the producer in choosing children's TV content in Surgeon-General, 1972.

CAREY, J. (1969), The communications revolution and the professional communicator in P. Halmos, 1969.

CARTER, R.E. (1958), Newspaper 'gatekeepers' and their sources of news, 'Public Opinion Quarterly', vol.22, pp.133-44.

CASEY and COPELAND (1958) Use of foreign news by 19 Minnesota dailies, 'Journalism Quarterly', Winter.

CATER, D. (1964), 'The Fourth Branch of Government', New York, Random House.

CAUTE, D. (1971), 'The Illusion: An Essay on Politics, Theatre and the Novel', London, Deutsch.

CHANEY, D. (1972), 'Processes of Mass Communication', London, MacMillan.

CICOUREL, A.V. (1964), 'Method and Measurement in Sociology', New York, Free Press.

COHEN, B.C. (1965), 'The Press and Foreign Policy', New Jersey, Princeton University Press.

COHEN, S and YOUNG, J. (1973), 'The Manufacture of News, Deviance, Social Problems and the Mass Media', London, Constable.

COLEMAN, T. (1970), Terry Coleman interviews Hugh Carlton Greene, 'The Guardian', 22 August, p.7.

COMMISSION ON THE FREEDOM OF THE PRESS (1947), 'A Free and Responsible Press', University of Chicago Press.

COX, Sir G. (1973), Television coverage of the October 1968 demonstration in London, 'EBU Review', vol.XXIV, no.5, September.

CREWE, I. (ed.) (1974), 'British Political Sociology Yearbook - Volume 1: Elites in Western Democracy', London, Croom Helm.

CROLL, P. (1973), 'The Future of Broadcasting', University of
Leicester, Centre for Mass Communication Research.
CROLL, P. and GOLDING, P. (1972) The sociology of television,
Letter responding to G.W. Goldie's review of P. Elliott, 1972 in
'Listener', 26 October.
CROSLAND, A. (1956), 'The future of Socialism', London, Cape.
CROSSMAN, R.H.S. (1952), Psychological warfare, 'Journal of the
Royal United Service Institution'.
CROSSMAN, R.H.S. (1968), The politics of viewing: the granada
lecture, 'New Statesman', 25 October.
CROSSMAN, R.H.S. (1971), The BBC, Labour and the public, 'New
Statesman', 16 July.
CURRAN, C. (1971), Researcher/broadcaster cooperation: problems
and possibilities in J.D. Halloran and M. Gurevitch, 1971.
CUTLIPP, S.M. (1954), Content and flow of AP news - from trunk to
TTS to reader, 'Journalism Quarterly', Fall.
DAY, Robin. (1970), Troubled reflections of a television journalist,
'Encounter', May.
DEARLOVE, J. (1974), The BBC and politicians, 'Index', no.1.
DELMER, S. (1962), 'Black Boomerang', London, Secker and Warburg.
DENZIN, N.K. (1970), 'Sociological Methods: A Sourcebook', London,
Butterworths.
DEXTER, L.A. and WHITE, D.M. (eds) (1964), 'People, Society and Mass
Communications', New York, Free Press.
DIMBLEBY, D. (1972), A broadcaster's hopes, 'The Listener', vol.88,
16 November.
DREW, D.G. (1972), Roles and decision making of three television
best reporters, 'Journal of Broadcasting', Spring.
DOMHOFF, G.W. (1967), 'Who Rules America?', New York, Prentice-Hall.
DONAHEW, L. (1967), Newspaper gatekeepers and forces in the news
channel, 'Public Opinion Quarterly', pp.61-80.
DONNELLAN, P. (1972), Internal influences on broadcasting in F.S.
Badley, 1972.
DONOHUE, G. et al. (1972), Gatekeeping: mass media systems and
information control in F.G. Kline and P.J. Tichenor, 1972.
DOUGALL, R. (1974), 'In and Out of the Box', London, Harvill Press.
DOWSE, R.E. and HUGHES, J.A. (1972), 'Political Sociology: A
Reader', London, John Wilsy.
DUNNE, J.G. (1970), 'The Studio', London, J.H. Allen.
EDELSTEIN, A.S. (1966), 'Perspectives in Mass Communications', Kiner
Mercks Forlag.
EDWARDS, D. (1962), 'News and Current Affairs', London, BBC.
ELLIOTT, P. (1970), Selection and communication in a TV production
in J. Tunstall, 1970.
ELLIOTT, P. (1972), 'The Making of a Television Series: A Case Study
in The Sociology of Culture', London, Constable.
ELLIOTT, P. (1972), 'The Sociology of the Professions', London,
MacMillan.
ELLIOTT, P. (Forthcoming)
ELLIOTT, P. and CHANEY, D. (1967), Towards a theoretical framework
for the study of the production process in the TV medium, University
of Leicester, Centre for Mass Communication Research.
ELLIOTT, P. and CHANEY, D. (1968) A sociological framework for the
study of television production, University of Leicester, Centre for
Mass Communication Research.

EMMETT, B. (1971), A brief history of broadcasting research in the
United Kingdom 1936-1965 in H. Egushi, and M. Ichinche, (eds).
'International Studies of Broadcasting - With Special Reference to
the Japanese Studies', Nippon Hoso Kyoksi.
EMMETT, B. (1972), The television and radio audience in Britain in
D. McQuail, 1972.
EPSTEIN, E.J. (1973), 'News from Nowhere: Television and the News',
New York, Random House.
EPSTEIN, E.J. (1973), The values of newsmen, 'Television Quarterly',
Winter.
EVERSOLE, P. (1971), Concentration of ownership in the communica-
tions industry, 'Journalism Quarterly', Summer.
FAIRLIE, H. (1959), The BBC in H. Thomas, 1959.
FAULKNER, G. (1974), The mass media and socialization, Unpublished
PhD dissertation, University of Leicester.
FLEGEL, R.C. and CHAFFER, S.H. (1971), Influence of editors, readers
and personal opinions on reporters, 'Journalism Quarterly', vol.48,
pp.645-51.
FLEMING, D. and BAILYN, B. (eds) (1969), 'The Intellectual Migra-
tion', Cambridge, Mass., Harvard University Press.
FRANK, T.M. and WEISBAND, E. (1974),'Secrecy and Foreign Policy',
Oxford University Press.
FRANKS, Lord (1972), 'Franks Report', Departmental Committee on
Section 2 of the Official Secrets Act 1911: Volume 1 - Report.
Volume 4 - Miscellaneous Evidence.
FREEPROP/FCG (1971), 'Television and the State', Pamphlet no.1,
January.
FRIENDLY, F.W. (1967), 'Due to Circumstances Beyond Our Control',
New York, Random House.
GALTUNG, J. and RUGE, M.H. (1965), The structure of foreign news:
the presentation of the Congo, Cuba and Cyprus Crises in four
foreign newspapers, 'Journal of International Peace Research',
vol.1, pp.64-90.
GANNON, F.R. (1971), 'The British Press and Germany 1936-1939',
Oxford University Press.
GANS, H.J. (1966), The shaping of mass media content: a study of the
news, Mimeo, expanded version of paper delivered at ASA 1966.
GANS, H.J. (1967), The creator-audience relationship in the mass
media: an analysis of movie making in Rosenburg and White, 1967.
GANS, H.J. (1971)', The sociologist and the television journalist:
observations on studying TV news in J.D. Halloran and M. Gurevitch,
1971.
GANS, H.J. (1972), The famine in American mass communications
research: comments on Hirsch, Tuchman and Gecas, 'American Journal
of Sociology', vol.77, no.4, January.
GELLES, R.J. (1971), The television news interview: a case study in
the consturction and presentation of social reality, Paper delivered
at ASA Annual Meeting.
GELLES, R.J. (1972), The Agnew theory: an examination of distortion
in television news, Paper delivered at Eastern Sociological Society,
April 21-3.
GERBNER, G. (1956), Toward a general model of communications,
'Audio-Visual Communication Review', vol.IV, no.5.
GERBNER, G. (1961), Psychology, psychiatry and mental illness in the

mass media: a study of trends 1900-1959, 'Mental Hygiene', vol.45, January.

GERBNER, G. (1964), Ideological perspectives and political tendencies in news reporting, 'Journalism Quarterly', vol.41, Autumn.

GERBNER,GG. (1969), Institutional pressures upon mass communicators, in P. Halmos, 1969.

GERBNER, G. (1972), Mass media and human communication theory in D. McQuail, 1972.

GERBNER, G. (forthcoming) 'Current Trends in Mass Communications, Mouton.

GIEBER, W. (1956), Across the desk: a study of 16 telegraph editors, 'Journalism Quarterly', Fall.;

GIEBER, W. (1960), How the 'gatekeepers' view local civil liberties news, 'Journalism Quarterly', vol.37, Spring, pp.199-205.

GIEBER, W. (1960), Two commicators of the news: a study of the roles of sources and reporters, 'Social Forces', vol.39, pp.76-83.

GIEBER, W. (1961), A city editor selects the news, Paper presented to ASA.

GIEBER, W. (1961), The political communicator: a model of mass media oriented communications behaviour, Association for Education in Journalism, August.

GIEBER, W. (1963), 'I' am the news in V.A. Daneilson, 'P.J. Deutschmann Memorial Papers in Mass Communications Research', Cincinatti, Scripps-Howard Research.

GIEBER, W. (1963), The private vs the public role of the newsman, Department of Journalism, SF State, Paper presented to Association for Education in Journalism.

GIEBER, W. (1964), News is what newspapermen make it, in L.A. Dexter and D.M. White, 1964.

GIEBER, W. (1964), The city desk: a model of news decisions, Paper presented to Association for Education in Journalism, August.

GIEBER, W. (1965), Personal and social communication systems of political correspondents, Paper presented to Association for Education in Journalism, August.

GIEBER, S. and JOHNSON, W. (1961), The city hall 'beat': a study of reporter and source roles, 'Journalism Quarterly' vol.38, pp.289-302.

GOLDIE, G.W. (1972), The sociology of television, 'Listener', 19 October. Review of P. Elliott, 1972.

GOLDING, P. (1970), The concept of 'gatekeeping' in mass communication research - a critique and illustrative study, MA Dissertation, University of Essex.

GOLDING, P. (1973), Open night, University of Leicester, Centre for Mass Communication Research.

GOLDING, P. (1974), News, 'Intermedia', July.

GOLDING, P. (1974b), 'The Mass Media', London, Longman.

GOLDSTEIN, W. (1967), Network television and political change: two issues in democratic theory, 'Western Political Quarterly'.

GOVERNORS OF THE BBC (1971), 'Yesterday's Men' - a statement by the board of governors of the BBC, 'Listener', 15 July.

GREEN, M. (1969), 'Television News: Anatomy and Process', Belmont, California, Wadsworth Publishing Company Inc.

GREENBERG, B.S. and TANNENBAUM, P.M. (1962), Communicator performance under cognitive stress, 'Journalism Quarterly', vol.39, Spring, pp.169-178.

GREENE, H.C. (1961), Foreword in G. Ross, 1961.
GREENE, H.C. (1969), The BBC since 1958, 'BBC Handbook'.
GREENE, H.C. (1969), 'The Third Floor Front: A View of Broadcasting in The Sixties', London, Bodley Head.
GREENE, H.C. (1971), Lord Reith: a personal view, 'Observer', 20 June, p.9.
GREENE, H.C. (1972), The future of broadcasting in Britain, 'New Statesmen', 20 October, pp.549-54.
GREENE, H.C. (1974), And, Faith, he'll prent it (Review of C. Hill, 1974) 'New Statesman', 20 September.
GRISEWOOD, H. (1968), 'One Thing At A Time', London, Hutchinson.
GUREVITCH, M. (1971), An Overview in J.D. Halloran and M. Gurevitch, 1971.
GUREVITCH, M. and BLUMLER, J. (1975), Linkages between the mass media and politics: a model for the analysis of political communication systems in G. Gerbner, 1975.
HALL, R.H. (1967), Some organisational considerations in the professional-organisational relationship, 'Administrative Science Quarterly',vol.12, December.
HALL, S. (1971), Deviancy, politics and the media, British Sociological Association Conference.
HALL, S. (1972a), The limitations of broadcasting, 'Listener', 16 March.
HALL, S. (1972b), The external dialectic in broadcasting: television's double-bind, in F.S. Bailey, 1972.
HALL, S. (1973a) Encoding and decoding in the television discourse, University of Leicester, Centre for Mass Communication Research.
HALL, S. (1973b) The 'structured communication' of events, Paper for 'Obstacles to Communication', Symposium, UNESCO, Division of Philosophy.
HALLORAN, J.D. (1970), 'The Effects of Television', London, Panther.
HALLORAN, J.D. (1971), 'The Effects of Mass Communication: with special reference to television', Leicester University Press, for the TVRC.
HALLORAN, J.D. (1974), 'Mass Media and Society - The Challenge of Research. An Inaugural Lecture', Leicester University Press.
HALLORAN, J.D. and CROLL, P. (1971), TV programmes in GB: content and control - with special reference to violence and sex', in Surgeon-General, 1971.
HALLORAN, J.D. and GUREVITCH, M. (1971), 'Broadcaster/Researcher Cooperation in Mass Communication', University of Leicester, Centre for Mass Communication Research.
HALLORAN, J.D. et al (1970), 'Demonstration and Communications: A Case Study', Harmondsworth, Penguin.
HALMOS, P. (ed) (1969), 'Sociology of Mass Media Communicators Sociological Review Monograph 13', University of Keele.
HAMMOND, P.E. (1964), 'Sociologists at Work', New York, Basic Books.
HARDCASTLE, W. (1971), The BBC's backbone, 'Listener', 15 July.
HARTMAN, P. and HUSBAND, C. (1973), 'Racism and the Mass Media', London, Davis-Poynter.
HMSO (1923), 'Broadcasting Committee Report', Cmd 1951 (1923) - (The Sykes Committee Report).
HMSO (1925), 'Report of theBroadcasting Committee': Cmd 2599 (1925) - (Crawford Committee Report).

HMSO (1951), 'Report of the Broadcasting Committee': Cmd 8116
(1949) - (Beveridge Report).
HMSO (1956) 'Report of the Select Committee on Broadcasting', H.C.
288 (1955-6).
HMSO (1962), 'Report of the Committee on Broadcasting': Cmd 1753
(Pilkington Report).
HILL, C. (1974), 'Behind the Screen. The Broadcasting Memoirs of
Lord Hill', London, Sidgwick & Jackson.
HILL, D. (1961), And the next tonight ...? 'Contrast', August.
HIMMELWEIT, H. (1963), An experimental study of taste development in
children in L. Arons and M.A. May, 1963.
HOCH, P. (1974), 'The Newspaper Game: The Political Sociology of
The Press', London, Calder & Boyers.
HOCKING, W.E. (1947), 'Freedom of the Press: A Framework of
Principle', University of Chicago Press.
HOOD, S. (1967), 'A Survey of Television', London, Heinemann.
HOOD, S. (1968), Crisis broadcasting: review of H. Grisewood, 1963,
'Listener', 28 March.
HOOD, S. (1972), 'The Mass Media', London, MacMillan.
HOOD, S. (1972), The politics of television in D. McQuail, 1972.
HOROWITZ, I.L. (ed.) (1967), 'Power, Politics and People: The
Collected Essays of C.W. Mills', Oxford University Press.
HUACO, G.A. (1965), 'The Sociology of Film Art', New York, Basic
Books.
HYDE, H.M. (1973), 'Baldwin: The Unexpected Prime Minister', London,
Hart-Davis, MacGibbon.
ITA (1972), News and current affairs programmes, January.
JAMES, R.R. (1969), 'Memoirs of a Conservative, J.C.C. Davidson's
Memoirs and Papers, 1910-1937', London, Weidenfeld & Nicholson.
JANOWITZ, M. (1967), 'The Community Press in an Urban Setting: The
Social Elements of Urbanism', Phoenix, Ariz., Phoenix Books.
JARVIE, I.C. (1970), 'Towards a Sociology of the Cinema', London,
Routledge & Kegan Paul.
JAY, A. (1971), 'Corporation Men', London, Jonathan Cape.
JAY, A. (1972), What's to become of the BBC? 'Sunday Times'
19 November.
JOHNSON, K.G. (1963), Dimensions of judgment of science news
stories, 'Journalism Quarterly', vol.40, pp.315-22.
JOHNSTONE, J.W.C. et al. (1973-4), The professional values of
American newsmen, 'Public Opinion Quarterly', Winter.
JONES, B. (ed.) (1973), 'Broadcasting and Society': Proceedings of
the Fifth symposium on Broadcasting Policy, University of Manchester,
Department of Extra-Mural Studies.
JONES, R. et al. (1961), News selection patterns from a state TT3-
wire, 'Journalism Quarterly', vol.38, pp.303-12.
JUDD, R.P. (1961), The newspaper reporter in a suburban city,
'Journalism Quarterly', vol.38, pp.35-42.
KARL, P. (1970), 'Kiss Kiss Bang Bang', London, Calder & Boyers.
KATZ, E. (1957), The two-step flow of communication, 'Public
Opinion Quarterly', Spring.
KATZ, E. (1971), Platforms and windows: broadcasting's role in elec-
tion campaigns, 'Journalism Quarterly', Summer, pp.304-14. (Also in
McQuail, 1972).
KEE, R. (1971), BBC errors, 'Listener', 22 July.

KEELEY, J. (1971), 'The Left-Leaning Antenna: Political Bias in Television', New York, Arlington House.

KEFAUVER, E. (1955), Television and juvenile delinquency, US Senate Committee on Judiciary, Sub-Committee on Juvenile Delinquency, Hearings, Spring 1955.

KERRICK, J. et al. (1964), Balance and writer's attitude in news stories and editorials, 'Journalism Quarterly', vol.41, pp.207-15.

KLAPPER, J.T. (1948), Mass media and the engineering of consent, 'American Scholar', vol.17, August, pp.419-29.

KLAPPER, J.T. (1960), 'The Effects of Mass Communications', Chicago, Free Press.

KLINE, F.G. and TICHENOR, P.J. (1972), 'Current Perspectives in Mass Communications Research', London, Sage.

KRACAUER, S. (1947), 'From Caligari to Hitler: A Psychological History of the German Film', Princeton University Press.

KUMAR, K. (1974), Holding the middle ground: the BBC, the public, and the professional broadcaster, Paper presented for the Workshop on 'The Political Role of the Mass Media': European Consortium for Political Research, Strasbourg, March 28 - April 2 1974.

LAMB, K. (1970), 'The BBC and Its Public', BBC Lunchtime Lectures, Eighth Series, 30 April.

LAMB, K. (1974), Disclosure, discretion and disemblement: broadcasting and the national interest in the perspective of a publicly owned medium in T.M. Frank and E. Weisband, 1974.

LANE, R.E. (1962), 'Political Ideology: Why The American Common Men Believes What He Does', New York, Free Press.

LANG, K. and LANG G. (1952), The unique perspective of television and its effect: a pilot study in W. Schrann, 1960.

LANG, K and LANG, G. (1955), The inferential structure of political communications, 'Public Opinion Quarterly', Summer.

LANG, K. and LANG, G. (1968), 'Politics and Television', Chicago, Quadrangle Books.

LASSWELL, H. (1960), The Structure and function of communication in society in W.G. Schrane, 1960.

LAZARFELD, P. (1963), Afterword in G. Steiner, 1963.

LAZARSFELD, P. et al. (1964), 'The People's Choice', New York, Duell, Sloan & Pearce.

LAZARSFELD, P. and MERTON, R.E. (1948), Mass communication, popular taste and organised social action in BRYSON, 1948.

LEVIN, B. (1972), 'The Pendulum Years: Britain and the Sixties', London, Pan Books.

LEWIN, K. (1943), Psychological ecology in K. Lewin, 1951.

LEWIN, K. (1947), Frontiers in group dynamics, 'Human Relations'.

LEWIN, K. (1948), Channels of group life in 'Human Relations', vol.1, no.2.

LEWIN, K. (1951), 'Field Theory in Social Science', New York, Harper.

LIPPMAN, W. (1922), 'Public Opinion', New York, MacMillan (revised 1929).

LLOYD, T.O. (1970), 'Empire to Welfare State: English History 1906-1967', Oxford University Press.

LOVELL, T. (1972), Sociology of aesthetic structures and contextualism in P. McQuail, 1972.

LUSTY, R. (1974), Six weeks that shook the BBC, 'New Statesmen', 6 September.

LUSTY, R. (1975), 'And Who May I Say Called?', London, Jonathan Cape.
MACKENZIE, P.R. (1969), Eden, Suez and the BBC - a reassessment, 'Listener', 18 December.
MACNEIL, R. (1968), 'The People Machine', Eyre & Spottiswoode.
MARTEL, M. and McCALL, G.J. (1964), Reality orientation and the pleasure principle: a study of American mass periodical fiction (1890-1955) in L.A. Dexter and D.M. White, 1964.
MATEJKO, A. (1970), Newspaper staff as a social system in J. Tunstall, 1970.
McCOMBS, E.M. (1972), Mass communication in political campaigns: information, gratification and persuasion in F.G. Kline and P.J. Tichenor, 1972.
McDONALD, D. (1971), Is objectivity possible? 'The Center Magazine', September-October, vol.4, pp.29-43.
McLEOD J.M. and MAWLEY, Jr, S. (1964), Professionalisation among newsmen, 'Journalism Quarterly', vol.4, pp.529-38.
McNELLY, J.T. (1959), Intermediary communicators in the international flow of news, 'Journalism Quarterly', vol.36, pp.23-6.
McQUAIL, D. (1969), 'Towards a Sociology of Mass Communications', London, Collier-Macmillan.
McQUAIL, D. (1972), 'Sociology of Mass Communications', Harmondsworth, Penguin.
MERTON, R.K. (1957), The sociology of knowledge and mass communications, in R.K. Merton, 'Social Thoery and Social Structure', Chicago, Free Press.
MEYER, T.P. (1972), News reporter Bias: a case study in selective perception, 'Journal of Broadcasting', Spring.
MICKELSON, S. (1972), 'The Electric Mirror: Politics in an Age of Television', New York, Dodd, Mead.
MILIBAND, R. (1972), The problem of the capitalist state: a reply to Poulantsas, in R. Blackburn, 1972.
MILIBAND, R. (1973), 'The State in Capitalist Society: The Analysis of the Western System of Power, London, Quartet Books.
MILLER, K. (1969), Dissent, disobedience and the mass media - the achievement of Sir Hugh Greene, 'Listener', 24 April, pp.557-60.
MILLS, C.W. (1967), See I.L Horowitz, 1967.
MITCHELL, A. (1973), The decline of current affairs television, 'Political Quarterly', vol.44, no.2, pp.127-36.
MOLOTCH, H. and LESTER, M. (1972), Accidents, scandals and routines: resources for conflict methodology, ASA Paper, August.
MOLOTCH, H. and LESTER, M. (1974), News as purposive behaviour: on the strategic use of routine events, accidents and scandals, 'American Sociological Review', vol.39, pp.101-12.
MOODY, R.J. (1970), The armed forces broadcast new system: Vietnam version, 'Journalism Quarterly', Spring.
MORRISON, D. (1976), 'Paul Lazarsfeld: Biography of an Institutional Innovator', University of Leicester.
MURDOCK, G. (1972), The ownership and control of the mass media in contemporary Britain: patterns and consequences, University of Leicester, Centre for Mass Communication Research.
MURDOCK, G. (1974), Mass media and the class structure, University of Leicester, Centre for Mass Communication Research.
MURDOCK, G. and GOLDING, P. (1974) For a political economy of mass communications in R. Miliband and J. Saville, 'The Socialist Register 1973', London, Merlin Press.

NIXON, R.B. and WARD, J. (1961), Trends in newspaper ownership, 'Journalism Quarterly', Winter.

NORMANBROOK, Lord,(1965), The functions of the BBC's governors, London, BBC, 15 December.

O'HIGGINS, P. (1972), 'Censorship in Britain', London, Nelson.

OLIEN, C.N. et al. (1968), The community editor's power and the reporting of conflict, 'Journalism Quarterly', vol.45.

PARKIN, F. (1972), 'Class Inequality and POlitical Order', St. Albans, Paladin.

PALETZ, D.L. and DUNN, R. (1969), Press coverage of civil disorders: a case study of Winston-Salem, 1967, 'Public Opinion Quarterly', Fall.

PAULU, B. (1961), 'British Broadcasting in Transition', University of Minnesota Press.

PELLING, H. (1974), 'Winston Churchill, London, Macmillan.

PENNIMAN, H.R. (1974), 'Britain at the Polls: The Parliamentary Election of February 1974', American Enterprise Institute for Public Policy Research, Washington, DC.

PETERSON, T. (1956), The social responsibility theory in F.S. Siebert et al., 1956.

PETERSON, T. (1968), Commercial control of the mass media, Talk at YMCA - YMCA Faculty Forum, University of Illinois, November 8.

POLSKY, N. (1971), 'Hustlers, Beats and Others', Harmondsworth, Penguin.

POOL, I. de S. and SHULMAN, I. (1959), Newsmen's fantasies, audience and news-writing, 'Public Opinion Quarterly', vol.23, pp.145-48.

POULANTZAS, N. (1972), The problem of the capitalist state in R. Blackburn, (ed.), 1972.

PRATTEN, C.F. (1970), 'The Economics of Television', London, PEP Broadsheet, No. 520.

PRESS COUNCIL (1970), 'Distribution of Advertising Revenue by Media in the UK. 1965-1969' Report.

PUTNAM, R.D. (1973), 'The Beliefs of Politicians: Ideology, Conflict and Democracy', Yale University Press.

RAFFERTY, K. and JERMAIN, L.L. (1954), College backgrounds of staffs of American daily newspapers, 'Journalism Quarterly', Fall.

REITH, Lord (1963-4), Forsan, 'Parliamentary Affairs', Winter.

REX, J. (1974), Capitalism, elites and the ruling class in P. Stanwroth and A. Giddens, 1974.

RILEY, J.W. and RILEY, M.W. (1959), Mass communication and the social system in R.K. Merton, et al. 'Sociology Today', New York, Basic Books.

ROBINSON, J.P. (1969), Television and leisure time: yesterday, today, and (maybe) tomorrow, 'Public Opinion Quarterly', Summer.

ROSS, G. (1961), 'Television Jubilee: The Story of 25 Years of BBC Television', London, S.H. Allen.

ROSS, L. (1962), 'Picture', Harmondsworth, Penguin.

RYDBECK, O. (1970), Impartiality - Utopia or reality? 'EBU Review', May, pp.10-13.

SACHSMAN, D.B. (1970), A test of loading: news measure of bias 'Journalism Quarterly', Winter.

SCHRAMM, W. (1954), How communication works in W. Schramm and D.F. Roberts, 1954.

SCHRAMM, W. (1957), 'Responsibility in Mass Communication', London, Harper & Row.
SCHRAMM, W. (1960), 'Mass Communications: A Book of Readings', Urbana, University of Illinois Press.
SCHRAMM, W. and ROBERTS, D.F. (1954), 'The Processes and Effects of Mass Communication', Urbana, University of Illinois Press.
SEELMAN, H.L. (1971), Keeping the gates at the 'Chicago Defender' 'Journalism Quarterly', Summer.
SELENICK, P. (1957), 'Leadership in Administration', New York, Harper & Row.
SEYMOUR-URE, C. (1968), 'The Press, Politics and the Public', London, Methuen.
SEYMOUR-URE, C. (1969), Editorial policy-making in the press, 'Government and Opposition', Autumn.
SEYMOUR-URE, C. (1974), 'The Political Impact of Mass Media', London, Constable.
SHAW, D.L. (1967), News bias and the telegraph: a study of historical change, 'Journalism Quarterly', vol.38, pp.3-12.
SHULMAN, M. (1973a), 'The Least Worst Television in the World', London, Barrie and Jenkins.
SHULMAN, M. (1973b), 'The Ravenous Eye: the Impact of the Fifth Factor', London, Cassell.
SIEBERT, F.S. etaal. (1963), 'Four Theories of the Press', Urbana, University of Illinois Press.
SIGELMAN, L. (1973), Reporting the news: an organisational analysis 'American Journal of Sociology', vol.79, no.1, July.
SILVERMAN, D. (1968), Formal organisations or industrial sociology: towards a social action analysis of organisations, 'Sociology', vol.2, no.2, May.
SILVEY, R. (1963), 'Reflections on the Impact of Broadcasting', BBC Lunchtime Lectures, 13 February.
SIMON, H.A. (1957), 'Administrative Behaviour', Chicago, Free Press.
SIMON, Lord (1953), 'The BBC From Within', London, Gollancz.
SMALL, W. (1970), 'To Kill A Messenger: TV News and The Real World' New York, Hastings House.
SMITH, A. (1972), Internal pressures in broadcasting, 'New Outlook', no.4.
SMITH, A. (1972), Internal pressures in broadcasting in F.S. Badley, 1972.
SMITH, A. (1972), Television coverage of Northern Ireland, 'Index', Summer, vol.1, no.2.
SMITH, A. (1972), The 'Yesterday's Men' affair, 'New Statesman', 16 June.
SMITH, A. (1973), Broadcasting - the origins of a conflict, 'New Humanist', vol.88, no.10, February.
SMITH, A. (1973), 'The Shadow in the Cave: The Broadcaster, The Audience and the State', London, Allen & Unwin.
SMITH, A. (1974), 'British Broadcasting', Newton Abbot, David & Charles.
SOCIAL MORALITY COUNCIL (1973), 'The Future of Broadcasting', London, Eyre-Methuen.
STANWORTH, P. and GIDDENS, A. (1974), 'Elites and Power in British Society', Cambridge University Press.
STARK, R.W. (1962), Policy and the pros: an organisational analysis

of a metropolitan newspaper, 'Berkeley Journal of Sociology',
vol.7, pp.11-31.
STEINER, G. (1963), 'People Look at TV', New York, A. Knopf.
STREET, H. (1972), 'Freedom, the Individual and the Law', Harmonds-
worth, Penguin.
STUART, C. (ed.) (1975), 'The Reith Diaries', London, Collins.
SURGEON-GENERAL (1972), 'Television and Social Behaviour', US De
Department of Health, Education and Welfare.
SWALLOW, N. (1963), Instant truth: some reflections on current
affairs television, 'Contrast', Summer.
SWALLOW, N. (1966), 'Factual Television', London, Focal Press.
SWANN, M. (1974), A year at the BBC, 'Listener', 17 January.
SWANSON, C.E. (1949), Midcity Daily: the news staff and its relation
to control, 'Journalism Quarterly', vol.26, pp.20-8.
SYMONS, J. (1957), 'The General Strike', London, Cresset Press.
THOMAS, H. (ed.) (1959), 'The Establishment', London, Blond.
THOMPSON, E.P. (1973), An open letter to Lessek Kolakowski in
Miliband and Haville, 1973.
THORNE, B. (1970), 'The BBC's Finances and Cost Control', London,
BBC Publications.
TRENAMAN, J. and McQuail, D. (1961), 'Television and the Political
Image', London, Methuen.
TUCHMAN, G. (1972), Objectivity as strategic ritual: an examination
of newspapermen's notions of objectivity, 'American Journal of
Sociology', vol.77, no.4, January.
TUCHMAN, G. (1973a), The technology of objectivity: doing 'objective'
TV news film, 'Urban Life and Culture', vol.2, no.1.
TUCHMAN, G. (1973b), Making news by doing work: routinising the
unexpected, 'American Journal of Sociology', vol.79, no.1, July.
TUDOR, A. (1970), Film, communication and content, in J. Tunstall,
1970.
TUNSTALL, J. (1970), 'Media Sociology: A reader', London, Constable.
TUNSTALL, J. (1970), 'The Westminster Lobby Correspondents', London,
Routledge & Kegan Paul.
TUNSTALL, J. (1971), 'Journalists at Work: Specialist Correspondents.
'Their News Organisations, News Sources, And Competitor Colleagues',
London, Constable.
TYRELL, R. (1972), 'The Work of the Television Journalist', London,
Focal Press.
VALLEAU, J.F. (1952), Oregon legislative reporting: the newsmen and
their methods, 'Journalism Quarterly', vol.29, Spring, pp.158-70.
WAKEFORD, J. et al. (1974), Some social and educational character-
istics of selected elite groups in contemporary Britain: a research
note based on a 'K Means' cluster analysis, in I. Crewe, 1974.
WARNER, M. (1971), Organisational context and control of policy in
the television newsroom: a participant observation study, 'British
Journal of Sociology', vol.XXII, no.3, September.
WEBELL, E.G. (1968), 'Broadcasting and Public Policy', London,
Michael Joseph.
WEBELL, E.G.(1970), 'Structures of Broadcasting: A Symposium',
Manchester University Press.
WESTERSTAHL, J. (1970), Objectivity is measurable, 'EBU Review',
May, pp.13-17.
WESTLEY, B.H. and MACLEAN, M.S. (1957) A conceptual model for com-
munications research, 'Journalism Quarterly', vol.34, no.1.

WHALE, J. (1969), 'The Half-Shut Eye', London, Macmillan.
WHELDON, H. (1973), 'Tastes and Standards in BBC Programmes', London, BBC Publications.
WHITE, D.M. (1950), The 'Gatekeeper': a case study in the selection of news, 'Journalism Quarterly', vol.27, no.4.
WILLIAMS, D. (1965), 'Not In The Public Interest', London, Hutchinson.
WILLIAMS, F. (1957), 'Dangerous Estate', London, Longmans.
WILLIAMS, G.A. (1960), Gramsci's concept of 'Egemonia', 'Journal of the History of Ideas', vol.21, no.4.
WILLIAMS, M. (1972), 'Inside No.10', London, Weidenfeld & Nicholson.
WILLIAMS, R. (1965), 'The Long Revolution', Harmondsworth, Penguin.
WILLIAMS, R. (1966), 'Communications', London, Chatto & Windus.
WILLIAMS, R. (1971), Literature and sociology, 'New Left Review' no.67, May/June.
WILLIAMS, R. (1974), 'Television: Technology and Cultural Form', London, Fontana.
WILSON, C. (ed.) (1970), 'Parliaments, People and Mass Media', London, Cassell.
WILSON, D. (1968), 'Broadcasting: Vision and Sound', Oxford, Pergamon Press.
WILSON, H. (1971), 'The Labour Government 1964-1970: A Personal Record', Weidenfeld & Nicholson, and Michael Joseph.
WINCHESTER, S. (1974), 'In Holy Terror: Reporting the Ulster Troubles', London, Faber.
WINDLESHAM, Lord (1966), 'Communication and Political Power', London London, Cape.
WOLFE, T. (1973), 'The New Journalism', New York, Harper & Row.
WORSLEY, T.C. (1970), 'Television: The Ephemeral Art', London, Allan Ross.
ZUCKERMAN, H. (1972), Interviewing an ultra-elite, 'Public Opinion Quarterly', Summer.

INDEX